T0220805

Communications in Computer and Information Science 1763

More information about this series at https://link.springer.com/bookseries/7899

Nilay Khare · Deepak Singh Tomar ·
Mitul Kumar Ahirwal · Vijay Bhaskar Semwal ·
Vaibhav Soni (Eds.)

Machine Learning, Image Processing, Network Security and Data Sciences

4th International Conference, MIND 2022
Virtual Event, January 19–20, 2023
Proceedings, Part II

Springer

Editors
Nilay Khare ⓘ
Maulana Azad National Institute
of Technology
Bhopal, India

Deepak Singh Tomar ⓘ
Maulana Azad National Institute
of Technology
Bhopal, India

Mitul Kumar Ahirwal ⓘ
Maulana Azad National Institute
of Technology
Bhopal, India

Vijay Bhaskar Semwal ⓘ
Maulana Azad National Institute
of Technology
Bhopal, India

Vaibhav Soni ⓘ
Maulana Azad National Institute
of Technology
Bhopal, India

ISSN 1865-0929   ISSN 1865-0937 (electronic)
Communications in Computer and Information Science
ISBN 978-3-031-24366-0   ISBN 978-3-031-24367-7 (eBook)
https://doi.org/10.1007/978-3-031-24367-7

This Springer imprint is published by the registered company Springer Nature Switzerland AG
The registered company address is: Gewerbestrasse 11, 6330 Cham, Switzerland

Preface

On behalf of the department of Computer Science and Engineering, Maulana Azad National Institute of Technology, Bhopal, India, we are pleased to present the proceedings of the 4th International Conference on Machine Learning, Image Processing, Network Security and Data Sciences (MIND 2022). First, we would like to express our appreciation to the organizing committee for their constant efforts in managing this conference. The first edition in the MIND conference series (MIND 2019) was organized at NIT Kurukshetra, with the second and third editions (MIND 2020 and 2021) organized by NIT Silchar and NIT Raipur, respectively.

This conference was planned to highlight the wide range of engineering research work carried out in different industries and academic institutions, focusing on machine learning and computational intelligence, data sciences, image processing and computer vision, and network and cyber security. The MIND 2022 conference tracks represented distinct platforms for the discussion and exchange of ideas amongst national and international research scholars and professionals, successfully disseminating interdisciplinary knowledge in each track.

The MIND 2022 conference provided a wide-ranging view of the current state of the art, along with inspiration and motivation to attendees which we hope will help them to develop suggestions and strong recommendations to understand and further recent research topics and their challenges.

In response to the call for papers, MIND 2022 received 399 submissions from which only 119 papers were selected by the Program Committee (PC) for presentation. Out of these, only 64 papers were selected for publication in the proceedings (Springer CCIS Volumes 1762 and 1763). Each submission was reviewed (single blind) by at least three PC members or invited reviewers, experts in their fields, in order to supply detailed and helpful comments.

The conference featured three invited lectures:

- Genci Capi (Assistive Robotics Laboratory, HOSEI University, Japan) addressed "Machine Learning and Computational Intelligence",
- Akhtar Kalam (Victoria University, Melbourne, Australia) covered "Data Science & Engineering", and
- Youngshik Kim (Department of Mechanical Engineering, Hanbat National University, South Korea) spoke about "Neural Network-based state estimation for robotic systems".

We would like to thank the keynote speakers and all members of all the conference committees, especially the reviewers who worked very hard in reviewing papers and suggesting valuable comments to the authors for improvement of their work. We also would like to express our gratitude to the authors for contributing their research work to the conference. Special thanks go to the CCIS team at Springer for publishing the conference proceedings.

January 2023

Nilay Khare
Deepak Singh Tomar
Mitul Kumar Ahirwal
Vijay Bhaskar Semwal
Vaibhav Soni

Organization

Program Chairs

Nilay Khare (Chair)   MANIT Bhopal, India
Deepak Singh Tomar (Co-chair)   MANIT Bhopal, India

General Chairs

Meenu Chawla   MANIT Bhopal, India
Rajesh Kumar Pateriya   MANIT Bhopal, India

Publication Chairs

Mitul Kumar Ahirwal   MANIT Bhopal, India
Vijay Bhaskar Semwal   MANIT Bhopal, India
Vaibhav Soni   MANIT Bhopal, India

Founding Chairs

Gyanendra Verma   NIT Raipur, India
Rajesh Doriya   NIT Raipur, India

Advisory Board

Meenu Chawla (Chair)   MANIT Bhopal, India
Jyoti Singhai (Convenor)   MANIT Bhopal, India
Ram Bilas Pachori   IIT Indore, India
G. K. Singh   IIT Roorkee, India
Daniel Thalmann   EPFL, Switzerland
Zoran Bojkovic   University of Belgrade, Serbia
Salah Bourennane   École Centrale de Marseille, France
Pasanta K. Jana   IIT Dhanbad, India
G. C. Nandi   IIIT Allahabad, India
O. P. Vyas   IIIT Allahabad, India
Shekhar Verma   IIIT Allahabad, India
Anupam Shukla   IIIT Pune, India
Durga Prasad Mahapatra   NIT Rourkela, India
Harnath Kar   MNNIT Allahabad, India

Dheeresh K. Mallick	BIT Mesra, India
N. D. Londhe	NIT Raipur, India
Anil Kumar	IIIT Jabalpur, India
Pabitra Mohan Khilar	NIT Rourkela, India
Pavan Chakraborty	IIIT Allahabad, India
Satish Kumar Singh	IIIT Allahabad, India
Dilip Singh Sisodia	NIT Raipur, India
Bui Thanh Hung	Ton Duc Thang University, Vietnam
Balas Valentina Emilia	Aurel Vlaicu University of Arad, Romania
Ruben Gonzalez Crespo	UNIR, Spain
Zheng Xu	Shanghai University, China

Program Committee

Rajesh Kumar Pateriya (Chair)	MANIT Bhopal, India
Sanyam Shukla (Convenor)	MANIT Bhopal, India
Vasudev Dehalwar	MANIT Bhopal, India
Manish Pandey	MANIT Bhopal, India
Jyoti Bharti	MANIT Bhopal, India
Manasi Gyanchandani	MANIT Bhopal, India
Sweta Jain	MANIT Bhopal, India
Sri Khetwat Saritha	MANIT Bhopal, India
B. N. Roy	MANIT Bhopal, India
Ghanapriya Singh	NIT Uttarakhand, India
Shivram Dubey	IIIT Allahabad, India
Somesh Kumar	IIITM Gwalior, India
Debanjan Sadhya	IIITM Gwalior, India
Santosh Singh Rathore	IIITM Gwalior, India
Rajesh Wadhvani	MANIT Bhopal, India
Sanyam Shukla	MANIT Bhopal, India
Akhtar Rasool	MANIT Bhopal, India
Jaytrilok Choudhary	MANIT Bhopal, India
Dhirendra Pratap Singh	MANIT Bhopal, India
Namita Tiwari	MANIT Bhopal, India
Pragati Agrawal	MANIT Bhopal, India
Rajesh Doriya	NIT Raipur, India
Rahul Semwal	IIIT Nagpur, India
Jay Prakash	NIT Calicut, India
Basudeb Behra	NIT Jamshedpur, India
Kukil Khanikar	IIIT Guwahati, India
Badal Soni	NIT Silchar, India
Tirath Prasad Sahu	NIT Raipur, India
Sanjay Kumar	NIT Raipur, India

Rekh Ram Janghel   NIT Raipur, India
Deepak K. T.   IIIT Dharwad, India
Rajendra Hegadi   IIIT Dharwad, India
Urmila Shrawankar   G. H. Raisoni College of Engineering, Nagpur,
                               India
Rajesh Wadvani   MANIT Bhopal, India
Pooja Jain   IIIT Nagpur, India
Anupam Biswas   NIT Silchar, India
Somendu Chakraborty   IIIT Lucknow, India

Additional Reviewers

Daniel Thalmann   Swiss Federal Institute of Technology Lausanne,
                               Switzerland
Zoran Bojkovic   University of Belgrade, Serbia
Salah Bourennane   École Centrale de Marseille, France
Ram Bilas Pachori   IIT Indore, India
José Mario De Martino   University of Campinas, Brazil
Félix J. García Clemente   Universidad de Murcia, Spain
Marcelo Sampaio de Alencar   Universidade Federal de Campina Grande, Brazil
Wei-Chiang Hong   Asia Eastern University of Science and
                               Technology, Taiwan
Dimitrios Alexios Karras   National and Kapodistrian University of Athens,
                               Greece
Alexandre Carlos Brandao Ramos Universidade Federal de Itajubá, Brazil
Kamran Arshad   Ajman University, UAE
Pradip K. Das   IIT Guwahati, India
Pascal Lorenz   University of Haute-Alsace, France
Zhao Yang   Pacific Northwest National Laboratory, USA
Tomasz Rak   Rzeszow University of Technology, Poland
Uttam Ghosh   Vanderbilt University, USA
Pradip Sharma   Aberdeen University, UK
Arpad Gellert   Lucian Blaga University of Sibiu, Romania
José Antonio Marmolejo Saucedo Universidad Panamericana, Mexico
Raffaele Pizzolante   University of Salerno, Italy
Georgia Garani   University of Thessaly, Larissa, Greece
Adem Alpaslan Altun   Selçuk Üniversitesi, Turkey
Rajeev Shrivastava   IIT BHU, India
Viranjay M. Srivastava   University of KwaZulu-Natal, Durban,
                               South Africa
Ashutosh Kumar Singh   NIT Kurukshetra, India
Sabe Abd-Allah   Beni-Suef University, Egypt
Eugénia Moreira Bernardino   Polytechnic of Leiria, Portugal

Rajiv Misra	IIT Patna, India
Carlos Becker Westphall	Federal University of Santa Catarina, Brazil
Dinesh K. Vishwakarma	Delhi Technological University, India
Miroslav Škorić	University of Novi Sad, Serbia
H. K. Sardana	CSIR Chandigarh, India
K. K. Shukla	IIT BHU, India
Shuai Zhao	Amazon Alexa AI, USA
Manoj Kumar Singh	Banaras Hindu University, India
S. M. Warusia Yassin	Universiti Teknikal Malaysia Melaka, Malaysia
Annappa	NIT Surathkal, India
Madhusudan Singh	Yonsei University, South Korea
Pabitra Mitra	IIT Kharagpur, India
Abdul Jalil M. Khalaf	Ministry of Higher Education and Scientific Research, Iraq
Subhrakanta Panda	BITS Pilani, Hyderabad, India
Ajay Kumar Lal	Nepal Engineering College, Bhaktapur, Nepal
Reham R. Mostafa	Mansoura University, Egypt
Dimitrios A. Karras	National Technical University of Athens, Greece
Korhan Cengiz	Trakya University Edirne, Turkey
Sherif S. Rashad	Morehead State University, USA
Vishal Passricha	Central University of Haryana, India
Reeta Sony	JNU New Delhi, India
Satish Kumar Singh	IIIT Allahabad, India
Syed Taqi Ali	VNIT Nagpur, India
A. C. S. Rao	IIT Dhanbad, India
Tarachand Amgoth	IIT Dhanbad, India
Pilli Emmanuel Shubhakar	MNIT Jaipur, India
G. R. Gangadharan	NIT Trichy, India
Pratik Chattopadhyay	IIT BHU, India
Veenu Mangat	UIET Panjab University, India
Bhupesh Kumar Singh	GBPUAT Pantnagar, India
Shyam Lal	NIT Karnataka, India
Ravi Panwar	IIITDM, Jabalpur, India
Poonam Saini	PEC Chandigarh, India
M. P. S. Chawla	SGSITS Indore, India
Anshul Verma	Banaras Hindu University, India
Vibha Vyas	College of Engineering Pune, India
S. Sridevi	Thiagarajar College of Engineering, India
K. Anitha Kumari	PSG College of Technology, India
Narendra Kohli	HBTU Kanpur, India
Ashish Khare	Allahabad University, India
Pankaj Pratap Singh	CIT Kokrajhar, India

Koushlendra Kumar Singh	NIT Jamshedpur, India
Aakanksha Sharaff	NIT Raipur, India
Vijay Bhaskar Semwal	MANIT Bhopal, India
Srinivas Koppu	VIT Vellore, India
Debajyoti Choudhuri	NIT Rourkela, India
Jayapandian N.	Christ University, India
Veena Anand	NIT Raipur, India
D. Jude Hemanth	Karunya Institute of Technology and Sciences, India
Vinutha D. C.	Vidyavardhaka College of Engineering, India
A. Muthumari	University College of Engineering, Ramanathapuram, India
Sravani Devi Y.	G Narayanamma Institute of Technology and Science, India
Dhanaraj	SMS College of Arts and Science, India
Akhilesh Tiwari	MITS Gwalior, India
Naresh Babu Muppalaneni	NIT Silchar, India
Tripti Goel	NIT Silchar, India
Sachin K. Jai	IIITDM Jabalpur, India
Deepak Gupta	NIT Arunachal Pradesh, India

Publicity and Website Committee

Saritha Khetawat (Chair)	MANIT Bhopal, India
Vijay Bhaskar Semwal (Convenor)	MANIT Bhopal, India
Mitul Kumar Ahirwal	MANIT Bhopal, India
Vishwanath Bijalwan	Institute of Technology Gopeshwar, India
Koshlendra Kumar	NIT Jamshedpur, India
Arun Kumar	NIT Rourkela, India
Lakshman Mahato	IIIT Dharwad, India
Jagadish Devagoda	IIIT Dharwad, India
Arun Kumar	IIITM Gwalior, India
Raul Kumar Chaurasiya	MANIT Bhopal, India

Organizing Committee

Narendra Singh Raghuwanshi	MANIT Bhopal, India
Manisha Dubey	MANIT Bhopal, India
Nilay Khare	MANIT Bhopal, India
Deepak Singh Tomar	MANIT Bhopal, India
Vijay B. Semwal	MANIT Bhopal, India
Mitul K. Ahirwal	MANIT Bhopal, India
Vaibhav Soni	MANIT Bhopal, India

Organizing Institution

Computer Science and Engineering Department, Maulana Azad National Institute of Technology, Bhopal, India

Contents – Part II

Network and Cyber Security

Contents – Part I

Data Sciences

Image Processing and Computer Vision

Leveraging CNN and Transfer Learning
for Classification of Histopathology Images

Achyut Dubey[1]([✉]) [iD], Satish Kumar Singh[1] [iD], and Xiaoyi Jiang[2] [iD]

[1] Department of Information Technology, IIIT Allahabad, Prayagraj, India
achyut.dubey6.4@gmail.com, sk.singh@iiita.ac.in
[2] Faculty of Mathematics and Computer Science, University of Münster, Münster, Germany
xjiang@uni-muenster.de

Abstract. This paper aims to build a hybrid convolutional neural architecture by leveraging the power of pre-trained ResNet 50 (trained on ImageNet dataset) through transfer learning. The proposed work has achieved state-of-the-art performance metrics on the BreakHis dataset, containing microscopic histopathological images of benign and malignant breast tumours. The model incorporates global average pooling, dropout and batch normalisation layers on top of the pre-trained ResNet50 backbone. This methodical superimposing of the GAP layer in tandem with Resnet50's knowledge and training is the proposed novelty taking our model the extra mile. As a result, the binary classification problem between benign and malignant tumours is handled gracefully by our proposed architecture despite the target imbalance. We achieve an AUC of 0.946 and an accuracy of 98.7% which is better than the previously stated standard.

Keywords: Histopathology Images · BreakHis · Convolutional Neural Network (CNN) · Transfer Learning · Breast Cancer

1 Introduction

Breast cancer is known to be one of the major medical problems facing modern women. The tumours [6] affect the milk producing ducts among many other functionalities of a female breast, and are deadly if not detected and treated in time. Followed by the traditional methods resorting to CAD-based techniques, state-of-the-art deep learning architectures have opened up a whole new avenue for automated and effective detection of benign and malignant tumours.

1.1 Histopathological Image Analysis

It is widely known that Histology or Histopathology deals with unravelling the structure of tissues at a microscopic level. This field of analysis becomes vital because understanding biological functions at the sub-cellular and tissue levels plays a huge role in identifying disease progression and prognosis. The morphological characteristics of tissue is also something that pathologists focus on to detect the presence/onset of cancer,

N. Khare et al. (Eds.): MIND 2022, CCIS 1763, pp. 3–13, 2022.
https://doi.org/10.1007/978-3-031-24367-7_1

while analysing histological images under a microscope. The biopsy sample is processed, and its sections are placed on glass slides for examination under a microscope.

This pathologist's diagnosis is subjective and depends greatly on the observer variations amidst different personnel. As a result, quantitative evaluation of these images is critical for objective diagnosis. Thus, traditional methods like Computer Assisted Disease Diagnosis (CAD) and modern frameworks built out of Machine Learning (ML) & Deep Learning (DL) have carved out an entirely new avenue in histopathological imaging and diagnostics. On way or the other, Histology remains the foundation stone for preliminary clinical research, practice and future advancements.

1.2   Contributions of This Work

By using ResNet50 architecture as the backbone of our transfer learning model, we have tried to classify microscopic histopathological images into the known classes of benign and malignant respectively. Let's understand the contributions of this work in further detail.

- On top of the backbone, we have added the GAP layer to substitute (via pooling operation) fully connected layers in classical CNNs.
- We have topped it off with a dropout layer to prevent overfitting and a two-neuron output layer for binary classification which has resulted in an improved standard on all relevant performance metrics.
- The novelty in our proposed architecture is the usage of Global Average Pooling (GAP) layer in tandem with Resnet50's knowledge and training.
- The GAP layer manages to aggressively summarise the feature presence in image, prevents overfitting since there is no parameter to be optimised, and therefore, makes for a unique pairing with the Resnet backbone.
- This added subtlety of the native convolution structure enabling correspondences between feature maps and categories takes our model the extra mile.

2   Related Works

Since the former traditional approaches utilized a more manual outlook for feature extraction, CNNs took over the landscape due to their ability to extract features from input images themselves. Falling in line, Benzheng Wei et al. [17] deployed his the BiCNN model and achieved accuracy in upwards of 97% on the BreakHis dataset. However, the need for significantly large datasets and the subsequent tuning of a plethora of parameters are some of the major roadblocks facing CNNs. Moreover, the complexity of learning that comes with histopatho-logical breast tissue images asks for deep CNN architectures and large amounts of data. This is where Transfer Learning [20] enters the picture to provide an effortless solution to this ensuing dilemma [12].

What makes transfer learning indispensable for complex histopathology analysis is that it enables us to use a deep pre-trained CNN model developed for another similar application [5] and tune the weights and learning rates to perform classification on the images of our choice. One of the very first implementations of such a technique was done by Spanhol et al. [14] who used it on the BreakHis dataset.

Moving on the trails, Erkan Deniz et al. [1] leveraged the pre-trained AlexNet and a hybrid AlexNet-VGG-19 model on the same dataset, and vouched to deploy CNN models & data augmentation for improved classification accuracy in the future. Another interesting endeavour by Tripathi et al. [15] applied transfer learning to classify different types of cell nuclei in histopathological images (dealing with colon cancer) by using pre-trained (on ImageNet) AlexNet, VGG16, and VGG19 architectures. In research endeavours that followed, Tripathi et. al. used Hybrid O_L ConvNet [16] which integrates the interpretability of traditional object-level features and generalization of deep learning features for Cell Nuclei Classification in Histopathological Images.

Tracing back to the roots of the aforementioned works, we find that it all started when Yann LeCun et al. [4] introduced the vintage LeNet-5 architecture which showcased impressive performance on the MNIST database. Alexnet, introduced by Alex Krizhevsky et al. [3] also assessed the performance of this network on ImageNet dataset and it also obtained great results on the classic ImageNet dataset. Moreover, when Karen Simonyan et al. [10] introduced VGG-16 during the ILSVRC-14 classification challenge, their network's 7.3% test error was the second best in the competition. Finally, the birth of Residual network or ResNet by He et al. [2] was a welcome addition in a line of advanced convolutional network architectures.

3   Methodology and Workflow

3.1   Experimental Setup

The computational setup involved heavy use of Google Collaboratory and Jupyter Notebook to build, train and test Machine Learning models. As of recently, Google Colab provided a single 12 GB NVIDIA Tesla K80 GPU that could be used up to 12 h continuously. However, recent upgrades in Colab has also started offering free TPU. This enabled us to run code notebooks in GPU or even TPU backed deep learning environment, with zero configuration and easy sharing.

Colab notebooks allowed us to combine executable code and rich text in a single document, and save real-time progress on the cloud at all times.

3.2   Dataset

The BreakHis database [13] contains 7909 microscopic histopathological images (classified into benign and malignant breast tumours) that were collected over a batch of 82 patients. Breast tissue biopsy slides that were stained with the standard H&E (Hematoxylin and Eosin) gave the final samples. The final resultant images are present as the standard RGB color space using magnifying factors distributed across magnitudes of $40\times$, $100\times$, $200\times$, and $400\times$, corresponding to objective lenses of respective magnifications. Each image is in PNG format with dimensions of 460×700 pixels.

Table 1 shows the image distribution in the entire dataset into four magnification factors and two classes. And for our experiment, we have only used images from the BreakHis 400× dataset BreakHis's partial sample of 400× optical zoom, because previous studies [18] suggested that a higher magnification factor meant improved accuracy.

Table 1. Number of images in different magnifications and classes

Magnification	Begin	Malignant	Total
40×	625	1370	1995
100×	644	1437	2081
200×	623	1390	2013
400×	588	1232	1820
Total	2480	5429	7909
#Patients	24	58	82

Taking a look at the sample images in Fig. 1, it becomes clear that manual classification of the microscopic biopsy images into the two categories, benign and malignant, can only be done by a specialist pathologist and requires elite precision. This is where deep learning methods can come in handy.

3.3 ResNet50

In 2015, Kaiming He et al. introduced ResNet (also known as Residual Network) [2]. Since deep neural nets were hard to train, they introduced a residual learning framework (considerably deeper) to soften the training, by reformulating layers as learning residual functions. On a broader scale, these residual networks were effortlessly optimisable and obtained increased accuracies.

Moreover, the motivation (or rather intuition) behind the addition of more layers was that they'd be able to progressively learn more complex features that were previously overlooked in shallower architectures.

Another vital nuance was that the inner working of ResNets was the information from the initial layers being passed to deeper layers by simple matrix addition, where the operation doesn't impose any additional parameters while information is being forwarded. Moreover, the 'skip connections' act as direct connections which tend to skip some arbitrary layers and are a core feature of the residual blocks. To implement ResNet with 50 layers (ResNet 50), we simply use the function from Keras.

3.4 Transfer Learning and Added Layers

The backbone of our model is based on the pre-trained ResNet50 model which takes input shape of $224 \times 224 \times 3$. We have leveraged the learning of this model (trained on ImageNet dataset) and added our layers to obtain results for the BreakHis 400× dataset.

It is widely known that the standard 2D Averaging Block reduces the size of the data (in some sense through reduction of quantity of parameters), much like scaling down the size of an image. Not only does it drastically reduce the amount of computation needed

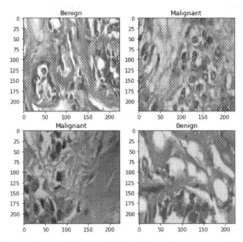

Fig. 1. Sample images from BreakHis 400×

but at the same time, controls over-fitting during model training. In our case, we have taken a step further with our proposed model architecture and added Global Average Pooling (2D) right after the backbone, which can be regarded as performing the same operation as the 2D Average pooling system. One glaring exception is that the pool size (which is a product of the horizontal pooling factor and vertical pooling factor) is equal to the size of the entire input of the block, which means our GAP layer is computing a singular average value for each of the input channels.

This GAP layer acts as a viable substitute (via pooling operation) for fully connected layers in classical CNNs. The core idea being that rather than stacking fully connected layers over the feature maps, we pull the feature map's resultant average and the resulting vector is supplied into the sigmoid (activation) layer. A clear upside of this substitution is that it enforces a more native convolution structure by enabling correspondences between feature maps and categories. This way, we can easily interpret the feature maps as categories confidence maps. Moreover, the lack of optimisable parameters in this approach makes sure that overfitting is completely avoided at this layer. Also, it is GAP's inherent nature to sum out the spatial information making it more robust and responsive to spatial transitions and translations of the input.

We have further added a dropout layer which randomly or arbitrarily nullifies some input units to 0 with a pre-defined frequency of rate (set to 0.5) during the training stage, and thereby helps prevent overfitting. We have implemented for a two-neuron output layer as this is a binary classification problem (between benign and malignant) and the activation function used is sigmoid.

3.5   Training and Testing

The training set and test set have been divided into two folders: benign and malignant. The training set consists of 371 images in the benign folder and 784 images in the malignant folder. On the other hand, the test set contains 176 images in the benign folder and 369 images in the malignant folder. We have trained our model with a benchmark batch size of 16, coupled with a learning rate of 0.0001 for 20 epochs.

3.6 Evaluation Metrics

In order to measure the performance of a model, it needs to be tested on all relevant scales from a conceptual standpoint and also for a comprehensive objective comparison with other works. Moreover, choosing the right evaluation metric (other than just accuracy percentage as a benchmark) becomes even more important for an imbalanced dataset. Also, Deep learning models deployed for biomedical purposes aim to minimise false negatives as they can prove to be lethal for the patient with an underlying condition.

So it makes sense to go over the evaluation metrics used to measure the effectiveness of our model in this research endeavour:

Precision: In a mathematical sense, Precision is calculated by dividing the correctly positive predicted observations by the total positive predicted observations, and as the name suggests, it gives us a measure of how precise our model is. A high precision value generally means low false positive count.

$$\textbf{Precision} = \textbf{TP}/(\textbf{TP} + \textbf{FP})$$

Recall: In a similar sense as above, Recall is obtained as the ratio of correctly predicted positive observations to the number of observations that are actually present in the positive class. The mathematical intuition behind Recall means that it is often used to measure the coverage of the minority class in an imbalanced learning setting.

$$\textbf{Recall} = \textbf{TP}/(\textbf{TP} + \textbf{FN})$$

F1-score: Mathematically stating, F1-score falls as the weighted average (also, harmonic mean) of Precision and Recall. F1 Score is the apt metric to pursue if we want to strike the right balance between precision and recall, as well as handle uneven class distribution.

$$\textbf{F1 Score} = 2 * (P * R)/(P + R)$$

TPR, FNR, TNR, FPR: It should also be noted that Rate serves as another important measure while evaluating the confusion matrix. And a perfectly trained model ensures high TPR & TNR and at the same time, low FNR & FPR.

- True Positive(TP): Values that are positive in reality and predicted positive as well, i.e., **TPR = TP/(TP + FN)**
- False Positive(FP): Values that are negative in reality but are predicted as positive, i.e., **FPR = FP/(TN + FP)**
- False Negative(FN): Values that are positive in reality but predicted as negative. i.e., **FNR = FN/(TP + FN)**
- True Negative (TN): Values that are negative in reality and predicted negative as well, i.e., **TNR = TN/(TN + FP)**

AUC ROC: In theory, an ideally trained model must have AUC as near to 1 as possible indicating a respectable measure of separability, whereas a poor model has a respective AUC value near 0 indicating a bad sense of separability. The resultant ROC curve is plotted with TPR (True Positive Rate) against the FPR (False Positive Rate) on the y-axis and x-axis respectively.

4 Results

After training our model on 1155 images and testing on a set of 545 images from both classes, we achieve an impressive accuracy of 98.7% which outruns the latest recorded accuracy standard on the BreakHis 400× dataset by Soumik et al. [16].

Even though the standard accuracy percentage is a great metric for evaluation of any deep learning model, we know that our dataset houses sizeable imbalance, and therefore we need the help of other functional performance metrics to better evaluate the quality of our model and check for biasness during training.

4.1 Confusion Matrix: Type I Type II Errors

The Confusion Matrix as shown in Fig. 2 is a matrix of size 2 × 2 for binary classification, and clearly depicts vital information like true positive (TP), true negative (TN), false negative (FN), and false positive (FP), assuming malignant as + ve and benign as −ve in our case). False Positive (also known as Type I error) gives the wrong prediction of the negative class (which means actual negative is predicted positive) and in our case 16 units fall in that category. On the other hand, False Negative (also known as Type II error) wrongly predicts the positive class (which means actual positive is predicted negative) and in our case, 6 units fall in that category.

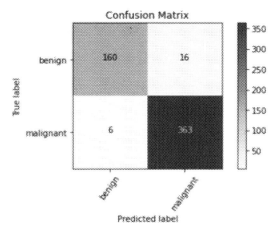

Fig. 2. Confusion Matrix: True vs Predicted

Table 2. Evaluation Metrics

	Precision	Recall	F1-score
Values	0.957	0.983	0.969

4.2 Precision, Recall, F1 and More

Using the values of TN, TP, FN and FP, we calculate precision, recall, F1-score, and the results (Table 2) lead us to believe that our model is generalising well to the test set and handling the dataset imbalance gracefully.

Furthermore, an extra added measure to check if the model is working well despite data imbalance is that the values of TPR and TNR should be high, and FPR and FNR should be as low as possible. Table 3 enlists the results required and provides further positive evidence of model performance.

4.3 AUC Value

Since this is a binary classification problem with target imbalance in the dataset, the significance of a good AUC value increases manifold. Interestingly enough, the ROC curve (plotted TPR vs FPR) gives an AUC value of **0.946**.

This metric outperforms the latest recorded AUC standard on the BreakHis 400× dataset by Parvin et al. [7]. Table 4 gives a bird's eye view comparison of our proposed model on grounds of more relevant metrics (precision, recall, F1score) used in classification problems, and lists the values obtained from each pre-trained architecture (used on the 400×flavour of the BreakHis dataset only).

Table 3. Type I and Type II errors

	TPR	TNR	FPR	FNR
Values	0.983	0.90	0.090	0.016

4.4 Accuracy Comparisons

During the performance measurement stage of the experimental results obtained by our deep learning model, another important avenue worth peeking at is the accuracy obtained during binary classification. Table 5 gives a comprehensive understanding of the accuracy values obtained by various state-of-the-art methods and architectures, and that our proposed model performs fairly better than current standards. Figure 3 shows some of the random samples picked from the complete lot of test images and marked with their respective actual labels and predicted labels.

Table 4. Comparison with state-of-the-art architectures

	Backbone	AUC	Precision	Recall	F1-score
	LeNet-5	50	34	50	41
	AlexNet	85	88	85	86
Parvin et al. [7]	VGG-16	80	82	80	81
	ResNet-50	50	33	50	40
	Inception-V1	88	89	88	89
Proposed Model	**Resnet-50**	**94.6**	**96**	**98**	**97**

Table 5. Accuracy comparison with state-of-the-art methods

	Backbone	Accuracy(%)
	LeNet-5	70
	AlexNet	89
Parvin et al. [7]	VGG-16	83
	ResNet-50	66
	Inception-V1	90
Xiang et. al. [18]	CNN	95.1
Deniz et al. [1]	AlexNet	91.3
Soumik et al. [11]	Inception-V3	98.5
Proposed Model	**Resnet-50**	**98.7**

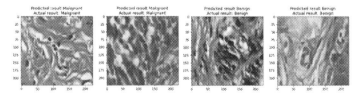

Fig. 3. Sample Predictions: Test set

5 Conclusion

The hybrid deep learning architecture that leveraged the power of pre-trained neural network like ResNet 50 via Transfer Learning was able to break through the current standard in the BreakHis 400× dataset classification problem. This was majorly made possible by the functional superimposing of additional layers on the ResNet model. The use of Global Average Pooling layer as a viable substitute for fully connected layers ensured a more native convolution structure by enforcing correspondence between feature maps and categories. Moreover, since there are no optimisable parameters in the global average pooling concept, it takes care of over-fitting in a seamless fashion. Moreover, the skip connections in the ResNet architecture skip some of the layers (as the name suggests) in the neural network and feed the output of one layer as the input to some arbitrary next layer. This takes care of the'degradation problem' which arises when deep networks start to converge, i.e., accuracy gets saturated with increasing depth and then degrades drastically.

6 Future Scope

Future works can look to incorporate deep learning segmentation models [8] as an up-and-coming wing of digital pathology, where models can combine multiscale features in the encoder and the decoder stages itself. Furthermore, foraying deeper into multi-scale neural networks [19] for DL-based histopathological image classification/analysis is also an exciting avenue, since much of the work is concentrated around single-scale neural networks. Such a multi-scale network can be structured on a ResNet50 model, and seamlessly take care of degradation issues [2] with increasing depth. Another potential path is offered by General Adversarial Networks (GANs) which are known to handle the resolution problem. Widening residual blocks and leveraging self-attention [9] in tandem with GAN's Wasserstein Gradient Penalty has already shown to achieve impressive results on breast histopathology images.

References

1. Deniz, E., Şengür, A., Kadiroğlu, Z., Guo, Y., Bajaj, V., Budak, Ü.: Transfer learning based histopathologic image classification for breast cancer detection. Health Inf. Sci. Syst. **6**(1), 1–7 (2018)
2. He, K., Zhang, X., Ren, S., Sun, J.: Deep residual learning for image recognition. In: Proceedings of the IEEE Conference on Computer Vision and Pattern Recognition, pp. 770–778 (2016)
3. Krizhevsky, A., Sutskever, I., Hinton, G.E.: Imagenet classification with deep convolutional neural networks. Adv. Neural Inf. Process. Syst. **25** (2012)
4. LeCun, Y., Bottou, L´., Bengio, Y., Haffner, P.: Gradient-based learning applied to document recognition. Proc. IEEE **86**(11), 2278–2324 (1998)
5. Liang, H., Fu, W., Yi, F.: A survey of recent advances in transfer learning. In: 2019 IEEE 19th International Conference on Communication Technology (ICCT), pp. 1516–1523. IEEE (2019)
6. Nagpure, R., Chandak, S., Pathak, N.: Breast cancer detection using neural network mammogram. In: 2020 International Conference on Convergence to Digital World Quo Vadis (ICCDW), pp. 1–6 (2020)
7. Parvin, F., Al Mehedi Hasan, Md.: A comparative study of different types of convolutional neural networks for breast cancer histopathological image classification. In: 2020 IEEE Region 10 Symposium (TENSYMP), pp. 945–948. IEEE (2020)
8. Samanta, P., Raipuria, G., Singhal, N.: Context aggregation network for semantic labeling in histopathology images. In: 2021 IEEE 18th International Symposium on Biomedical Imaging (ISBI), pp. 673–676 (2021)

9. Shahidi, F.: Breast cancer histopathology image super-resolution using wide-attention gan with improved wasserstein gradient penalty and perceptual loss. IEEE Access **9**, 32795–32809 (2021)
10. Simonyan, K., Zisserman, A.: Very deep convolutional networks for large-scale image recognition. arXiv preprint arXiv:1409.1556 (2014)
11. Israk Soumik, M.F., Bin Aziz, A.Z., Ali Hossain, Md.: Improved transfer learning based deep learning model for breast cancer histopathological image classification. In: 2021 International Conference on Automation, Control and Mechatronics for Industry 4.0 (ACMI), pp. 1–4. IEEE (2021)
12. Israk Soumik, M.F., Ali Hossain, Md.: Brain tumor classification with inception network based deep learning model using transfer learning. In: 2020 IEEE Region 10 Symposium (TENSYMP), pp. 1018–1021. IEEE (2020)
13. Spanhol, F.A., Oliveira, L.S., Petitjean, C., Heutte, L.: A dataset for breast cancer histopathological image classification. IEEE Trans. Biomed. Eng. **63**(7), 1455–1462 (2015)
14. Spanhol, F.A., Oliveira, L.S., Petitjean, C., Heutte, L.: Breast cancer histopathological image classification using convolutional neural networks. In: 2016 International Joint Conference on Neural Networks (IJCNN), pp. 2560–2567. IEEE (2016)
15. Tripathi, S., Singh, S.: Histopathological image classification: Defying deep architectures on complex data. In: Santosh, K.C., Hegadi, R.S. (eds.) RTIP2R 2018. CCIS, vol. 1036, pp. 361–370. Springer, Singapore (2019). https://doi.org/10.1007/978-981-13-9184-2_33
16. Tripathi, S., Singh, S.K.: Cell nuclei classification in histopathological images using hybrid *OL* convent. ACM Trans. Multim. Comput. Commun. Appl. **16**(1s), 1–22 (2020)
17. Wei, B., Han, Z., He, X., Yin, Y.: Deep learning model based breast cancer histopathological image classification. In: 2017 IEEE 2nd International Conference on Cloud Computing and Big Data Analysis (ICCCBDA), pp. 348–353. IEEE (2017)
18. Xiang, Z., Ting, Z., Weiyan, F., Cong, L.: Breast cancer diagnosis from histopathological image based on deep learning. In: 2019 Chinese Control and Decision Conference (CCDC), pp. 4616–4619. IEEE (2019)
19. Xie, P., Li, T., Li, F., Zuo, K., Zhou, J., Liu, J.: Multi-scale convolutional neural network for melanoma histopathology image classification. In: 2021 IEEE 3rd International Conference on Frontiers Technology of Information and Computer (ICFTIC), pp. 551–554 (2021)
20. Zhuang, F., et al.: A comprehensive survey on transfer learning. Proc. IEEE **109**(1), 43–76 (2020)

Lane Detection and Distance Estimation Using Computer Vision Techniques

Alan Henry[1]([envelope]), R. Rahesh[2], Kuntal Das Barman[3], and R. Sujee[1]

[1] Department of Computer Science and Engineering, Amrita School of Engineering, Amrita Vishwa Vidyapeetham, Coimbatore, India
cb.en.p2aid20010@cb.students.amrita.edu, r_sujee@cb.amrita.edu
[2] Center for Computational Engineering and Networking, Amrita School of Engineering, Amrita Vishwa Vidyapeetham, Coimbatore, India
[3] Volvo Group India Private Limited, Bangalore, India
kuntal.das.barman@volvo.com

Abstract. In the realm of computer vision, the term "autonomous driving" has become a buzzword. The main goal of the autonomous driving is to reduce human efforts while driving. However, dealing with measurements of distance raises numerous obstacles, both in terms of equipment and approach. The use of cameras to measure the distance of an object is practical and popular for obstacle avoidance and navigation.. This work focuses on vehicle distance measuring of traffic signs and cars, which is a critical task in the image processing domain. In this research, the suggested system employs two cameras installed in the hosting vehicle in front, to obtain the data and estimate distance. The proposed pipeline starts with YOLO v3 and YOLOv2 algorithms for detecting traffic signs and cars in the video frames. The distances of the detected objects are measured using triangle similarity approach. In final phase, lane segmentation and grid marking are added along with these results. As a result, it will assist drivers in making decisions prior to reaching signs, potentially resulting in improved safety decisions.

Keywords: Object detection · Lane segmentation · Collision avoidance · YOLO · Self-driving

1 Introduction

Over the last two decades, self-driving cars have grown in importance in the research domain, and they are expected to take the place of humans in a range of industries by completing a variety of missions. The development of autonomous vehicles has become one of the most important areas in the field of automotive research, owing to the growing traffic challenges in most regions of the world. As a result, there's a good chance that relieving drivers of driving responsibilities in part or totally will improve road safety and driving comfort.. Because driver responsibilities can be automated, collisions can be reduced, and road safety can be improved.

Because of the complex and dynamic environment,, as well as the complex movement in a short period of time, researchers in the field of self-driving face numerous challenges.

N. Khare et al. (Eds.): MIND 2022, CCIS 1763, pp. 14–26, 2022.
https://doi.org/10.1007/978-3-031-24367-7_2

The automated cars must be able to detect other vehicles of any shape or sort. As a result, numerous techniques such as detection of vehicle and licence plate along with its speed and distance could be useful for the system to avoid collision. Automated vehicles use the data gathered from these algorithms to make decisions like avoiding other vehicles, shifting their path, or increasing their speed.

Measuring the distance between the cars is a hot topic in autonomous vehicles. As a result, determining nearby vehicle information in real time is an essential and tough task.. There are two basic ways for measuring distance in the literature: active and passive approaches.

The active technique sends distance-measuring signals to the object. Systems that search for items using sensors such as laser scanners, structured light, ultrasound, or time-of-flight are being developed to boost environmental awareness beyond what humans are capable of. The disadvantage of these systems is the high cost of implementation. As a result, replacing these equipment with cameras and computer vision techniques saves both time and money.

Passive techniques, on the other hand, rely on the object's location being determined by passive measures of the scene, such as camera photos. Object distance measurement via image processing is one of the most important research fields in computer vision. The implications of extracting useful data from photographs and video footage have applications in robotics, virtual reality, remote sensing, and industrial automation, among other fields. The passive approach offers the advantages of being able to work in a variety of weather and lighting circumstances, having a high resolution, and being able to use low-cost cameras.

Also, the main purpose of finding the objects is to avoid the collision by tracking the movement of the objects in a series of frames. Objects can be classified based on their dynamic nature. The first one is stationery objects, which maintains its location regardless of frame or time. For example, traffic signs, barricades, and parked cars. The second one is moving objects, as time passes, their position changes. For example, moving cars. The YOLOv3 and YOLOv2 algorithm is used in this work to detect traffic signs as well as vehicles passing in front of the hosting vehicle. The distance is calculated using the triangle similarity approach, which uses the calculated focal length to derive the distance. In the final output video, lane segmentation is incorporated alongside the gridlines. The main novelty of the research, is that, it focuses on using pure computer vision and deep learning algorithms to recognise traffic signals and automobiles in front of the hosting vehicle, as well as estimate the distance between them. As a result, the system alerts the camera hosting vehicle even before it reaches the appropriate traffic sign site.

The following is a breakdown of the paper's structure. The purpose is discussed in the following section. The third section discusses the difficulties encountered when implementing the project. Following the problems, the next section explains the work on autonomous vehicle distance estimate and how objects are detected using YOLOv3 and YOLOv2 algorithms.The study then goes into detail on novelty and the dataset that was used. The next part goes over the experiment's several steps, what happens during them, and the outcomes. The final section discusses the conclusion as well as the future scopes.

2   Methodology

Fig. 1. Proposed methodology

The implementation of the proposed system is done different stages (Fig. 1):

2.1   Data Collection

The data was collected in transit between Bangalore and Calicut during daytime in proper lighting conditions. The video was continuously recorded and stored in cloud-based platform during the transit. There were challenges during this journey like pedestrian crossing, diversion of routes. Etc. Two monocular cameras were placed on the left and right corners of the windshield of the hosting bus to capture data. The video footage from the right camera is used for the study. The camera was able to capture a dataset with resolution of 1280*720. To make computation easier, a 2-min video was extracted from the dataset was used. The raw footage is then fed into pre-processing stage for further steps.

2.2   Camera Calibration

The camera's lens curvature causes radial distortion in the images it captures. This causes the image's straight lines to appear twisted or curled in an unnatural way. The distortion in an image frame degrades image quality and has an impact on estimating distances between objects in the image. Camera calibration procedures can help to eliminate this distortion. To eliminate distortions, checkerboard calibrating technique is used in the dataset. First 7*7 checkerboard was used in this project, but the results were disappointing. However, when compared to the 7*7 checkerboard, the 9*9 checkerboard produced correct findings (Fig. 2).

Fig. 2. 9*9 distorted image(left), 9*9 undistorted image (right)

2.3   Object Detection of Traffic Sign and Cars

Object detection is a way for applying deep learning algorithms to determine the location of a target in an image. For object detection, there are numerous state-of-the-art algorithms. R-CNN, SSD, FCN, YOLO, and so forth. The complexity and architecture of these algorithms varies. Because it is highly rapid at detecting objects, YOLOv2, YOLOv3 was considered for this study. You Only Look Once, Version (YOLO) is a real-time object identification system that detects specific objects in an image or videos. YOLO uses deep convolutional neural network to detect an item from an image frame. CNNs are classifier-based systems that can recognise patterns in incoming images and interpret them as organised arrays of data. YOLO much faster compared to other frameworks or networks without sacrificing accuracy. During test time the model is evaluated and predictions are made based on the image's overall context. YOLO and other convolutional neural network algorithms "score" regions by comparing them to preset categories. Positive detections of the class with which they most closely identify are highlighted in high-scoring areas. A single-stage real-time object detection model is called YOLOv2 or YOLO9000. By using Darknet-19 as a foundation, batch normalisation, a high-resolution classifier, anchor boxes to forecast bounding boxes, and other features, it outperforms YOLOv1 in a number of ways. In terms of class speed, precision, and specificity, YOLOv3 [9] differs significantly from earlier versions. Darknet-19 was chosen because it is the most widely used architecture worldwide. In terms of accuracy, speed, and architecture, YOLOv2 and YOLOv3 are poles apart. YOLOv3 is the improved version of YOLOv2 and YOLOv1 (Figs. 3 and 4).

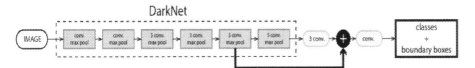

Fig. 3. YOLO v2 architecture

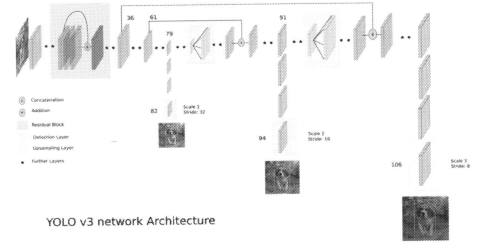

YOLO v3 network Architecture

Fig. 4. YOLO v3 architecture

For traffic sign and vehicle detection, the YOLOv3 and YOLOv2 algorithms was employed using pre-trained weights. These pretrained weights were trained on images of traffic signs and cars respectively. Traffic signs output classes are categorised into labels such as prohibitive, harmful, obligatory, and others. Among YOLO algorithms, YOLOv3 performed much better compared to the YOLOv2. The bounding box and associated confidence scores are used to detect traffic signs.

To get the actual proximity distance of an object from the hosting vehicle distance are measured manually. Distance guidelines are marked based on the manual distance measurement as seen on Fig. 5

Fig. 5. Distance guidelines 5m(top-left), 10m(top-right),15m (bottom-left), 20m (bottom-right)

The distance is calculated using the triangle similarity method. This is how the triangle similarity resembles each other: Consider a item or marker with a known width W. After that, we set this item at a distance D from the camera. The camera takes a snapshot of the object and then determines P is the apparent width of the object in pixels. This allows to calculate the camera's apparent focal length F.

$$F = (P \times D)/W$$

The distance is calculated based on the focal length provided. In this study, the average width of cars as a marker for car detection and width of the traffic signs as marker for traffic sign detection. In India, the average width of cars is 1700mm and that of the traffic signs is 900 mm. These measurements are considered for the corresponding detections. The width of the bounding box equals the pixel width of the object detected. It is then used to figure out how far away the observed object is based on the focal length which is calculated using triangle similarity algorithm. The focal length of the guideline closest to the base of the bounding boxes is considered.

2.4   Lane Segmentation Along with Grids

There are different phases done inorder to get a lane detection result. First, the picture frames from the video are delivered to the camera calibration component. The distortions in the image frames are eliminated after applying the camera caliberation parameters. After applying camera calibration, the output is supplied into the perspective transformation section, where the picture is transfromed depending on the source and destination coordinates and warped perspective is applied to that image frame.

Following the acquisition of the warp perspective image, the image is subjected to thresholding. For lane line markings, photos are either changed to white or black based on a specified threshold value. Lanelines are embedded on the image after thresholding. The extracted laneline is then superimposed on top of the original photos. The final video is created by combining these original photos (Fig. 6).

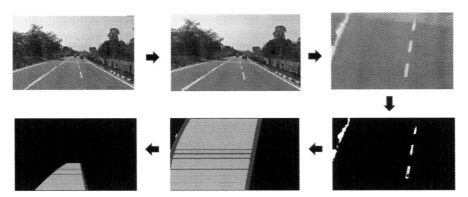

Fig. 6. Lane segmentation phases

3   Purpose

In recent years, distance measurement in vehicles has gained a lot of attention in various fields. Vehicle automation is one of the most important trends in automotive research and development. The idea is to relieve drivers of some or all of their driving responsibilities while also improving road safety and comfort. Autonomous driving may involve several kinds of challenging factors such as dynamic environment, complex, and high-speed movement. The vehicle must detect the positions of other automobiles in any type of traffic, which includes object detection, relative speed estimation, and distance. In order for the vehicle to adjust its path and/or speed, these variables must be determined.

Object distance calculation is becoming increasingly important in autonomous systems. Recognizing their environment correctly and quickly is one of the most critical and hardest tasks for autonomous systems. There are two methods for measuring distance: active and passive. The majority of researchers have used active approaches inorder to obtain precise vehicle distance measurements. The disadvantage of these systems is the high cost of implementation. As a result, saving money can be achieved by using cameras and computer vision algorithms instead of these high cost equipments.

So, instead of using a lidar sensor or other sensors, this re are employing cameras to estimate the distance of a traffic sign. Initially the traffic sign and car is detected using the object detection algorithm like YOLO, and then the triangle similarity method to calculate the distance and then embed lane segmentation and along with the grid marking for ease of use.

4   Major Research Findings

This work [1] focuses on inter-vehicle distance measuring, which is a difficult task in the domain of image processing. It's employed in a variety of systems, including DSSS (Driving Safety Support Systems), traffic mobility, and autonomous driving. In this research, image-based self-driving vehicle inter-vehicle distance measurement system have been presented. As one stereo camera, the suggested solution uses two cameras positioned in the hosting car behind the rear-view mirror. First, a single camera is used to detect vehicles, and a recent effective study from the literature is used. The similar car is then spotted in the image acquired by the second camera using the template matching technique. As a result, a basic algorithm based on the vehicle's position in both cameras, geometric derivations, as well as technical information such as camera distance and particular angles is used to estimate the inter-vehicle distance.. The results of the extensive testing revealed that the suggested method is more accurate than earlier works in the literature, and it allows for efficient measurement of vehicles' distances from the hosting vehicle. Furthermore, independent of the object kinds, this method might be employed in real time in a variety of systems from various disciplines. The studies were carried out using a TERASIC VEEK-MT2S equipped with a Hardware Processor System (HPS).

Self-driving automobiles serve individuals in a variety of fields by reducing human error and completing diverse missions. They've become a hot topic in both industry and academia when it comes to automotive research and development. However, dealing with distance measurement and cost poses numerous obstacles, both in terms of equipment and approach. The use of a stereo camera to measure the distance of an object is convenient and frequent for obstacle avoidance and navigation. Vehicles that operate on their own. When calculating distance, angle is considered. The image pixel, the distance between cameras, and the distance between the cameras. This research [2] presents a trigonometry-based approach for measuring object distance is confronted by a self-driving automobile that uses image processing and stereo vision for high precision, cheap cost, and quick computing. Using this method, you can measure distance with a high level of precision of up to 20 m. It can be utilised in real-time computer systems to calculate the safe driving distance between obstacles.

Using a single black-box camera placed in an automobile, this research [3] proposes a method for detecting and measuring the distance of a vehicle travelling in front. It was important to reduce throughput and speed up processing in order to adapt the suggested technology to autonomous vehicles. This is accomplished using the suggested method, before obtaining the aggregated channel information, which breaks down the input image into various images for real-time analysis (ACFs). The goal was to extract only the most vital information from photographs of varied sizes in an uniform manner.

From a bird's eye view, inverse perspective mapping (IPM) was used to build a system for recognising an item and establishing a vehicle's distance. In the proposed technique, ACFs were used to develop the AdaBoost-based vehicle detector. The ACFs were derived using the sedge gradient,LUV colour, and orientation of the input image (histograms of oriented gradients). The distance between the recognised vehicle and the autonomous vehicle was computed using IPM and the creation of a three-dimensional image from a two-dimensional input image. In a real-world road situation, the suggested method yielded precise results for vehicle detection and proximity estimation in real-time processing. As a result, we were able to demonstrate that our technology can be used in driverless vehicles.

In recent years, artificial intelligence technology has advanced at a breakneck pace. The goal of this paper [4] is to use this to calculate the distance to an object. Two independent photographs of the object from the identical angles will be taken to determine the distance. It compares the sizes of the same thing in two imagesThis was done in real time using object identification technologies from Artificial Intelligence on a cell phone. A method for calculating the distance between two images is provided in this paper. On iOS, the proposed method was tested as a prototype. Experiments were carried out in diverse situations to assess the performance of distance measurement. The empirical data produced various inconsistencies with the actual measurement in the experiments. This was due to faults in the object detection procedure, which caused the true dimensions of the item to be estimated incorrectly. Despite these shortcomings, this object recognition method could be widely used in instances when accurate measurements aren't necessary, such as navigation systems for the blind people.

As humans,we are rather skilled at deducing information from the three-dimensional world in which we inhabit. We accomplish this by fusing data from many senses with our prior understanding of the geometry of the thing. Therefore, the assumption will be almost accurate even if an object is obscured! Contrary to how robots and self-driving cars work, humans often combine stereo and monocular clues to detect the presence of an object and localise it. Understanding and collecting third-dimension data from a global coordinate system is difficult. The issues can be solved by active sensors like LiDAR. The lack of data and expensive cost of such sensors inhibit the development of such applications. Understanding depth from 2D photographs is a promising subject of research that could someday lead to 3D reconstruction and 3D item detection. Since unsupervised learning doesn't require ground truth for training, it is gaining popularity. In this study [5], unsupervised learning was used to propose a DNN for depth estimation. The proposed approaches are then assessed using KITTI standard metrics, demonstrating a potential path forward for autonomous vehicles. The proposed techniques outperform the most recent methods for depth estimation in unsupervised learning with over 75% less training data and a lower input resolution.

The introduction of self-driving cars and AI technology altered the transportation infrastructure. The current generation of self-driving cars require accurate and trustworthy data from a variety of functional modules. Object detection and categorization is one of the main modules included in vehicles. In this study [6], a method for slow-moving electric vehicle platforms is created for speed bump identification. The created technique divides the speed bump using a GAN network from monocular photos as input. The outcomes of the novel approach demonstrate that the GAN network can accurately separate different kinds of speed bumps. This novel alternative method demonstrates GANs' suitability for use in self-driving car speed bump detection.

For intelligent and precise farming, autonomous agricultural machinery is crucial. Adopting autonomous path planning technologies to replace the time-consuming task of manually steering vehicles might significantly improve agricultural machinery efficiency and precision, saving farmers time and reducing driver fatigue. This paper's [7] goal is to create a stereo vision-based path planning system for an autonomous onion harvester. The proposed method comprises employing semantic segmentation based on deep learning to recognise crop rows in images broadcast by a stereo vision camera. In order to determine the harvester's navigation waypoints is determined by segmentation information along with image depth map. An Indian onion field dataset was used to construct and test the produced system, and it provides accurate results.

The purpose of the paper [8] is to classify faults in a fabric material using deep learning and neural network techniques. Rust, Hole, Grease, Broken Filament, Oil Stain, and Slough are the six types of faults discussed in this work. The YOLOv2 model and the YOLOv3 Tiny model were made independently in this study, with the identical fabric data set(six different sorts of faults) and pre-trained convolutional weights on the Imagenet dataset. Both models had a high success rate in finding flaws in the fabric, which was observed and documented.

5   Discussion

The first and foremost is obtaining a dataset. Since the dataset is not readily available. The dataset is gathered from video footage of the bus.Road conditions can play a vital role in determining the distance.Since we are not using sensors, distance can be inaccurate in sometimes. Computational cost is high. Vibration during the travel of the bus can affect the quality of the data.Weather condition can also affect the computation of the distance.Computation expense is high due to the large size of data. Radial distortion present in most of the images. While detecting the traffic signs, the model misclassified some of the items in the frames, even though they are not actual traffic signs. This means there are a lot of false positives. In lateral view, the algorithm miscalculates the distance between cars when it comes to car detection. Because lane lines are not always visible on Indian roadways, the most difficult part of lane segmentation was determining lane line markers. It could be caused by a buildup of dust on the road, faded lane lines, or poor illumination.

6   Results

The proposed method is fed with a two-minute video from the original video to test its effectiveness, and it was able to correctly detect traffic signs and vehicles on the roads, as well as the approximate distances between traffic signs and the host vehicle and the vehicles moving in front. In terms of detection and confidence ratings, YOLOv3 surpassed YOLOv2 among detection algorithms. After detection, the proposed method was able to segment lane lines in each frame and embed grid markings along with it (Figs. 7, 8, 9, and 10).

Fig. 7. Traffic sign detection

The model misclassified some of the objects in the frames while detecting the traffic signs, even though they are not actual traffic signs. This indicates a high rate of false positives. Retraining the model with a better dataset can help decrease this. When it comes to car detection, the algorithm miscalculates the distance between cars in lateral view due to the static width of the back (1700 mm). The bounding box's pixel width is greater than the pixel width of the car's rear. As a result, the distance is associated with a small error. In the case of lane segmentation, the most difficult component was identifying lane line marking on Indian highways, because lane lines are not always visible. It could be due to an accumulation of dust on the road, faded lane markings, or bad lighting conditions.

Fig. 8. Car detection(YOLOv2)

Fig. 9. Car detection result(YOLOv3)

Fig. 10. Lane segmentation result

7 Conclusion and Future Research Work

The proposed method successfully was able to detect traffic signs and car detection. After detection, the model was able to estimate the approximate distances between the targets. Lane lines are segmented after distance measurement, and grid markers are incorporated in the output frame. The proposed method for measuring object distance that relies solely on cameras yields good results. This method can help establish safe driving distance by measuring the distance between the hosting vehicle and cars and traffic signs. Even though the proposed approach was able to predict the approximate distances, it was lacking on some other aspects like more false positivity rates, irregular lane markings etc.

Stereo vision, which can replace the existing active approach and perceptual systems, can improve this research even more.The approach proposed in this work simply utilises one of the two cameras to capture the front obstructions. The produced results can be applied in driving assistance systems by adding them on local maps and driver dashboards. This helps the drivers to make better decisions and prevent the vehicle from collisions. Similar technology could be utilised with more cameras or 360° cameras in the future to detect problems in more directions.

References

1. Zaarane, A., Slimani, I., Al Okaishi, W., Atouf, I., Hamdoun, A.: Distance measurement system for autonomous vehicles using stereo camera. Array 5, 100016 (2020)
2. Salman, Y.D., Ku-Mahamud, K.R., Kamioka, E.: Distance measurement for self-driving cars using stereo camera. Int. Conf. Comput. Informat. 1(105), 235–242 (2017)
3. Kim, J.B.: Efficient vehicle detection and distance estimation based on aggregated channel features and inverse perspective mapping from a single camera. Symmetry 11(10), 1205 (2019)
4. Lee, J.M.: Real distance measurement using object detection of artificial intelligence. Turkish J. Comput. Math. Educ. (TURCOMAT) 12(6), 557–563 (2021)
5. Harisankar, V., Sajith, V.V., Soman, K.P.: Unsupervised depth estimation from monocular images for autonomous vehicles. In: 2020 Fourth International Conference on Computing Methodologies and Communication (ICCMC), pp. 904–909. IEEE (2020)
6. Patil, S.O., Variyar, V.S., Soman, K.P.: Speed bump segmentation an application of conditional generative adversarial network for self-driving vehicles. In: 2020 Fourth International Conference on Computing Methodologies and Communication (ICCMC), pp. 935–939. IEEE (2020)
7. Sinalkar, S., Nair, B.B.: Stereo vision-based path planning system for an autonomous harvester. In: Reddy, V.S., Prasad, V.K., Wang, J., Reddy, K.T.V. (eds.) ICSCSP 2019. AISC, vol. 1118, pp. 499–510. Springer, Singapore (2020). https://doi.org/10.1007/978-981-15-2475-2_46
8. Sujee, R., Shanthosh, D., Sudharsun, L.: Fabric defect detection using YOLOv2 and YOLO v3 tiny. In: Chandrabose, A., Furbach, U., Ghosh, A., Kumar, A.M. (eds.) ICCIDS 2020. IAICT, vol. 578, pp. 196–204. Springer, Cham (2020). https://doi.org/10.1007/978-3-030-63467-4_15
9. Redmon, J., Farhadi, A.: Yolov3: An incremental improvement. arXiv preprint arXiv:1804.02767 (2018)

10. https://www.pyimagesearch.com/2015/01/19/find-distance-camera-objectmarker-using-pyt hon-opencv/#:~:text=In%20order%20to%20determine%20the,going%20to%20utilize%20t riangle%20similarity.&text=For%20example%2C%20lets%20say%20I,camera%20and% 20take%20a%20photo
11. Emani, S., Soman, K.P., Sajith Variyar, V.V., Adarsh, S.: Obstacle detection and distance estimation for autonomous electric vehicle using stereo vision and DNN. In: Wang, J., Reddy, G.R.M., Prasad, V.K., Reddy, V.S. (eds.) Soft Computing and Signal Processing. AISC, vol. 898, pp. 639–648. Springer, Singapore (2019). https://doi.org/10.1007/978-981-13-3393-4_65
12. Nabati, R., Qi, H.: Radar-camera sensor fusion for joint object detection and distance estimation in autonomous vehicles. arXiv preprint arXiv:2009.08428 (2020)

Using Deep Transfer Learning to Predict Student Engagement in Online Courses

Naeem Ahmad[1]([✉]) [iD], Anirudh Gupta[1], and Deepak Singh[2]

[1] Department of Computer Applications, National Institute of Technology Raipur, C.G., Raipur, India
nahmad.mca@nitrr.ac.in, anirudh.nitrr@gmail.com
[2] Department of Computer Science and Engineering, National Institute of Technology Raipur, C.G., Raipur, India
dsingh.cs@nitrr.ac.in

Abstract. The use of online courses is growing worldwide that has opened the door for the interested students to learn comfortably from their locations especially, during Covid-19 pandemic. However, an important aspect of traditional classroom is real-time students' feedback for content delivery and interactive sessions, which is missing in online courses. The aim of this work is to bridge this gap by providing an automatic recognition system for engagement level of the students during online courses using deep transfer learning. In this paper, a CNN based method is proposed to predict the level of engagement while watching online class sessions. The CNN based method consists of two different modalities including: (1) pre-trained network based transfer learning for feature extraction from image data, (2) support vector machine (SVM) classifier for classification. Ten different pre-trained networks are used in the proposed method. The superiority of the method is evaluated on the dataset created using images of graduate students. Of all pre-trained networks, Resnet50 and VGG16 achieved highest classification accuracy of 72.34% and 71.77% using the proposed approach respectively.

Keywords: Deep Learning · MOOCs · Student engagement · E-learning · Deep transfer learning

1 Introduction

In recent years, online courses (e.g. Coursera, Byjus) have changed system of education by providing for personalized delivery of course contents. Online literacy has become common place in education, ranging from Massive Open Online Courses (MOOCs) to Virtual Learning Environments (VLEs) and Learning Management Systems (LMSs) [16]. Although such systems are indicative of positive progress in education system, online platforms have a long way to go before they approach the experience of traditional classroom tutoring. Online education platforms are presently lacking real-time students' feedback for content delivery during online lectures, which is an important aspect. For example, an instructor may ask students if they are not properly engaged in the class or they are having doubts pertaining to any topic. In such cases, an instructor needs to know engagement level of students or their interests. In online platforms, most of the times students' feedback is absent thus resulting in a startling powerhouse rate nearly 93% [13]. Courses consist of static material, thus it is up to the student to research any questions they may have online or through other channels of communication like posting to the instructor or in class forums, which can usually take a while to react. Giving the system feedback on the behaviour of the students seeing the lectures online is an efficient way to bridge the gap between regular classrooms and online courses. Behavioural states may include engagement, confused, frustration etc. This knowledge could either be given to the teacher, who could make adjustments as needed, or it could be constructed with enough supporting materials that could be chosen at any time within a single lecture based on the student who is listening to it. The widespread usage of mobile devices, such as smart phones and tablets, as well as the inclusion of cameras in similar mobile devices, play a crucial role in making it possible for similar feedback. The front-facing web cameras of these devices could be used by online courses to monitor students during online lectures [16].

Table 1. Different pre-trained networks used for the study

Pre-trained networks	Depth	Number of layers	Final 3 layers replaced
Googlenet	22	144	loss3-classifier, prob, output
Alexnet	8	25	fc8, prob, output
Vgg16	16	41	fc8, prob, output
Vgg19	19	47	fc8, prob, output
Resnet101	101	347	fc1000, prob, Classification Layer predictions
Resnet50	50	177	fc1000, fc1000 Softmax, Classification Layer fc1000
Resnet18	18	72	fc1000, prob, Classification Layer Predictions
Squeezenet	18	68	pool10, prob, Classification Layer Predictions
Inceptionv3	48	316	predictions, predictions Softmax, Classification Layer Predictions
Densenet201	201	709	fc1000, fc1000 Softmax, Classification Layer fc1000

Engagement may be regarded as the most fundamental behavioural state in a learning environment among the many other possible behavioural states. Every other effective state, including boredom, confusion, tiredness etc., affects a student's level of engagement. Students' engagement while viewing course content is one of the major issues [11]. This study enhances the feedback system in e-learning environments by rating online lectures on a scale of three involvement levels. Although it is possible to get the conclusion that eye contact is a sign of engagement, this method of determining engagement has two significant flaws. First, eye-tracking is a very challenging task. Second, eye contact with the instructor is not a only criterion for involvement during online lectures. For instance, a student may be engaged in analysis while avoiding eye contact. Although the students' engagement is very helpful in e-learning, it can also be used in other application areas such as advertisement where it may help advertisers better understand the interests of consumers.

We then put forth a cutting-edge method of engagement recognition that uses information from crowdsourced labels to enhance the system's overall effectiveness. The experimental outcomes of our approach are then displayed, and they are encouraging. Over 10% more accuracy is gained in performance using our suggested methods. The remaining sections of this study are structured as follows: We discuss related work that has already been done in Sect. 2 in the area of engagement detection, not just for students but also for other contexts like marketing. The proposed methodology for engagement recognition is described in Sect. 3. The obtained results are discussed in Sect. 4. Finally, We conclude our work in Sect. 5.

Table 2. Image database details used for the proposed study

Class type	Engagement level	Number of images	Class contribution (%)
1	No Engagement	400	13.75
2	Minimal Engagement	2245	46.99
3	Full Engagement	1763	39.25

2   Related Works

Due to covid-19 pandemic, online course got exponential growth in popularity, which also attracted the research community to work in this domain make the suitable for education. Early research of this domain focus on using the machine learning techniques to develop the real-time adaptive learning system for MOOCs courses [17,20]. The personalized curriculum [8], adaptive evaluation [7] and learners' preferences based recommendation system [18] have played an important role in the development of online courses. Various research efforts have been devoted to this domain, which utilizes the machine learning as in [9,14]. However, very handful of works is done in predicting the behavior pattern of student during online course such as engagement level, student interest for courses using deep learning and convolutional neural networks.

Most of the studies mainly presented the use of computer vision to determine student engagement based on the six basic expressions (happiness, fear, anger, sadness, surprise etc.) and the facial action units associated with them [23,24]. However, recent studies has focused on using the deep learning and CNN for image classification due to its self-learning ability [6,15]. Authors in [10] proposed the automatic recognition system to measure the engagement level of TV viewers using fuzzy-Support Vector Machines (SVMs). In [12], a multiple geometric features extraction method and SVM is applied on a custom dataset to determine the engagement level of a TV viewer as a binary classification problem. In the same work, authors used single coder to create and labeled the small dataset, which may introduce the personal bias. Also the study ignores the subject awareness of experiment objectives while creating the dataset. On the similar line, a study of engagement level is carried out in [22] to deal with the real-time issues of online courses using the custom dataset, which had the same issue of subject awareness. The dataset is not revealed in case both the studies for future research works.

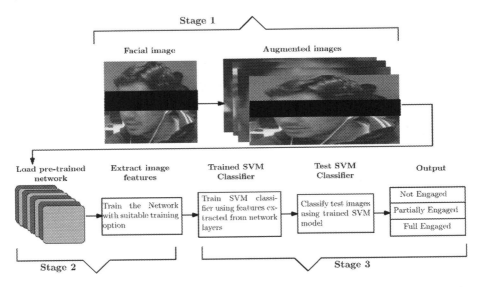

Fig. 1. Classification process of students based on their engagement level using transfer learning and pre-trained CNN network

In order to address the said issues, we have an effort by proposing the deep learning and CNNs based method. We used the dataset created as subjects watch videos in online courses considering the Hawthorne effect in its design. Another aspect of the proposed work is determine the engagement level of the students in real-worlds application, which is not in the commercial applications like Emotient [1], Emovu [2] and SightCorp [5]. These application had only provided the similar affective state, for example attentiveness. Another issue is their performance of these applications, which is not satisfactory for the challenging real-world videos. For instance, eye tracking used in SightCorp [5] is only the parameter to determine the engagement level. It is seen that eye-tracking is not directly related to the attentiveness especially in online classes because the student can carefully hear the voice of the instructor for better understanding without looking at the system screen during the online class [1]. It has motivated us to extend the present work to the other aspects of engagement levels. Hence, This work presented deep transfer learning based automatic engagement level recognition system to address the said issues. We have used open source data downloaded from https://github.com/e-drishti/wacv2016. This data is captured for subjects watch videos in online courses and labeled using crowdsourcing with varying option of engagement labels.

3   Proposed Methodology

It is seen that CNN is an ideal solution for image classification because of its self-learning capability of features. It is also one of the best option for the problems of multi-class classification. The primary building block of CNN are convolution layer (Conv) and ReLU, Pool and batch normalization. The final layer of CNN consists fully connected layer dropout, softmax and classification output layers. In CNN, the filters of convolutional layer determine the different patterns of images. Here, we have used ten different pre-trained networks which are shown in Table 2 along with the details of their parameters. These pre-trained networks were used to determine the best model for the 8-class problem in different studies [4]. Later, evaluation of the method was done using the following two strategies: (1) pre-trained network based transfer learning, (2) pre-trained network for feature extraction of image data.

3.1   Transfer Learning Using Pre-trained Networks

Transfer learning utilizes the pre-trained networks fine-tuned over a new task for better learning [19,21]. Figure 1 depicts the classification process of students based on their engagement level using transfer learning and pre-trained CNN network, which is done using the following steps:

1. Create facial images from the input videos
2. Image augmentation is applied on the dataset as it contains both types of images:colored images and black & white images.
3. The low-level features are generated from the lower layers of diverse pre-trained network.
4. Low-level features are passed to the upper layers to extract high-level features from the augmented images.
5. Dataset of facial images is categorized into 3 classes for training images.
6. Trained networks are tuned on the validation data and tested on tuned models for the test images.

In Table 1, 10 different pre-trained networks are shown, which are used to for the study. Here, these network are used on different parameters such as network depth, number of layers, required image input size, and suitable last 3 layers. The learning rate is set 1e−3, 1e−4, 1e−5 and 1e−6 to accurately test the models such as stochastic gradient descent with momentum (sgdm), root mean square propagation (rmsprop), and adaptive moment estimation (adam) optimizer [4].

3.2   Extract Image Features Using Pre-trained Network

Pre-trained deep networks are found to be the easiest and fastest way to extract the features. Therefore, for the study of engagement level, a pre-trained networks are used to extract the lower level features from the images those are passed to the SVM classifier for image classification [3]. The feature extract and classification process is shown in Fig. 1. Here first stage is used for inputting image and applying the image augmentation techniques. Image augmentation changes the size of the images as dataset contains both colored and black & white images. In second stage, pre-trained networks are loaded where higher-level features at the deeper layers are constructed using the lower-level features of earlier layers. In third stage, the features collected from the previous layers are used to train the SVM classifier, while features extracted from the test images are used to evaluate the SVM model.

3.3   Contributions of Training and Testing Image Datasets

We have used open source data. This data is captured for subjects watch videos in online courses and labeled using crowdsourcing with varying option of engagement labels. Dataset contains facial images of students to study the engagement level of the students, which is divided into 70% and 30% for training and testing stage respectively as shown in Table 2. Trained dataset is used to train the SVM classifier at radial basis kernel function. In order to evaluate the performance, classification accuracy is used in this study. The simulation set up is run 10 times and average results are reported.

4   Results and Discussion

This section presents obtained results of classification for the transfer learning and feature extraction techniques. In Fig. 2, the classification accuracy is shown

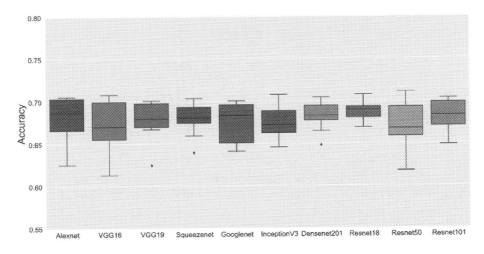

Fig. 2. Classification accuracy using transfer learning and pre-trained CNN network

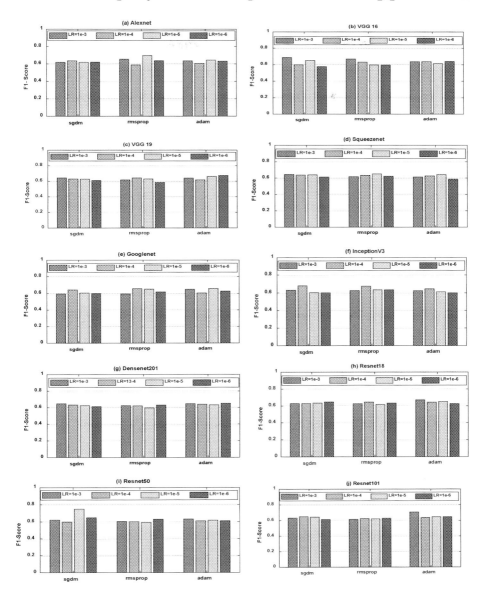

Fig. 3. F1-scores using transfer learning and pre-trained CNN network at different learning rate and solvers

for transfer learning technique at different solvers and learning rates. Figure 3 depicts the obtained F1-Score on various transfer learning model with varied learning rule and solver method. The highest F-1 score of 68.70% is achieved using Resnet50 model in case of SGDM solvers at learning rates 1e−6. The highest F1-score of 68.34% and 68.17% is achieved using Vgg16 and Vgg19 models in case of SGDM solvers at learning rates 1e−5 respectively. The highest F1-Score of 0.70 is achieved by Resnet101 at learning rates 1e−4, while Inceptionv3 model outperforms with learning rate 1e−5 with highest F-Score of 0.69 using RMSPROP solvers by Alexnet respectively. VGG16 achieved the highest F-Score of 0.68 at learning rate 1e−3 using SGDM solvers. The highest F-Score of Resnet50 and Resnet101 with the solvers 0.67 is achieved at learning rate 1e−3 and 1e−4. Resnet18 using solver ADAM has 0.67 at learning rate 1e−4. Overall, pre-trained networks and solvers works well at learning rate 1e−4. Additionally, summarized results of all pre-trained networks on different performance metrics are presented in Table 3. Of all pre-trained networks, Resnet50 and VGG16 achieved highest classification accuracy of 72.34% and 71.77% using transfer learning and extract image features approach respectively.

Table 3. Summarized results for pre-trained networks

Pre-trained networks	Solvers	LR	Accuracy	Sensitivity	Specificity	Precision
Alexnet	rmsprop	1e−3	0.7052	0.7084	0.8472	0.6400
VGG16	rmsprop	1e−3	0.7177	0.7127	0.8765	0.6703
VGG19	rmsprop	1e−6	0.7005	0.6716	0.8371	0.6295
Squeezenet	rmsprop	1e−6	0.7032	0.7197	0.8584	0.6585
Googlenet	adm	1e−3	0.7003	0.7379	0.8696	0.7325
InceptionV3	sgdm	1e−4	0.7075	0.7442	0.8432	0.6568
Densenet201	rmsprop	1e−6	0.7041	0.6934	0.8473	0.6369
Resnet18	adm	1e−3	0.7073	0.7289	0.8449	0.6525
Resnet50	sgdm	1e−5	0.7234	0.7864	0.8879	0.6926
Resnet101	adm	1e−3	0.7074	0.7297	0.8453	0.6908

5   Conclusion

In online courses, determining the engagement level of students is an intuitive process to human. This study is an attempt to model this intuitive process. Here, we have proposed a deep transfer learning approach including CNN, SVM and combination of all layers to predict the level of students' engagement while watching online class sessions. The said method uses facial images from the input videos to extract low-level features from the video sessions as the available dataset is not sufficient for deep learning. Furthermore, these low-level features are utilized to extract high-level features with the help of novel layer combinations for temporal dynamics modelling. The superiority of the proposed method is evaluated on the dataset created using images of graduate students. In future, this work can be extended to video segments for determining the engagement level instead of using images.

Acknowledgement. This work is part of major project of MCA students supported by Department of Computer Applications, NIT Raipur, India.

References

1. Emotient. http://emovu.com/e/. Accessed 26 Jul 2022
2. Emovu. http://www.emotient.com/. Accessed 26 Jun 2022
3. Extract image features using pretrained network. https://tinyurl.com/mryjsfv7. Accessed 4 Jul 2022
4. Pretrained deep neural networks. https://tinyurl.com/3m9cnmbz. Accessed 4 Aug 2022
5. Sightcorp. http://www.sightcorp.com/. Accessed 20 Jun 2022
6. Barbhuiya, R.K., Ahmad, N., Akram, W.: Application of convolutional neural networks in cancer diagnosis. In: Raza, K. (ed.) Computational Intelligence in Oncology. SCI, vol. 1016, pp. 95–109. Springer, Singapore (2022). https://doi.org/10.1007/978-981-16-9221-5_5
7. Baylari, A., Montazer, G.A.: Design a personalized e-learning system based on item response theory and artificial neural network approach. Expert Syst. Appl. **36**(4), 8013–8021 (2009)
8. Chang, Y.C., Li, J.W., Huang, D.Y.: A personalized learning service compatible with moodle e-learning management system. Appl. Sci. **12**(7), 3562 (2022)
9. Ciloglugil, B., Alatli, O., Inceoglu, M.M., Erdur, R.C.: A multi-agent based adaptive e-learning system. In: Gervasi, O., et al. (eds.) ICCSA 2021. LNCS, vol. 12951, pp. 693–707. Springer, Cham (2021). https://doi.org/10.1007/978-3-030-86970-0_48
10. Ding, Y., Chen, X., Zhong, S., Liu, L.: Emotion analysis of college students using a fuzzy support vector machine. Math. Prob. Eng. **2020**, 8931486 (2020)
11. Fredricks, J.A., Blumenfeld, P.C., Paris, A.H.: School engagement: potential of the concept, state of the evidence. Rev. Educ. Res. **74**(1), 59–109 (2004)
12. Hernandez, J., Liu, Z., Hulten, G., DeBarr, D., Krum, K., Zhang, Z.: Measuring the engagement level of tv viewers. In: 2013 10th IEEE International Conference and Workshops on Automatic Face and Gesture Recognition (FG), pp. 1–7. IEEE (2013)
13. Jordan, K.: Initial trends in enrolment and completion of massive open online courses. Int. Rev. Res. Open Distrib. Learn. **15**(1), 133–160 (2014)
14. Kamath, A., Biswas, A., Balasubramanian, V.: A crowdsourced approach to student engagement recognition in e-learning environments. In: 2016 IEEE Winter Conference on Applications of Computer Vision (WACV), pp. 1–9. IEEE (2016)
15. Khan, A., et al.: Predicting emerging trends on social media by modeling it as temporal bipartite networks. IEEE Access **8**, 39635–39646 (2020)
16. Kurtz, G., Kopolovich, O., et al.: Impact of an instructor's personalized email intervention on completion rates in a massive open online course (MOOC). Electron. J. e-Learn. **20**(3), 325–335 (2022)
17. Li, L., Tong, Y., Qiao, L.: Eye tracking and its applications in the field of intelligent education. In: Wang, W., Wang, G., Ding, X., Zhang, B. (eds.) Artificial Intelligence in Education and Teaching Assessment, pp. 161–174. Springer, Singapore (2021). https://doi.org/10.1007/978-981-16-6502-8_15

18. Rahhali, M., Oughdir, L., Jedidi, Y., Lahmadi, Y., El Khattabi, M.Z.: E-learning recommendation system based on cloud computing. In: Bennani, S., Lakhrissi, Y., Khaissidi, G., Mansouri, A., Khamlichi, Y. (eds.) WITS 2020. LNEE, vol. 745, pp. 89–99. Springer, Singapore (2022). https://doi.org/10.1007/978-981-33-6893-4_9

19. Singh, D., Shukla, A., Sajwan, M.: Deep transfer learning framework for the identification of malicious activities to combat cyberattack. Futur. Gener. Comput. Syst. **125**, 687–697 (2021)

20. Sunitha, P., Ahmad, N., Barbhuiya, R.K.: Impact of covid-19 on education. In: Kumar, A., Mozar, S. (eds.) ICCCE 2021. LNEE, vol. 828, pp. 1191–1197. Springer, Singapore (2022)

21. Szegedy, C., ET AL.: Going deeper with convolutions. In: Proceedings of the IEEE Conference on Computer Vision and Pattern Recognition, pp. 1–9 (2015)

22. Whitehill, J., Serpell, Z., Lin, Y.C., Foster, A., Movellan, J.R.: The faces of engagement: automatic recognition of student engagement from facial expressions. IEEE Trans. Affect. Comput. **5**(1), 86–98 (2014)

23. Wu, C.H., Huang, Y.M., Hwang, J.P.: Review of affective computing in education/learning: trends and challenges. Br. J. Edu. Technol. **47**(6), 1304–1323 (2016)

24. Zeng, Z., Pantic, M., Roisman, G.I., Huang, T.S.: A survey of affect recognition methods: audio, visual, and spontaneous expressions. IEEE Trans. Pattern Anal. Mach. Intell. **31**(1), 39–58 (2008)

Performance Analysis of First Order Optimizers for Plant Pest Detection Using Deep Learning

T. Saranya[1](✉), C. Deisy[1], S. Sridevi[1], Kalaiarasi Sonai Muthu[2],
and M. K. A. Ahamed Khan[3]

[1] Thiagarajar College of Engineering, Madurai, India
saranshakthi09@gmail.com
[2] Multimedia University, Melaka, Malaysia
[3] UCSI University, Kuala Lumpur, Malaysia

Abstract. Several of the major issues affecting food productivity are a pest. The timely and precise detection of plant pests is crucial for avoiding the loss of agricultural productivity. Only by detecting the pest at an early stage can it be controlled. Due to the cyclical nature of agriculture, pest accumulation and variety might vary from season to season, rendering standard approaches for pest classification and detection ineffective. Methods based on machine learning can be utilized to resolve such issues. Deep Learning, which has become extremely popular in image processing, has recently opened up a plethora of new applications for smart agriculture. Optimizers are primarily responsible for the process of strengthening the deep learning model's pest detection capabilities. In order to detect pests on tomato plants, this study compares the performance of a few gradient-based optimizers, including stochastic gradient descent, root means square propagation, adaptive gradient, and adaptive moment estimation, on a proposed deep convolution neural network architecture with augmented data. In comparison to other optimizers, the evaluation findings demonstrate that the Adam optimizer performs better with an accuracy of 93% for pest identification.

Keywords: Deep Learning · Optimizers · Convolution Neural Network

1 Introduction

Agriculture is an important sector for supplying food to the world. As the population grows, it is necessary to increase food productivity, but this is complicated by the accumulation of various pests on crops. [1, 2] Pest can appear in various parts of the plant body, even from the root to the tip, causing severe yield loss.

The pest consumes the majority of the product, lowering productivity. The presence of pests in the plant body can reduce the amount of sunlight available to the plant, resulting in nutrient deficiency and the development of fungus and bacteria-based diseases. Early detection and classification of pest types may aid in the implementation of control measures.

The traditional or conventional method is incapable of detecting and classifying pests because the rules of the algorithm must frequently be changed whenever the class level

N. Khare et al. (Eds.): MIND 2022, CCIS 1763, pp. 37–52, 2022.
https://doi.org/10.1007/978-3-031-24367-7_4

changes or increases. [3, 4, 19, 21] Using Artificial Intelligence techniques like Deep Learning (DL) based Convolution Neural Networks (CNN) would help solve issues with the existing technique and deliver intelligent classification and detection.

Deep Learning is critical for early pest classification and detection. [20, 22] Deep learning is a subfield of Machine Learning that paves the way for Artificial Intelligence (AI). Although DL models work well for image classification, they are still susceptible to lose/cost. The misclassification in the model is represented by the loss, which is the difference between predicted and actual data. The loss also has an impact on the model's accuracy. [5–7] The optimizer is used to reduce loss and improve model prediction accuracy. The optimizers would perform well in order for the CNN model to generalize better for previously unseen data.

When combined with pesticide recommendations, the DL-based pest classifications system can be extremely beneficial to farmers. Pesticides were recommended based on pest prediction, so the model should be highly optimized to classify without any misclassification or error, otherwise, the system will recommend incorrect pesticides, so optimizing the CNN model is one of the most important roles.

The aim of this paper is to performance analysis of CNN using gradient-based optimizers such as Stochastic Gradient Descent (SGD), Root Mean Square Propagation (RMSPROP), Adaptive Gradient (ADAGRAD), and Adaptive Momentum Estimation (ADAM).

The rest of this paper is structured as follows: Sect. 2 discusses optimization for DL, Sect. 3 discusses various gradient-based optimizers, Sect. 4 presents the methodology for CNN-based pest classification, Sect. 4 discusses performance evaluation metrics, Sect. 5 discusses results and discussion, and Sect. 6 concludes the paper.

2   Optimization for Deep Learning

[8] A deep learning model tries to generalize the data and makes predictions about data that has not yet been observed. [9, 10] The loss inherent in the predictive model often denotes the fact that the results predicted by the DL model do not match the output from the real world. Loss in deep learning refers to how poorly the model is performing. Its goal is to use this loss to train our network to perform better. [11] Loss reduction is achieved by optimization. In designed to reach global minima with the very lowest loss, optimization techniques will adjust the neural network's weights and learning rate. [14] Once the loss is reduced the model predictions became more accurate.

The optimization methods can be classified into two types such as deterministic and stochastic based methods. The neural network utilizes stochastic based model and the stochastic based method is further split into two types as Gradient based method and Newton based method. The gradient-based optimizers work based on first-order derivatives and Newton-based optimizer work based on higher-order derivatives. The DL model is optimized either by gradient or Newton method but more probably it is optimized based on the gradient method due to its simplicity in computation. Figure 1 depicts the gradient-based optimizers analyzed in this paper.

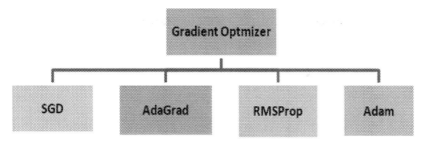

Fig. 1. Gradient Based Optimizer.

3 Gradient Based Optimizers

3.1 Gradient Descent (GD)

One of the most well-liked neural network optimizers is gradient descent. It will lower the loss and arrive at the global minima by using the learning rate and the derivative of the loss function. The gradient descent works effectively for convex optimization problems but not for non-convex optimization. It will compute every record in the whole dataset for each epoch and perform forward and backward propagation. When the data size is very little, it is a good neural network optimizer, but when the data size is larger, it requires more processing, takes longer to update the weights, and has slower convergence. SGD optimizer was used to lessen these issues.

$$W_{\text{new}} = W_{old} - \eta(\partial L/\partial W_{old}) \tag{1}$$

The Eq. (1) shows the weight updating on NN where W_{old} denotes the old weight, W_{new} denotes new weight, η denotes learning rate, ∂L is the derivative of loss $\partial L/\partial W_{old}$ is called gradient descent and ∂W_{old} is the derivative of old weight.

3.2 Stochastic Gradient Descent (SGD)

This is a Gradient Descent optimizer variant that has the extra ability to work with non-convex optimization problems. SGD solves the GD problem by randomly selecting a batch size of data for each iteration rather than the entire dataset. [12] Because only a few samples of data were used, SGD appears to be noisier than GD. SGD uses more iterations to reach local optima, which increases computation time. Even as the number of iterations increases, the computation cost remains less than GD.

The batch size is defined in mini-batch SGD, the convergence is not as smooth as in SGD, and the weight updating is not equal but somewhat close to SGD, but the reason for using mini-batch SGD is that it requires fewer resources and less computation expense. To reduce noise, the SGD with momentum is used, and the exponentially weighted average is used for smoothing.

3.3 ADAGRAD

[13] The ADAGRAD optimizer's learning rate is mostly fixed and identical. If the variable is close to its optimum, a low learning rate is required and a high learning rate is required for the variable that is far from the optimum point to resolve this issue ADGRAD optimizer is used. AdaGrad is useful when manually selecting the learning rate is difficult. During the learning process, the learning rate keeps on decreasing, and no longer effectively updating on weight is one of the problems while using this optimizer but it is good for the small neural network. This can be resolved by the Root Mean Square Error optimizer.

$$W_t = W_{t-1} - \eta'_t (\partial L / \partial W_{old}) \qquad (2)$$

The Adagrad is similar to Eq. (1) but the learning rate is slightly modified as η'_t instead of η_t. The base t denotes the time stamp. Where η'_t is computed as below:

$$\eta'_t = \eta_t / \sqrt{\alpha_t} + \varepsilon \qquad (3)$$

where η_t is the initial learning rate, ε small positive value used to avoid zero because if $\alpha_t = 0$ then the total will become zero, the α is the square of the previous loss derivative the purpose of doing this is to have a bigger value so that when dividing η'_t with α_t we will obtain less η'_t value.

$$\alpha_t = \sum\nolimits_{i=1}^{t} (\partial L / \partial W_{t-1})^2 \qquad (4)$$

3.4 RMSPROP

RMSPROP is similar to GD with momentum. [14, 15] It avoids the oscillations towards the vertical direction and takes longer steps towards the horizontal direction so that it would converge faster than SGD. The value of momentum will usually be set to 0.9. The monotonically decreasing problem in Adagrad is resolved by RMSPROP. In RMSPROP the new learning rate is computed as:

$$\eta'_t = \eta / \sqrt{sdw_t} + \varepsilon \qquad (5)$$

where sdw_t is the exponentially weighted average and computed as

$$sdw_t = \beta sdw_{t-1} + (1 - \beta)(\partial L / \partial W_{old})^2 \qquad (6)$$

β is the hyperparameter value usually set to 0.9 or 0.95; (1-β) is used to restrict the value of sdw_t to be only in small value, therefore in Adagrad the value of α_t is high so there is not much change in new weight so to resolve this (1-β) is applied.

3.5 ADAM

Adaptive Moment estimation is the combination of momentum and RMSPROB. [16, 17] The momentum takes care of smoothening and RMSPROB for the estimation of the learning rate. The advantage of these combinations in ADAM makes it a more powerful optimizer and solves most of the complex problems in the real world.

4   Methodology

This paper develops a CNN model for pest multi-classification and compares the performance of gradient-based optimizers such as SGD, RMSPROB, ADAGRAD, and ADAM. The preprocessed data is divided into two parts: 80% for training and 20% for validating. Figure 2 depicts the overall process.

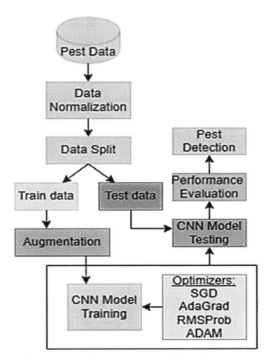

Fig. 2.   Overall Process Flow of Pest Detection.

4.1   Pest Dataset

[23] The dataset involved in this work is sourced from the Mendeley data set. The dataset contains eight types of pests that commonly feed on 100 + plant species. It consists of 4263 pest images. Table 1. Shows the types of pests in the dataset.

4.1.1   Pest Image Preprocessing

Image preprocessing involved in this work is normalization and augmentation. Normalization aids in having a similar data distribution so that training converges faster. For image data, the pixel should be positive, and the normalized data should be scaled in the range of 0 to 1.

Table 1. Types of Pests (Class Label)

S. No	Pest Name (Label)	S. No	Pest Name (Label)
1	Bemisia Argentifolii (BA)	5	SpodopteraLitura(SL)
2	HelicoverpaArmigera HA)	6	Thrips Palmi (TP)
3	MyzusPersicae (MP)	7	TetranychusUrticae (TU)
4	Spodoptera Exigua(SE)	8	Zeugodacus Cucurbitae(ZC)

[19] Because of data scarcity and overfitting, the augmentation technique could be used. Figure 3 shows the augmented image. This technique will generate more data by making slight changes to the original data, such as random flipping, random rotating, zooming, and so on.

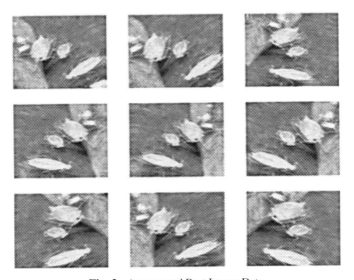

Fig. 3. Augmented Pest Image Data.

4.1.2 Proposed CNN Architecture for Pest Classification

CNN is similar to NN in that it employs a series of convolutional layers. [18] The CNN is composed of three layers: the convolution layer, the pooling layer, and the fully connected layer. CNN2D is used in the convolution layer to classify the pest, with a filter of 3*3, stride set to 1, and activated by ReLU. In the pooling layer, max-pooling 2D is used to extract high-intensity values that are needed for pest classification. It flattens the output layer of convolution in the fully connected layer and performs mathematical operations by computing the sum of the product of weight with its respective input and passing that information into the activation function. The softmax activation function is used at the final layer due to the multi-class pest classification.

ReLU Activation Function: One of the well-liked non-linear activation functions in deep learning is the Rectified Linear Unit (ReLU). ReLU has the advantage of not activating all of the neurons simultaneously. ReLU has the benefit of requiring less computation and solving the vanishing gradient problem.

Max-pooling2D: Max-Pooling2D, which extracts higher intensity pixels, is utilized in plant pest data since the pest can occur in any area of the plant and needs to be extracted effectively.

Dropout Layer: Only a small subset of neurons in the neural network is likely ignored during training neural network. This prevents the model from overfitting when a deep neural network is constructed. The probability p = 0.2 has been set in the CNN model.

The CNN architecture for performance analysis of gradient-based optimizer for pest classification has four CNN2D layers each layer has been followed with Max-pooling 2D, a dropout layer is added to the output of the final max-pooling layer and finally, the layer is flattened and classified using softmax classifier. Figure 4 depicts the proposed CNN architecture.

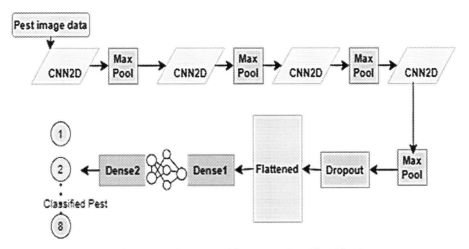

Fig. 4. Proposed CNN Architecture or Pest Classification

5   Evaluation Metrics

The performance analysis of the optimizer is evaluated by accuracy and loss. For loss categorial cross-entropy is used and it is expressed as:

$$CE_{loss} = -\sum T_i log(f(sm)_i) \tag{7}$$

where CE$_{loss}$ is the categorical cross-entropy loss, T$_i$ is the target, f(sm)$_i$ is the softmax output.

The performance of the model across all classes is measured by accuracy and it is defined as:

$$Accuracy = TP + TN/TP + TN + FP + FN \qquad (8)$$

where TP is a true positive in which both actual and predicted are true, TN is a true negative in which both actual and predicted are false, FP is a false positive in which actual is false but predicted as true, and FN is a false negative in which actually is true but predicted as false.

6   Results and Discussion

The CNN model for pest classification has a total of 2,117 992 trainable parameters. The layer type and output shape are given in Table 2. Table 3 shows the hyper-parameter selection utilized in this work. Table 4 show the performance analysis of optimizers for plant pest classification which was run up to 25 epochs.

Table 2. CNN layer types and output shape.

Layer	Output shape
Input size	180, 180, 3
CNN 2D_1	180, 180, 16
Max_Pooling	90, 90, 16
CNN 2D_2	90, 90, 32
Max_Pooling	45, 45, 32
CNN 2D_3	45, 45, 64
Max_Pooling	22, 22, 64
CNN 2D_4	22, 22, 128
Max_Pooling	11, 11, 128
Dropout	11, 11, 128
Flatten	15488
Dense_1	128
Dense_2	8

This section compares the performance of pest detection optimizers such as SGD, AdaGrad, RMSprop, and Adam. Figures 5, 7, 9, and 11 depict the accuracy and loss of the CNN model during training and validation for each optimizer. Figures 6, 8, 10, and 12 depict the confusion matrix multi-class pest classification.

Validation accuracy and loss are 76.41% and 0.714% for SGD optimizer, 88.26% and 0.48% for AdaGrad, 91.3% and 0.394% for RMSProp, and 93.43% and 0.218% for Adam. The numerical results show that the Adam optimizer performs better than other optimizers for pest image classification.

Table 3. Hyper-parameter of the model.

Hyper parameter	Value
Epoch	25
Batch size	32
Activation	ReLU
Optimizer	SGD, RMSProp, Adagrad, Adam
Dropout	0.2
Momentum	9
Learning rate	0.001
Beta1	0.99
Beta2	0.999
Epsilon	-

Table 4. Numerical Outcomes of Optimizers.

Optimizer	Accuracy %	Loss %
SGD	76.41	0.7
AdaGrad	88.26	0.48
RMSProp	91.31	0.39
Adam	93.63	0.28

Because each record requires forward and backward propagation, SGD takes some time to converge, which causes the SGD optimizer to become trapped in local minima and never reach the ideal point. Furthermore, the global minimal path gets very noisy, making it difficult to generalize the pest classes SL, HA, TP, and TU.

Although AdaGrad is superior to SGD, it is not fully generalized. In AdaGrad, a squared term is added with each iteration. The learning rate is constantly declining and, as it is always positive, has the potential to become infinitely small. Monotonically diminishing is a problem of AdaGrad. RMSProp optimizers generalize the model better than SGD and AdaGrad but still, it is not well good for classifying SE, and TP classes. Adam combines the advantages of RMSProp and AdaGrad.

Adam is an adaptive gradient descent technique that maintains a learning rate for each parameter. It also tracks the moving averages of the first and second moments of the gradient. Adam can therefore use the first and second moments to directly estimate the parameter changes in an unscaled manner. Finally, despite the development of newer optimization techniques, Adam is still a trustworthy optimizer for image classification and detection. From the comparative graph Figs. 13 and 14 shows that the Adam model outperforms all others because it uses the combination of both momentum for smoothing and RMSprob for learning rate.

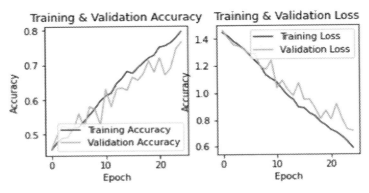

Fig. 5. Accuracy and Loss of SGD.

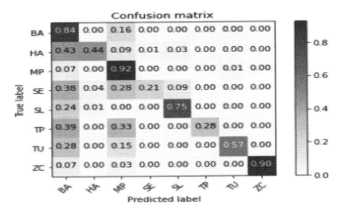

Fig. 6. Confusion Matrix of SGD.

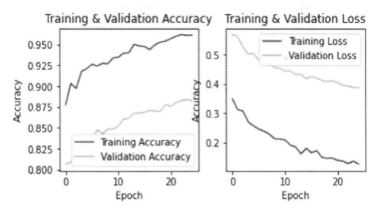

Fig. 7. Accuracy and Loss of ADAGRAD.

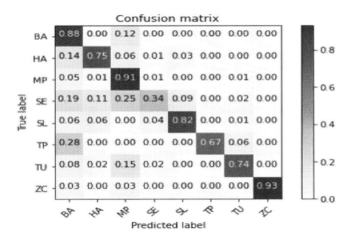

Fig. 8. Confusion Matrix of ADAGRAD.

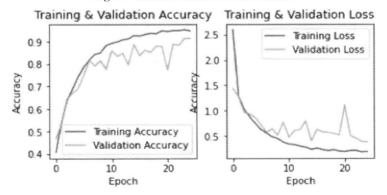

Fig. 9. Accuracy and Loss of RMSPROP

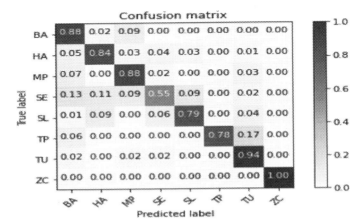

Fig. 10. Confusion Matrix of RMSPROP

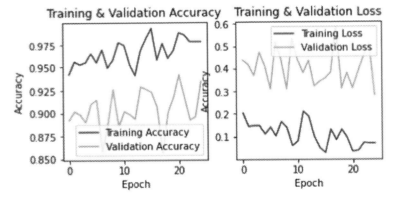

Fig. 11. Accuracy and Loss of ADAM.

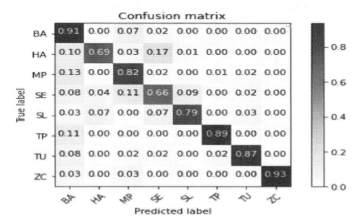

Fig. 12. Confusion Matrix of ADAM.

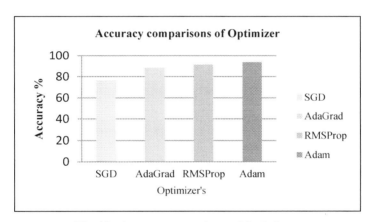

Fig. 13. Accuracy comparisons of Optimizers.

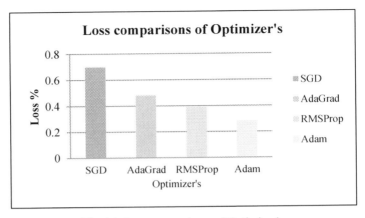

Fig. 14. Loss comparisons of Optimizer's.

7   Conclusion

One of the biggest issues in agriculture is pests. Agriculture is fluctuating, which complicates and impairs the ability to detect pests using traditional methods. These problems are solved by DL, which is more effective at identifying and detecting unseen pests. By increasing the reliability of pest detections, optimization of the DL model makes the model more resilient. This study examined the effectiveness of gradient-based optimizers on proposed deep convolution neural network architecture with augmented data, including stochastic gradient descent, adaptive gradient, root mean square propagation, and Adam. The results and discussions revealed that the Adam optimizer has a 93% accuracy rate for multi-class pest classification, outperforming all other optimizers.

Acknowledgment. The authors express their gratitude to the Thiagarajar College of Engineering (TCE) for supporting us to carry out this research work Also, the financial support from TCE under Thiagarajar Research Fellowship scheme (File.no: TRF/Jul-2022/01) is gratefully acknowledged.

References

1. Turkoglu, M., Yanikoğlu, B., Hanbay, D.: PlantDiseaseNet: Convolutional neural network ensemble for plant disease and pest detection. SIViP **16**(2), 301–309 (2022)
2. Malathi, V., Gopinath, M.P.: Classification of pest detection in paddy crop based on transfer learning approach. Acta Agricult. Scand. Sect. B Soil Plant Sci. 71(7): 552–559 (2021)
3. Sheema, D., Ramesh, K., Renjith, P.N., Lakshna, A.: Comparative study of major algorithms for pest detection in maize crop. In: 2021 International Conference on Intelligent Technologies (CONIT), pp. 1–7. IEEE (2021)
4. Radha, N., Swathika, R.: A polyhouse: plant monitoring and diseases detection using CNN. In: 2021 International Conference on Artificial Intelligence and Smart Systems (ICAIS), pp. 966–971. IEEE (2021)

5. Dubey, S.R., Chakraborty, S., Kumar Roy, S., Mukherjee, S., Kumar Singh, S., Baran Chaud-huri, B.: diffGrad: an optimization method for convolutional neural networks. IEEE Trans. Neural Netw. Learn. Syst. 31(11), 4500–4511 (2019)
6. Lachgar, M., Hrimech, H., Kartit, A.: Optimization techniques in deep convolutional neuronal networks applied to olive diseases classification. Artif. Intel. Agricult. (2022)
7. Abdullahi, H.S., Sheriff, R.E.: Introduction to deep learning in precision agriculture: Farm image feature detection using unmanned aerial vehicles through classification and optimiza-tion process of machine learning with convolution neural network. In: Deep Learning for Sustainable Agriculture, pp. 81–107. Academic Press (2022)
8. Zohrevand, A., Imani, Z.: An empirical study of the performance of different optimizers in the deep neural networks. In: 2022 International Conference on Machine Vision and Image Processing (MVIP), pp. 1–5. IEEE (2022)
9. Luo, Y., Fan, Y., Chen, X.: Research on optimization of deep learning algorithm based on convolutional neural network. J. Phys. Conf. Ser. **1848**(1), 012038 (2021). IOP Publishing
10. Bera, S., Shrivastava, V.K.: Analysis of various optimizers on deep convolutional neural network model in the application of hyperspectral remote sensing image classification. Int. J. Remote Sens. **41**(7), 2664–2683 (2020)
11. Postalcıoğlu, S.: Performance analysis of different optimizers for deep learning-based image recognition. Int. J. Pattern Recognit Artif Intell. **34**(2), 2051003 (2020)
12. Chaudhury, S., Yamasaki, T.: Robustness of adaptive neural network optimization under training noise. IEEE Access **9**, 37039–37053 (2021)
13. Zhang, N., Lei, D., Zhao, J.F.: An improved Adagrad gradient descent optimization algorithm. In: 2018 Chinese Automation Congress (CAC), pp. 2359–2362. IEEE (2018)
14. Kumar, A., Sarkar, S., Pradhan, C.: Malaria disease detection using cnn technique with sgd, rmsprop and adam optimizers. In: Dash, S., Acharya, B.R., Mittal, M., Abraham, A., Kelemen, A. (eds.) Deep learning techniques for biomedical and health informatics. SBD, vol. 68, pp. 211–230. Springer, Cham (2020). https://doi.org/10.1007/978-3-030-33966-1_11
15. Saadna, Y., Boudhir, A.A., Ahmed, M.B.: An analysis of ResNet50 model and RMSprop opti-mizer for education platform using an intelligent chatbot system. In: Ahmed, M.B., Teodor-escu, H.-N.L., Mazri, T., Subashini, P., Boudhir, A.A. (eds.) Networking, Intelligent Systems and Security. SIST, vol. 237, pp. 577–590. Springer, Singapore (2022). https://doi.org/10. 1007/978-981-16-3637-0_41
16. Mehta, S., Paunwala, C., Vaidya, B.: CNN based traffic sign classification using Adam opti-mizer. In: 2019 International Conference on Intelligent Computing and Control Systems (ICCS), pp. 1293–1298. IEEE (2019)
17. Ilboudo, W.E.L., Kobayashi, T., Sugimoto, K.: Robust stochastic gradient descent with student-t distribution based first-order momentum. IEEE Trans. Neural Netw. Learn. Syst. (2020)
18. Mikołajczyk, A., Grochowski, M.: Data augmentation for improving deep learning in image classification problem. In: 2018 International Interdisciplinary PhD Workshop (IIPhDW), pp. 117–122. IEEE (2018)
19. Mrudula, K., Jain, H.R., Bhansali, J., Sejal, S.N.: Plant-Wise Comparison of Various CNN Algorithms for Detection of Pest Infestation. In: 2021 IEEE Pune Section International Conference (PuneCon), pp. 1–7. IEEE (2021)
20. Mondal, B.: Artificial intelligence: state of the art. In: Recent Trends and Advances in Artificial Intelligence and Internet of Things, pp. 389–425 (2020)

21. Mondal, B., Patra, O., Satapathy, A., Behera, S.R.: A comparative study on financial market forecasting using AI: a case study on NIFTY. In: Hassanien, A.E., Bhattacharyya, S., Chakrabati, S., Bhattacharya, A., Dutta, S. (eds.) Emerging Technologies in Data Mining and Information Security. AISC, vol. 1286, pp. 95–103. Springer, Singapore (2021). https://doi.org/10.1007/978-981-15-9927-9_10
22. Singh, S.K., Mondal, B.: A fuzzy-based clustering and data collection for internet of things based wireless sensor networks. In: 2021 International Conference on Innovation and Intelligence for Informatics, Computing, and Technologies (3ICT), pp. 303–308. IEEE (2021)
23. Huang, M.L., Chuang, T.C.: A database of eight common tomato pest images. In: Mendeley Data (2020)

A Review on Skin Pigment and Vein Pattern Detection Techniques

Komal Kharakwal$^{(\boxtimes)}$, Y. P. Raiwani$^{(\boxtimes)}$, and Rohan Verma$^{(\boxtimes)}$

Department of Computer Science and Engineering, H. N. B. Garhwal University, Srinagar,
Uttarakhand, India
komalkharkwal10@gmail.com, yp_raiwani@yahoo.com,
rohanvermahnb@gmail.com

Abstract. Over the past few years, image processing has dominated work in
suspect detection, medical science, and meteorology. Facial recognition, finger
knuckles, Relatively Permanent Pigmented or Vascular Skin Marks (RPPVSM),
vein patterns, and biometrics are all included in this review paper. Unlike birthmarks, RPPVSM is inherited, whereas birthmarks are acquired. The two primary
elements of RPPVSM are matching and detection. Consequently, it is improba-
ble that redundant evidence could produce a vein pattern. Several cases involving
child sexual assault or disharmony have been resolved by using RPPVSMs as a
biometric attribute for recognition. In this paper, we also give a review on findings
and results of various authors.

Keywords: RPPVSM · Vein · Criminal · Identification · Biometric

1 Introduction

In situations such as criminal investigations, it may not always be possible to obtain
biometric information such as a person's face or fingerprint. Vascular colors and skin
markings are quite helpful in such circumstances. Especially when minors are involved,
when there has been sexual abuse, etc. Examining recognized skin traits on the face and
in the facial records is one way. In order to identify face features, any facial recognition
algorithm would crop off any landmarks or distinguishing features from a subject's
image. The programmer may evaluate features including the part's size or shape, as well
as the nose, cheekbones, and jaw. It is connected to other biometric modalities, such
fingerprint or voice detection systems, in the majority of security mechanisms. It's also
gaining popularity as a tool for branding businesses in marketing campaigns. The search
for photographs that meet the requirements is then conducted using these.

Image processing is a technique for enhancing unprocessed images obtained from
satellite cameras, spacecraft, airplanes, or photos taken for a variety of everyday reasons.
There have been many different image processing methods created during the last four to
five decades. Most of the methods are used to enhance photos from unidentifiable satel-
lites, space experiments, and military identification missions. Image processing systems
are becoming increasingly widespread as large-screen personal computers, graphics

N. Khare et al. (Eds.): MIND 2022, CCIS 1763, pp. 53–67, 2022.
https://doi.org/10.1007/978-3-031-24367-7_5

applications, and other software become more widely available. Before compressing the face data, other techniques normalize a collection of face photos, saving only the info there is an image that is useful for a face identification. After that, the facial data is compared to a probe image. Template matching, which generates compressed representations of faces based on salient facial traits, was one of the earliest successful approaches.

Skin Recognitions Framework is a computer application that uses a digital image or video to detect or authenticate an individual from a visual source. Another option is to use the body and face databases to separate the various skin features. It's a type of biometric similar to fingerprints or the iris of the eye that's often employed in security systems. It's also growing more popular as a marketing and branding tool for businesses.

Geometry separates an image into values and compares them to templates to get rid of variance. Using photometric technology, an image is broken down into values, and the values are then compared with templates to get rid of variations in the image. Three-dimensional skin identification is an allegedly more accurate trend that has just emerged. This method utilized 3D sensors to gather data regarding a face's shape. The distinguishing characteristics of the skin's surface can then be determined using this information. One benefit of 3D skin identification is that, unlike previous methods, it is not impacted by variations in lighting. A skin can be recognized from a variety of viewing angles, including profile view. Skin identification accuracy is greatly increased by using three-dimensional skin data points. The advancement of sophisticated sensors that better capture 3D skin imaging benefits 2D research. Structured light is projected onto the face by the sensor to operate. These image sensors, each of which catches a distinct portion of the spectrum, can be arranged in groups of up to twelve or more on the CMOS chip.

1.1 Author's Contribution

This research paper tries to address the findings and results of different authors. We try to present a method for identifying RPPVSM by an automated system, as human identification of RPPVSM is time-consuming and requires considerable effort. In this paper Algorithms are used to detect RPPVSMs, detect them, and match them with skin segmentation. The technique was tested using back photos from a variety of subjects in a variety of poses and viewpoints. To handle identification with limited numbers of RPPVSM, a fusion scheme with inferred vein patterns is also proposed. The results indicate that RPPVSM detection in all body parts improves with the fusion, but the improvements are dependent on the number of veins detected.

1.2 Organization of the Paper

The remainder section of this paper is structures as follows. Section 2 is about the literature review of RPPVSM detection techniques. Section 3 is about skin texture analysis which converts the distinctive lines, patterns, and spots that are found on a person's skin into mathematical space. Section 4 is about methodology and preprocessing. Section 5 is about discussion and result. Sections 6 and 7 describes our conclusion and future scope.

2 Literature Review

X. Yan et al. [1] additionally, they discuss a unique palm vein detection technique that utilizes local invariant features as well as a multi-sampling and feature-level fusion method. If a SIFT algorithm is applied to extract features on a palm vein image directly, it will be difficult to collect enough features for effective recognition. This is due to the poor contrast and fuzzy nature of the majority of contactless palm vein photos. In order to ensure that more characteristics are extracted from the feature extraction procedure, the authors suggest using the entire palm as a Region of Interest (ROI) and implementing updated hierarchical augmentation on the ROI. The registered template is then generated through feature-level fusion from the many samples obtained during the registration stage. Finally, a mechanism for reducing mismatches is proposed: bidirectional matching. The suggested method outperforms the other methods in recognition performance, especially when it comes to palm vein image recognition during significant posture changes, based on experiments utilizing the CASIA Palm Vein Picture Database and palm vein database acquired during posture transformation. For the two datasets discussed above, the Equal Error Rates (EERs) were 0.17% and 0.72%, respectively.

Using the generalized Gabor direction pattern (GGDP) and the weighted discrepancy measurement model (WDMM), T. Chen et al. [2] proposed a method to describe texture features that is both responsive to sound and able to acquire more detailed direction information. A novel patch-structure direction pattern (PDP) is developed in order to obtain rich feature information without generating buzz. The need for a description approach that can investigate richer and more discriminating texture features while minimizing the high dimension problem of the local Gabor feature vector has pushed us to improve PDP in order to build the GGDP methodology with multi-channel Gabor space. In addition, WDMM, which can effectively estimate the feature distance between two images, is introduced for image classification and identification. The suggested method outperforms existing traditional methods in simulated tests on the Yale B face database, the Carnegie Mellon University posture, illumination, and expression (CMUPIE), and the Olivetti research laboratory (ORL) face databases.

X. Li et al. developed a method for identifying dorsal hand vein patterns [3]. To increase the identification ratio, the venous skeleton must be separated with little distortion. The technique then employs a variety of steps, such as scaling and grey normalization, to produce a clean, single-pixel-broad skeleton with the least amount of distortion. Average and low passing Gaussian filters. Segmentation of the local Niblack dynamic threshold. Then a function vector is obtained from the seven modified moment invariants of the vein skeleton. The authors found that the algorithm had a 95% identification rate after running numerous tests.

Due to their biological characteristics, A. Nurhudatiana et al. [4] identified "Relatively Permanent Pigmentation or Vascular Skin Signs" (RPPVSM). Males: 144 men of different racial backgrounds, including Caucasians, Asians, and Latinos, provided torso photographs. With the assistance of a dermatologist, their RPPVSMs were manually identified. The observation results indicate that RPPVSM variations are distributed randomly and consistently in 80% of the population. Asians and Latinos have fewer RPPVSMs than Caucasians do.

Criminals that engage in child trafficking or sexual assault frequently disguise or mask their names and scars so that they cannot be identified. The natural skin markings on their neck, chest, and back are typically visible up close. Manual RPPVSM can be laborious and challenging to find. An automatic RPPVSM recognition methodology is provided that makes use of RPPVSM detection and matching techniques. Nurhudatiana, A., and coworkers [5]. Three learning-based techniques have been developed to recognize RPPVSMs in color photos automatically. To evaluate these algorithms, 215 backside pictures of 120 individuals were used. Their findings imply that the unique RPPVSM identification approach has a high level of identification accuracy as well as great criminal investigative potential.

A straightforward and quick face detection algorithm was created by X. Hu et al. [6]. Instead of using both chrominance Cr and Cb data at first, only chrominance Cr is used to look for specific points of interest that mark skin patches in the data. Instead, the presence of a face near the recognized points of interest was checked using the AdaBoost algorithm. 400 facial patches were decreased to 137 after being converted to the YCbCr vacuum since it was discovered that 400 of them overlapped with the non-skin Cr histogram. From a pool of 105 individuals, 220 facial photographs from the LFW collection were randomly selected to test the proposed methodology. The single Cr technique discovered all of the face regions while using the fewest interest points and the quickest overall detection time when compared to other methods for detecting interests. The proposed method of facial detection can therefore be judged to be successful.

Large skin scars and marks are used, but in some legal situations they are unsuccessful since the skin in the evidence photographs lacks any markings or skin marks that may be used to identify the person. Vein markings were formerly difficult to employ in forensic investigation since they were not evident in colored images. This article describes an algorithm for identifying human identity patterns in colour skin-skin pictures. Vein markings were formerly difficult to employ in forensic investigation since they were not evident in coloured images. An algorithm for identifying personnel by revealing Skin vein structures are shown in colour imaging was proposed by C. Thang et al. [7]. The author simulates the reverse phase of skin colour development in an image using principles from optics and skin biophysics, and uses colour photographs to provide spatial distributions of biophysical parameters where vein patterns can be seen. The outcomes of experiments have been quite positive. The resulting images have vein shapes that are as clear as, if not clearer than, near-infrared representations.

According to Y. Peng et al. [8], recognizing suspects and offenders from photos of skin from various body locations is a novel and challenging topic. Since there are no recognizable faces or body marks in this case, it is hard to identify the person since skin images, especially in some forensic circumstances, do not show evident qualities. Many solutions based on blood vessel and skin mark patterns have been proposed to deal with this issue. However, these techniques disregard the fact that the image is frequently inaccurate, with incorrect skin markings and blood vessels. Androgenic hair variations work well in low resolution, but synchronization hasn't been taken into account, and the match is unstable when the point of view shifts. It was proposed that a novel the propagation of the skin texture phenomena was the focus of this feature pattern. be utilized to define contour lines in geography. An architecture with sliding blocks is designed to enhance rotation and discrimination. The experimental findings show that the suggested approach is effective and slightly boosts rotational invariance.

Sensitive biometrics, like skin markings, are important in forensic identification because they can act as a backup if hard biometrics are not accessible, in addition to the fact that hard biometrics do not always ensure complete identification success. Due to the fluctuating illumination, pose and little changes in skin markings are difficult to see. For forensic identification tasks, P. Yu et al. [9] developed algorithm-compatible meta-recognition-based skin marks. A collection of skin marks and knowledge of their positions are required for the procedure, which also uses geometrical knowledge of spatial variability to identify the relationship between two photos. The skin marks are placed in an overlapping pattern with multiple levels, and a meta-recognition method is used to aggregate values at different stages.

Relatively Permanent Pigmented or Vascular Skin Marks (RPPVSM) are a class of skin marks proposed by A. Nurhudatiana, A.W.-K. Kong, K. Matinpour, D. Chon, L. Altieri, S.Y. Cho, and N. Craft et al. [10] as a biometric feature for forensic investigations. The uniqueness was examined to establish the theoretical foundations of employing RPPVSM patterns as a novel biometric feature. 269 male subjects' backs with RPPVSM were evaluated. They discovered that RPPVSM tends to form clusters in high density patterns while independent and uniform distributions are more common in intermediate to low density patterns. For the independently distributed and uniformly distributed RPPVSM patterns, they provide an individuality model in their study. This model closely matches the empirical distribution when compared to the empirical evidence. Finally, it reports the anticipated error rates for authentication and verification.

A multilayer framework for high resolution face recognition that takes advantage of information at various scales is introduced by the authors D. Lin and X. Tang et al. [11]. The four layers that make up each face image are the overall appearance, the facial organs, the skins, and the irregular details. They use Multilevel PCA and Regularized LDA to represent facial organs and overall look. The requirement for creating new representations arises from the description of skin texture and infrequent details, for which traditional vector representations are insufficient. Discriminative Multiscale Texton Features and SIFT-Activated Pictorial Structure, which characterize skin and fine details, respectively, are presented as solutions to the problem. They also develop a metric fusion algorithm that adaptively prioritizes the highly confident layers in order to efficiently merge the information supplied by all layers. They identify the various functions performed by the layers through methodical studies and clearly demonstrate that by exploiting their complementarities, their framework achieves notable improved performance.

For better face picture matching and retrieving efficiency, Unsang Park and Anil K. Jain et al. [12] recommend using demographic data (such as gender and ethnicity) and facial marks (such as scars, moles, and freckles). In order to locate the main facial features (such as the eyes, nose, and mouth), the active appearance model, the Laplacian-of-Gaussian blob detection, and morphological operators are all used in an automatic facial mark detection approach that has been created. The use of soft biometric traits can enhance the face-recognition performance of a state-of-the-art commercial matcher, according to experimental results based on the FERET database (426 images of 213 subjects) and two mugshot databases from the forensic domain (1225 images of 671 subjects and 10,000 images of 10,000 subjects, respectively).

A unique approach is presented by C. Tang, A. W. Kong, and N. Craft [13] to explore the potential for leveraging texture data from facial skin regions for biometric identification of people. When a person cannot be identified using their whole facial image, as could be the case in forensic analysis, this data is still useful. Since they are likely to be distinguishable even in partially occluded face images, four facial regions—the forehead, right cheek, left cheek, and chin—were examined in this study. In order to make it easier to extract these facial regions of interest, facial landmarks are automatically discovered. To find areas with significant skin content, a skin detection technique is used.

S. Hoque, F. Deravi, H. Alsufyani [14], Their work offers a fresh framework for examining the potential for biometric identification of people using texture data from facial skin regions. When a person cannot be identified using their whole facial image, as could be the case in forensic analysis, this information is still useful. Since they are likely to be distinguishable even in partially occluded face images, four facial regions—the forehead, right cheek, left cheek, and chin—were examined in this study. In order to make it easier to extract these facial regions of interest, facial landmarks are automatically discovered. To find areas with significant skin content, a skin detection method is used. Then, utilizing features based on Local Binary Patterns and Gabor wavelet filters, each skin region is processed separately. Before classifying the photos, feature fusion of the sub-regions is employed. In order to assess the effectiveness of the skin detection technique and biometric recognition, experiments were conducted utilizing the publicly accessible Skin Segmentation database and the XM2VTS databases, respectively. The outcomes demonstrate that the skin detection algorithm delivered outcomes on par with other cutting-edge methods. The forehead and chin areas of the regions under investigation were discovered to be a rich source of biometric data.

To find properties in frontal images of upright faces, S. Milborrow and F. Nicolls et al. [15] employ the Active Shape Model of Cootes et al. [16] and some simple additions to it. Researchers show through solid test results that the Active Shape Model correlates favorably with more advanced methods after upgrades. Extensions include (i) fitting more landmarks than necessary (ii) utilizing two-dimensional landmark prototypes rather than one-dimensional ones (iii), introducing noise to the training set (iv), relaxing the shape model when appropriate (v), reducing partial derivatives by setting most entries to zero (vi), and rearranging two Active Shape Models in sequence.

Venugopal K R, L M Patnaik, Ramesha K, and K B Raja et al. [17] They suggested the TBMDFR method, which uses a face image with at least one mole to identify personnel. For the mole to be clearly visible, light adjustment utilizing homomorphic filtering is carried out. When a mole's intensity value and position are compared to predetermined NCC threshold values, NCC matching with the complement of a Gaussian template is utilized to identify the mole. The co-ordinates of the identified moles are compared to the Grab-Cut segmented image to determine the validity of the mole, and any mole found in the skin region is recognized as valid. The suggested approach performs better in face recognition with a minimum of one mole because the NCC values of TBMDFR are higher than those of the current SDAFR algorithm.

The following is a summary of key findings and results from the various authors (Table 1):

Table 1. Comparison table of results and findings of the various authors

Author	Year	Methods	Findings
X. Yan et al. [1]	2015	SIFT, bidirectional matching	EER: 0.16 and 0.73
T. Chen et al. [2]	2016	GDPP & WDMM	WDMM is presented for classifying and identifying images. The feature separation between two pictures can be determined by it
X. Li et al. [3]	2010	Average filtering and Gaussian low passing, niBlack threshold	Recognition Rate 95.5
A. Nurhudatiana et al. [4]	2011	PPVSM	RPPVSM variations that are distributed continuously and independently in 80% of the population are present
A. Nurhudatiana et al. [5]	2013	RPPVSM	It is possible to achieve good identification accuracy using the RPPVSM identification method
X. Hu et al. [6]	2014	CbCr based face detection	The Cr method detects face regions and has the shortest overall detection time per face region, along with fewer interest points
C. Thang et al. [7]	2011	In colour images, vein structures from the skin are shown	An image of veins is as clear as an image of near-infrared
Y. Peng et al. [8]	2017	Sliding block framework	Proposed algorithm is efficient and increases rotational invariance slightly
P. Yu et al. [9]	2018	Meta-recognition-based skin marks for forensic identification	In terms of rank-1 accuracy, there was a 22% improvement

(*continued*)

Table 1. (*continued*)

Author	Year	Methods	Findings
Cheng Tang Pan et al. [18]	2019	Near Infrared (NIR) Light	Low-cost vein finder prototypes utilizing camera assisted near infrared (NIR) light technology
Beata Marciniak et al. [19]	2021	Digital Image Correlation (DIC)	Detecting skin micro shifts caused by pulsation of vein
Vijay Bhaskar Semwal et al. [20]	2021	SVM, ANN and XGBoost-based machine learning algorithms	The challenges associated with gait-based person identification, the CASIA-A, B, and C5data set is investigated for the view, clothing, and speed invariant person identification

3   Skin Texture Analysis

Another new trend makes advantage of the skin's visual features as they appear in common digital or scanned photos. Skin texture analysis is a method that converts the distinctive lines, patterns, and spots that are found on a person's skin into mathematical space. Tests have indicated that adding skin texture analysis can improve face recognition ability by 20 to 25%. Using thermal cameras is an alternative method of gathering data for face recognition; during this process, the cameras will only identify the contour of the head and will ignore any subject accoutrements, such as glasses, hats, or make-up. The fact that there aren't many face recognition databases makes using thermal images for face recognition problematic. Ferroelectric electric sensors with low sensitivity and low resolution are used in the study to capture long wave thermal infrared.

4   Preprocessing

The system design includes a system module specifically intended for comprehending and gathering the input samples. Figure 1 depicts the whole study-proposed system. An analysis unit, a modulation unit, and a segmentation unit make up this system. Retrieving the input sample and comparing it to the system's training data sets is its main goal. The pigment analysis and extraction, which is enlarged to a higher level of organ analysis covering the arms, back, and shoulders, improves the pattern analyses of our system. The system architecture is made up of system train data sets that are collected from people who are suspected of being guilty, including criminals who are being held in jail or on remand, and are then stored and preserved in a safe location. Input samples from the crime scene were taken by the system and fed into it for processing. We retrieved and examined data samples in a MATLAB environment for a better understanding of the procedure. The system also has a decision-making component for assessing and identifying patterns in the collected data. In Fig. 2, a thorough architecture diagram is displayed.

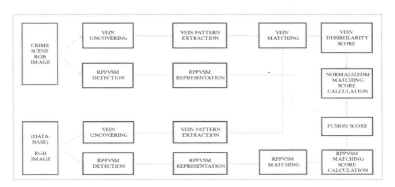

Fig. 1. System architecture diagram

It describes the many tasks carried out throughout the preprocessing step.

- The RGB image can be split into the Red, Green, and Blue channels.
- A YCbCr color space model is created from an RGB image.
- Luminance (Y) channel, Chrominance (Cb) channel, and Chrominance (Cr) channel can all be created from the YCbCr picture.
- Applying the Gray World technique will improve the YCbCr output image.
- All three channels of the YCbCr image are subjected to a Mean/Average Filter, and a resulting normalized RGB image is produced.

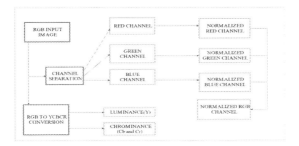

Fig. 2. Preprocessing Flowchart

Rotational and translational fluctuations cause the images to be jittery. It goes through preprocessing stages in order to get rid of these variations. Image enhancement is the technique that goes into it. Histogram equalization is used to improve the image for better visualization. The pixel value distribution of an image is expanded via histogram equalization to boost the perceptual information. After histogram equalization, the histogram fills the entire range of 0 to 255, improving the visualization effect. Contrast Limited Adaptive Histogram Equalization (CLAHE) is used to further improve the image.

The contrast limited adaptive histogram equalization (CLAHE) method is widely used in biological image processing because it is very good at enhancing the visibility of the prominent regions that are often of interest. The image is divided into several sections, and local histogram equalization is used in each zone. The regions' borders are then removed using a bilinear interpolation. The primary goal of this approach is to specify a point transformation within a small local window whose intensity value is taken to be a staunch representation of the local distribution of the intensity value of the entire image. The progressive change in intensity between the image centers and edges is considered to have no impact on the local window. The point transformation distribution is centered on the window's mean intensity and spans the full image's intensity range.

Consider a running sub picture W of N X N pixels that is centered on a pixel P (i,j). Using the equation below, the image is filtered to create another sub image P of N X N pixel.

$$p_n = 255. \left(\frac{[\varnothing_w(p) - \varnothing_w(Min)]}{[\varnothing_w(Max) - \varnothing_w(Min)]} \right) \tag{1}$$

where

$$\varnothing_w(p) = \left[1 + exp\left(\frac{\mu_w - p}{\sigma_w} \right) \right]^{-1} \tag{2}$$

where Max and Min are the highest and lowest intensity values throughout the entire image, while μ_w and σ_w stand for the mean and standard deviation of the local window, respectively, which are defined as:

$$\mu_w = \frac{1}{N^2} \sum_{(i,j) \in (k,l)} p(i,j) \tag{3}$$

$$\sigma_w = \sqrt{\frac{1}{N^2} \sum_{(i,j) \in (k,l)} (p(i,j) - \mu_w)^2} \tag{4}$$

This adaptive histogram equalization makes the side that was poorly lighted in the input image brighter in the output image while leaving the side that was strongly illuminated the same brightness or decreasing it.

5 Discussion and Result

In order to identify offenders in these skin images, this study suggests an automated RPPVSM identification system that consists of skin segmentation, RPPVSM detection, and RPPVSM matching algorithms. The culprits' vein patterns are also retrieved and merged with the RPPVSM. The system architecture consists of system train data sets, which are obtained from users under suspicion, such as offenders in jail and on remand, and are stored and preserved in a secure area. The system collected input samples from the crime scene and fed them into the system to be processed. For a better understanding, the processing was done in a MATLAB environment, and we retrieved and analyzed data samples. A decision-making unit is also included in the system for evaluating and extracting patterns from the sampled data. SVM classification method has been used in the testing phase to classify the images based on the features obtained. Different images of same person were matched with each other and hence we achieved high recognition rate and accuracy. The accuracy achieved has been up to 96.77% accuracy (Figs. 15 and 17).

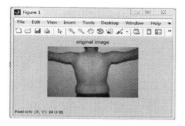

Fig. 3. Input Image

Fig. 4. Color space converted to YCbCr

Figure 4 shows the color space converted image where the input image has been converted to YCbCr color space using built it MATLAB functions.

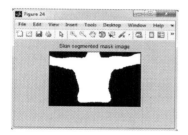

Fig. 5. Skin Segmented mask image

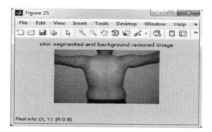

Fig. 6. Skin Segmented & Background Removed image

Figure 5 shows the mask image obtained for skin areas. This mask is then applied on the complete image to obtain skin parts sans the background as shown in Fig. 6. The skin segmented image in original form is shown in Fig. 7. Normalized blue channel Image (Fig. 8) is then processed to obtain the LoG filtered image shown in Fig. 9. The threshold image is shown in Fig. 10. This threshold image is then used to enhance the portions of the skin image. The results of skin enhanced image obtained as a result is shown in Fig. 11 and Fig. 12 respectively. The Vein extraction method is then applied to this enhanced image which results in uncovering the underlying vein pattern which is shown in Fig. 13. Figure 14 represents the LBP features obtained from the uncovered vein pattern.

The Vein pattern and LBP pattern features are then put in the database. Any test image is then subjected to the same procedure. When a successful match is made, the results of vein matching are shown in Fig. 15. When the test image is discovered to be unrelated to the database photos, the findings are shown in Fig. 16.

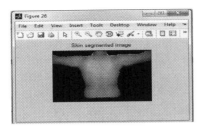

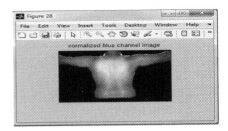

Fig. 7. Skin Segmented image   **Fig. 8.** Normalized Blue Channel Image

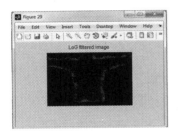

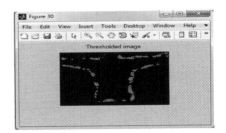

Fig. 9. LoG filtered Image   **Fig. 10.** Threshold Image

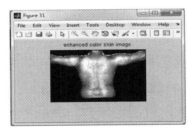

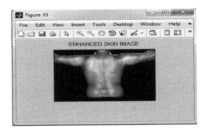

Fig. 11. Enhanced Color Skin Image   **Fig. 12.** Enhanced Skin Image

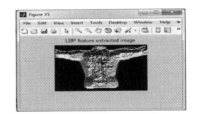

Fig. 13. Vein Extracted Pattern   **Fig. 14.** LBP Feature extracted Image

Figure 17 shows a snapshot of MATLAB command prompt with the results of classification and accuracy obtained. Table 2 shows the comparison of accuracy results for images of different persons in the database. Figure 18 shows the accuracy chart of the obtained accuracy results for all the persons in the database.

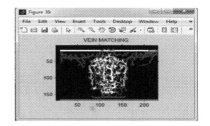

Fig. 15. Vein Matching (Matched)   **Fig. 16.** Vein Matching (Not Matched)

Command Window

```
Skin Matched
This skin belongs to criminal person-1

ans =

Accuracy of using SVM classifier is: 96.7742%
```

Fig. 17. Classification Result

Table 2. Comparison table

Person	Accuracy
Person 1	96.7742%
Person 2	95.1613%
Person 3	96.7742%
Person 4	95.1613%

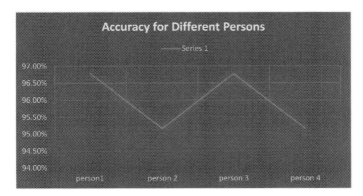

Fig. 18. Accuracy Chart

6 Conclusion

In this paper, a review of the various existing methods related to vein pattern and skin pigment-based detection methods has been presented. A number of techniques have been suggested by the researchers including RPPVSM, androgenic hair patter, NIR based techniques. The details of the methods have been thoroughly studied and their key findings have been compiled. The RPPVSM is combined with the vein patterns of the offenders. The system architecture is made up of system train data sets that are collected from people who are suspected of being guilty, including criminals who are being held in jail or on remand, and are then stored and preserved in a safe location. Input samples from the crime scene were taken by the system and fed into it for processing. While the faces of the culprits in evidence photographs of child sexual assault, masked gunmen, and rioting are rarely visible, their non-facial body parts are frequently visible. Relatively Permanent Pigmented or Vascular Skin Marks (RPPVSMs) have lately been proposed as a biometric characteristic for identification in situations when the evidentiary images only show the perpetrators' or victims' non-facial body parts, such as in child sexual abuse and riots. An automated RPPVSM identification approach is necessary since manual RPPVSM identification takes a lot of time and effort.

7 Future Work

The method for creating RPPVSM patterns from back skin photos was provided in the current work. In the future, skin scans from different body parts, such as the legs, arms, etc., can be utilized to assess the system's precision. Future study may involve developing a model for identifying skin images from any part and examining the vein and RPPVSM underpinnings. In addition to the currently employed methods, this can be used as another biometric characteristic for person identification.

References

1. Yan, X., Kang, W., Deng, F., Wu, Q.: Palm vein recognition based on multi-sampling and feature-level fusion. Neurocomputing, **151**(2), 798–807 (2015). ISSN 0925-2312
2. Chen, T., Zhao, X., Dai, L., Zhang, L., Wang, J.: A novel texture feature description method based on the generalized gabor direction pattern and weighted discrepancy measurement model. Symmetry **8**, 109 (2016)
3. Li, X., Liu, X., Liu, Z.: A dorsal hand vein pattern recognition algorithm. In: 2010 3rd International Congress on Image and Signal Processing, Yantai, pp. 1723–1726 (2010)
4. Nurhudatiana, A., Kong, A.W., Matinpour, K., Cho, S.-Y., Craft, N.: Fundamental statistics of relatively permanent pigmented or vascular skin marks for criminal and victim identification. In: 2011 International Joint Conference on Biometrics (IJCB), Washington, DC, 2011, pp. 1–6 (2011)
5. Nurhudatiana, A., Kong, A.W., Altieri, L., Craft, N.: Automated identification of relatively permanent pigmented or vascular skin marks (RPPVSM). In: 2013 IEEE International Conference on Acoustics, Speech and Signal Processing, Vancouver, BC, pp. 2984–2988 (2013)

6. Hu, X., Peng, S., Yan, J., Zhang, N.: Fast face detection based on skin color segmentation using single chrominance Cr. In: 2014 7th International Congress on Image and Signal Processing, Dalian, pp. 687–692 (2014)

7. Tang, C., Kong, A. W. K., Craft, N.: Uncovering vein patterns from color skin images for forensic analysis. In: CVPR 2011, Providence, RI, pp. 665–672 (2011). https://doi.org/10.1109/CVPR.2011.5995531

8. Peng, Y., Su, H.: A method of leg skin recognition based on distribution of skin texture. In: 2017 2nd International Conference on Robotics and Automation Engineering (ICRAE), Shanghai, pp. 415–419 (2017)

9. Yu, P., Kong, A.W.: A meta-recognition based skin marks matching algorithm with feature fusion for forensic identification. In: 2018 International Conference on Biometrics (ICB), Gold Coast, QLD, pp. 111–117 (2018)

10. Nurhudatiana, A., et al.: The individuality of relatively permanent pigmented or vascular skin marks (RPPVSM) in independently and uniformly distributed patterns. IEEE TIFS8(6), 998–1012 (2013)

11. Lin, D., Tang, X.: Recognize high resolution faces: from macrocosm to microcosm. In: Proceedings of the IEEE CVPR, pp. 1355–1362 (2006)

12. Park, U., Jain, A.K.: Face matching and retrieval using soft biometrics. IEEE Trans. Inf. Forens. Secur. 5, 3 (2010)

13. Tang, C., Kong, A.W., Craft, N.: A knowledge-based algorithm to remove blocking artifacts in skin images for forensic analysis. In: 2011 IEEE International Conference on Acoustics, Speech and Signal Processing (ICASSP), Prague, pp. 1928–1931 (2011). https://doi.org/10.1109/ICASSP.2011.5946885

14. Alsufyani, H., Hoque, S., Deravi, F.: Exploring the potential of facial skin regions for the provision of identity information. In: 7th International Conference on Imaging for Crime Detection and Prevention (ICDP 2016), Madrid, pp. 1–6 (2016). https://doi.org/10.1049/ic.2016.0084

15. Milborrow, S., Nicolls, F.: Locating facial features with an extended active shape model. In: Forsyth, D., Torr, P., Zisserman, A. (eds.) ECCV 2008. LNCS, vol. 5305, pp. 504–513. Springer, Heidelberg (2008). https://doi.org/10.1007/978-3-540-88693-8_37

16. Cootes, T.F., Taylor, C.J., Cooper, D.H., Graham, J.: Active shape models — their training and application. CVIU 61, 38–59 (1995)

17. Ramesha, K., Raja, K.B., Venugopal, K.R., Patnaik, L.M.: Template based mole detection for face recognition. Int. J. Comput. Theory Eng. 2(5), 1793–8201 (2010)

18. Pan, C.-T., Francisco, M.D., Yen, C.-K., Wang, S.-Y., Shiue, Y.-L.: Vein pattern locating technology for cannulation: a review of the low-cost vein finder prototypes utilizing near infrared (NIR) light to improve peripheral subcutaneous vein selection for phlebotomy. Sensors. 19, 3573 (2019). https://doi.org/10.3390/s19163573

19. Lutowski, Z., Bujnowski, S., Marciniak, B., Kloska, S., Marciniak, A., Lech, P.: A novel method of vein detection with the use of digital image correlation. Entropy 23(4), 401 (2021). https://doi.org/10.3390/e23040401

20. Semwal, V.B., Mazumdar, A., Jha, A., Gaud, N., Bijalwan, V.: Speed, cloth and pose invariant gait recognition-based person identification. In: Pandey, M., Rautaray, S.S. (eds.) Machine Learning: Theoretical Foundations and Practical Applications. SBD, vol. 87, pp. 39–56. Springer, Singapore (2021). https://doi.org/10.1007/978-981-33-6518-6_3

Brain Tumor Classification Using Deep Learning Techniques

K Susheel Kumar[1]([⊠]), Amishi Bansal[2], and Nagendra Pratap Singh[2]

[1] Gandhi Institute of Technology and Management, Bangalore, Karnataka, India
skalyani@gitam.edu
[2] National Institute of Technology, Hamirpur, Himachal Pradesh, India
nps@nith.ac.in

Abstract. Technology and the rapid expansion of brain imaging technologies have always played an important role in evaluating and focusing new perspectives on the architecture and functioning of the brain. To improve treatment outcomes and the likelihood of patient survival, it is essential to arrive at an accurate diagnosis of a brain tumor. However, performing a manual analysis of the multiple magnetic resonance imaging (MRI) images that are produced in a medical facility can be difficult to accomplish. As a direct result of this, there is a demand for methods of computer-based tumor detection that are more precise. In recent years, a significant amount of time and energy has been dedicated to researching traditional machine learning methods that can automate this process. Recently, there has been a resurgence of interest in the use of deep learning methods as a method of diagnosing brain tumors that is both more accurate and reliable. In the field of medical science, the method of image processing is used extensively to improve early diagnosis and therapy phases. Up to this point, deep neural networks, also known as DNNs, have demonstrated exceptional performance in classification and segmentation tasks. Using MRI images, our goal is to categorize different types of brain tumors. The model was trained and tested with a high level of accuracy after using a dataset of brain MRI images.

Keywords: Brain image segmentation · Brain imaging · Brain tumor detection · Cancer detection · Image processing · MRI scans · ResNet

1 Introduction

A brain tumor is an abnormal or unusual growth that occurs in the brain. Due to the complexity of brain images, extracting brain tumors and analyzing their characteristics is a challenging task in the domain of medical image processing. On the other hand, manually evaluating the number of generated MRI images can be challenging. As a consequence of this, there is a demand for computer-based tumor detection methods that are more accurate. In the field of medical science, the method of image processing is extensively used to improve early diagnosis and therapy phases. To this point, Deep Neural Networks have demonstrated remarkable success in the classification and segmentation tasks they have been given.

© The Author(s), under exclusive license to Springer Nature Switzerland AG 2022
N. Khare et al. (Eds.): MIND 2022, CCIS 1763, pp. 68–81, 2022.
https://doi.org/10.1007/978-3-031-24367-7_6

In recent years, there has been a lot of interest in deep neural networks, abbreviated as DNN. The purpose of this research is to design and create a system that will assist in the diagnosis and identification of brain tumors by utilizing MRI scans of the brain and applying the image classifier approach that has been suggested as a potential method. The early detection of a cancerous region is always helpful in making an early diagnosis of a patient, which is one of the factors that contribute to the reduction of the risk of death. The approach of image processing has gained popularity across the board in the industry, and the utilization of image processing mechanisms has increased over the past few years. Imaging the brain with magnetic resonance, or MRI, is a well-established medical technique that can analyze and diagnose a wide range of neurological conditions, such as brain tumors, multiple sclerosis, epilepsy, and many others.

Medical image dataset interpretation has always been time-consuming and difficult. This paper aims to find simple deep learning techniques for the detection of brain tumors. The suggested Resnet-50 classifier has a high accuracy rate. Its accuracy and statistical measure are much better than non-deep learning approaches. It would be fascinating to combine this deep neural network with others and see the impact on the same brain MRI dataset.

1.1 Image Segmentation and MRI

Image segmentation is a technique that involves breaking up a digital image into a variety of different subgroups referred to as image segments. It helps in reducing the complexity of the image, which makes it easier to perform further processing or analysis on the image. Simply put, segmentation is the process of assigning labels to pixels. A standard label is given to each of the picture's components that fall into the same category. Take, as an illustration, a challenge in which the picture itself must be supplied as part of the input for object recognition. Instead of processing the entire image, the detector can have a region that has been selected by a segmentation algorithm as its input. It saves time. It will prevent the detector from processing the entire image, which will result in a reduction in the amount of time required for inference. Figure 1 shows a simplified process of image segmentation.

Fig. 1. The process of image segmentation

The magnetic resonance imaging (MRI) scanner is a very useful instrument for conducting brain analysis investigations and is also frequently used to provide and transfer anatomical information. In addition to being non-intrusive, it has a very fine spatial resolution. However, one of the challenges is separating different parts of the brain images. Image segmentation is essential for a variety of applications, including the detection of anomalies and the planning of surgical procedures. However, noise is the primary obstacle that leads to the failure of the majority of segmentation algorithms. The MRI images themselves are susceptible to a significant amount of noise as a consequence of noise introduced during transmission or recording to the medium, quantization error, and other factors. There is also the problem that medical images don't have enough contrast, which makes it hard to segment the image.

The process of brain imaging segmentation is difficult and involves a lot of complex methods to get accurate results. However, if accuracy is preserved throughout the segmentation work, it will significantly contribute to the cancer detection process. The identification of brain structures using MRI is essential in the field of neuroscience. Studies on the development of the brain, neuroanatomical studies of the brain, and other types of research can all benefit from this technique. As a consequence of this, MRI pictures are utilized almost exclusively to comprehend and carry out research analysis in the field of medical image segmentation. When it comes to analyzing images of the brain, MRI segmentation learning procedures, and pattern recognition strategies are quite effective. In a nutshell, the method involves making a parametric model based on a density function and taking certain factors into account.

1.2 Upcoming Sections

In the upcoming section of this paper, we will discuss previous work and research pertinent to the topic of tumor identification. In the Sect. 3, we will be giving information regarding the suggested method as well as the various ways in which it can be utilized. In the Sect. 4, we will talk about the simulation and results of the experimental model. Section 5, contains a generalized and comprehensive picture of the subject this study presented, along with future research directions and limitations.

2   Background and Related Works

2.1 Related Research Work

Image segmentation is an essential task in the field of machine learning and a vitally important application in the field of medicine. The process of image segmentation and analysis has been extensively researched by a great number of academics. Classifying brain MRI images with the help of Deep Wavelet Autoencoder-Based Deep Neural Networks, Mallick et al. [2] provided a comprehensive review of the various methods that can be used to detect cancer. They developed a model to classify brain MRI images and validated their model by using the results of a variety of experiments.

In addition, Hiralal and Menon [3] provided a comprehensive overview of the numerous different methods of brain image segmentation that are used in brain MRI images. They stressed how important it was to have a clear conversation about how to choose a segmentation method for MRI brain images so that they could be analyzed and a prognosis could be made. The algorithms known as Fuzzy C-Means (FCM) and Support Vector Machine (SVM) were utilized in the development of an image segmentation algorithm by Xiao and Tong [4]. They combined the two algorithms mentioned above and proposed a segmentation method that was shown to benefit from high noise and high bias fields in a brain MRI scan. This technique was successful in reducing noise and improving bias fields.

Another extensive survey on brain MRI image segmentation was conducted by Nayak *et al.* [6], who then provided a comprehensive review of the technique used to detect brain tumors using brain MRI images. The Fuzzy c-means and k-means algorithms were combined in a method proposed by Jose *et al.* [5] to detect brain tumors and the areas where they had spread using brain MRI images. Shen *et al.* proposed a method for the detection of brain tumors that was based on MRI fuzzy segmentation and neural network optimization. It was able to accomplish this by utilizing a one-of-a-kind optimization strategy in conjunction with neighborhood attraction, which assisted in the accurate detection of brain tumors based on images.

In 2015, Damodharan and Raghavan [7] focused their research on the segmentation of brain tissue. The proposed method worked well and quickly when it came to separating brain tissue and tumors, as well as in other situations where feature extraction and classification were needed. In a separate piece of research, Rehmad *et al.* [8] developed a computer-aided tumor detection model that classified brain tumors by combining three distinct CNN models (VGG16, GoogLeNet, and AlexNet) with an embedded transfer learning and data augmentation technique. The proposed accuracy of the VGG-16 was the highest possible, coming in at a value of up to 98.69 percent. [1] introduced an automated method to detect and segment multi-sequence brain MRI using a GoogleNet architecture, and the classification results showed that the GoogleNet performance was superior to that of other machine learning methods [9–13].

2.2 Existing Methods for Brain Tumor Classification

2.2.1 Fusion Based

This method involves superimposing an image of the victim's test subject on an image of a test subject of the same age group to identify the tumor. This method has been mentioned by A Selvapandian and K Manivannan in their paper. [14]

In the fusion-based method, the negative aspects include the fact that the overlapping generates complexit y as a result of the different dimensions of both images. Moreover, this procedure requires a lot of time.

2.2.2 Canopy Based

The application of Canny Based edge detection is recommended as the superior method for overcoming the challenge of detecting the edges. This method has been mentioned by A Zhang *et al.* [15]

This technique does not support color images. It causes an increase in the amount of time required to find the best solution.

3 Proposed Methodology

3.1 Dataset Used

The proposed methodology varies from the existing research based on its accuracy. In addition, the proposed model can be deployed in a real-world scenario with an immediate effect on brain tumor classification. The information gathered on brain tumors is extensively analyzed for a variety of purposes, including educational, medical, and personal ones. To conduct the experimental research for this paper, a dataset measuring 2.48 gigabytes in size was used. The data consists of several grayscale MRI images of various types of brain tumors, specifically pituitary, meningioma, and glioma tumors. The image is contained in the training data.pickle file has three channels and is represented as RGB. The dataset is called the Brain Tumor Classification MRI Dataset and is available to anyone who wants to use it for research and testing in various authors [17–23].

3.2 Dataset Management

Downloading and extracting the dataset was the initial step in training the model. After that, we proceeded to visualize the dataset. The dataset consisted of a collection of 3064 images in total (Fig. 2).

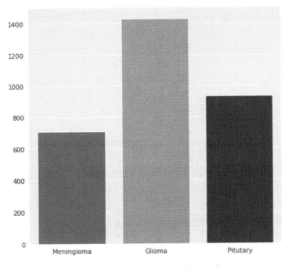

Fig. 2. Visualization of the three classes

The sample contains 3 classes namely, Meningioma, Glioma, and Pituitary, each containing 4 samples. In total the number of scans associated with each tumor is as follows:

- Meningioma: 708
- Glioma: 1426
- Pituitary: 930 (Figs. 3, 4 and 5)

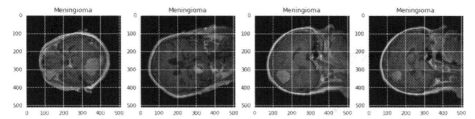

Fig. 3. Class: meningioma

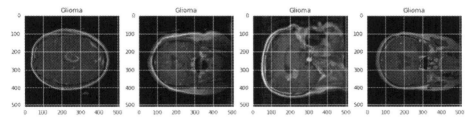

Fig. 4. Class: glioma

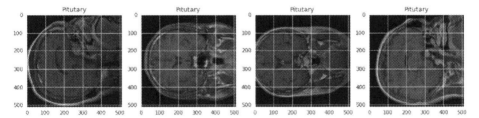

Fig. 5. Class: pituitary

3.3 Model Used - RESNET 50

The term "ResNet," which is an abbreviation for "Residual Networks," refers to a traditional neural network that serves as the foundation for many computer vision tasks. Before the development of ResNet, it was challenging to train very deep neural networks because of the problem of vanishing gradients. Increasing the network depth, on the other hand, cannot be accomplished by merely piling on additional layers. Training deep neural networks is notoriously difficult because of a problem known as the vanishing gradient problem. This issue arises when the gradient is back-propagated to earlier layers; at this point, repeated multiplication may cause the gradient to become extremely negligible, which leads to the aforementioned problem. As a consequence of this, the performance of the network begins to degrade and eventually reaches a point where it is unable to support any additional users. The sample contains 3 classes namely, Meningioma, Glioma, and Pituitary, each containing 4 samples. In total the number of scans associated with each tumor is as follows (Fig. 6):

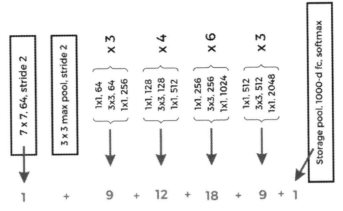

Fig. 6. The 50 layers of Resnet-50 model

3.3.1 Skip Connections in RESNET

The concept of skipping a connection was initially presented by ResNet. The skip connection is depicted in the diagram that follows. The figure on the left illustrates the process of piling convolution layers on top of one another in sequential order. On the right, we add the initial input to the output of the convolution block in addition to stacking convolution layers as we did before. It is referred to as skipping the connection (Fig. 7).

Fig. 7. Skip connection

After combining the identity and convolution blocks programmed in the notebook, a ResNet-50 model with the architecture shown below is produced. The ResNet-50 model is composed of five stages, and each stage has a convolution block and an Identity block within it. Each convolution block and identity block has three convolution layers that make up their respective structures. In addition, there are three convolution layers contained within every convolution layer. The ResNet-50 contains more than 23 million trainable parameters in its database (Fig. 8).

The following is an explanation of the ResNet-50 model presented above:

- **Zero-padding:** When the input is padded with a pad of (3, 3)
- **Stage 1:** Known as the 2D Convolution, consists of 64 filters of shape (7, 7) and a stride of (2, 2). It is known by the name "conv1." The channels axis of the input has

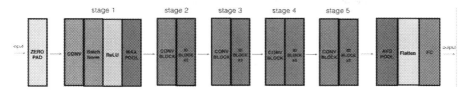

Fig. 8. Resnet-50 model

the BatchNorm filter applied to them. MaxPooling operates with a window of size (3, 3) and a stride of size (2, 2).

- **Stage 2:** The convolutional block has a size of 64 × 64 × 256, an f value of 3, a s value of 1, and the letter "a" as its block letter. The two identity blocks are denoted by the letters "b" and "c," and they each make use of three sets of filters that have the dimensions 64 × 64 × 256.
- **Stage 3:** The convolutional block has a size of 128 × 128 × 512, an f value of 3, a s value of 2, and the block itself is denoted as "a." The three identity blocks are denoted by the letters "b," "c," and "d," and they use three sets of filters with dimensions of 128 by 128 by 512.
- **Stage 4:** The convolutional block has a size of 256 × 256 × 1024, a filter size of $f = 3$, a filter size of $s = 2$, and the block's letter is "a." The five identity blocks have the following names: b, c, d, e, and f. They each use three sets of filters that are 256 by 256 by 1024 pixels in size. $f = 3$.
- **Stage 6:** The convolutional block has the following parameters: $f = 3$, $s = 2$, and the block's letter is "a." The size of the filters used is 512 × 512 × 2048. The two identity blocks are denoted by the letters "b" and "c," and they each make use of three separate sets of filters that have the dimensions 256 × 256 × 2048.

A window with the shape (2, 2) is used in the 2D Average Pooling algorithm, and its name is "avg pool." The flatten operation lacks both hyperparameters and a name parameter. Through the utilization of a softmax activation, the input of the Fully Connected (Dense) layer is reduced to the number of classes. The correct name for it is 'FC' plus str (classes).

3.3.2 Residual Block

A residual block is a stack of layers that are configured in such a way that the output of one layer is taken and added to another layer that is deeper in the block. This process continues until the output of the last layer in the stack is used. This procedure is carried out multiple times until the block is finished. The non-linear effect is then applied to the signal after the output of the corresponding layer in the main path is added to the original signal before the addition. This occurs after the addition (Fig. 9).

3.3.3 Identity and Convolutional Block

In ResNets, the identity block serves as the template for the standard block that is used. This section of the diagram corresponds to the scenario in which the input activation

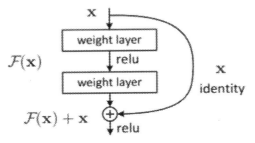

Fig. 9. Residual block in resnet-50

and the output activation both have the same dimension. On the other hand, when the input dimensions and output dimensions do not correspond to one another, we can use a convolutional block. One key difference between the shortcut path and the identity block is the presence of a CONV2D layer in the former (Fig. 10).

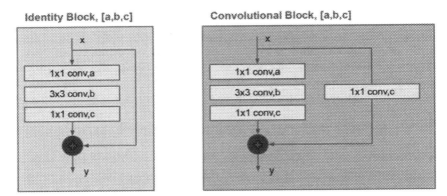

Fig. 10. Identity and convolutional block architecture

ResNets is an efficient Neural Network Architecture because they retain a low error rate deep in the network. Feature extraction, semantic segmentations, and different Generative Adversarial Network designs all perform well with deep neural networks. These may be utilized to construct AI-equipped Computer Vision systems for extracting detailed details or increasing picture and video quality. Standard models do not adapt a residual block technique which makes Resnet-50 more efficient and suitable for this research.

4   Performance Analysis and Results

The training of the model was finished after a run of 15 epochs. After training, the testing data was run, and it was discovered that the experimental results matched the expected results with an accuracy of 96.875 percent. It was because the dataset had been split into two parts previously.

4.1 Running Different ResNet Models

We ran the model on different ResNet models with different layers and judges their accuracy. However, the best results were achieved by the ResNet-50 model, and hence our final experiment incorporated the same.

ResNet model	Accuracy	Loss	Remarks
ResNet 18	92.1875%	0.1411%	Less accuracy as compared to other ResNets
ResNet 34	96.875%	0.1320%	Deviation in accuracy in every epoch
ResNet 50	95.3125%	0.1548%	Consistent accuracy and lesser time
ResNet 101	98.875%	0.1162%	Takes a longer time but has deviations in accuracy

4.2 Plotting Different Graphs for Analysis

See Figs. 11, 12, 13 and 14.

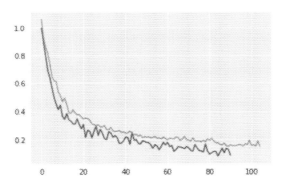

Fig. 11. Graph of loss vs MiniBatch

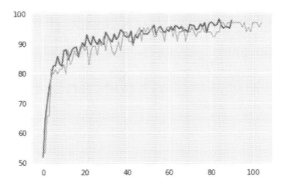

Fig. 12. Graph of accuracy vs MiniBatch

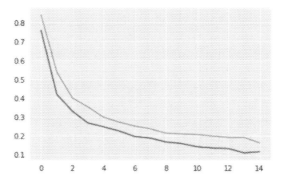

Fig. 13. Graph of loss vs epoch

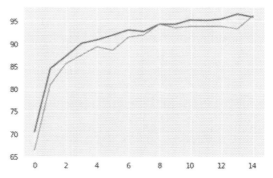

Fig. 14. Graph of accuracy vs epoch

4.3   Tumor Detection

See Figs. 15, 16 and 17.

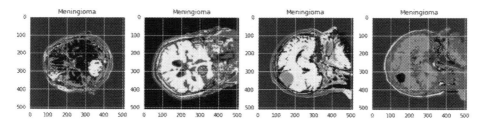

Fig. 15. Meningioma tumour detection

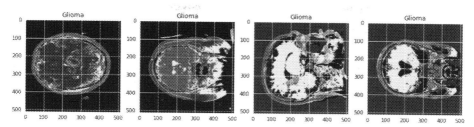

Fig. 16. Glioma tumour detection

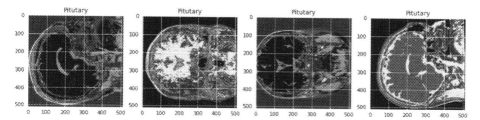

Fig. 17. Pitutary tumour detection

5   Conclusion and Future Work

The interpretation of medical image datasets has traditionally been a process that takes a lot of time, and dealing with them in and of themselves presents a challenge. The solutions that are presented in this paper prompted us to think about employing deep learning strategies. Regarding the accuracy of classifiers, the Resnet-50 classifier that was proposed performed exceptionally well. The results of the technique that was proposed show that its accuracy and statistical measure are significantly more competitive than those of any other techniques that do not involve deep learning. It would be much more interesting to investigate the possibility of combining this deep neural network with other networks and then observing the effect or performance on the same brain MRI dataset. Specifically, it would be far more interesting to do so.

However, the proposed model has limitations that still need to be resolved. Even with an accuracy rate as presented in the results, there is a scope for improvement in the model using hybrid deep learning techniques. A combination of different models can be explored in more detail in upcoming research and study phases.

References

1. Ehret, F., Kaul, D., Clusmann, H., Delev, D., Kernbach, J.M.: Machine learning-based radiomics in neuro-oncology. In: Staartjes, V.E., Regli, L., Serra, C. (eds.) Machine Learning in Clinical Neuroscience, pp. 139–151. Springer, Cham (2022). https://doi.org/10.1007/978-3-030-85292-4_18
2. Mallick, P.K., Ryu, S.H., Satapathy, S.K., Mishra, S., Nguyen, G.N., Tiwari, P.: Brain MRI image classification for cancer detection using deep wavelet autoencoder-based deep neural network. IEEE Access. **7**, 46278–46287 (2019)

3. Hiralal, R., Menon, H.P.: A survey of brain MRI image segmentation methods and the issues involved. In: Corchado Rodriguez, J., Mitra, S., Thampi, S., El-Alfy, E.S. (eds.) ISTA 2016. AISC, vol. 530, pp. 245–259. Springer, Cham (2016). https://doi.org/10.1007/978-3-319-47952-1_19

4. Xiao, J., Tong, Y.: Research of brain MRI image segmentation algorithm based on FCM and SVM. In: The 26th Chinese Control and Decision Conference (2014 CCDC), pp. 1712–1716. IEEE (2014)

5. Jose, A., Ravi, S., Sambath, M.: Brain tumor segmentation using k-means clustering and fuzzy c-means algorithms and its area calculation. Int. J. Innov. Res. Comput. Commun. Eng. 2(2) (2014)

6. Nayak, S., Karali, Y., Panda, S.: A study on brain MRI image segmentation techniques. Int. J. Res. Stud. Comput. Sci. Eng. 2(9), 4–13 (2015)

7. Damodharan, S., Raghavan, D.: Combining tissue segmentation and neural network for brain tumor detection. Int. Arab J. Inf. Technol. (IAJIT) 12(1) (2015)

8. Rehman, A., Naz, S., Razzak, M.I., Akram, F., Imran, M.: A deep learning-based framework for automatic brain tumors classification using transfer learning. Circuits Syst. Signal Process. 39(2), 757–775 (2020)

9. Sharma, K., Kaur, A., Gujral, S.: Brain tumor detection based on machine learning algorithms. Int. J. Comput. Appl. 103(1), 7–11 (2014)

10. Amin, J., Sharif, M., Yasmin, M., Fernandes, S.L.: A distinctive approach in brain tumor detection and classification using MRI. Pattern Recogn. Lett. 139, 118–127 (2020)

11. Borole, V.Y., Nimbhore, S.S., Kawthekar, D.S.S.: Image processing techniques for brain tumor detection: a review. Int. J. Emerg. Trends Technol. Comput. Sci. (IJETTCS) 4(2), 1–14 (2015)

12. Amin, J., Sharif, M., Raza, M., Saba, T., Anjum, M.A.: Brain tumor detection using statistical and machine learning method. Comput. Methods Programs Biomed. 177, 69–79 (2019)

13. Abdalla, H.E.M., Esmail, M.: Brain tumor detection by using artificial neural network. In: 2018 International Conference on Computer, Control, Electrical, and Electronics Engineering (ICCCEEE), pp. 1–6. IEEE (2018)

14. Selvapandian, A., Manivannan, K.: Fusion based glioma brain tumor detection and segmentation using ANFIS classification. Comput. Methods Programs Biomed. 166, 33–38 (2018)

15. Zhang, C., Shen, X., Cheng, H., Qian, Q.: Brain tumor segmentation based on hybrid clustering and morphological operations. Int. J. Biomed. Imaging 2019 (2019)

16. Abiwinanda, N., Hanif, M., Hesaputra, S.T., Handayani, A., Mengko, T.R.: Brain tumor classification using convolutional neural network. In: Lhotska, L., Sukupova, L., Lacković, I., Ibbott, G.S. (eds.) World Congress on Medical Physics and Biomedical Engineering 2018, pp. 183–189. Springer, Singapore (2019). https://doi.org/10.1007/978-981-10-9035-6_33

17. Paul, J.S., Plassard, A.J., Landman, B.A., Fabbri, D.: Deep learning for brain tumor classification. In: Medical Imaging 2017: Biomedical Applications in Molecular, Structural, and Functional Imaging, vol. 10137, pp. 253–268. SPIE (2017)

18. Muhammad, K., Khan, S., Ser, J.D., Albuquerque, V.H.C.d.: Deep learning for multigrade brain tumor classification in smart healthcare systems: a prospective survey. IEEE Trans. Neural Netw. Learn. Syst. 32(2), 507–522 (2021)

19. Saleh, A, Sukaik, R, Abu-Naser, S.S.: Brain tumor classification using deep learning. In: 2020 International Conference on Assistive and Rehabilitation Technologies (iCareTech), pp. 131–136. IEEE (2020)

20. Mohsen, H., El-Dahshan, E.S.A., El-Horbaty, E.S.M., Salem, A.B.M.: Classification using deep learning neural networks for brain tumors. Future Comput. Inform. J. 3(1), 68–71 (2018)

21. Patil, P., Kumar, K.S., Gaud, N., Semwal, V.B.: Clinical human gait classification: extreme learning machine approach. In: 2019 1st International Conference on Advances in Science, Engineering and Robotics Technology (ICASERT), pp. 1–6 (2019)

22. Bijalwan, V., Semwal, V.B., Singh, G., Crespo, R.G.: Heterogeneous computing model for post-injury walking pattern restoration and postural stability rehabilitation exercise recognition. Expert. Syst. **39**(6), e12706 (2022). https://onlinelibrary.wiley.com/doi/abs/10.1111/exsy.12706

23. Jain, R., Semwal, V.B., Kaushik, P.: Deep ensemble learning approach for lower extremity activities recognition using wearable sensors. Expert Syst. **39**(6), e12743 (2022). https://onlinelibrary.wiley.com/doi/abs/10.1111/exsy.12743

Automatic Image Caption Generation Using ResNet & Torch Vision

Vijeta Verma[✉], Sri Khetwat Saritha, and Sweta Jain

Maulana Azad National Institute of Technology, Bhopal, India
vijetaverma444@gmail.com

Abstract. Image captioning is a task through which a textual description can be generated that illustrated the action performed in the image. It is one of the most complicated research areas where only the machine learning approach can intervene. In the area of image captioning, a system should be intelligent enough to understand the semantic knowledge to recognize the object present in the image and the situation that evolves with it. In the proposed work an image captioning system has been generated using ResNet along with CNN and RNN. CNN is used as an encoder and RNN is used as a decoder. The system is able to infer the situation precisely for MSCOCO benchmark. The model has been trained with ResNet152 which effectively utilizes the layers and minimizes the computational time. ResNet skips the convolutional layers that solved the gradient exploding problem, that is why it is also known as skip connection. System perceived better Bilingual Evaluation Understudy (BLEU), METEOR, CIDEr, and Rouge score as compared to the previously implemented model. BLEU score has been evaluated with four parameters as B1, B2, B3 and B4 i.e., 0.57, 0.404, 0.279, 0.191 respectively. METEOR, CIDEr and Rouge have been depicted as 0.195, 0.396 and 0.6 respectively. Model has been better utilized to train the samples by reducing the size of the image and enhancing the brightness with pillow. System also uses the Torch Vision library to enhance the model for better predicting the situation.

Keywords: Image captioning · ResNet · CNN · RNN · MSCOCO · BLEU · Machine learning

1 Introduction

Image captioning is the process of extracting textual description from an image by recognizing the objects present in the image and the action supposed to be performed there. It can be done using Computer Vision as well as Natural Language Processing. There are several datasets available that challenges researchers to generate the caption that better describes the actions which are present in the image. Convolutional Neural Network (CNN) has been adopted as an encoder that extracted the features from an input image. The hidden states of the CNN layers are connected with the decoder i.e., Recurrent Neural Network (RNN). RNN works as a language processing model that initiates the textual extraction from pertained features. Extracting the accurate or precise caption is still a challenge in the field of image processing or artificial intelligence. The extracted caption should be grammatically and semantically correct. Many researchers are looking for a better prediction model that can generate an accurate caption. Facebook is working on image captioning for their users for getting post their pictures with automated generated captions where users are not required to intervene manually write the caption. Facebook proposed a torch vision package that works for natural language processing. Torch vision is especially designed for analyzing the situation present in the image along with object recognition.

Fig. 1. Image captioning inferences [1]

Figure 1 shows various examples of image captioning inferences. In the previous works, systems were lacking somewhere and were not able to precisely describe the image and pertain low BLEU score. BLEU is a technique through which the candidate caption and reference caption can be compared and accuracy can be calculated. System also compares the caption result with Meteor, Rouge and CIDEr metrics. The procurement and examination of visual data is one of the solutions through which; this world can be analyzed or to be getting more familiar with the world by using machines. Image captioning is an examination that transmutes the images into comprehension. There are two phases involved in this field where first phase involves feature extraction of the image. It can also be called as object identification where objects in the image pertains certain kind of information related to its own features or textures that signify the objects. Once the features has been extracted then system is able to classify the object and it can extract what kinds of objects are available in the image. In the second phase; system pertains the information about the activities that have been predicted as per the object information and activity involved in the image. This is also called semantic information where information has been extracted in the form of keywords that later combines and form a sentence that describe the image which is called as image caption. There is no particular region of interest (ROI) because whole image is considered as ROI where system is responsible for attaining all the information about foreground and background of the image. Image caption is very effective and there are so many applications for the same. The most popular application is human computer interface where interaction become easier and it can also be used for inserting subtitle in the videos [2].

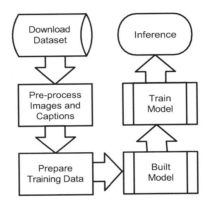

Fig. 2. Block diagram of basic model processing

Figure 2 shows the basic process model for image captioning. The image dataset is first downloaded and pre-processed. The captions are also pre-processed for preparing the training data. Later, the system build the model and complete the training for inferences.

2   Related Works

Several researches have been done in the field of image caption generation where various methodologies have been used for attaining precise information related to the image. K. Vijay et al. [2] introduced a method that is related to stemming algorithm. Stemming algorithm is a natural language processing algorithm for obtaining the image caption from different kind of images. It is a conventional method which is not related to the machine learning approach. It is based on morphological variant approach that makes a relation among similar kind of words. It is template matching based approach which is not proficient to attain better level of accuracy with precise captions. Xinru Wei et al. [3] introduced a method that is related to DenseNet. System uses CBIR benchmark that contains 10,000 images. DenseNet is very complex in nature, as it is a densely populated network where layers are high in range which makes the system more complex, resulting in degraded computation efficiency and it requires more memory to store the trained weight model. It takes very long time to accomplish the training phase. DenseNet is very slow due to complex layers. Network should be lighter in weight and use proficient pre-processing techniques through which it can be compiled as faster network as compared to the ResNet, VGG-16, RNN and many more. Niange Yu et al. [4] introduced a method that is related to Order Embedding algorithm. In this kind of algorithm, system intended to extract the image features and keywords and embed the keywords according to the topic related to the field. The embedding technique is bit poor because it can work with high quality images. High quality images pertain precise caption but poor resolution based images suffer due to the low pixel intensities that degrade the object classification method. Min Yang et al. [5] introduced a method that is related to MLADIC which is a multitasking learning algorithm. They used two phases algorithm for pertaining information from the source image to the target information. The image amalgamation task utilizes the restrictive generative antagonistic network to incorporate conceivable images dependent on text depictions. In C-GAN, a generative model G orchestrates conceivable images given text depictions and a discriminative model attempts to recognize the images. The dual learning mechanism of image caption structural model contains CNN, image synthesis and LSTM models. Image synthesis contains various convolutional layers. Mathematically every convolutional layer has been computed as:

$$Z_{out} = F(Z_{in}, W_i) + Z_{in} \tag{1}$$

where Z_{in} and Z_{out} are input and output vectors of layers and $F(Z_{in}, W_i)$ denotes the mapping function of the system.

Ren C. Luo et al. [6] introduced a method that is related to Template augmentation method. They used sentence based template where image features have been extracted first and later the strings are compared with the templates and result is obtained accordingly.

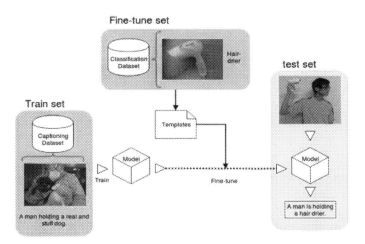

Fig. 3. Template based augmented model [6]

The system has been fine-tuned by enhancing the object recognition method. Figure 3 shows the flow of this method where template based augmented model is used for classifying the object and generating the caption. In this paper they focused on object recognition for recognizing the correct object and generate the captions accordingly. But template based method is very conventional method where machine learning is not involved. Conventional method is returning the result on the basis of pre-defined templates. Yanagimoto et al. [7] introduced a method that is related to attention mechanism. It is a multiple perceptive generator for controlling the caption flow. Attention is a weight model that has been used in encoding phase and for decoding the features, LSTM is used. System uses VGG16 because multiple perceptive model can be formed with VGG16 which uses 16 layers for evaluating the performance of the system. They used 128 bit dimension vectors for encoding the input data and use 14×14 segments for tensors. VGG16 is a heavy weight model that requires more time for training the network. It has vanishing gradient problem that leads to higher error and this may degrade the performance of the system. Network should be light in weight and small filter scan be used to decrease the computation time. There are several hidden states in LSTM such as cell state ct, input state it, output state ot and forget state ft.

$$i_t = \sigma \left(K_{ia} a_t + K_{ih} h_{t-1} + n_i \right) \tag{2}$$

$$f_t = \sigma \left(K_{fa} a_t + K_{fh} h_{t-1} + n_f \right) \tag{3}$$

$$o_t = \sigma \left(K_{oa} a_t + K_{oh} h_{t-1} + n_o \right) \tag{4}$$

Megha J Panicker et al. [8] introduced transfer learning algorithm that is related to the Convolutional Neural network (CNN). This system used hybrid model by combining two distinct approaches for generating captions. This system used CNN along with LSTM for better precision. They have used Flickr8K for performing the testing phase and obtaining the result accordingly. They used Bilingual Evaluation Understudy for comparing the

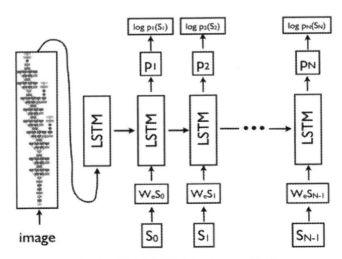

Fig. 4. CNN & LSTM structure model [8]

result with extracted text. System generated the scores as per the image description output and keywords that have been extracted and compared with the ground truth values. They tested 2000 images from Flickr8K dataset and trained with 6000 images. There are certain drawbacks of LSTM because it takes longer time to train the model as compared to the other machine learning approaches. It also requires more memory due to bulky network. Dropout is more complex to implement.

Figure 4 shows the CNN and LSTM hybrid model where two tasks have been performed, first one is encoder where text has been extracted and second one is decoder where final translation has been performed to build a meaningful sentence.

Muhammad Abdelhadie Al-Malla et al. [9] proposed an image captioning model using attention and object features. In this study, authors introduced and demonstrated the efficiency of an attention-based encoder-decoder image captioning model that employs two feature extraction techniques: an image classification CNN (Xception) and an object identification module (YOLOv4). They introduced the significance factor, which favours high-confidence items over low-confidence ones and prioritizes foreground large objects over background ones, and they showed how it affects score growth. They demonstrated how the approach raised scores and contrasted it with other research in terms of score growth, particularly the CIDEr metric. But in object identification YOLOv4 has more localization error and struggle to identify the close objects as well as the small ones. It suffers if objects are not recognized correctly. Object identification plays an important role in the field of image caption generation because if an object is not recognized

Table 1. Models comparison

Method	Finding
CNN+LSTM	Longer time to train.
	Requires more memory,
	Bulky network.
	Dropouts.
VGG-16	Heavy weight model.
	Requires more time for training.
	Vanishing gradient problem.
Template Augmentation	Very conventional method
	No machine learning involved.
	Result on the basis of pre-defined templates.
Order Embedding	Poor technique because it can work with high quality images.
	Does not effectively work with poor image.
DenseNet	Slow due to complex layers.
	Network should be lighter in weight and use proficient pre-processing techniques through which it can be compiled faster.

correctly then the image can not be described properly, so it is not able to pertain the efficient score as compared to the other machine learning models.

Table 1 shows the drawbacks of certain models through which image captioning can be implemented with satisfying precisions.

3 Proposed Work

Proposed system is based on ResNet to train model for image caption generation. ResNet utilizes the layers effectively because of skip connections. ResNet is able to train the model with hundreds or thousands of layers and still able to acquire better performance as compared to the other models. It has great potential to represent the model with object recognition, classification and regression. There are several networks that suffer from the vanishing gradient problem where layers get unstable and not able to back propagate the information to the layers. ResNet is very much effective to tackle vanishing problems and makes model more powerful. ResNet stands for Residual Network that is better recognized as identical shortcut connection which is also known as skip connections (Fig. 5).

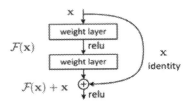

Fig. 5. Residual connection network [9]

where x is considered as identity and f(x) is the activation function and f(x) + x is the forward identity function. Here the system uses the residual blocks for calibrating the model for training and the input of the system goes through the weight connections as well as the skip connections which is commonly known as identity shortcut. Let Ml is considered as output and l is the number of residual blocks, k is the mapping function and b is the random variable;

$$M_l = ReLU \ (b_l * k_l(M_{l-1}) + id\,(M_{l-1})) \tag{5}$$

It can be considered as normal ReLU block if bl is equal to 1. But if bl is equal to 0 then it would be;

$$M_l = ReLU \ (id\,(M_{l-1})) \tag{6}$$

Let s_l be the survival probability of the system;

$$M_l = ReLU \ (s_l * k_l(M_{l-1}) + id\,(M_{l-1})) \tag{7}$$

The resulting rule for survival probability as;

$$S_l = 1 - \frac{l}{L}(1 - S_L) \tag{8}$$

where S_L is considered as the survival probability of the system and L is considered as total number of blocks in the model.

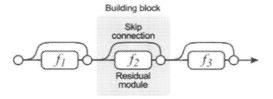

Fig. 6. Three block ResNet (Conventional ResNet Model) [10]

Figure 6 shows the conventional model of ResNet that contains 3 layers with skip connection where input data can be skipped when required or similar output encounters continuously. ResNet is considered as the best deep learning approach as per the experiments done because of its skipping nature that makes the model light and effective.

A. Encoder& Decoder
Proposed system uses CNN for encoding the data for machine translation. The length of the input sequence as well as the output sequence could be different. An example can be pertained as (Fig. 7);

Fig. 7. Caption: a person is riding the surfboard in the ocean [11]

Machine encodes and decodes the vectors; one at a time. Machine starts encoding and decoding with a vector and calculate till the last conditional probability distribution (Fig. 8).

$$P(y_t = j|y_1^{t-1}, I) \text{ is the probability distribution}$$

Here system encodes the input image into vectors and that vectors can be recognized and decoded later. $Fc_n(I)$ is the representation model of an image.

$$S_1 = \sigma(M_{S_0} + U_{X_1} + b) \tag{9}$$

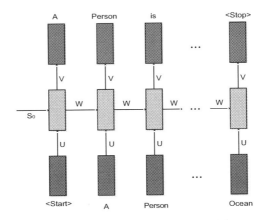

Fig. 8. Encoding and decoding model

$$S_2 = \sigma(M_{S_1} + U_{X_2} + b) \tag{10}$$

$$S_n = \sigma(M_{S_{n-1}} + U_{X_n} + b) \tag{11}$$

where S_1 is the next version of S_0, similarly S_2 is the next version of S_1. It can be stated that all input are dependent on previous layer output. CNN encodes images into vectors and forward it to the next layer for traversing all vectors. Here Recurrent Neural Network (RNN) is used to decode the vectors into a word and sequentially arrange the words for meaningful sentence using attention mechanism.

$$S_0 = h_T \tag{12}$$

Where T is the length of input

$$S_t = RNN\left(S_{t-1}, e\left(\hat{y}_{t-1}\right)\right) \tag{13}$$

$$P\left(y_t = j \middle| y_1^{t-1}, x\right) = softmax\left(V_{S_t} + b\right) \tag{14}$$

$y_1, y_2, y_3, y_4, \ldots, y_{t-1}$ are hidden decoding states.

In every probability there is a loss function considered as log p, certain words can be missed, so it is required to reduce the negative log probability of the model while decoding the input image.

$$L(\theta) = \sum_i^t L_t(\theta) = -\sum_{t=1}^t logP\left(y_t = j \middle| y_1^{t-1}, x\right)$$

$L(\theta)$ is considered as the loss function $\tag{15}$

Figure 9 shows the architecture of encoder and decoder whereas CNN is used to encode the data and RNN is used to decode the vectors into the meaningful captions.

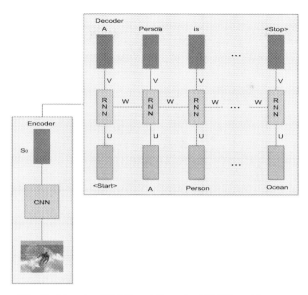

Fig. 9. Encoder (CNN) and Decoder (RNN) architecture

Proposed work is able to generate image captions automatically with high preciseness. System is based on ResNet-152 for building network model. It also uses Torch Vision library for enhancing the performance. System uses MSCOCO dataset for training and testing the model and it has been trained with 82,783 images along with ground truth captions. 40,504 images are available for validation process and system tested with 39,622 images with 5 captions for each image. Figure 15 shows the flowchart of training where firstly dataset is loaded with ground truth captions then data is prepared by resizing the images (224 * 224) before encoding. Once the data has been prepared then CNN encodes the image into feature vectors then training and validation can be done using ResNet-152 model. Once the feature learning has been done then decoding module can be initiated using RNN. System predicts the objects containing in the image along with action performed over there. Prediction is started with first word and goes till the end word has not been encountered. If system depicts new word which is not available in ground truth caption then system appends that word and searches the word till end word has not been encountered. After the caption has been generated a model is finally built, then inference can be performed. The batch size of the training model is 128 with 20 epochs, the beam size is 5 with maximum length 20. System also uses TorchVision model for addressing certain tasks such as object detection, object classification, semantic segmentation and many more. Torch vision is embedded with ResNet and Torch vision has potential to obtain accuracy up to 94.046% for object detection and classification. Both the model solved the vanishing gradient problem and pertained better level of accuracy in the field of image captioning along with better BLEU, Meteor, CIDEr and Rouge scores.

Here CNN has been used to extract the features and ResNet is responsible for classifying the features. Feature extraction process includes various convolutional layers.

The output of one layer is transferred to next layer in the form of feature maps. Feature mapping is the process of representing image features that has been extracted by model in the form of graph. The representation of the image is based on RGB (Red Green Blue) colour model and each channel has its own pixel values that would be in the range of 0 to 255.

Fig. 10. Original image (From MSCOCO)

Fig. 11. Pixelate image

Figure 10 shows the original image that has been picked up from MSCOCO dataset and Fig. 11 shows the pixelate of referenced image where pixel boxes are appeared that contained RGB pixel intensities.

$$I = \begin{bmatrix} r_{11}g_{11}b_{11} & r_{12}g_{12}b_{12} & r_{13}g_{13}b_{13} & r_{14}g_{14}b_{14} \\ r_{21}g_{21}b_{21} & r_{22}g_{22}b_{22} & r_{23}g_{23}b_{23} & r_{24}g_{24}b_{24} \\ r_{31}g_{31}b_{31} & r_{32}g_{32}b_{32} & r_{33}g_{33}b_{33} & r_{34}g_{34}b_{34} \\ r_{41}g_{41}b_{41} & r_{42}g_{42}b_{42} & r_{43}g_{43}b_{43} & r_{44}g_{44}b_{44} \\ r_{51}g_{51}b_{51} & r_{52}g_{52}b_{52} & r_{53}g_{53}b_{53} & r_{54}g_{54}b_{54} \\ r_{61}g_{61}b_{61} & r_{62}g_{62}b_{62} & r_{63}g_{63}b_{63} & r_{64}g_{64}b_{64} \end{bmatrix}$$

I is considered as the input RGB image containing three channel pixel intensities and network model is responsible to compute the mean value of the all three channels.

$$R_{mean} = \left(\frac{1}{P}\right) \sum_{p=1}^{P} R(p) \tag{16}$$

$$G_{mean} = \left(\frac{1}{P}\right) \sum_{p=1}^{P} G(p) \tag{17}$$

$$B_{mean} = \left(\frac{1}{P}\right) \sum_{p=1}^{P} B(p) \tag{18}$$

where R, G and B are red, green and blue channels resp. Mean is the average value of respective channel. P is the pixel value of respective channels.

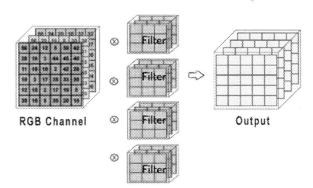

Fig. 12. Convolutional layer output (Color figure online)

Figure 12 shows the convolutional layer output of three distinct channels by computing its average and further filters are applied to render the image feature maps (Figs. 13 and 14).

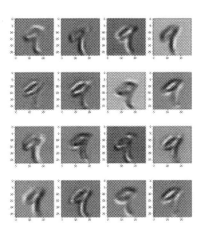

Fig. 13. Feature map

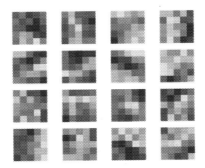

Fig. 14. Filters used to create fature maps

Figure 16 shows the flowchart of testing model where system firstly loaded the encoder and decoder model then system loaded ResNet model and input data too for extracting the captions. Inference can be done from start word to the end word if any of the decode error has not been encountered. Once the end word reached then decoded words can be achieved and caption can be generated using attention mechanism for sequentially arranging the words for pertaining meaningful caption. Once the candidate caption has been achieved then it can be compared with the reference caption for computing certain parameters such as BLEU, Meteor, CIDEr and Rouge scores. These metrics can decide the precision of the system that how much candidate caption is similar or different from the reference caption. System pertained better scores as compared to the previous template augmentation model.

ResNet has great potential to learn the complex function with high preciseness and shortly. While performing the training; the model's performance can drop down that degrads the system, this is called degradation problem. Skip connection solved the degradation problem that is why it can be considered as the better model as compared to the others. ResNet as a skip connection or identity block can skip certain layers and minimize the load of the model and output of one layer is directly transferred to the next layer of the model. Table 2 explain the steps involved in the model for training and testing module.

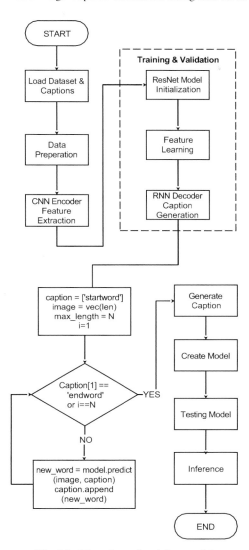

Fig. 15. Flowchart of training model

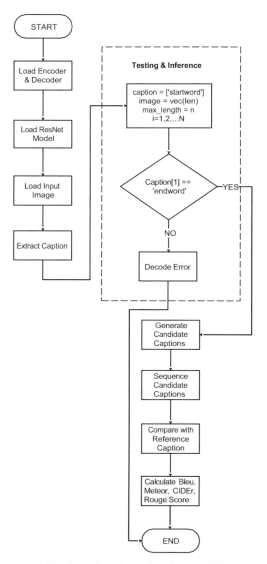

Fig. 16. Flowchart of testing model

4 Experimental Result

Experimental result is based on candidate captions as well as the reference captions. MSCOCO dataset has been used to train and test the model and result has been pertained by comparing the captions. Result is based on non fine tuned data. BLEU, METEOR, CIDEr and Rouge have been computed for evaluating the result as:

Bn as BLEU Score, M as METEOR, R as Rouge, C as CIDEr.

Table 2. Proposed algorithm

ResNet-152 Image Captioning Algorithm

Initialization

Input: Set of Image $X=(x_1, x_2, x_3,\ldots\ldots x_N)$ with ground truth data $Y=(y_1, y_2, y_3 ,\ldots\ldots y_N)$

Output: Image Caption

Step 1: Input image

Step 2: Normalize image by resize

$$(w_{new}, h_{new}) = \frac{R}{max(w, h)} (w, h)$$

Where (w_{new}, h_{new}): the new width and height of the image, R is the replacing value, $max(w, h)$ is the maximum value

Step 3: Define the identity block

f(x)+x

Step 4: Initialize beam size, batch size and no. of epochs, W_h as weight model for hidden layers, W_b as weight for output layer and B_h, B_a as bias for hidden and output layer resp.

Step 5: Compute output of each convolutional layer

$$M_l = ReLU\left(b_l * k_l(M_{l-1}) + id(M_{l-1})\right)$$

It can be considered as normal ReLU block if b_l is equal to 1. But if b_l is equal to 0 then it would be;

$$M_l = ReLU\left(id(M_{l-1})\right)$$

Step 6: Calculate survival probability

$$S_l = 1 - \frac{l}{L}(1 - S_L)$$

Where S_L is considered as the survival probability of the system and L is considered as total number of blocks in the model.

Step 7: Calculate probability distribution

$$P(y_t = j|y_1^{t-1}, I)$$

Step 8: Generate model

Step 9: Load model

Step 10: Decode data

$$S_t = RNN\left(S_{t-1}, e(\hat{y}_{t-1})\right)$$

$y_1, y_2, y_3, y_4,\ldots\ldots,y_{t-1}$ are hidden decoding states

Step 11: Generate caption by attention mechanism

Step 12: Compare candidate caption with reference caption

Step 13: Compute BLEU, METEOR, CIDEr and Rouge

Step 14: End

METEOR (Metric for Evaluation of Translation with Explicit ORdering) is a metric that can express the result of machine translation. In this evaluation; the result is based on harmonic mean with precision and recall. It has been designed to solve the problem of BLEU metric to correct the correlation.

$$p = \frac{m}{w_t}$$

where m is the unigram of the candidate that is available in reference translation. Wt is the no. of unigram in candidate (Fig. 17).

the cat sat on the mat

on the mat sat the cat

Fig. 17. METEOR evaluation example

BLEU (Bilingual Evaluation Understudy) is an evaluation that can be used for computing the quality of machine translation. It analyses the generated captions compared with the reference caption (Fig. 18).

$$\frac{No.\ of\ candidate\ words\ in\ the\ reference\ translation}{Total\ no.\ of\ words\ in\ the\ candidate\ translation}$$

Candidate 1: the the the the the the the.
Candidate 2: the cat is on the mat
Reference: The cat is on the mat.

Fig. 18. BLEU evaluation example

The Precision for candidate 1 is 2/7(28.5%). The Precision for candidate 2 is 1 (100%).

CIDEr (Consensus-based Image Description Evaluation) measures the similarity between the candidate captions with the reference caption. It is an important evaluation in the field of image captioning. It also measures the quality of generated captions as per the ground truth.

$$CIDEr = \frac{1}{KN} \sum_{k=1}^{K} \sum_{n=1}^{N} g_c(c, c_n^k)$$

where N is the annotated ground truth, K is the similar images, c is the caption.

ROUGE is a set of metric that generates the precision, recall, and F-score of a candidate with respect to references. ROUGE stands for Recall-Oriented Understudy for Gisting Evaluation.

$$F - Score = \frac{Precision * Recall}{Precision + Recall}$$

Table 3. Experimental results

Dataset	B_1	B_2	B_3	B_4	M	R	C
MSCOCO (Non Fine Tuned)	0.579	0.404	0.279	0.191	0.195	0.396	0.600

As per the experimental results; BLEU scores have been obtained as 0.579, 0.404, 0.279 and 0.191 respectively. METEOR as 0.195, ROUGE as 0.396 and CIDer as 0.600. The obtained result is better than the previous work that has been considered as base paper. Good scores represent that the system is good enough to generate relevant captions for a particular dataset.

Table 4. Result comparison

	B_1	B_2	B_3	B_4	M	R	C
Ren C. Luo [6]	0.238	0.109	0.050	0.022	0.096	0.249	0.143
Proposed	0.57	0.404	0.279	0.191	0.195	0.396	0.600

Table 3 represents the result obtained for all metrics and Table 4 shows the result comparison with Template Augmentation Method.

Table 5. Proposed caption result

Image	Image Caption
Ground Truth: A couple of giraffe standing next to each other	Candidate Caption: a couple of giraffe standing next to each other a couple of giraffes standing next to each other a couple of giraffes that are standing in the dirt a couple of giraffe standing next to each other on a field a couple of giraffe standing next to each other on a dirt ground

Table 5 represents the proposed candidate caption generation of an image and its reference caption. The preciseness of the system is better as compared to the template augementation method (Fig. 19).

Graph I Result Comparison

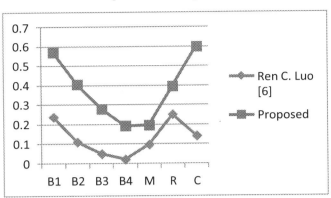

Fig. 19. Result comparison

5   Conclusion and Future Scope

Image captioning is a challenging task in the field of artificial intelligence. There are various models through which image captioning can be implemented but it is required to obtain better precision along with less processing time. Proposed system is based on ResNet as main training model, Torch Vision as library, CNN as encoder and RNN as decoder. ResNet is able to utilize the layers by skip connection method. System pertained high precision as compared to the earlier proposed model like Template Augmentation Method. System detained MSCOCO benchmark and trained model for the same and acquired better efficient model for image captioning. The limitation of the proposed work is to generate the caption from very old pictures that pertains low index because they are not even black and white image but are also missing in index values. In future different dataset can be trained with ResNet and can acquire better precision. ResNet can be ultilized bit more in future and precision can be enhanced. There are several datasets available such as CBIR, Flickr8k, Flickr30k, VizWiz and many more, these datasets can be trained with ResNet and pertain better metrics.

References

1. Popular Mechanics, Google's Image-Captioning AI Is Getting Scary Good. .https://www.popularmechanics.com/technology/robots/a23019/google-aicaptioning. Accessed 28 March 2022
2. Vijay, K., Ramya, D.: Generation of caption selection for news images using stemming algorithm. In: International Conference on Computation of Power, Energy, Information and Communication (ICCPEIC), pp. 0536–0540 (2015)
3. Wei, X., Qi, Y., Liu, J., Liu, F.: Image retrieval by dense caption reasoning. IEEE Visual Commun. Image Process. **2017**, 1–4 (2017). https://doi.org/10.1109/VCIP.2017.8305157
4. Yu, N., Hu, X., Song, B., Yang, J., Zhang, J.: Topic-oriented image captioning based on order-embedding. IEEE Trans. Image Process. **28**(6), 2743–2754 (2019). https://doi.org/10.1109/TIP.2018.2889922

5. Yang, M., et al.: Multitask learning for cross-domain image captioning. IEEE Trans. Multimedia **21**(4), 1047–1061 (2019). https://doi.org/10.1109/TMM.2018.2869276
6. Luo, R.C., Hsu, Y.-T., Wen, Y.-C., Ye, H.-J.: Visual image caption generation for service robotics and industrial applications. IEEE Int. Conf. Indust. Cyber Phys. Syst. **2019**, 827–832 (2019). https://doi.org/10.1109/ICPHYS.2019.8780171
7. Yanagimoto, H., Shozu, M.: Multiple perspective caption generation with attention mechanism. In: 2020 9th International Congress on Advanced Applied Informatics (IIAI-AAI), pp. 110–115 (2020). https://doi.org/10.1109/IIAI-AAI50415.2020.00031
8. Panicker, M.J., Upadhayay, V., Sethi, G., Mathur, V.: Image caption generator. Int. J. Innov. Technol. Explor. Eng. **10**(3) (2021). ISSN: 2278–3075
9. Al-Malla, M.A., Jafar, A., Ghneim, N.: Image captioning model using attention and object features to mimic human image understanding. J. Big Data **9**, 20 (2022). https://doi.org/10.1186/s40537-022-00571-w
10. Lazar, D.: Building a ResNet in Keras (2020). https://towardsdatascience.com/building-a-resnet-in-keras-e8f1322a49ba. Accessed 04 Mar 2022
11. Feng, V.: An Overview of ResNet and its Variants (2017). https://towardsdatascience.com/an-overview-of-resnet-and-its-variants-5281e2f56035. Accessed 04 Mar 2022
12. Soheyla, A., Khaled, R., Thiab, T., Hamid, A.: Automatic Generation of Descriptive Titles for Video Clips Using Deep Learning (2021)
13. Jagannath, A.: Image captioning using deep learning. Int. J. Res. Appl. Sci. Eng. Technol. **8**. 1430–1435 (2020). https://doi.org/10.22214/ijraset.2020.6232
14. Vijay, K., Ramya, D.: Generation of caption selection for news images using stemming algorithm. In: 2015 International Conference on Computation of Power, Energy, Information and Communication (ICCPEIC), pp. 0536–0540 (2015). https://doi.org/10.1109/ICCPEIC.2015.7259513
15. Varsha, K., Vaidehi, M., Megha, K.: Deep Learning based Automatic Image Caption Generation, pp. 1–6 (2019). https://doi.org/10.1109/GCAT47503.2019.8978293
16. Amritkar, C., Jabade, V.: Image caption generation using deep learning technique. In: 2018 Fourth International Conference on Computing Communication Control and Automation (ICCUBEA), pp. 1–4 (2018). https://doi.org/10.1109/ICCUBEA.2018.8697360
17. Xi, S.M., Cho, Y.I.: Image caption automatic generation method based on weighted feature. In: 2013 13th International Conference on Control, Automation and Systems (ICCAS 2013), pp. 548–551 (2013). https://doi.org/10.1109/ICCAS.2013.6703998
18. Pranay, M., Aman, G., Aayush, Y., Anurag, M., Nand, B.: Camera2Caption: a real-time image caption generator, pp. 1–6 (2017). https://doi.org/10.1109/ICCIDS.2017.8272660
19. Kuznetsova, P.,Ordonez, V., Berg, T.L., Choi, Y.: Treetalk: composition and compression of trees for image descriptions. ACL (2014)
20. Priyanka, K., Malde, N., Aromal, N., Saurabh, P., Sharma, G.: Visual Image Caption Generator Using Deep Learning (ICAST-2019) (2019)
21. Aker, A., Gaizauskas, R.: Generating Image Descriptions Using Dependency Relational Patterns. Annual Meeting of the Association for Computational Linguistics, pp. 1250–1258 (2010)
22. Vinyals, O., et al.: Show and tell: a neural image caption generator. In: Computer Vision and Pattern Recognition. IEEE (2015)
23. Wadhwa, T., Virk, H., Aghav, J., Image, S.B.: Captioning using deep learning. Int. J. Res. Appl. Sci. Eng. Technol. **8**(VI) (2020)
24. Kaviyarasu, B., .Krishnakumar, B., Kousalya, K., Gokul, S., Karthikeyan, R.: Image caption generator using deep learning. Int. J. Adv. Sci. Technol. **29**(3s), 975–980 (2020)
25. Hoxha, G., Melgani, F., Slaghenauffi, J.: A New CNN-RNN Framework For Remote Sensing Image Captioning. In: 2020 Mediterranean and Middle-East Geoscience and Remote Sensing Symposium (M2GARSS), pp. 1–4 (2020)

Consistency Comparison of Machine Vision Images Based on Improved ORB Algorithm

Yong Huang[✉]

School of Information and Engineering, Henan Institute of Science and Technology,
Xinxiang 453003, Henan, China
huangyong2022@126.com

Abstract. In recent years, with the continuous development of society, people's exploration in the field of machine vision images has gradually increased the demand for machine vision and digital image processing. Only the consistency comparison research of machine vision images based on the improved ORB algorithm, in order to obtain more complete image information. Based on the improved ORB algorithm, this paper conducts research by improving the consistency comparison of machine vision images, and meets the requirements of accuracy and precision for the obtained machine vision images and so on. This paper briefly introduces the technology and development trend of machine vision image consistency comparison, studies the machine vision image consistency comparison, and through a series of experiments to prove that the machine vision image consistency comparison based on the improved ORB algorithm is effective in To a certain extent, it has certain feasibility in terms of precision and accuracy. Analysis and comparison based on different image stitching methods were carried out. The final results of the research show that the accuracy of the five-consistency comparison of machine vision images is 98.7% when the distance of image five is 83.4 km. Experimental data show that the accuracy of machine vision image consistency comparison has always been maintained at a stable level, that is, 97%. It shows that the accuracy of machine vision image consistency comparison does not decrease with the increase of distance.

Keywords: ORB algorithm · Machine vision · Image consistency · Comparison research

1 Introduction

With the development of science and technology, the demand for high-definition panoramic images has become more and more urgent, and the machine vision image consistency technology has become the focus of many researchers at home and abroad, and the speed and effect of the corresponding stitching algorithms have been improved and improved for a long time. Because the quality of image stitching algorithm is directly determined by the image registration process [1]. Therefore, with the advantages of high efficiency and fast speed, feature-based image stitching methods have become the focus of current research, and have achieved relatively fruitful research results, but in the field of UAV remote sensing image stitching, such stitching methods There are still deficiencies in the performance of accuracy and real-time performance.

Many researchers have explored the consistency comparison of machine vision images based on the improved ORB algorithm. For example, Chen K believes that the subsidence caused by the mining process is very critical to the stability of buildings and production equipment, so it is very necessary to carry out subsidence data before mining [2]. Feng Y believes that an algorithm is used to detect feature points, and then the binary ORB feature descriptors corresponding to these feature points are extracted, and then combined with two-way matching and algorithms to complete image registration, and finally fade-in and fade-out image fusion is performed. The overall stitching speed and stitching effect are both It has been greatly improved [3]. At present, many scholars at home and abroad have done a lot of research on the consistency comparison of machine vision images. These theories and practices provide the basis for the research of this paper.

This paper is based on the theoretical basis of human-based improved ORB algorithm. With the advantages of high efficiency and fast speed, the feature-based image stitching method has become the focus of current research, and has achieved relatively fruitful research results. In the field of remote sensing image stitching, such stitching methods are still insufficient in accuracy and real-time performance. In order to meet the dual requirements of high precision and high real-time performance of UAV remote sensing image stitching, this paper proposes a UAV remote sensing image stitching algorithm with improved ORB features, and verifies the practicability of this algorithm through a series of comparative experiments.

2   Related Theoretical Overview and Research

2.1   Design and Research of Machine Vision Measuring System

(1) Principle and performance parameters of machine vision measurement system

After selecting a camera with suitable pixels and resolution, select the corresponding type of optical lens according to the requirements of magnification and field of view. The focal length is calculated according to the working distance. The working distance of the lens is the distance from the object to be measured to the front surface of the lens in the optical lens. Considering that the traditional lens is prone to produce parallax effect, the hardware platform uses a telecentric lens. When the measured object is within the working distance of the lens, its image magnification is relatively stable. Before image acquisition, the cable needs to be processed into a sample of specified length [4, 5]. The telecentric lens has a good depth of field effect, which can eliminate the influence of some errors caused by sample preparation on the image acquisition effect.

(2)Structural composition of machine vision images

In the target image, the characteristics of the knife mark texture and the need for texture removal are analyzed, and a method for removing the knife mark texture based on bilateral filter is proposed. Bilateral filter is a good nonlinear spatial smoothing filter that can protect edge information and remove noise [6]. The basic principle is to smooth the image through a neighborhood template, the center point pixel in this area is determined by the pixel value in the neighborhood, and the weight of the influence of the pixel point in the neighborhood on the value depends on the spatial proximity and pixel value similarity of the two pixels. However, the consistency comparison of machine vision images based on the improved ORB algorithm can be sensitive to noise and other problems through the hard clustering method represented by mean clustering, and it is difficult to ensure the effectiveness and adaptability of the algorithm, and even cause the image segmentation task to fail. With the development of fuzzy theory, fuzzy theory is gradually applied to clustering algorithms, forming fuzzy mean clustering. In recent years, fuzzy mean clustering has also been widely used in the field of image segmentation to solve the problem of traditional hard clustering methods. It is difficult to achieve denoising of images containing a large amount of uneven noise, and achieve effective segmentation of noisy images.

(3)Software Design of Machine Vision Measuring System

The nonlinear support vector machine for machine vision image consistency comparison is more suitable for solving nonlinear problems, and has strong application potential in solving practical engineering problems, so it is widely used. Due to the low computational complexity of using the radial basis function to project sample points, few parameters to be set, and strong implementation stability, it is not easy to receive interference. Therefore, the radial basis function is often regarded as the best The kernel function is aimed at the linearly inseparable problem in the sample space[7, 8]. The main idea of solving this problem is to project the sample points to a higher dimension by establishing a linear mapping, so that it is linearly separable in the new dimension, and this mapping method usually requires With the help of the projection method based on the kernel function, this method is called nonlinear support vector machine.

Based on the machine vision image consistency comparison based on the improved ORB algorithm, other types of machine vision image consistency comparison features are not effective in removing features [9]. The cross-sectional images of different types of sample cable cores have differences in the number and distribution of knife marks. Knife mark texture presents complex distribution characteristics in the airspace, but the analysis shows that the knife mark texture has the characteristics of directional consistency. This chapter analyzes the knife mark texture from the perspective of the frequency domain. The many and complex knife mark textures in the air domain appear as a directional long strip highlight area in the frequency domain, and the main direction of the texture is related to the strip highlight There is a vertical relationship between the regions.

2.2 Theoretical Introduction of Improved ORB Algorithm

With the increasing application of feature matching algorithms, the requirements for the running speed and memory usage of the algorithms do not increase, so researchers have proposed more feature matching algorithms [10]. A large number of misjudgments will occur in the dynamic background. An improved Vibe algorithm with ORB feature point matching is proposed to realize the detection of moving objects in the dynamic background. In this paper, the feature points are detected and matched according to the ORB algorithm, the matching point pairs are screened by the RANSAC method and the transformation matrix parameters are calculated, the global motion compensation image is obtained through the perspective transformation, and the sample frames matched by the ORB feature points are dynamically updated [11]. ORB algorithm has been applied in many fields such as remote sensing image matching, target localization and tracking due to its high detection efficiency and less system memory occupation.

Image Consistency Algorithm for Machine Vision Based on Improved ORB Features. The traditional ORB algorithm has good real-time performance, which will lead to low image registration accuracy and spatial dislocation [12]. In view of the above problems, this paper improves the ORB algorithm for feature point extraction, so as to improve the registration accuracy of machine vision images while retaining the high real-time performance of the ORB algorithm. Image block processing. Since the actual non-machine vision images obtained are generally larger in size, in order to improve the centralized distribution of ORB feature points and ensure that more feature points are detected in the image, the machine vision images to be spliced are first processed into blocks. Constructing improved machine vision images. The traditional ORB algorithm does not have scale invariance, which reduces the number of matchable feature points and the matching accuracy of machine vision images when they contain scale changes. In order to further purify the initial matching point pair set and solve the machine vision image model with higher accuracy at the same time.

3   Experiment and Research

3.1   Experimental Method

Bilateral filter has the characteristics of image denoising and preserving edge information, in which two functions that generate filter convolution kernel determine the effect of filter denoising. The function to generate the convolution kernel is based on the two parameters of the pixel's Euclidean distance and the grayscale difference:

$$g(i,j) = \frac{\sum_{k.,l} f(k,l) * w(i,j,k,l)}{\sum_{k,l} w(i,j,k,l)} \tag{1}$$

$$d(i, j, k, l) = \exp(-\frac{(i-k)^2 + (j-l)^2}{2\sigma_d^2}) \tag{2}$$

g(i, j) is the pixel value output after filtering, f(k, l) is the pixel point in the image to be processed, and w(i, j, k, l) is the bilateral filter template. Coordinates (k, l) represent the center pixel of the template, coordinates (i, j) represent other pixels of the template, and d is the standard deviation of the function.

3.2   Experimental Requirements

Based on the improved ORB algorithm, this experiment analyzes the consistency comparison of machine vision images, and analyzes the characteristics of the knife mark texture and the requirements for texture elimination in the target image, and proposes a method for eliminating knife mark texture based on bilateral filter. Bilateral filter is a kind of nonlinear spatial smoothing filter that can protect edge information and remove noise. The basic principle is to smooth the image through a neighborhood template, the center point pixel in this area is determined by the pixel value in the neighborhood, and the weight of the influence of the pixel point in the neighborhood on the value depends on the spatial proximity and pixel value similarity of the two pixels.

4 Analysis and Discussion

4.1 Consistency and Accuracy Analysis of Machine Vision Image Based on ORB Algorithm

This experiment is based on the machine vision image consistency comparison study of the improved ORB algorithm. By detecting the relationship between the push distance and the accuracy, the experimental data are as follows, As shown in Table 1 and Fig. 1.

Table 1. Machine vision image consistency accuracy analysis table

Image item	Distance (km)	Accuracy (%)
Image one	25.6	97.6
Image two	34.8	98.6
Image three	44.5	95.4
Image four	56.7	96.8
Image five	83.4	98.7

From the above data analysis, it can be seen from the results that when the distance of image 1 is 25.6 km, the accuracy of machine vision image consistency comparison is 97.6%. When the distance of the second image is 34.8 km, the accuracy of the machine vision image consistency comparison is 98.6%. When the distance of image three is 44.5 km, the accuracy of the three-consistency comparison of machine vision images is 95.4%. When the distance of image 4 is 56.7 km, the accuracy of machine vision image 4 consistency comparison is 96.8%. When the distance of image 5 is 83.4 km, the accuracy of machine vision image 5 consistency comparison is 98.7%. Experimental data show that the accuracy of machine vision image consistency comparison has always been maintained at a stable level, that is, 97%. It shows that the accuracy of machine vision image consistency comparison does not decrease with the increase of distance.

4.2 Accuracy Analysis of Machine Vision Image Consistency System

By analyzing the accuracy of the machine vision image consistency system, the accuracy of the data fitting parameters is relatively high. In this experiment, the 5 pieces of data captured by the machine vision image can be obtained by using the system analysis to obtain their accuracy comparison. The experimental data as shown below:

As shown in Fig. 2, by analyzing the accuracy of the machine vision image consistency system, the data analysis can be seen. The pixel widths of the four sets of data are 2.1 mm, 1.6 mm, 1.8 mm, and 1.5 mm, and the pixel lengths of the four sets of data are 3.4 mm, 2.9 mm, 3.2 mm, and 3.2 mm, respectively. The four sets of data all have only a small fluctuation, and the change is not large.

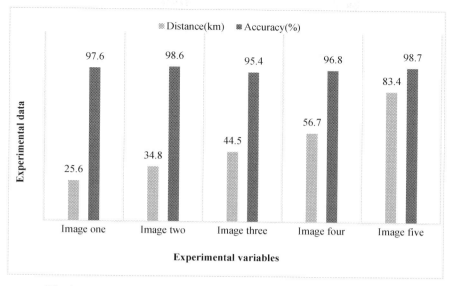

Fig. 1. Analysis of the consistency and accuracy of machine vision images

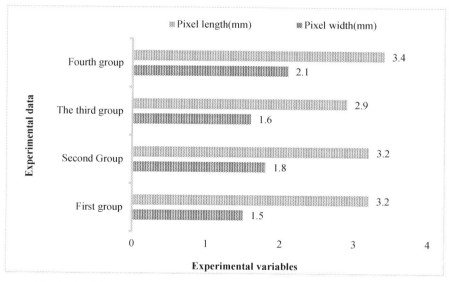

Fig. 2. Precision analysis diagram of machine vision image consistency system

5   Conclusions

Based on the background of the improved ORB algorithm, this paper first studies the consistency comparison of machine vision images, that the consistency comparison of machine vision images based on the improved ORB algorithm is accurate and accurate to a certain extent From the experimental data analysis of the impact of machine vision image consistency comparison on system accuracy, the accuracy of machine vision image consistency comparison has been maintained at a stable level, that is, 97% fluctuation. It shows that the accuracy of machine vision image consistency comparison does not decrease with the increase of distance. System analysis can obtain the data representation of the accuracy control shown, and as the line width increases, the impact on the system accuracy also increases. By analyzing the accuracy of the machine vision image consistency system, it is used to compensate the accuracy analysis of the machine vision image consistency comparison, and finally the machine vision image consistency comparison research based on the improved ORB algorithm is added to have higher accuracy. In order to improve the ORB algorithm implementation, a set of machine vision image model experimental data processing system based on the improved ORB algorithm is developed, which meets the requirements of accuracy and precision for the obtained machine vision images, and has the value of popularization and application.

Acknowledgements. Fund Project: No.22A210013, Development of Fog Cultivation System in All Artificial Light Plant Factory.

References

1. Iketani, A., Nagai, A., Kuno, Y., et al.: Real-time surveillance system detecting persons in complex scenes. Real-Time Imaging **7**(5), 433–446 (2021)
2. Kanade, T.: A system for video surveillance and monitoring. In: VSAM Final Report Carnegie Mellon University Technical Report, vol. **59**(5), pp. 329–337 (2020)
3. Stauffer, C.: Research on an image mosaic algorithm based on improved ORB feature combined with SURF. In: 2018 Chinese Control And Decision Conference (CCDC), vol. **13**(1), pp. 59–96 (2018)
4. Barnich, et al.: Research on energy efficiency management of Forklift based on improved YOLOv5 algorithm. J. Math. **2**(3), 1–22 (2021)
5. Droogenbroeck.: Research on image feature point matching based on ORB and RANSAC algorithm. J. Phys. Conf. Ser. **1651**(1), 89–152 (2020)
6. Solem, J.E., et al.: Methods for Navigating Through a Set of Images, US20170200293A1. **5**(15), 9–32 (2017)
7. ViBe.: Research on stereo matching algorithm based on improved steady-state matching probability. J. Phys. Conf. Ser. **1004**(1), 48–93 (2018)
8. Paquot, O.: Image matching research based on improved SIFT algorithm. In: VSIP 2019: 2019 International Conference on Video, Signal and Image Processing, vol. **2**(1), pp. 3–18 (2019)
9. Tico, M.: Research on the recovery of shredding based on matching algorithm. Int. Conf. Comput. Technol. Electron. Commun. **5**(2), 12–36 (2017)
10. Vehvilainen, M.: Research on feature importance evaluation of wireless signal recognition based on decision tree algorithm in cognitive computing. Cogn. Syst. Res. **5**(5), 882–890 (2018)
11. Wang, H., Jin, H., Xue, F.: Research on improvement of the decision tree algorithm based on information gain. Revista de la Facultad de Ingenieria **32**(2), 126–136 (2017)
12. Cormer, M., et al.: Towards an improved vision-based web page segmentation algorithm. Conf. Comput. Rob. Vis. IEEE Comput. Soc. **2021**(3), 1–10 (2017)

Application Analysis of Digital Special Effects Technology in Film and Television Post-production Based on Neural Network Algorithm

Hongxing Qian[✉]

School of Media and Communication, Changchun Humanities and Sciences College,
Changchun, Jilin, China
hongxing_1223@163.com

Abstract. The leap in film and television special effects technology has updated a series of film production methods. Post-production using the most advanced computer graphics technology stimulates the creativity of the producers, simplifies the post-production process, and improves the quality of the entire film. The purpose of this paper is to study the application of digital special effects technology in film and television post-production based on neural network algorithm. First, the digital technology used in the widely used film and television post-production is introduced, and then some applications and problems of artificial neural networks are introduced. Then the PointNet network structure is introduced, which is a deep learning network in 3D point cloud. Framework, which eliminates the ambiguity caused by the disorder and rotation of point clouds by introducing T-net and utilizing max-pooling, and finally we introduce an encoder-decoder network for 3D human reconstruction, which encodes The network extracts the features, and uses the decoding network to learn the transformation between the template and the input point cloud, so as to complete the deformation fitting between the template and the point cloud.

Keywords: Neural networks · Film and television · Post production · Digital special effects technology

1 Introduction

In today's film and television industry, industry competition is becoming more and more fierce, and film and television professionals must provide high-quality services in a short period of time. Film art has a lot of room for development. Traditional film production has a clear division of labor. Directors, photographers, editors, and photographers are slow to execute their work. Sometimes they lose their jobs or quarrel due to lack of coordination, waste production costs and a lot of time [1, 2]. Under the conditions of digitalization, the division of labor of film and television crews began to become chaotic. With the help of advanced advanced equipment and drawing technology, photography,

photography, and editing can be done on the same computer, improving the quality of visual effects and saving costs [3, 4].

Frame interpolation is the process of inserting new frames between existing frames in a video sequence [5]. It has become an algorithmic module in cinematography. Kokaram reviews techniques for creating smooth frames and provides a framework for Bayesian frame interpolation algorithms using interpolation theory. Performance is also measured using the highest quality aftermarket equipment in the industry. All successful techniques were found to use motor-based interpolation, while commercial versions of Bayesian methods performed well [6]. Some scholars have analyzed that there are many problems with the new technology visual effects in Korean films, such as lack of scientific knowledge and operational technical know-how, improper production time and cost. Explore the expression techniques and visual effects production process of Korean films, and propose a more effective production method and alternatives for the problems that arise in the use of new films [7]. With the help of advanced special effects equipment and computer graphics technology, photography, art, editing can be done on the same computer, and films can be produced independently, producing the best visual effects, improving quality and saving costs [8].

This article subdivides the types of digital technologies used in film and television reproduction through a comparative study. It compares and studies traditional special effects and modern special effects, lists the advantages and disadvantages of early special effects, and further analyzes special effects from shallow to deep, as well as the types and uses of digital special effects in movies. Analyze the use, production process and far-reaching impact of 3D digital effects that affect aesthetics. The artificial neural network algorithm process is used to exemplify and practice the 3D reconstruction of the human body. The application of neural network algorithms has changed the quality of digital special effects technology and the art of post-production movies.

2   Research on the Application of Digital Special Effects Technology in Film and Television Post-production Based on Neural Network Algorithm

2.1   Traditional Special Effects and 3D Digital Special Effects

Special effects are an important part of a movie. Traditional special effects include model special effects, support special effects, etc. Examples of special effects include: characters, monsters, buildings, etc. [9, 10]. When moving traditional models, we have to use mechanical, electrical and human controls, which are more complex and cumbersome. In 3D digital modeling, this can be easily solved using bone articulation or motion mapping. We can use the download action or emoji download to complete the action [11, 12].

3D digital special effects are not a technical form of unattainable vision. It is easy to improve the quality of micro-movies by applying the intervention of 3D digital special effects, which can save more time and effort, save a lot of money and manpower and material resources. And bad utilization will produce twice the result with half the effort [13, 14].

2.2   Digital Technology Used in Film and Television Post-production

Computer digital imaging technology refers to the general term of computer image processing (the technology of combining motion and shape with computer) and digital image synthesis [15].

Digital special effects: The full name of digital special effects is computer numerical control technology. It is an advanced film production medium represented by digital image synthesis, digital image processing and 3D animation production.

Digital image processing technology: Digital image processing technology refers to computer-generated images or computer-generated images that are processed and processed according to the needs of the film. These include image color processing, image synthesis texture processing, and image shape distortion processing [16].

Non-linear editing technology: Non-linear processing technology is related to traditional linear processing, specifically refers to the processing method that does not need to follow the linearity of time, any combination of time and space on the screen. This editing method is based on images and sounds, which can be read and cut at any time [17].

2.3   Neural Networks

Artificial neural network is generally referred to as neural network, which is inspired by the central nervous system of living organisms: the working principle. Neural networks are generally used as computational models for machine learning [18].

The mathematical essence is a computational model. Similar to the biological nervous system, the interleaved connections of artificial neurons form a neural network. The function of the artificial neuron is the same as that of the neuron in the living body to transmit information. The structure of the artificial neuron: each neuron transmits the information $(x1, x2, \ldots, xn)$ from other neurons according to its own rules. For processing, it is actually a function θi (generally called transfer function or excitation function); the pairwise connection between neurons represents the weighted value of the signal connected by one neuron to another neuron, which is called weight, This is used to represent the neural network system's impression of this neuron.

After a large amount of information transmission between neurons, the output reaches the final output. The neural network itself is usually used as an approximation of other functions or algorithms or to demonstrate a logical strategy. Neural network is an adaptive network system, which continuously learns and changes itself by continuously accepting external knowledge, and improves itself step by step. A modern neural network is a nonlinear statistical data modeling tool that is often used for modeling or deep mining of data of varying complexity.

3   Investigation and Research on the Application of Digital Special Effects Technology in Film and Television Post-production Based on Neural Network Algorithm

3.1   3D Human Reconstruction Digital Effects Technology Based on Neural Network

For the training data, there are two cases. One is to know the correspondence between the point cloud and the grid template, that is, the supervised case. We learn the encoding network and the decoding network through the following reconstruction error function:

$$L^{\text{sup}} = \sum_{i=1}^{N} \sum_{j=1}^{P} \left| D_\theta(p_j; E_\varphi(S^{(i)})) - q_j^{(i)} \right|^2 \tag{1}$$

That is, the sum of the errors of the P points on all N training data. For those who do not know the correspondence between the point cloud and the grid template, we use the following loss function:

$$L^{un\,\text{sup}} = L^{CD} + \lambda_{LB} L^{LB} + \lambda_E L^E \tag{2}$$

LCD is the Chamfer distance of the input cloud and the reconstructed cloud, i.e. the Euclidean distance of the input cloud and the output cloud and the closest point of the output cloud and the input cloud. Its purpose is to make the deformed template is the same as the Laplace operator of the original template, that is, to make the deformation as equidistant as possible, LE is the edge item in the triangular mesh, which is to promote the edges on the triangular mesh before and after the deformation. The ratio of the length to 1.

3.2   Data Set

In order for our algorithm to be able to train, we need a lot of human data. Therefore, we train our model by artificially synthesizing some data using the SMPL model. To obtain realistic human shape and pose parameters from the model, we randomly sample $2 \bullet 10^5$ parameters in the SURREAL dataset and the FAUST dataset. To overcome the limitation of the dataset due to not including any bent people, we generate bent human data by manually estimating 5 key parameters from the 20 joints in the SMPL skeleton. Finally we got $2 \bullet 10^5$ human data with different poses and shapes.

4   Analysis and Research on the Application of Digital Special Effects Technology in Film and Television Post-production Based on Neural Network Algorithm

4.1   Network Structure of Digital Special Effects Technology for Human Reconstruction

Our goal is to learn the deformation of the human template through a neural network, given an input human scan point cloud, to deform the template onto the target point cloud.

In this regard, we use an encoding and decoding network as shown in Fig. 1. For the input human point cloud S, we first extract features from the input point cloud through a feature extraction network similar to PointNet to obtain a feature vector, Then, the coordinates of each point on the human body template plus the feature vector obtained by the encoding network are used as the input of the decoding network, and finally a decoding network is used to map the input points to the reconstructed surface.

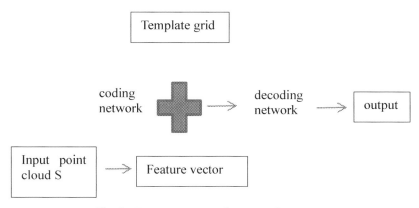

Fig. 1. Human reconstruction network structure

For the encoding network E, the input is first preprocessed with a T-net structure, and then a convolutional neural network with hidden feature sizes of 60, 120, and 1000 is used, and then the features at all points are maximized to get a A 1000-dimensional feature vector, and the obtained feature plus the coordinates of the point on the human template as the input of the decoding network to train and predict the position of the corresponding point in the input point cloud. This decoding network is a multi-layer perceptron with hidden layer sizes of 1000, 500, 200, 100, followed by a hyperbolic tangent activation function, and finally 3D point coordinates. Through training, the network learns the transformation between the grid template and the input point cloud, and completes the 3D human body reconstruction.

4.2 Experimental Results

For the input point cloud, the reconstruction results obtained by using the low-resolution point cloud and the original point cloud can be seen that using this multi-resolution method can improve the reconstruction accuracy, and this method is faster than the traditional method. Fast and without the need to mark the location of key points. However, this method is sensitive to the selection of the initial value. When the selection of the initial value is not suitable, the reconstruction result is not very good, so we further optimize the output result. We add a regression network after the decoding network, utilize the Chamfer distance to further refine the results, and employ a multi-resolution approach.

Table 1. Importance of subsequent optimizations

Method	Error on FAUST dataset	Error on SURREAL dataset
No regression layer	5.62	6.92
With regression layer	4.02	5.05
With regression layer + uniform sampling	2.86	3.15
There are regression layers + uniform sampling + high resolution	1.05	1.36

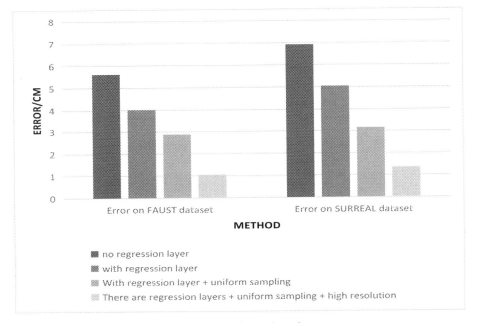

Fig. 2. Experimental results

The specific steps are: (a) optimize the latent features to minimize the Chamfer distance between the input and output (regression layer); (b) use better and more uniformly sampled data when training the network; (c) use a high-resolution template Rate sampling (about 100,000 vertices) for the nearest neighbor step is shown in Table 1, and the experimental results are shown in Fig. 2.

5   Conclusions

Digital technology is applied to the fidelity in the post-production process. Special effects technology is an important technology in non-linear editing technology. It will be used to enhance the visual effect of video editing and better express the intention of the creator. This paper conducts a deeper analysis and research on 3D digital special effects and human body reconstruction through the application of 3D digital special effects in movies, and summarizes the use of artificial intelligence to improve the post-production quality of human reconstruction movies. It is analyzed that the 3D digital special effects intervention film based on 3D human body reconstruction can enhance the artistic beauty. I hope to involve more 3D digital special effects in the post-production of the film in the future. Make the video quality higher and make the video more artistic.

References

1. Faber, J.M., Visscher, A.J.: The effects of a digital formative assessment tool on spelling achievement: results of a randomized experiment. Comput. Educ. **122**(JUL.), 1–8 (2018)
2. Sime, J.E., et al.: The effects of digital predistortion in a CO-OFDM system – a stochastic approach. IEEE Photon. Technol. Lett. **PP**(99), 1–1 (2020)
3. Blythman, T., Vinen, N.: SFX super digital sound effects module part 2: construction and set-up. Everyday Pract. Electron. **48**(9), 32–37 (2019)
4. Economics: Effects of digital transformation and network externalities in the telecommunication markets. Economics. **7**(2), 31–42 (2019)
5. Huseynli, S.: E-commerce and tax audit; the effects of digital goods on tax auditing. J. Curr. Deb. Soc. Sci. **4**(1), 33–47 (2021)
6. Kokaram, A., Singh, D., Robinson, S., et al.: Motion-based frame interpolation for film and television effects. IET Comput. Vision **14**(6), 323–338 (2020)
7. Oliver, P.: Production and post in 2018. Dig. Video Mag. **26**(1), 22–25(2018)
8. Caston, E.: The pioneers get shot: music video, independent production and cultural hierarchy in Britain. J. Br. Cine. Tel. **16**(4), 545–570 (2019)
9. Aitaki, G.: Television drama in Israel: identities in post-TV culture. Histor. J. Film Radio Tel. **39**(2), 1–2 (2019)
10. Goode, I.: The unsatisfactory medium: the transition from mobile cinema to television in the post-war highlands and islands. Northern Scotland **11**(1), 23–41 (2020)
11. Zhabskiy, M.I.: Film production in postsoviet Russia: seven factors of investment risk. Sot͡siologicheskie Issledovanii͡a. **2018**(4), 127–137 (2018)
12. Molek-Kozakowska, K., Nicieja, S.: Imagining a "post-carbon" future? climate change as represented by media and film industries. Świat i Słowo **34**(1), 47–62 (2020)
13. Dankwah, J.R., Baah, E.O., Dankwah, J.B., et al.: Production of iron nuggets from the Akpafu-Todzi iron ore and artisanal ferrous slag using post consumer thermosets (waste electrical sockets) as reductants. Ghana Mining J. **19**(2), 41–49 (2019)
14. Bramslw, L., Naithani, G., Hafez, A., et al.: Improving competing voices segregation for hearing impaired listeners using a low-latency deep neural network algorithm. J. Acoust. Soc. Am. **144**(1), 172–185 (2018)
15. Elsisi, M., et al.: An improved neural network algorithm to efficiently track various trajectories of robot manipulator arms. IEEE Access. **PP**(99), 1–1 (2021)
16. Skuratov, V., Kuzmin, K., Nelin, I., et al.: Creation of a neural network algorithm for automated collection and analysis of statistics of exchange quotes graphics. EUREKA Phys. Eng. **3**(3), 22–29 (2020)
17. Mohammed, M.J., Mohammed, E.A., Jarjees, M.S.: Recognition of multifont English electronic prescribing based on convolution neural network algorithm. Bio-Algorithms Med-Syst. **16**(3), 182–190 (2020)
18. Smys, S., Wang, H., Basar, A.: 5G network simulation in smart cities using neural network algorithm. J. Artif. Intell. Capsul. Net. **3**(1), 43–52 (2021)

Video Image Analysis of Sports Skill Training on Account of Fuzzy Clustering Algorithm

Zhongwen Lu[✉]

School of Physical Education, Yili Normal University, Yining, Xinjiang, China
lzwyili@yeah.net

Abstract. With the development of Internet and audio and video technology, a large amount of training in the field of sports is stored in audio and video formats in various image analysis files. Professionals edit and optimize the audio and video of various activities in a large number of sports fields, which allows most netizens to check and watch, and refine the processing of this kind of video. In order to meet the market demand, all kinds of audio and video resources are modified, processed, and carefully packaged, so that the product has a new look. Sports skills training video image analysis application in the development of the Internet and audio and video technology to break through the obstacles of various important social issues in the field of video image analysis and application. This article studies a series of theories and knowledge of image analysis application in sports field, reveals the concept and definition of fuzzy clustering algorithm, and carries on application case disposal to sports skills training video image analysis application. By analyzing the actual effect of video images, based on fuzzy clustering algorithm for sports skills training video image analysis application study, test result shows that sports skills training based on fuzzy clustering algorithm video image analysis application in sports skill training video image analysis applications in image processing complexity, collaborative filterability, The efficiency of denoising and spatial accuracy is 83.32%, 90.01%, 92.25% and 98.10%.

Keywords: Fuzzy clustering algorithm · Sports skills · Training video · Image analysis application

1 Introduction

The video coding technology carries on the image processing to the processing object and carries on the multidirectional encryption and encapsulation to the processing object. In the past, video technology did not have the latest advantages, and the picture processing was more complicated. Video processing technology is based on semantic segmentation algorithm to process the image and part of the image. In the image segmentation in the professional field released a lot of ways, many of which are scientific segmentation in image processing. The method of motion video image segmentation based on fuzzy clustering algorithm improves the sharpness and viewing effect of image processing. This set of video technology through video segmentation, image optimization, video precision processing and other aspects of the movement analysis of sports training, so as to provide technical assistance in sports, motor skills and other fields. As for the application of communication learning based on fuzzy clustering algorithm in sports training video image analysis, it is necessary to strengthen the theoretical research and practical application ability based on fuzzy clustering algorithm, fuzzy clustering algorithm, to solve many problems in sports application training video image analysis.

As for the research based on fuzzy clustering algorithm, many scholars at home and abroad have studied it. In foreign studies, AminantoME etc., proposed a two-stage fuzzy anomaly detection system. In the first phase, the training phase, ACA is proposed to determine the clustering. In the second stage, the classification stage, a fuzzy method is used to detect anomalies in new monitoring data by combining two distance-based methods. The hybrid approach was validated using the KDDCup'99 dataset. The results show that the hybrid method has higher detection rate and lower false positive rate compared with the traditional and new methods [1]. Dhalkge CAL. Proposed a histogram based fuzzy clustering (HBFC) technique, which adopted an improved version of firefly algorithm (FA). The proposed method is rigorously compared with several state-of-the-art natural optimization algorithms (NIOA) and traditional clustering techniques. Numerical results show that this method is superior to the traditional NIOa-based clustering method in terms of segmentation accuracy, robustness and quality of segmentation results [2]. Alammge CAL. Proposed a kernel fuzzy C-means algorithm (GKFCM) based on genetic algorithm to cluster documents in the library. After the user enters the keyword as the input of the system, the system will use WORDNET ontology to process the keyword and realize the neighborhood keyword and synset keyword. Documents within the cluster are first released as result-related documents for the query key, and these documents have clusters with maximum matching score values. Experimental results show that the system based on GKFCM has better performance than the existing methods [3]. However, the application of sports skill training video image analysis based on fuzzy clustering algorithm is still in the initial stage, and there is still a certain gap compared with foreign systems.

In order to further improve the fuzzy clustering algorithm in China, we must start from the following points: First, deepen the research of fuzzy clustering algorithm system; Secondly, the application data model based on fuzzy clustering algorithm is optimized. Finally, strengthen the exchange and communication with foreign countries, improve the video image analysis and application ability.

2 Research on the Application of Sports Skill Training Video Image Analysis Based on Fuzzy Clustering Algorithm

2.1 Based on Fuzzy Clustering Algorithm

According to the selection of known parameters, fuzzy clustering algorithm is processed by data model. Compared with the effect, the traditional algorithm model has better effect on hard clustering and fuzzy clustering algorithm of data and better performance of random distribution of data [4, 5]. All data samples are processed by clustering analysis algorithm to optimize the image. Various other theories have been proposed in cluster analysis methods, including fuzzy set theory [6, 7]. Based on the classification of fuzzy clustering algorithm, this kind of algorithm is divided into methods and optimized and processed in the field of data application [8, 9].

Based on the objective function, this kind of problem is conditioned, and this kind of data model is optimized. The algorithm model has clear structure and strong practical application, which can be used for theoretical research and disposal of clustering. With the progress of computer technology and the rapid development of other data models, related image processing technology based on objective function algorithm has become the core method in this field [10, 11]. The objective function is used to process the sports images, and the fuzzy clustering algorithm is used to analyze the data of the images, and the expected effect of the images is disposed according to the details of the images.

Compared with previous clustering, clustering algorithm is the absolute division of the processed objects, and the principle of this division is very clear [12, 13]. Image processing analysis is strictly processed by fuzzy set theory, and algorithm users use this theory for image processing [14, 15]. The fuzzy clustering algorithm deals with the sample degree of the processed object and introduces each part of the partition [16].

Fuzzy clustering algorithm contains many clustering methods. In view of the various relations of the image, the algorithm gathers all the relevant data, processes the data set based on the constructed data model, and finally forms the image processing result. This method has many conditions, cannot meet the principle of image processing, in the application field is not typical, therefore, this method of image processing analysis is not many times. In the actual image processing practice, there may be a lot of bad effects in this way of image processing. The shortcomings of this algorithm model in image processing can be improved by continuous experiments in practical practice, and the model can be optimized to a certain extent.

2.2 Application of Sports Skill Training Video Image Analysis

The coordinate value of the processing object in the training video image can be changed, and the numerical performance of some pictures is irregular, so the performance in the image processing is fuzzy, and the processing boundary cannot be clear. In view of this phenomenon, we can carry out layer extraction of images and technical disposal of positions and pixels of different images. This algorithm model is used to process the image frames in sequence. According to the change of coordinate value of the object, the corresponding data model is constructed and the image is blurred (Fig. 1).

3   Research on the Application Effect of Sports Skill Training Video Image Analysis Based on Fuzzy Clustering Algorithm

3.1   Content Analysis Method

In this paper, content analysis method is adopted to dynamically observe samples and construct sample point model for all samples. The application of clustering algorithm for sports training image processing, data records for each test points, data analysis. Effect data comparison is mainly used to process data of two groups based on fuzzy clustering algorithm and non-algorithm respectively. Remove or optimize unreasonable data, and use data model to train all sample points.

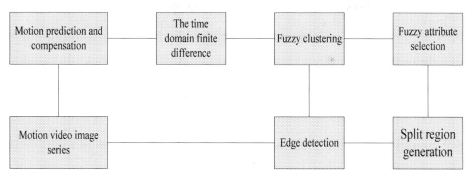

Fig. 1. Sports image processing block diagram

3.2 Brief Description

In this paper, the content analysis method is used to analyze and process the image, and the sample points are trained and processed. The effect of sports skill training video image analysis and application is analyzed through data sample image formation.

3.3 The Formula

$$J(U, V) = \sum_{k=1}^{N} \sum_{i=1}^{C} [u_i(X_k)]^\lambda d_{ik}{}^2 \tag{1}$$

$$m_d{}^4 = \frac{1}{N} \sum_{\eta(x,y)} [d(x) - \overline{m}]^4 \tag{2}$$

U represents the set of membership function, refers to the distance between pixel points and the cluster midpoint, represents the sample points of unclustered pixels, belongs to the ith class of membership degree, represents a fourth-order matrix, is the pixel points covered in the process of movement, is the average pixel point.

3.4 Calculation Principles

Sports images based on clustering algorithm analysis the influence factors analysis and deal with them one by one, the overall effect of the image integration, part of the resolution images, through this process, using the data model, to be blurred images, finally through the model best effect design, and the sports skills training video image analysis application related parameters optimization.

4 Investigation and Research on the Application of Sports Skill Training Video Image Analysis Based on Fuzzy Clustering Algorithm

4.1 Test Effect

The test object is divided into image analysis application based on algorithm and non-algorithm effect comparison and analysis. Take video of sports events for processing, and deal with various data of the events. Respectively on two groups of testing data, sort out the improvement effect of image analysis application, sports skill training video image analysis applied to actual performance data record: in content analysis, sports skill training can video image analysis application effect to sports skill training video image analysis and application's goal to ascend, according to the results of image analysis application effect is very obvious. The key and difficult problems in strengthening the application of image analysis have played a good role, and the results are shown in Table 1 and Fig. 2.

Table 1. Physical training image data sheet

	Image complex processing performance	Synergistic filtration	Noise iterativeness	Spatial accuracy
Numeric value	160	320	487	654
Proportion	83.32%	90.01%	92.25%	98.10%
Percentage	91	93	96	99

The application effect of sports skill training video image analysis based on fuzzy clustering algorithm is better than that of the traditional method. In the image complexity processing, collaborative filtering, denoising and spatial accuracy to achieve high efficiency, in the model effect data processing and application of testing and analysis, sports skills training video image analysis application performance of various aspects of data processing and analysis. It focuses on the distribution performance of various sample points encountered in the modeling process, including sample number, sample generation model, sample point optimization, model verification and evaluation. The horizontal orientation focuses on the classification of modeling ability from the level and law of human cognitive development. The intensified research and development of sports skill training video image analysis and application based on fuzzy clustering algorithm is conducive to a great breakthrough in the field of sports skill training video image analysis and application.

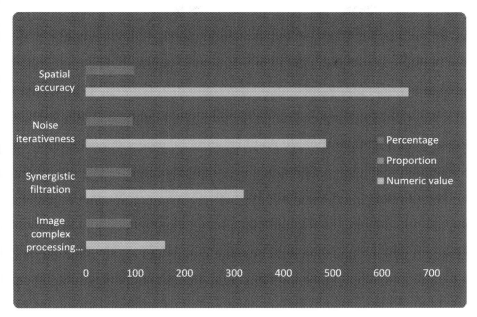

Fig. 2. Sports training video image application data chart

5   Conclusions

Fuzzy clustering algorithm is good at image processing and optimization in sports field. Compared with traditional audio and video processing technology, this method achieves high efficiency in image complexity processing, collaborative filtering, denoising and spatial accuracy, etc. This method plays an important role in the demonstration of test data. Sports training video image analysis helps sports lovers to grasp the inner law of sports picture accuracy, and provides help for sports career, athletes' fitness and other progress. This paper studies the category and practice of sports skill training video image analysis and application, and provides optimization solutions for sports skill training video image analysis and application. Through a full range of sports skills training video image analysis and application process analysis and research, for sports skills training video image analysis and application of various fields play an important role, and deepen the pace of technological progress in the field of sports.

References

1. Aminanto, M.E., Kim, H.J., Kim, K.M., et al.: Another fuzzy anomaly detection system based on ant clustering algorithm. IEICE Trans. Fundam. Electron. Commun. Comput. Sci. **100**(1), 176–183 (2017)
2. Dhal, K.G., Das, A., Ray, S., et al.: Randomly attracted rough firefly algorithm for histogram based fuzzy image clustering. Knowl. Based Syst. **216**(1), 106814 (2021)
3. Alam, M.G., Baulkani, S.: Reformulated query-based document retrieval using optimised kernel fuzzy clustering algorithm. Int. J. Bus. Intell. Data Mining **12**(3), 299–318 (2017)

4. Wang, X., et al.: Clustering effect on mechanical properties and failure mechanism of open hole high modulus carbon fiber reinforced composite laminates under compression. Comp. Struct. **229**(Dec.), 111377.1–111377.12 (2019)
5. Atal, V., Sanglas, A., Triantafyllou, N.: LIGO black holes and dark matter: the effect of spatial clustering. J. Cosmol. Astropart. Phys. **2020**(11), 036 (2020)
6. Kapoutsis, C.A., Mulaffer, L.: A logical characterization of small 2NFAs. Int. J. Found. Comput. Sci. **28**(05), 445–464 (2017)
7. Cohen, L., Constable, R.L.: Intuitionistic ancestral logic. J. Log. Comput. **29**(4), 469–486 (2019)
8. Nagli, P., Pernu, F., Likar, B., et al.: Adopting higher-order similarity relations for improved estimation of optical properties from subdiffusive reflectance. Opt. Lett. **42**(7), 1357 (2017)
9. Jain, A.K., Gupta, B.B.: Detection of phishing attacks in financial and e-banking websites using link and visual similarity relation. Int. J. Inf. Comput. Secur. **10**(4), 398–417 (2018)
10. Bahl, B., et al.: Time-series aggregation for synthesis problems by bounding error in the objective function. Energy. **135**(sep.15), 900–912 (2017)
11. Liu, Y., Teng, J., Xu, T., et al.: Robust time-domain full waveform inversion with normalized zero-lag cross-correlation objective function. Geophys. J. Int. **209**(1), 106–122 (2017)
12. D'Urso, P., Lafuente-Rego, B., Vilar, J.A.: Quantile autocovariances: a powerful tool for hard and soft partitional clustering of time series. Fuzzy Sets Syst. **340**(JUN.1), 38–72 (2017)
13. Prokic, I., Pantovic, J.: Characterization of generalized S-threshold functions by nomura parameters. J. Mult. Value. Logic Soft Comput. **33**(3), 271–290 (2019)
14. Dang, E., Luk, R., Allan, J.: A principled approach using fuzzy set theory for passage-based document retrieval. IEEE Trans. Fuzzy Syst. **29**(7), 1967–1977 (2021)
15. Pandey, B.: A method for classification of red, blue, and green galaxies using fuzzy set theory. Month. Notices Royal Astron. Soc. Lett. **499**(1), L31–L35 (2020)
16. Jang, J., Hitchcock, D.B.: Model-based cluster analysis of democracies. J. Data Sci. **10**(2), 297–319 (2021)

Real Estate Display System Based on Virtual Reality Technology

Bing Du[✉] and Lin Zhou

School of Management, Shenyang Jianzhu University, Shenyang 110168, Liaoning, China
yunong5566@126.com

Abstract. The main purpose of the real estate display system is to promote the sales of real estate, so its key point is how to attract the attention and attention of potential customers, and virtual reality technology can bring users into a realistic real estate community situation. Therefore, this paper takes a virtual real estate community as an example, develops a virtual real estate display system with the help of modeling software AutoCAD, 3Ds MAX and virtual reality engine VPR-platform, introduces the creation of virtual real estate scene model in detail, and tests the beauty of the system display effect. In addition, 30 users were asked about their satisfaction with using the system to visit the virtual real estate scene, and finally realized the system roaming interaction mode.

Keywords: Virtual reality technology · Real estate display system · Modeling software · Roaming interaction

1 Introduction

The traditional real estate marketing model is generally promoted through posters. As virtual reality technology becomes more and more mature, real estate developers are committed to using virtual reality technology to develop real estate display systems. In the system, there are a large number of floor plans and three-dimensional virtual scenes. Marketing can not only promote real estate products, but also allow users to have a real viewing experience.

There are many related research results on the design and implementation of real estate display system based on virtual reality technology. For example, a laboratory has developed a virtual roaming system, which breaks through the barriers that cannot be interacted in the past, allowing users to watch at will in the system. The system has been widely used in construction, tourism and other fields. It brings a virtual stereo vision experience [1, 2]. A scholar uses a virtual roaming algorithm to generate a real estate display roaming system. The system establishes a 3D real estate scene, which has the characteristics of interactivity and virtuality, allowing users to have tactile, visual and auditory communication when visiting the real estate model, realizing a real presence. Its environment viewing experience [3]. Although many scholars have studied the design of real estate display system based on virtual reality technology, to make the real estate display more realistic, it is necessary to play the role of virtual reality technology.

N. Khare et al. (Eds.): MIND 2022, CCIS 1763, pp. 123–130, 2022.
https://doi.org/10.1007/978-3-031-24367-7_11

This paper firstly pays attention to modeling the three-dimensional model of real estate, including building model, indoor building model, residential tree model, sky model, etc., and then analyzes the non-functional requirements of the system, and then uses modeling software to design a real estate display system, test System performance, analyze the realization of system roaming interaction function.

2 Real Estate 3D Modeling and System Requirements Analysis

2.1 3D Modeling of Real Estate

In the virtual reality scene, the 3D modeling of objects requires designers to grasp the 3D modeling as a whole and deeply describe the details of the model. At the same time, it is necessary to accurately grasp and strictly describe the appearance characteristics of many objects in the virtual reality scene. Through personal careful observation and rational thinking, we can discover the characteristics of the objects and produce a sufficient number of details [4].

(1) Building modeling

Before making a building model, it is first necessary to examine and analyze the structure and layout of the building. After analyzing the structure of the building and its characteristics, it was finally decided which general method to use to create the model. For example, for a building, the main building should be built first, and then the multi-level buildings; for the garden villa area, based on the same idea, the main building should be built first, and then the sub-buildings, attics, garages, balconies, yards and other places should be built. The system is modeled by the synthesis method [5]. Specifically, it is to split the entire building, including the walls, the upper part of the house, doorsteps and other structures, and to do specific modeling for each part. Especially for some single buildings with simple structure or appearance, one wall can be built directly from one wall, and then each wall can be added together to form the physical layout of the building. After the main body of the appearance is formed, the top of the house and the steps at the door are gradually added [6].

(2) Indoor architectural modeling

The interior architecture is different from the building architecture, and it has its own characteristics. A huge indoor scene can be divided into many small scenes, each of which is invisible to each other. Therefore, it is necessary to divide indoor scenes according to this characteristic, and treat different rooms as small scenes [7]. First, analyze the layout of the indoor scene, select an appropriate division method according to its function or orientation, divide a large scene into multiple small rooms, and then build the specific structure of each small room. Following this guideline, at all times, the system should only display a view of the room or the environment that the user can see. This reduces the number of models displayed at any one time, while effectively reducing the computational complexity of indoor scenes [8].

(3) Modeling of residential trees

In the large-scale visualization of 3D terrain, ground objects are also a very important part. Trees, as common objects in nature, are indispensable natural elements in virtual geographic environment. On the one hand, the simulated plants can greatly enhance the realism of the scene. On the other hand, in some specific virtual research fields, the plants themselves are important research objects or reference objects. In this case, the plants in the scene are required to have a high degree of realism [9]. The system adopts the plant modeling method of image model. This method replaces the tree model with an image. Its essence is to use the tree image to perform texture mapping in a rectangular area of space to express the tree, but because one or more intersecting two-dimensional planes with tree texture maps Indicates trees, which loses the spatial distribution characteristics of trees, and the lighting effect of trees cannot be expressed, and the effect is not ideal when viewed from a close point of view. In general, this generation method has a faster calculation speed and simpler geometry, but if there are too many types of trees, more textures are required, which requires a higher texture cache of the display device [10, 11].

(4) Sky modeling

In real life, the blue sky and white clouds above people's heads will make people feel happy and refreshed. In the virtual environment, if the effect of the sky can be added, the immersive realism of the system will be significantly improved. There are two common sky modeling methods: the sky box method and the celestial sphere method [12]. The skybox method is to use five images, represent them on each inner surface of a rectangular box, and simulate the effect of the real sky through different textures of five different inverted surfaces. However, this approach has an obvious limitation of the image used per surface. For example, the image must be in bitmap (BMP) format, the size must be a specific size, the top edge of the image must be around and the surrounding image, and the top edge must be linked to the surrounding image. This places higher demands on the selection of images by creating a model [13]. Due to visual effects, the user is limited by the size of the scene in the virtual roaming scene, resulting in a feeling of being outside the environment. And the creation of the skyball method completes this "exit" limitation. The sky designed by the sphere method violates the limitation of space and also corresponds to the general visual effect of the intersection of heaven and earth [14].

2.2   Non-functional Requirements for System Design

System responsiveness needs to be at least ten frames per second. If it is required to be natural and continuous without impact, then it should reach more than 24 frames per second. At the same time, the shorter the human-computer interaction response time, the better, generally 0.5 s.

In terms of system operation, staff are required to be able to use it proficiently after short-term training. For potential customers, the operation is as simple as possible, so that users who are exposed to such systems for the first time can browse freely in a short period of time. In order to reduce the computer level requirements of the staff, the system is preferably free of installation and can be used directly.

In the aspect of system development, the system should have better support for the change and development of virtual technology. The underlying technology used by the system must conform to international standards or industry agreements. At the same time, the system needs to adapt to the development of the real estate display industry and can be easily expanded to meet the needs of users. This type of extension should be consistent with the design of the system architecture without substantially conflicting with the design implementation or product definition.

2.3   2D and 3D Model Data Association

In both 2D and 3D models, the primary task of data interconnection is to map the two coordinate systems together. The connection between the two can be made according to the center point. It is common practice to use the point in the lower left corner of the map as the coordinate source; any other point in both models refers to this coordinate principle to determine relative coordinates. Its conversion relationship can be expressed as:

$$\Delta X = (X - X_0)/n \tag{1}$$

$$\Delta Y = (Y - Y_0)/n \tag{2}$$

Among them, X and Y are the coordinate values of any point in 2D or 3D, X_0 and Y_0 are the origin of the coordinates, that is, the reference point, and n is the ratio between the 2D map and the 3D scene.

3   System Design

3.1   System Build Tools

According to the characteristics and requirements of the virtual display system based on 3D modeling, the main modeling software used in the system are AutoCAD, 3Ds MAX software and virtual reality engine VPR-platform. Taking the design drawings of the residential building as the actual research object, the three-dimensional virtual digital display of the building is realized to meet the application needs of commercial publicity. After completing the work in the 3Ds MAX space, the next task is how to import the model that has been done into the VR-Platform software. To solve this problem, we mainly use the 3DsMax-for-VRP plug-in. The function of this plug-in is to connect 3Ds MAX with VR-Platform without saving the 3Ds model as another model. It is easier to install the plugin.

3.2   System Function Design

According to the needs of understanding, discussing and analyzing the project, roughly the system can be divided into two modules. The first module is 3D modeling. Including the construction of 3D models, texture processing, overall model synthesis, complex

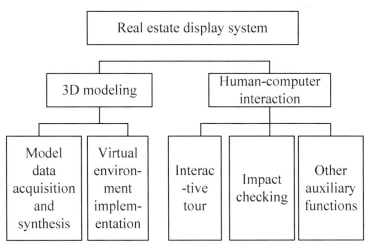

Fig. 1. Functional modules of real estate display system

scene blanking. The second module is human-computer interaction. It includes collision detection, roaming along a predetermined path, and interaction between 2D maps and 3D scenes. System function modules, as shown in Fig. 1.

For the 3D modeling module, it is not only necessary to display virtual objects such as buildings, plants, and fountains, but also to apply materials and textures to their surfaces. When a large number of models are synthesized together, part of the data must be removed using hidden techniques to reduce computation and increase realism. For human-computer interaction units, the system must allow the user to navigate in a predetermined way, so it must respond quickly to changes in virtual objects. When roaming, the user must determine his position in the virtual scene, that is, the interaction between the two-dimensional map and the three-dimensional scene. In order to achieve a more immersive purpose, collision detection is performed during the roaming process, so that the objective physical world can be simulated more realistically.

4   System Testing and Implementation

4.1   System Test

(1) Performance test

As shown in Table 1, the system's functionality and ease of use are tested. The functionality includes accuracy, interactivity, and aesthetics. The test values are 97%, 92%, and 95%, respectively. The reason for the low value is that during the test, it was found that the display system in a few computers did not display properly. For example, there is no animation effect and the introductory video cannot be shown, but through fault inquiry, it is found that the problem is the animation plug-in and the local video playback software, and the problem is solved after installing the corresponding plug-in and software. The ease of use includes ease of operation and ease of learning, with test values of 100% and 98%, respectively. Ease of operation reaches 100%, which means that the system is easy to operate, and it only needs a little guidance to get started.

Table 1. Performance Test Results

	Subfeature	Performance test value
Function	Accuracy	97%
	Interactivity	92%
	Aesthetics	95%
Ease of use	Easy to operate	100%
	Learnability	98%

(2) System user satisfaction test

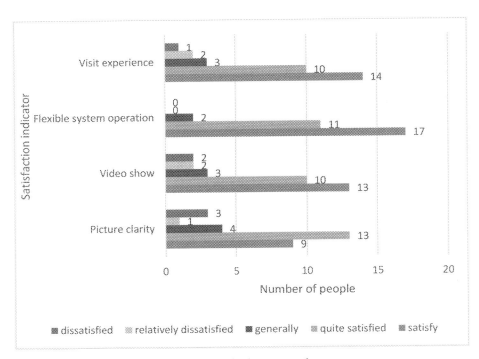

Fig. 2. Satisfaction test results

In this experiment, 30 users were selected to use the system to visit the real estate model. After visiting the exhibition, they were asked about the use of the system, including whether the pictures were clear, whether the video was displayed normally, whether the operations such as space rotation, forward and backward were flexible, and asked The overall feeling of their visit, the results are shown in Fig. 2. Among the 30 people, 4 were dissatisfied with the clarity of the displayed pictures, and 4 were dissatisfied with the video presentation. Although there are not many people, it is still necessary to improve the display effect of the system in these two aspects. The number of people who are dissatisfied with the flexible operation of the system is 0, indicating that the system is easy to use and easy to learn. There are 3 people who think that the visiting experience is dissatisfied, 24 people are satisfied, and 3 people are generally satisfied.

4.2   Implementation of System Roaming Interaction

The interaction with each part of the system consists of five parts: community introduction, room selection, commentary, help, and exit. Customers can easily operate by clicking the corresponding button according to their own needs. When browsing to a room, in addition to hearing the corresponding explanation, the user can also learn the corresponding room information through the text data. Text information provides room details. The user's interaction of room roaming can be controlled by mouse or keyboard operation. The basic modules of VRP provide different types of interaction modes. Our main 8 common virtual roaming actions: forward, backward, ascend, descend, look up, look down, move left, move right. It can be controlled by the W, A, S, D keys and the up, down, left and right keys on the keypad.

5   Conclusion

This paper focuses on the use of virtual reality technology to design a real estate display system. The design tools include AutoCAD, 3Ds MAX and other modeling software, and the virtual reality engine VPR-platform is added to the system to realize human-computer interaction. The system functionality and ease of use are tested. The test results show that the performance of the system is above 90%, and the user's satisfaction with the use of the system is also very high. The realization of the system interaction function also shows that the system meets the needs of users.

Acknowledgements. Supported by the Society Science Foundation of Liaoning province (Grant No. L16BJY028).

References

1. Benson, C.L., Benson, C.L., Mcdonald, C., et al.: Design and implementation considerations for virtual reality in human services. J. Technol. Hum. Serv. **39**(3), 215–218 (2021)
2. Lim, E.S., et al.: Implementation of a low-cost virtual reality system using smart phone. J. Dig. Contents Soc. **19**(7), 1237–1244 (2018)

3. Geltner, D., Kumar, A., Minne, A.: Riskiness of real estate development: a perspective from urban economics and option value theory. Real Estate Econom. **48**(2), 406–445 (2020)
4. Khobragade, A.N., Maheswari, N., Sivagami, M.: Analyzing the housing rate in a real estate informative system: a prediction analysis. Int. J. Civil Eng. Technol. **9**(5), 1156–1164 (2018)
5. Kirichek, Y.O., Grianyk, V.A.: State system of cadastral registration of real estate property. Bull. Prydniprovs'ka State Acad. Civil Eng. Arch. **5**, 42–46 (2018)
6. Caulfield, J.: Real estate learns to share. Build. Design Constr. **60**(5), 38–40, 42, 44 (2019)
7. Hartzell, D., Howton, S.D., Howton, S., et al.: Financial flexibility and at-the-market (ATM) equity offerings: evidence from real estate investment trusts. Real Estate Econom. **47**(2), 595–636 (2019)
8. Yrigoy, I.: State-led financial regulation and representations of spatial fixity: the example of the Spanish real estate sector. Int. J. Urban Reg. Res. **42**(4), 594–611 (2018)
9. Gibler, K.: 2018 international real estate society (IRES) awards. ARES Newsl. (Am. Real Estate Soc.) **33**(2), 3 (2018)
10. Saginor, J.: The real estate academic leadership (REAL) rankings for 2014–2018. J. Real Estate Lit. **26**(2), 255–261 (2018)
11. Ushatova, D.: Disbalance between tax assessments and market prices of real estate. Trakia J. Sci. **17**(Suppl. 1), 115–124 (2019)
12. Nirwana, H.D.: Sistem Kelayakan Investasi Real Estate Pada Perumahan Citra Garden. Jurnal Teknologi Berkelanjutan **8**(1), 30–35 (2019)
13. Aliyu, F., Talib, C.A.: Virtual reality technology. Asia Proc. Soc. Sci. **4**(3), 66–68 (2019)
14. Akdere, M., Acheson, K., Jiang, Y.: An examination of the effectiveness of virtual reality technology for intercultural competence development. Int. J. Intercult. Relat. **82**(1), 109–120 (2021)

Production of Film and Television Animation Based on Three -Dimensional Models Based on Deep Image Sequences

Panpan Li[✉]

Higher Vocational and Technical College, Chengdu Neusoft University, Chengdu 6111844, Sichuan, China
lipanpan@nsu.edu.cn

Abstract. In recent years, with the continuous development of my country's social science and technology, people's exploration in the field of film and television animation production in three-dimensional model is getting deeper, and the application needs of the three-dimensional model of film and television animation production research are gradually increased. Only to increase research and analysis efforts to achieve more complete and accurate film and television animation production processes. Based on the depth image sequence, the key to the three-dimensional model is the entry point, and the research on film and television animation production is carried out in a new perspective. This paper briefly introduces the current three-dimensional model of film and television animation and its development trend, and research on the existing three-dimensional model of film and television animation production, and passed a series of experiments to demonstrate film and television animation production based on deep image sequences. It has a specific advantage while performing a feasibility test of film and television animation production based on a three-dimensional model of a depth image sequence. The final result of the study shows that when the number of frames of the five animations is 97 times, the film and television animation of the three-dimensional model is 96.7%. By experimental data, it was found that the exposure of the three-dimensional model of the film and television animation was always maintained in a stable level, ie, horizontally floating between 96% levels. The exposure of the film and television animation of the three-dimensional model does not change as the number of frames changes.

Keywords: Depth image sequence · 3D Model · Film and television animation · Production research

1 Introduction

With the development of productivity and science and technology, the demand for the production of film and television animation of three-dimensional model is more urgent, and the establishment of a more stable and perfect film and television animation production process has become a focus on many researchers at home and abroad. From reasonable utilization, improving supplementation and re-creation, combined with domestic

N. Khare et al. (Eds.): MIND 2022, CCIS 1763, pp. 131–138, 2022.
https://doi.org/10.1007/978-3-031-24367-7_12

and foreign paintings to adaptive animation examples, surround film and television animations, including theme ideas, narrative structures, color light and shadow, character images, lens languages, and auditory languages, trying to summarize The film and television animation strategy of going out of origin is [1]. Looking for a re-creation method for the main purpose, I hope to give the animation worker clear revelation and inexhaustible motivation to promote the booming in my country's animation.

In recent years, many researchers have explored the research of film and television animation production based on deep image sequences and have achieved good results. For example, Hartzheim B H conducts in -depth thinking and analysis of the current technical problems, as well as the application design principles, content and design strategies of interior scene design under the Chinese aesthetic system [2]. YaHiaoui R believes that through three aspects of the creative process of three -dimensional animation and games, simplifying traditional three -dimensional animation production processes, and integrated 3D software technology, it can meet the needs of the "film game integration" development trend for the three -dimensional animation creative process [3]. At present, scholars at home and abroad have conducted a lot of research on the production of three -dimensional models. These previous theoretical and experimental results provided theoretical basis for the study of this article.

Based on the theoretical basis of the deep image sequence, this article reveals and define the research process of film and television animation production processes of three -dimensional models. From the perspective of film and television animation production market consumption, consumer population structure, and the consumption preferences of animation users, the current status of the three -dimensional model film and television animation consumption is analyzed. Under the trend of consumption guided by the three -dimensional model, due to the changes brought about by the innovation of the media and the innovation of communication channels, the current domestic film and television animation marketing strategy was analyzed. Insufficient content, dispersion channels, and unstable production level. It mainly makes suggestions on how to improve the effects of film and television animation from the perspective of audience needs.

2   Related Theoretical Overview and Research

2.1   Three -Dimensional Model Film and Television Animation Production Development Process

(1)   The current status of film and television animation production

Nowadays, the scale and quantity of film and television animation production have gradually exhibited large, and the production structure is more complicated. By understanding the dynamic behavior, this paper proposes an adaptive time-space segmentation algorithm for three-dimensional animation data, and uses time domain and airspace redundancy, the adaptiveness of the algorithm has enhanced the algorithm when facing the characteristic difference. Sex; proposed a compression optimization method based on boundary editing and a compression enhancement method based on matrix recombination [4]. By quantifying contrast and visual reconstruction errors, the experiment indicates that the spatial splitting method and its optimization algorithm have certain competitiveness and effectiveness on three-dimensional animation compression.

(2) Three -dimensional model film and television animation production structure composition

Three -dimensional animation enters the stage of film and television animation production. The model production is mainly based on high -precision models (hereinafter referred to as "high models"). There are many aspects. Multi -use polygon modeling methods are used to complete the creation of a model [5]. Essence Generally, the number of planes of a character model can reach thousands of planes, and the model of the entire scene is as many as tens of millions of places. The details are rich in structure and the effect of high -quality screens can meet the requirements of film and television levels. The game model requires a streamlined number. Most of the low -precision models (hereinafter referred to as the "low model") with small number of aspects can meet the needs of computer operation in the later production [6]. The game model needs to introduce real -time rendering in the game engine, and it can also save the rendering time of the model. Therefore, some game models with small number of face -to -face are not suitable for the production of three -dimensional animation.

(3) The process design of the film and television animation production of 3D model

The three-dimensional animation is an important part of the film and television industry. It is a kind of audience's vast animation form. Today, "moving tourism" is also the development of three-dimensional animation today. In terms of screen expressions and software technology, three-dimensional animation and three-dimensional games have many communication, and the development trend of 3D animation "video game" has laid the foundation in the creation process [7, 8]. As the creation of three-dimensional animation "movie-game integration", as a type of media integration, in the picture performance, theme expression, technology, production efficiency, communication channels, etc., more advantages, more advantageous in the past. Therefore, the development of "video game fusion" in three-dimensional animation is a new direction of three-dimensional animation creation.

Building the three -dimensional model of the ground objective target is the basis of the characteristics of the target characteristics of the ground and the research simulation of remote sensing imaging. In these studies, not only the high -precision three -dimensional geometric model is required, but also the three -dimensional model built with high accuracy [9]. The existing method is: the three -dimensional geometry model and the spectrum characteristics of the target material are obtained by using three -dimensional geometric modeling equipment and spectral measurement equipment, and then the measured material spectrum is associated with the three -dimensional geometric model through the target material classification to achieve the target three -dimensional geometry High -precision modeling with spectral characteristics. Based on the cross -area of high spectrometer imaging technology and three -dimensional imaging technology, this article proposes a three -dimensional model reconstruction method based on imaging spectrum measurement, which realizes the geometry and spectral models of the target three -dimensional model.

2.2 Theoretical Introduction to Depth Image Sequence

The image that has a certain relationship with a certain relationship is called a sequence image. The sequence image is an extension of a single digital image on the timeline. Each frame of the video in the video is a static image. When a series of static images are arranged and played in accordance with time, the video can be obtained [10, 11]. The number of frames contained in the video, the size and frame rate of each frame is an important indicator of measuring video images. The frame rate refers to the number of pictures contained in each second, that is, FPS, which can be regarded as the sample frequency of the sensor as a sensor; Value in the state of this sampling.

From physical space to images, there is a mapping relationship between the pictures collected from the three -dimensional space to the two -dimensional plane. And image coordinate system [12]. Combining the monitored structural displacement timing curve with structural vibration theory, using the principle of rapid Fourier transformation to achieve the structural frequency recognition method based on the displacement timing curve. Correspondingly, the order of each peak from left to right is the order of the structure from left to right, and the horizontal coordinates of the peak value are the frequency of each order of the structure. As a result, the complex problems that are not easy to find in the time domain to the frequency domain to better evaluate the structural health state.

3   Experiment and Research

3.1 Experimental Method

From the human sensing level, the human vision system may indirect image brightness and reflectivity separation when it is inferred image reflectance, so it is very important to handle image brightness and reflectance respectively. In the overall process, the image brightness component describes the global change of the image, reflecting the image dynamic range; the reflectivity component of the image represents the image contour details and color space information:

$$H_{i,c} = I_i R_{i,c} \tag{1}$$

$$L_i^y = \log(\sum_c W_c \exp(y_{i,c})) \tag{2}$$

The image brightness is i, and the image reflectance component is R. Among them $W = (0.213, 0.715, 0.072)$, Y is a reflectance.

3.2 Experimental Requirements

This experiment is based on the factor acquisition method of deep image sequence. The multi -exposure image fusion algorithm comes from the most basic idea of image fusion. It aims to integrate the different exposure LDR image sequences input and strengthen the proportion of the high -quality area of the image. The proportion of fusion in inferior areas is reduced, and an adaptive exposure image with a good visual effect is obtained after integration. The image is called HDR image. Multi -exposure fusion imaging algorithm is strong, which is less affected by the camera mapping curve. Therefore, not only has low requirements on the shooting environment during the imaging process, it can also minimize the impact of the camera's own parameters. At the same time, the images generated after the fusion of multiple exposure images often have more image details, showing better visual effects.

4   Analysis and Discussion

4.1   Analysis of the Exposure of the Film and Television Animation of 3D Model

The experiment is studied based on the exposure of the film and television animation of the three-dimensional model of the depth image sequence. The experimental data is shown in Table 1 by detecting the exposure of the film and television animation of the three-dimensional model.

Table 1. Exposure analysis of the film and television animation of the three-dimensional model

Animation item	Animation frame number	Exposure (%)
Animation one	36	96.5
Animation two	51	93.9
Animation three	65	96.8
Animation four	86	96.1

From the analysis of the above data, from the results, when the number of frames of the first animation is 36 times, the exposure of the film and television animation of the three -dimensional model is 96.5%. When the number of frames of No. 2 animation is 51 times, the exposure of the film and television animation of the three -dimensional model is 93.9%. When the number of frames of No. 3 animation is 65 times, the exposure of the three -dimensional model of film and television animation is 96.8%. When the number of frames of No. 4 animation is 86 times, the exposure of the three -dimensional model of film and television animation is 96.1%. Through the comparison of experimental data, it is found that the exposure of the film and television animation of the three -dimensional model has always maintained at a stable level, that is, it is maintained between 96%of the level. It shows that the exposure of the film and television animation of the three -dimensional model does not change with the change of frame numbers (in Fig. 1).

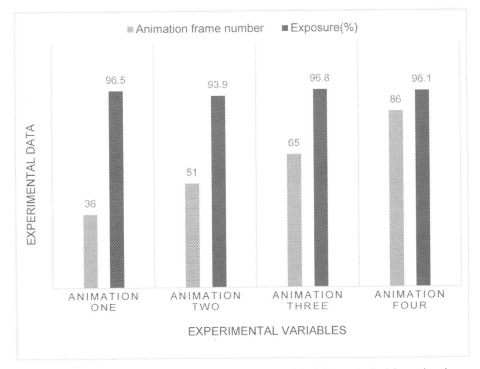

Fig. 1. Exposure analysis of the three-dimensional model of film and television animation

4.2 Analysis of the Clarity of the Film and Television Animation of 3D Model and Economic Applicability

Through the analysis of the clarity and economic applicability of the three-dimensional model, it helps to explore the film and television animation of the three-dimensional model to meet the sharpness of the economic applicability while satisfying the pursuit of economic applicability, thus judge the film and television animation of the three-dimensional model. Feasibility, experimental data as shown Fig. 2.

As shown in Fig. 2, a comparison analysis of the profit of the three-dimensional model of the film and television animation of the three-dimensional model is compared to the economic applicability data. When the four sets of three-dimensional model of film and television animation is 50%, 75%, 90% and 100% The corresponding economic applicability is 86.7%, 82.4%, 83.5% and 84.6%, respectively. The value of the four sets of three-dimensional model of film and television animation is different. The data is stable at the same level. Experimental data shows that the three-dimensional model has a better film and television animation economics, and economic applicability is not affected by clarity.

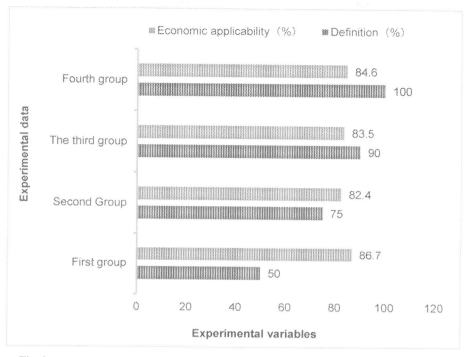

Fig. 2. Analysis of the clarity and economic applicability of the three-dimensional model

5 Conclusions

This paper first studies and analyzes the current three-dimensional model of the film and television animation production process based on the background of the depth image sequence. And clarity and economic applicability have certain feasibility, the experimental data of the exposure of the film through the 3D model can see that the exposure of the three-dimensional model of film and television animation is always maintained in a stable level, that is, maintained Floating between 96% levels. The exposure of the film and television animation of the three-dimensional model does not change as the number of frames changes. Moreover, the data of the clarity and economic applicability analysis of the film and television animation of the three-dimensional model, the film and television animation of the three-dimensional model is better, and the economic applicability is not affected by clarity. The research results of the three-dimensional model of the three-dimensional model have met the exposure and clarity and the requirements of economic applicability, and have the promotion application value.

References

1. Santos, R.B., Oliveira, U.: Analysis of occupational risk management tools for the film and television industry. Int. J. Ind. Ergon. **72**, 199–211 (2019)
2. Hartzheim, B.H.: Making of a Mangaka: industrial reflexivity and Shueisha's weekly Shnen jump. Tel. New Media **22**(5), 152–213 (2019)
3. Yahiaoui, R., et al.: Translating irony into Arabic –who's having the last laugh? Dubbing Monsters Inc.: Egyptian vernacular vs. modern standard Arabic. Eur. J. Hum. Res. **7**(4), 32–46 (2019)
4. Keiichi, S., Isao, A.: Composite Tungsten Oxide Film and Production Method Therefor, and Film Formation Base Material and Article Having Said Film: EP3812480A4, vol. 6(10), pp. 639–723 (2021)
5. Takeshi, A.: Retardation Film And Production Method: EP3633425A1, vol. 1651(1), pp. 012187 (7pp) (2020)
6. Mcclellan, P.: Production Design: Visual Design for Film and Television, vol. 5(15), pp. 329–352 (2020)
7. Benson-Allott, C.: The Stuff of Spectatorship: Material Cultures of Film and Television, vol. 1004(1), pp. 01209 (6pp) (2021)
8. Nakafuji, S.Y., et al.: Composition, Film, and Production Method of Patterned Substrate: US20200348595A1, vol. 55(6), 522–533 (2020)
9. Dean, M., Nordahl-Hansen, A.: Film and television representations of ASD: it's not just about Hollywood. Int. Meet. Autism Res. **46**(7), 987–993 (2020)
10. Raissi, P., Naghashzadeh, M., Raissi, S.: Designing a model for film production risk management. Honar--Ha-Ye-Ziba: Honar-Ha-Ye-Namayeshi Va Mosighi **24**(2), 33–42 (2019)
11. Camacho-Gómez, D., García Aznar, J.M., Gómez-Benito, M.J.: A 3D multi-agent-based model for lumen morphogenesis: the role of the biophysical properties of the extracellular matrix. Eng. Comput. **38**(5), 4135–4149 (2022)
12. Nguyen, V.V.L., Sam, T.U., Huynh, D.P., Cao, X.V., Bui, V.-T.: Methanol assisted-massive production of surfactant-free ordered honeycomb polycaprolactone film. J. Polym. Res. **29**(1), 1–6 (2021). https://doi.org/10.1007/s10965-021-02855-w

3D Printing Design Simulation of Ceramic Products Based on 3D Image Reproduction Technology

Lan Yao(✉)

Shanghai Art & Design Academy, Shanghai, China
lanlan95@126.com

Abstract. With the development of communication technology, people will be exposed to more and more graphics and images in the process of life and work. Like using digital devices such as camera, scanner and camera to obtain images, but these instruments and equipment can only obtain two-dimensional image information of objects, which is completely insufficient. In many fields, three-dimensional information of objects is necessary. In this paper, the 3D printing design of ceramic products is simulated based on 3D image reproduction technology. The satisfaction of users with the ceramic visual effect and hand-held comfort produced by 3D image reproduction simulation technology is investigated by means of questionnaire, and the computer vision technology and stereo matching technology are compared. The results show that more than 85% of users are very satisfied with the ceramic visual effect and hand-held comfort of three-dimensional image reproduction simulation technology, and less than 5% of users are not satisfied; The satisfaction of ceramic visual effect produced by computer vision technology and stereo matching technology is less than 60%, and the hand-held comfort is less than 70%.

Keywords: 3D image reproduction technology · Ceramic products · 3D printing design · Simulation research

1 Introduction

With the emergence of three-dimensional reproduction of two or more pictures and three-dimensional restoration of a single image. Modern 3D image reproduction technology provides an important technical means for 3D printing of Chinese ceramic products, which is of great significance to carry forward China's traditional culture and art. In recent years, with the rapid development of image-based 3D reproduction technology, people have been able to directly use the captured pictures for 3D reproduction, thus eliminating the problem of calibration in traditional reproduction technology.

Simulation Research on 3D printing design of ceramic products based on 3D image reproduction technology has been studied by many scholars at home and abroad. Seung Mok showed the implementation of 3D printer using DLP projector and the printing method of ceramic resin. 3D printers support 3D printing of their specific materials.

© The Author(s), under exclusive license to Springer Nature Switzerland AG 2022
N. Khare et al. (Eds.): MIND 2022, CCIS 1763, pp. 139–145, 2022.
https://doi.org/10.1007/978-3-031-24367-7_13

In order to develop powder resin for 3D printing, we use general DLP projector, high-precision servo control platform and blade to realize 3D printer. For the performance evaluation of ordinary resin and ceramic resin, the inner diameter and outer diameter of equal thickness and short length pipe manufactured by the implemented 3D printer were measured [1]. Kim h analyzed a new preparation method, which prepared porous bodies by adding slag and reinforcing metal. In order to reduce the cost, a method of using recyclable material slag is proposed. With the increasing demand for additive manufacturing using by-products, slag as a diversified recycled material of 3D printing technology has attracted attention [2].

On the basis of previous studies and combined with traditional technology, this paper proposes the application of 3D image reproduction simulation technology to 3D printing of ceramic products. 3D printing process is a cross-border combination of technology and art. Under the new ceramic forming process, the traditional production mode has changed from the relationship between man and mud to the relationship between man and machine, and the design method has also changed. For computer-aided design, in the implementation process, analyze and summarize the process characteristics and modeling characteristics [3, 4]. Using 3D image reproduction simulation technology, 3D printing process design enriches the style of ceramic products. It brings a new aesthetic feeling to the modeling of ceramic products - Mechanical aesthetic feeling, and a new visual taste to the ceramic product industry. The modeling of mechanical aesthetics is different from the modeling of existing ceramic products. The modeling process of ceramic products under the new process is a rational, orderly and planned implementation, while the modeling of traditional ceramic products is mostly the embodiment of experience or personality art [5].

2   Image Based 3D Reconstruction Technology

Materials can also be used to describe the correlation between the object surface and light. When the three-D model is formed, in addition to the default color of the object appearance, materials and maps must be used to show the actual color of the object. Make it consistent with the diffuse reflection color, so as to form a matte effect, so as to reduce the gloss of the material, change the projection angle direction of the original light source, and form a deviation of the original light source. Mapping can apply images, patterns, color adjustments, and other special effects to any place of the material, such as diffuse reflection or highlight. By simulating texture adjustment, reflection, refraction and other special effects, it can add details to the material without increasing the complexity of the material and effectively improve the appearance and realism of the material [6, 7].

Maps can be divided into 2D and 3D maps. 2D maps mainly include "bitmap", "checkerboard", "gradient" and other types. In modeling, the "coordinates" rollout of 2D mapping is particularly important. In the "tile" mapping, mapping directly on the model may lead to incorrect mapping graphics position or completely disordered orientation. At this time, UV coordinate settings need to be used. In the 2D graphics, move the mapping direction arbitrarily to make it "pasted" to the model surface completely [8, 9]. The so-called UV can be understood as X and Y axes in essence. The visualization of 3D images can be divided into two methods. One is to reconstruct the intermediate geometric units from the original 3D medical image data, and describe the 3D structure of the object through geometric unit splicing. This method is called surface rendering. Another method is to display the volume data directly to the plane, which is called volume rendering.

Surface rendering is also mainly divided into two methods: contour connection and isosurface extraction. In many cases, reconstructing the surface of the object can meet the needs of users. Of course, it is undeniable that in more cases, users prefer to see the internal characteristics of organs, so surface rendering is not often used as the choice of three-dimensional visualization. The main steps of the contour line connection method are as follows: the first step is to extract the contour line, which is mainly based on the information such as gray value or gradient value; The second step is to correspond the points on the contour line. The general method is to use the same number of marked points for the upper and lower layers, and use the same serial number points to mark the points on the contour line closest to the European style. The last step is surface fitting, which usually uses small triangular patches to fit smooth surfaces [10, 11]. At the same time, the normal vector of each facet is calculated, which will be used in optical effects. The second method of surface rendering is to extract the isosurface. The user defines a specific gray value, and then traverses each voxel to determine whether the eight vertices of the voxel are located inside or outside the isosurface, so as to determine the position of the patch in this voxel [12].

3   Research on 3D Printing Design Simulation of Ceramic Products

3.1   Selection of Test Materials

Based on the extrusion technology, the experiment forces the slurry to flow out of the printer nozzle by applying extrusion pressure on the slurry, prints layer by layer according to the path planned by the layered software, heats by the heating device to realize layer by layer solidification, and finally accumulates into a complete printing model. In order to improve the printing success rate, it is necessary to analyze the properties of the printing slurry and do a simple extrusion test before the formal printing test, which proves that the precursor ceramic slurry can meet the material properties of 3D printing.

(1)   After the slurry is configured, there are no particles and more bubbles.
(2)   Although the slurry has high viscosity, it can ensure good fluidity, which indicates that the slurry can flow out smoothly in the printing process and the bonding quality of molded parts is high.
(3)   Because the slurry has certain compressibility, it may have a certain impact on the response of discharge speed in the printing process.
(4)   The slurry has a suitable solidification range. The solidification temperature of the slurry in the printing process is between 120.00 °C and 150.00 °C. After applying a simple heat insulation device to the nozzle, it will not affect the slurry in the nozzle, will not solidify the slurry in the nozzle, and there is no plug phenomenon.
(5)   The slurry can be discharged under the condition of minimum pressure of 0.01Mpa.

3.2 Design Requirements for Slurry Extrusion Device of 3D Printer

The function of 3D printer for ceramic materials is mainly to solve the problem that ceramic materials are hard and brittle and difficult to process. By using 3D printing to add materials instead of cutting and reducing materials, 3D printing can quickly form ceramic parts with good performance, low cost and complex structure. The design requirements of 3D printer slurry extrusion device are as follows:

(1) A suitable slurry extrusion device for precursor ceramic slurry printing is designed and selected to ensure that the discharge is continuous and stable in the printing process and there is no problem of breaking and excessive discharge.
(2) The heating device is designed to realize the heating and curing of the extruded precursor ceramic slurry, but the ceramic slurry that has not been extruded can not be cured.
(3) Design printer nozzle with reasonable structure. Due to the high viscosity of precursor ceramic slurry, the nozzle adhesive can not affect the printing quality in the extrusion process. It can print ceramic parts with complex shape, and the printed parts should have high forming accuracy.

3.3 3D Ceramic Printing Simulation Algorithm

In the printing process, in order to discharge the pulp from the nozzle according to the printing speed requirements, the pulp to be extruded must be provided with appropriate pressure. This pressure can cause slight extrusion change of the slurry. Therefore, although the pressure is very small, it can not be ignored when using a nozzle with a diameter of about 0.6 mm. Therefore, it is necessary to detect the volume and elastic modulus of the slurry. Therefore, first detect the density of slurry under normal temperature and pressure, and then use the calculation formula of density (1):

$$\rho = \frac{m}{v} \tag{1}$$

where, is density, M is mass and V is volume. Then, the plunger extrusion device is used to apply pressure to complete the test of the bulk elastic modulus of the slurry. The plunger extrusion device uses a multi-stage reducer to squeeze the slurry, which has great control accuracy in the small volume deformation of the silo, and can meet the requirements of the test of the bulk modulus of the slurry. The patch pressure sensor is embedded in the plunger extrusion device with a capacity of 190 ml, and the discharge port is completely closed. According to the principle formula of liquid bulk modulus (2):

$$H = -\frac{V \Delta P}{\Delta V} \tag{2}$$

where h represents the bulk elastic modulus of liquid, V represents the initial volume value, pressure and total volume deformation.

4   Research on 3D Printing Design Simulation of Ceramic Products

In this paper, a questionnaire survey is conducted on the visual effects of ceramics produced by different technologies by ceramic users, and the computer vision technology and stereo matching technology are compared. The survey results are shown in Table 1 and Fig. 1

Table 1. Visual effects of different technologies for ceramic products

	Good visual effect	General visual effect	Poor visual effect
Computer vision technology	59%	38%	9%
Stereo matching technology	47%	26%	15%
3D image reproduction simulation technology	87%	24%	3%

The results showed that 87% of users thought that the ceramic visual effect of three-dimensional image simulation technology was very satisfactory, and only 3% of users were dissatisfied; The satisfaction of ceramic visual effect produced by computer vision technology and stereo matching technology is less than 60%.

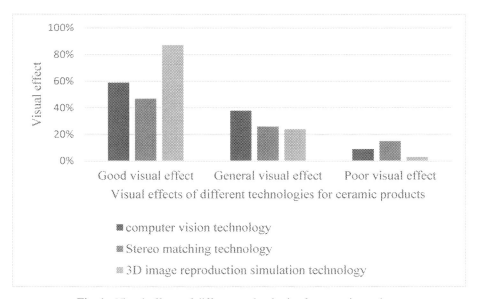

Fig. 1. Visual effects of different technologies for ceramic products

Next, the investigators conducted a questionnaire survey on the hand feel comfort of ceramic products made with different technologies. The survey results are shown in Fig. 2

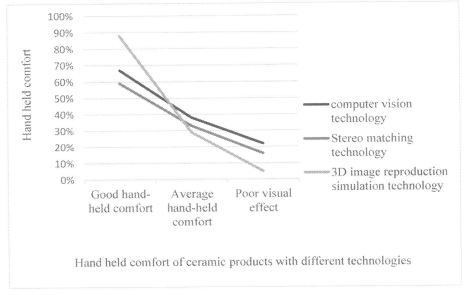

Fig. 2. Hand held comfort of ceramic products with different technologies

The experimental results show that the 3D image reproduction simulation technology used in this paper has better effect on 3D printing of ceramic products than computer vision technology and stereo matching technology. No matter in visual effect or hand comfort, it is obviously superior to the traditional technology, and the three-dimensional image reproduction simulation technology can effectively deal with the free-form surface in ceramic modeling, and the overall performance is high.

5   Conclusions

Because of its high temperature resistance, corrosion resistance, high strength and high hardness, composite ceramics have attracted widespread attention from all walks of life. Additive production technology is the trend of the development of production science and technology. The application of additive manufacturing technology to Chinese ceramic manufacturing breaks through the technical limitations of traditional composite ceramic processing technology, which is an important key technology in China. Composite ceramic 3D printing technology is an organic integration of new material production technology and traditional ceramic manufacturing. Compared with traditional ceramic processing and production technology, this technology has the advantages of low cost, high production efficiency, high forming accuracy and forming a large number of complex parts. In this paper, the 3D printing design simulation of ceramic products is studied and analyzed based on 3D image reproduction technology, the extrusion device of ceramic materials is deeply studied, the 3D printer of ceramic materials is made, and the printing equipment is improved to further improve the forming effect. However, the 3D printing equipment is still not mature enough. The ceramic materials used are traditional ceramics. The purpose of formed products after sintering can not be compared with engineering ceramics, so it needs further improvement and perfection. The printer needs further production processing.

References

1. Lee, S.-M., et al.: Implementation of 3D printer using DLP for ceramic resin. J. Korean Inst. Inf. Technol. **15**(8), 95–100 (2017)
2. Kim, H., Lee, S.: Printability and physical properties of iron slag powder composites using material extrusion-based 3D printing. J. Iron. Steel Res. Int. **28**(1), 111–121 (2020). https://doi.org/10.1007/s42243-020-00475-0
3. Strebelle, S.: Multiple-point statistics simulation models: pretty pictures or decision-making tools? Math. Geosci. **53**(2), 267–278 (2021). https://doi.org/10.1007/s11004-020-09908-8
4. Ta, A., Kth, B., Jhk, B.: Extrusion-based 3D direct ink writing of NiZn-ferrite structures with viscoelastic ceramic suspension. Ceram. Int. **46**(5), 6469–6476 (2020)
5. Rigante, M., Rocca, G.L., Lauretti, L., et al.: Preliminary experience with 4K ultra-high definition endoscope: analysis of pros and cons in skull base surgery. Acta Otorhinolaryngologica Italica Organo Ufficiale Della Società Italiana Di Otorinolaringologia E Chirurgia Cervico Facciale **37**(3), 237–241 (2017)
6. Karczewski, M.: 3D scanner working parameters – influence on an accuracy of mechanical vehicle element reproduction. J. KONES **25**(1), 215–223 (2018)
7. Balasubramanian, G., Nimje, M.T., Kutumbarao, V.V.: Conversion of aluminium industry wastes into glass-ceramic products. Soc. Sci. Electron. Publ. **2000**(9), 285–291 (2017)
8. Tatsuki, O.: Additive manufacturing of ceramic components—towards innovation of ceramic industry. Synthesiol. English Edn. **11**(2), 81–93 (2018)
9. Xu, H., Medina-Sánchez, M., Zhang, W., et al.: Human spermbots for patient-representative 3D ovarian cancer cell treatment. Nanoscale **12**(39), 20467–20481 (2020)
10. Bogdanov, S.P., Sychev, M.M., Lebedev, L.A.: Structural changes during sintering of Al 2 O 3 3D-ceramics. Refract. Ind. Ceram **59**(5), 466–470 (2019)
11. Yang, K., Xu, S., Li, B.: The influence mechanism of nano-alumina content in semi-solid ceramic precursor fluid on the forming performance: via a light-cured 3D printing method. RSC Adv. **10**(68), 41453–41461 (2020)
12. Fina, F., Goyanes, A., Gaisford, S., Basit, A.W.: Selective laser sintering (SLS) 3D printing of medicines. Int. J. Pharm. **529**(1–2), 285–293 (2017)

Artificial Intelligence of Internet of Things and Virtual Reality Technology in the Image Reconstruction of Film and Television Characters

Hanlin Guo[✉]

Division of Culture and Creativity, United International College,
Anshan 114000, Liaoning, China
g2592873296@163.com

Abstract. The animation market structure continues to be optimized, and the animation economic cake continues to grow. Character image building is a very important work content, this part of the work is the most important part of the whole film and TV series. Animation characters from the character, characteristics, character psychological activities, action and other aspects to show their own character image. All these features are innovative elements in film and television, which provide their own services for the development of film and television plot and make the development of film and television more visual. This paper studies the research on the image reconstruction of Internet of Things artificial intelligence and virtual reality technology in film and television character reconstruction, and points out the related content of the research on the image reconstruction of film and television character reconstruction. The test confirmed that artificial intelligence of the Internet of Things and virtual reality technology had excellent performance in the image reconstruction of film and television character role shaping.

Keywords: Internet of things artificial intelligence · Virtual reality technology · Film and television character shaping · Image reconstruction research

1 Introduction

In the process of film and television animation production, clothing is a very important accessory. The choice of clothing style and the change of clothing will always affect the shaping of characters in film and television animation. Therefore, the role of clothing must be considered in the shaping of characters. General clothing includes clothes, scarves, handbags, shoes and other external parts. Through these external parts to modify the character, so as to achieve the purpose of character image shaping. Artificial intelligence of the Internet of things and virtual reality technology are adopted to improve the technical foundation of the image shaping of film and television characters, so as to enhance the image shaping effect. The research on the image reconstruction of Internet of Things artificial intelligence and virtual reality technology in film and television character reconstruction is conducive to the in-depth development of the research on the image reconstruction of film and television character reconstruction.

As for the research on artificial intelligence and virtual reality technology of Internet of Things, many scholars at home and abroad have carried out research on it. In foreign studies, Rifa 'ia proposed the use of logistic regression, decision tree and random forest methods to evaluate the sensitivity of soil erosion in the Mayurakshi River Basin in eastern India, and verified the ROC curve and Kappa statistics [1]. CrossC has proposed the rapid development and improvement of ARTIFICIAL intelligence and deepfakes to create unique images, which are already evident. This paper argues that the adoption of these new technologies requires a rethinking of current preventive messaging, which focuses on promoting the use of Internet search (in particular reverse image search) to verify or refute the identity/scene presented. For those who choose to do so, it can be successful and avoid the initial financial loss or reduce the overall amount of damage to the offender [2]. AppelL proposed that the team develop the CVRrulum (CVR) project: a pilot project that recruits teachers to adapt traditional written work into a virtual reality format. A mixed approach was used to collect data from 5 faculty and 18 student participants. In this article, the implementation process is described, identified challenges are reported, and recommendations are provided to improve subsequent products. The team solved the challenges presented by creating a set of resources available on the CVR website [3].

The visual effect of film and television animation is constantly improving, and people's aesthetic appreciation is also constantly improving, which requires the design of characters to become more delicate and subtle [4, 5]. This paper describes the working principle of animation characters' decoration, action, preference and other aspects of display. Internet of Things artificial intelligence and virtual reality technology can assist in the successful realization of these tasks. Research on the image reconstruction of Internet of Things artificial intelligence and virtual reality technology in film and television character reconstruction promotes the efficient development of the image reconstruction of film and television character reconstruction [6, 7].

2 Design and Research on the Image Reconstruction Research of Internet of Things Artificial Intelligence and Virtual Reality Technology in the Role Shaping of Film and Television Characters

2.1 The Internet of Things

The Internet of Things refers to the use of a network to connect multiple objects in several ways [8, 9]:

First, the Internet of Things relies on the network, and develops and expands connectivity on the network.

Second, the essence of the Internet of Things is the exchange of information. Which relies on the technology is the network hardware, network access and so on.

2.2 Artificial Intelligence

Artificial Intelligence, abbreviated as AI [10, 11]. The study and development of theories, methods, techniques and application systems for simulating, extending and extending human intelligence.

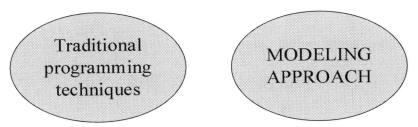

Fig. 1. Artificial intelligence algorithm on the computer implementation

There are two ways to realize artificial intelligence algorithm on computer, as shown in Fig. 1: one is to use traditional programming technology to make the system appear intelligent; One is the analog method, whose principle highlights the analogy or similarity between methods and biological mechanisms.

2.3 Virtual Reality Technology

Virtual reality technology refers to the use of information technology to create virtual objects or scenes in reality, its essence is to add other modification parts of reality, so as to achieve the effect of change technology.

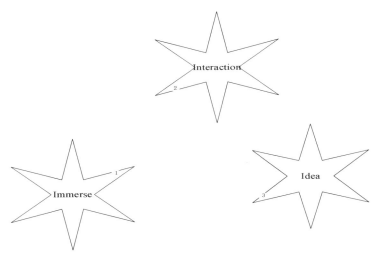

Fig. 2. Virtual reality technology having the following three main characteristics

Virtual reality technology has the following three main features, as shown in Fig. 2:

(1) Immersion. It refers to the use of computer-generated three-dimensional images, so that users feel surrounded by the virtual world, as in another world or environment, to give a person a sense of immersive. In immersion. Users' visual immersion, tactile immersion, auditory immersion, olfactory immersion and taste immersion should be considered [12, 13].
(2) Interactivity. In a virtual environment, people can interact with objects in the virtual world through sensing devices. For example, when users touch and grab objects in a virtual environment, they need to get the same sensation as in real life.

2.4 Research on Image Reconstruction of Internet of Things Artificial Intelligence and Virtual Reality Technology in Film and Television Character Shaping

Excellent character creation is often based on life and excellent in life. Artificial intelligence algorithm of the Internet of Things and virtual reality technology are adopted to analyze virtual personas from the following points, as releaved in Fig. 3.

Fig. 3. Film and television character role shaping techniques

Exaggerated [14, 15]. Higher than life is the effect of animation production, in the plot, the performance of the work will be more exaggerated, so as to meet the audience's curiosity, to achieve the desired good effect.

Bizarre. Weirdness is, in some ways, a form of exaggeration. The setting of characters often requires exploring unknown territory and realizing steps to achieve the desired effect of the audience.

Describe psychological characteristics [16, 17]. Psychology is a fluctuating abstract curve, and it is very common for characters to show this in a story. Therefore, the plot often needs to constantly grasp the psychological changes, always grasp the overall trend of the master.

3 Research on the Effect of Internet of Things Artificial Intelligence and Virtual Reality Technology in the Image Reconstruction of Film and Television Characters

Naive Bayes is established based on Bayes formula, which is as follows:

$$p(a|b) = \frac{p(b|a)p(a)}{p(b)} \tag{1}$$

$p(a|b)$ refers to the occurrence of b cases, the probability of a produced, such as p (cold | sneezing, fever) refers to sneeze at the same time, the probability of a cold fever cases in; $p(a)$ is the probability of a occurring without any of the prerequisites.

The concept of entropy comes from the theoretical concept of physics and expresses the uncertain probability of matter. The formula of entropy in artificial intelligence algorithm is as follows:

$$H(X) = -\sum_{x} p(x) \log p(x) = -\sum_{i=1}^{n} p(x_i) \log p(x_i) \tag{2}$$

In this formula, x is the random variable, $p(x)$ is the probability distribution of x.

In this paper, the Bayesian model of Internet of Things artificial intelligence algorithm is used to classify the image of film and television characters, and new characters are created through restrictions. At the same time, the virtual reality technology is used to realize the virtual technology of the original film and television characters, so as to create the image collection of film and television characters, and finally realize the reconstruction of characters.

3.1 Research on Image Reconstruction of Internet of Things Artificial Intelligence and Virtual Reality Technology in Film and Television Character Shaping

Professional design engineers will constantly adjust the relevant situation according to the differences of clothing itself. The adjustment can be analyzed from the following perspectives:

First, contrast. After costume design, there will be a comparison of effects, which is a necessary step after costume design. The purpose of comparison is to compare and deal with the visual effects of different styles of clothing and the transformation of the image of film and television characters. There are many kinds of characters in film and television animation, such as simple and extravagant clothes; Variety and monotony of dress; The fineness and roughness of clothing, etc. After a variety of designs, costumes tend to be more or less increased or decreased in the composition of drama, so as to show a variety of personalized characteristics.

Second, reflect the history and times. There are many animated films and television books that describe characters in different countries and different times. Among them, clothing is a prominent symbol to show this characteristic. Dress often can show the mark of history, can show the symbol of The Times. All kinds of historical features can be incisively and vividly displayed, such as the head hairpin of the Terracotta Warriors can show the roughness of the people in the northwest; Bing Dwen Dwen's image can clearly reflect the modern Chinese space technology advanced achievements.

Third, the importance of thinking and imagination. Creative designers often need to rely on their own imagination to figure out the atmosphere conveyed by clothing, grasp the appropriate accessories to express the emotion of a particular situation, which is a typical performance of character modeling. What is touching about the imagination here is the virtual reality scenes that are mixed in the imagination, making it easier for people to think of some kind of touching effect.

4 Investigation and Research Analysis of the Image Reconstruction of Internet of Things Artificial Intelligence and Virtual Reality Technology in the Role Shaping of Film and Television Characters

This paper uses test cases to test the effect of image reconstruction of film and television characters based on artificial intelligence of Internet of Things and virtual reality technology. This test uses four algorithms to verify the effect.

The operating platform of this test is Matlab. The operating system is Window 2010, the programming language is Java, and the database is MySQL. The processor is Pentium processor. Relevant test data are shown in Table 1.

Table 1. The state of the relevant test data

Algorithm	Efficiency	Accuracy	Degree of innovation
Artificial intelligence and virtual technology	1271	92%	100
HHR	720	70%	62

Table 1 shows two algorithms, Artificial Intelligence and Virtual Technology and HHR, a traditional technology. In the testing process, the two algorithms processed 1271,720 data sets of film and television character creation in unit time respectively. Accuracy was 92% and 70%, respectively; Innovation is 100 and 62, respectively. In terms of data, Artificial intelligence and virtual technology (Artificial Intelligence and Virtual Technology) has a better effect on the image reconstruction of film and television characters.

Figure 4 and 5 show the data of the efficiency, innovation and accuracy of the test algorithm. Figure 2 dark blue shows the test performance of ARTIFICIAL intelligence and virtual reality technology; Light blue indicates innovation test performance. Figure 3 shows the performance of algorithm accuracy. As can be seen from the figure, artificial intelligence and virtual reality technologies performed well.

The data show that the artificial intelligence of the Internet of Things and virtual reality technology perform efficiently in the image reconstruction of film and television characters.

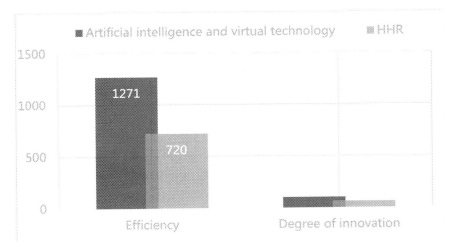

Fig. 4. Data on efficiency and innovation in the test

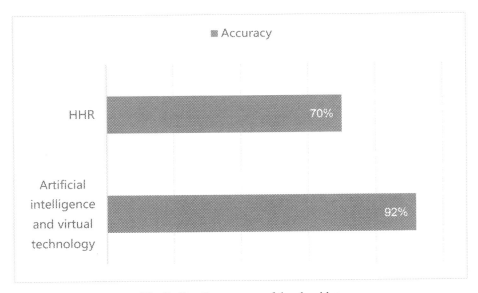

Fig. 5. Test the accuracy of the algorithm

5   Conclusions

Animation character portrayal of the media always more diversity, however, clothing as a very general material, shape of characters to played a role, it gives a person the visual effect is not only a simple dress, and I can give you more in-depth emotional triggers or declare or history of the era of straightforward. An excellent film and television is often inseparable from the portrayal of excellent characters, which more clearly show people the overall portrait of a character, show a person's physical characteristics. The research on the image reconstruction of Internet of Things artificial intelligence and virtual reality technology in film and television character reconstruction is conducive to the progress in the field of image reconstruction of film and television character reconstruction.

References

1. Rifa'I, A.: Sistem pemantauan dan kontrol otomatis kualitas air berbasis internet of things (IOT) menggunakan platform node-red untuk budidaya udang. JTT (Jurnal Teknologi Terapan) **7**(1), 19–19 (2021)
2. Cross, C.: Using artificial intelligence (AI) and deepfakes to deceive victims: the need to rethink current romance fraud prevention messaging. Crime Prev. Community Saf. **24**(1), 1–12 (2022)
3. Appel, L., Peisachovich, E., Sinclair, D.: CVRRICULUM program: benefits and challenges of embedding virtual reality as an educational medium in undergraduate curricula. Int. J. Innov. Educ. Res. **9**(3), 219–236 (2021)
4. Kumar, P., Gupta, G.P., Tripathi, R.: A distributed ensemble design based intrusion detection system using fog computing to protect the internet of things networks. J. Ambient. Intell. Humaniz. Comput. **12**(10), 9555–9572 (2020). https://doi.org/10.1007/s12652-020-02696-3
5. Eze, K.G., Akujuobi, C.M.: Design and evaluation of a distributed security framework for the internet of things. J. Signal Inf. Process. **13**(1), 23 (2022)
6. Ahmad, M.S.: Mitigating malicious insider attacks in the internet of things using supervised machine learning techniques. Scalable Comput. **22**(1), 13–28 (2021)
7. Nurwijayanti, K.N., Adhytyas, R.E.: Garbage bin monitoring system based on the internet of things at university Dirgantara Marsekal Suryadarma. Int. J. Educ. Manag. Eng. **11**(2), 1–12 (2021)
8. Agong, R.: Wireless sensor and mobile ad-hoc networks for the internet of things: a survey. J. Innov. Res. Solut. (JIRAS) **10**(1), 2 (2021)
9. Dhaif, R.A., Ibrahim, A.F., Elkatatny, S.: Prediction of surface oil rates for volatile oil and gas condensate reservoirs using artificial intelligence techniques. J. Energy Res. Technol. **144**(3), 1–14 (2021)
10. Fornasier, M.: The regulation of the use of artificial intelligence (AI) in warfare: between international humanitarian law (IHL) and meaningful human control. Revista Jurídica da Presidência **23**(129), 67 (2021)
11. Allam, S.Z.: Artificial intelligence intervention to urban building renewable energy modeling intervention for robust flexible communities. Int. J. Adv. Res. **9**(3), 314–321 (2021)
12. Lashin, M.: Using artificial intelligence for optimizing natural frequency of recycled concrete for mechanical machine foundation. Recycling **6**(3), 43 (2021)
13. Jabbarpour, M.R., Saghiri, A.M., Sookhak, M.: A framework for component selection considering dark sides of artificial intelligence: a case study on autonomous vehicle. Electronics **10**(4), 384 (2021)
14. Peer, P., Zelenkova, J., Filip, P., et al.: An estimate of the onset of beadless character of electrospun nanofibers using rheological characterization. Polymers **13**(2), 265 (2021)
15. Aniukwu, N.: Nollywood and the leaders of tomorrow: interrogating film content and character formation of the Nigerian child. UJAH Unizik J. Arts Humanit. **20**(3), 59–79 (2020)
16. Bae, S.Y.: The fall of the hysteric subject : analysis of the characters of the film parasite. J. Contemp. Psychoanal. **23**(1), 9–48 (2021)
17. Hubbard, T.D., Curran, K.: The importance of being earnest: the role of character, competence, and emotion in reputation change. Acad. Manag. Annu. Meet. Proc. **2021**(1), 15323 (2021)

Research on the Application of Virtual Reality Technology in Environmental Art Design

Wei Meng$^{(\boxtimes)}$, Han Ding, and Hui Liu

College of Fine Arts, Bohai University, Jinzhou, Liaoning, China
bdmyjys@163.com

Abstract. Virtual reality technology is a comprehensive display technology developed on the basis of visual simulation technology and multimedia technology. Through equipment simulation, a three-dimensional virtual world is generated, and visual, auditory and tactile sensing are realized, bringing a real experience and an immersive feeling. With the help of VR, designers can easily and quickly complete environmental scene simulation, effectively grasp the specific characteristics of the corresponding environmental scene, and effectively carry out the design. The related technologies of VR applied to environmental art design include environment modeling technology, stereoscopic display technology, haptic feedback technology, system interaction technology and system integration technology. In the process of realizing the design, we should give full play to the advantages of these technologies to improve and optimize the effect of environmental art design.

Keywords: Virtual reality technology (VR) · Environmental art design · Stereoscopic display technology · Haptic feedback technology · Interactive technology

1 Introduction

Virtual reality technology (VR) is a more comprehensive display technology developed on the basis of visual simulation technology and multimedia technology. Through device simulation, a three-dimensional virtual world is generated to realize visual, auditory and tactile induction, bringing real experience and natural human-computer interaction, and users have an immersive feeling [1]. Virtual reality is the highest stage of multimedia technology development. Under ideal conditions, virtual reality allows people to have all the perception capabilities of the real world, including sight, hearing, touch, taste and feeling. With the help of VR, designers can easily and quickly complete environmental scene simulation, effectively grasp the specific characteristics of the corresponding environmental scene, and effectively carry out the design [2, 3]. It is not necessary to complete the corresponding environmental art design in a real venue, which is conducive to saving environmental art design funds. The application of VR can effectively resolve risks, obtain the same inspection information and design effects as in the real environment, and effectively enhance the safety of design practice, which is conducive to promoting the sustainable development. Through the computer's strict control of the parameter

© The Author(s), under exclusive license to Springer Nature Switzerland AG 2022
N. Khare et al. (Eds.): MIND 2022, CCIS 1763, pp. 154–161, 2022.
https://doi.org/10.1007/978-3-031-24367-7_15

variables in the virtual environment, the designer can truly restore the environmental scene, save time and energy, and improve and optimize the effect of environmental art design.

2 Stereoscopic Display Technology of Virtual Reality

Table 1. Stereoscopic display technology

No	Technical name	Display mode	Theoretical basis	Advantages and disadvantages
1	Color separation technology	Passive	Three component theory	Advantages: mature technology, low cost, not limited by viewing position; Disadvantages: need to wear special glasses, and the display effect is not good
2	Spectroscopic technology	Passive	Polarized light theory	Advantages: The cost of glasses is low, no harm to the eyes, and the stereoscopic feeling is better; Disadvantages: The projection facilities and curtains are expensive
3	Time sharing technology	Active	Visual delay theory	Advantages: good stereo effect, low requirements for projection equipment; Disadvantages: ghosting problems cannot be completely eliminated, and hardware requirements are high
4	Grating technology	Active	Visual fusion theory	Advantages: It can be viewed with the naked eye, without the need to wear special 3D glasses; Disadvantages: Each eye can only receive half of the original light

Stereoscopic display technology is an important implementation of virtual reality. With the help of special auxiliary equipment, images and videos with a certain parallax are processed to generate stereoscopic vision. 3D stereoscopic display can show all the depth, level and position of the image, more directly understand the actual distribution of the image, and more comprehensively understand the image or display content. There are three main factors that affect the generation of stereo vision: information source, information reception and information integration. In the 21st century, with the screening of many movies, the development of stereoscopic display technology has reached a new climax, and many equipment manufacturers have launched stereoscopic display products. 3D stereo projection is a display method that appears to enhance the audience's real experience. It uses the visual difference and visual residue of the human eye to experience the three-dimensional picture effect on the two-dimensional screen. In multi-projection-based graphics display systems, video playback is widely used as a core function. Full-screen display of high-quality and high-resolution stereoscopic video can create an excellent visual experience and a strong sense of immersion for the audience [4, 5]. The currently used stereoscopic display technologies are mainly divided into four types, as shown in Table 1.

3 Haptic Feedback Technology of Virtual Reality

Haptics is one of the fastest growing fields, and in everyday life, as interacting objects shift from keyboards and mice to phones and car entertainment systems, the way you interact and receive feedback becomes even more important. Use haptic feedback technology to provide timely and useful information through haptic experience, so that the experience of haptic users can be upgraded. Especially for people with visual or hearing impairments, haptic feedback can serve as the main feedback mechanism, allowing them to receive information more timely in their life and work [6, 7]. Taking a computer touch screen as an example, the haptic feedback process is shown in Fig. 1.

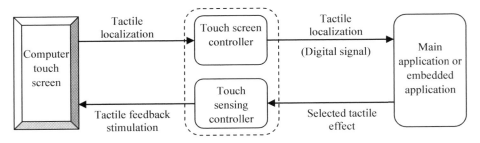

Fig. 1. Tactile feedback process of computer touch screen

Ultrasonic haptic feedback technology that allows people to touch objects in the virtual world. Provides different haptic feedback and virtual haptic shapes through ultrasonic haptic pulses or changing ultrasonic frequencies. Ultrasound changes shape and simulates an imaginary shape and force under pressure, known as "acoustic emission force," that makes human skin feel tactile. Varying the intensity of the ultrasonic waves, in turn, can produce more combinations of this sense of touch.

The sound radiation pressure P is proportional to the square of the sound pressure p:

$$P = \alpha E = \alpha \frac{I}{c} = \alpha \frac{p^2}{\rho c^2} \qquad (1)$$

For three-dimensional space, the sound pressure along the z-axis can be expressed as:

$$p = \rho c \frac{\pi}{\lambda} \frac{b^2}{z} |v_0| \quad (z \geq b) \qquad (2)$$

The relationship between the radiated sound power W of the transmitter and the initial velocity v_0 of the ultrasonic wave is:

$$W = S_0 \rho c r \frac{|v_0|^2}{2} \qquad (3)$$

The total radiation pressure produced by the array is:

$$F = PNS_0 = \alpha \frac{w}{c} NS_0 = \alpha \frac{W}{cS_0} NS_0 = \alpha \frac{NW}{c} \qquad (4)$$

The formula for calculating the focal diameter is:

$$W_f = \frac{4\pi r}{kNd} = \frac{2r\lambda}{Nd} = \frac{2rc}{Ndf} \qquad (5)$$

The formula for calculating the depth of focus is:

$$W_d = \frac{2rW_f}{Nd} = \frac{4r^2c}{N^2d^2f} \qquad (6)$$

The formula for calculating the resultant force at the focus is:

$$F = \frac{\alpha}{\rho c^2} \int_{-W_f/2}^{W_f/2} \int_{-W_f/2}^{W_f/2} \frac{|p(x_0, y_0)|^2}{2} dx_0 dy_0 \qquad (7)$$

4   Interactive Technology of Virtual Reality

In the design process of virtual reality interaction technology, it is necessary to further study the feedback of audience behavior. Taking the corresponding behavioral feedback as the starting point and standard for building a virtual world, the human-computer interaction experience can be further optimized. In the design process, it is necessary to comprehensively consider from the perspectives of virtual environment, audience objects, audience behavior and audience experience [8–11].

Pattern recognition is an important part of interactive technology, including methods based on template matching, methods based on machine learning and methods based on hidden Markov models. Based on the template matching method, the input image is matched with the template and classified according to the matching similarity. Based on the machine learning method, Markov process describing hidden states, widely used in machine learning and pattern recognition. HMM includes a Markov chain with state transition probabilities and a stochastic process that outputs observations, and states can only be represented by a stochastic process of observation sequences.

HMM is mathematically described by multiple model parameters:

N represents the number of states of the model, T represents the length of the observation sequence,

S represents the state set of the model, $S = \{S_1, S_2, \cdots, S_N\}$.

O represents the sequence of observations produced by the model in a certain period of time, $O = \{O_1, O_2, \cdots, O_T\}$.

A represents the state transition probability matrix of the model, denoted as $A = [a_{ij}]$, where:

$$a_{ij} = P\{q_{i+1} = S_j | q_t = S_i\}, 1 \le i, j \le N, \sum_{j=1}^{N} a_{ij} = 1 \tag{8}$$

B represents the output probability matrix of the model, denoted as $B = [b_j(k)]$, where:

$$b_{jk} = P\{O_t = v_k | q_t = S_j\}, 1 \le j \le N, 1 \le k \le M, \sum_{k=1}^{M} b_{jk} = 1 \tag{9}$$

$\prod$ represents the initial state probability matrix of the model, denoted as $\prod = [\pi_i]$, where:

$$\pi_i = P\{q_1 = S_i\}, 1 \le i \le N, \sum_{i=1}^{N} \pi_i = 1 \tag{10}$$

HMM is simplified to: $\lambda = (\prod, A, B)$.

How to adjust the parameters in the model so that the model produces the largest probability $P(O|\lambda)$ of the observed sequence,

According to the HMM definition, the most intuitive solution:

$$P(O|Q, \lambda) = \prod_{t=1}^{T} P(o_t|q_t, \lambda) = b_{q_1}(o_1) b_{q_2}(o_2) \cdots b_{q_t}(o_t) \tag{11}$$

The probability that the model produces a sequence of states can be written as:

$$P(Q|\lambda) = \pi_{q_1} a_{q_1 q_2} a_{q_2 q_3} \cdots a_{q_{r-1} q_r} \tag{12}$$

Since Q and O occur simultaneously, we get:

$$P(O|\lambda) = P(O|Q, \lambda) P(Q|\lambda) = \sum \pi_{q_1} b_{q_1}(o_1) a_{q_1 q_2} b_{q_2}(o_2) \cdots a_{q_{r-1} q_r} b_{q_r}(o_r) \tag{13}$$

The forward algorithm is expressed as:

$$a_t(i) = P(o_1 o_2 \cdots o_t, q_t = S_i | \lambda), 1 \le i \le N, 1 \le t \le T \tag{14}$$

Initialize $a_t(i)$, the initial value is:

$$a_1(i) = P(o_1, q_1 = S_i|\lambda) = \pi_i b_i(o_1), 1 \le i \le N \tag{15}$$

By induction on $a_t(i)$, we get:

$$a_{t+1}(i) = \left[\sum_{i=1}^{N} a_t(i) a_{ij} \right] b_i(o_{t+1}), 1 \le i \le N, 1 \le t \le T-1 \tag{16}$$

The end result is:

$$P(O|\lambda) = \sum_{i=1}^{N} P\{o_1 o_2 \cdots o_r, q_T = S_i|\lambda\} = \sum_{i=1}^{N} a_T(i) \tag{17}$$

The forward algorithm is expressed as:

$$\beta_t(i) = P(o_{t+1} o_{t+2} \cdots o_T, q_t = S_i|\lambda), 1 \le i \le N, 1 \le t \le T \tag{18}$$

The initial value of $\beta_t(i)$ is expressed as:

$$\beta_T(i) = 1, 1 \le i \le N \tag{19}$$

By induction on $\beta_t(i)$, we get:

$$\beta_t(i) = \sum_{j=1}^{N} a_{ij} b_j(o_{t+1}) \beta_{t+1}(j), 1 \le i \le N, T-1 \ge t \ge 1 \tag{20}$$

The end result is:

$$\beta_1(i) = P(o_2 o_3 \cdots o_r, q_1 = S_i|\lambda) \tag{21}$$

$$P(O|\lambda) = \sum_{i=1}^{N} \{P(o_2 o_3 \cdots o_r, q_1 = S_i|\lambda\} = \sum_{i=1}^{N} \beta_1(i) \tag{22}$$

5   Application of VR in Environmental Art Design

VR can not only improve the expressiveness of environmental art design and enhance the authenticity of the space, but also focus more on the subjective feelings of users, making what they see more realistic. VR has become a bridge between designers and users, it will also change the relationship between new materials and new technologies, and comprehensively improve the effect.

(1) Follow the basic principles of VR. In the process of applying VR, different design elements are involved. In order to improve the design effect, the following principles need to be followed: First, the principle of purpose. Pay attention to the content, elements and effects of environmental art design, and prevent designers from affecting the realization of design goals due to personal subjective judgments. Second, the principle of artistry. Highlight aesthetics and values, and stimulate the vitality of design projects through VR. Third, the principle of interactivity. Using VR, assist designers to realize the improvement and combination of software technology to meet the interactive needs of customers for design.

(2) VR is safer. The process is complex and involves many technologies. If a problem occurs in a detail, it will affect the overall design. In the specific design process, if many real environments and building layouts do not meet the requirements, they need to be adjusted or modified, and problems often occur in this process. Using VR, build a virtual situation, design the scene, and then adjust the data structure according to the visual experience to highly restore the real effect. In this process, there will be no dangerous behavior and no need to invest a lot of cost, which is one of the reasons for the popularization and promotion of VR.

(3) Improve the expressiveness of works through VR. Artistic expression is the appeal of artworks, including enhancing the rendering of the atmosphere, enhancing the visual impact and enhancing the depth of the picture. The VR is organically combined with reality, showing the most real fields, improving the satisfaction of user experience, giving full play to the artistic value of design in the works, and meeting the needs of users' life. The combination of virtual environment technology and reality fully stimulates the innovative potential of designers of modern environmental culture and art works, creates more realistic environmental art design scenes, improves the artistic expression of design works, and promotes the healthy development.

(4) Optimize the process through VR. At the stage of determining the design plan, VR is applied to simulate the design plan, and check the degree of compliance of the design plan with the customer's requirements and technical standards, so as to ensure the scientificity and effectiveness of the design plan. In the design practice stage, VR is applied to restore the environmental scene, accurately grasp the environmental information, and improve the design details. In the design acceptance stage, the VR is applied to explain the details of the design results to the users, so as to better complete the design handover.

6   Conclusion

Virtual reality is a "new world" that relies on computer processing to create or change. This new world looks real, but it is actually VR. Through the mirror nervous system in the human brain, through the two processes of "imagination" and "perception", a virtual scene is created by simulating people's previous experience. And through the external sensor equipment, the user operation data is fed back to make changes to the virtual environment. Solves the problem of tedious manual drawing accuracy and the problem of rough rendering of computer renderings. It has opened up a new way to meet the artistic and spiritual needs of human settlements for environmental art design.

References

1. Pack, A., et al.: University EAP students' perceptions of using a prototype virtual reality learning environment to learn writing structure. Int. J. Comput.-Assist. Lang. Learn. Teach. **10**(1), 27–46 (2020)
2. Steel, A., Robertson, C.E., Taube, J.S.: Current promises and limitations of combined virtual reality and functional magnetic resonance imaging research in humans: a commentary on Huffman and Ekstrom. J. Cogn. Neurosci. **33**(2), 1–8 (2020)
3. Berti, M., Maranzana, S., Monzingo, J.: Fostering cultural understanding with virtual reality: a look at students' stereotypes and beliefs. Int. J. Comput.-Assist. Lang. Learn. Teach. **10**(1), 47–59 (2020)
4. Bridget, C., et al.: Development of a virtual reality clinically oriented temporal bone anatomy module with randomised control study of three-dimensional display technology. BMJ Simul. Technol. Enhanc. Learn. **7**(5), 352–359 (2020)
5. Jianghao, X., et al.: Augmented reality and virtual reality displays: emerging technologies and future perspectives. Light: Sci. Appl. **10**(1), 216 (2021)
6. Vaghela, K.R., Trockels, A., Carobene, M.: Active vs passive haptic feedback technology in virtual reality arthroscopy simulation: which is most realistic? J. Clin. Orthop. Trauma **16**(1), 249–256 (2021)
7. Almousa, O., et al.: Virtual reality simulation technology for cardiopulmonary resuscitation training: an innovative hybrid system with haptic feedback. Simul. Gaming **50**(1), 6–22 (2019)
8. Ferraz-Torres, M., et al.: Passive or interactive virtual reality? The effectiveness for pain and anxiety reduction in pediatric patients. Virtual Reality **14**(2), 1–10 (2022). https://doi.org/10.1007/s10055-022-00633-7
9. Dimitrios, B., et al.: First assessment results of surveying engineering labs in immersive and interactive virtual reality. J. Surv. Eng. **148**(1), 388–396 (2022)
10. Yun, H., Jun, M.B.G.: Immersive and interactive cyber-physical system (I2CPS) and virtual reality interface for human involved robotic manufacturing. J. Manuf. Syst. **62**(1), 234–248 (2022)
11. Kaisa, L., et al.: Virtual reality for 3D histology: multi-scale visualization of organs with interactive feature exploration. BMC Cancer **21**(1), 1133 (2021)

Computer Vision and Pattern Recognition Technology on Account of Deep Neural Network

Yiming Ren[1(✉)], Jiake Han[2], Chongyu Chen[3], Yang Xu[1], and Tingxuan Bao[1]

[1] Shenzhen MSU-BIT University, Shenzhen 518172, Guangdong, China
ren4102212002@163.com
[2] Shanghai University, Baoshan District, Shanghai 201900, China
[3] Tianjin University of Science and Technology, 1038 Dagu South Road Tianjin Hexi, Tianjin 300222, China

Abstract. With the rapid development of computer, computer vision technology is also making rapid progress. In this paper, deep neural network algorithm is used to improve the technology of computer vision, improve the visual effect, and at the same time, innovative algorithm structure, improve the identification of pattern recognition. Computer vision and pattern recognition is a very cutting edge technology that has given people very advanced tools for vision and recognition. At present, the technology can control more accurate image resolution and improve the ability of pattern recognition. This article mainly explains the process of using deep neural network algorithm to improve computer vision and pattern recognition from the internal mechanism, and reveals the working principle and internal mechanism of computer vision and pattern recognition technology application. Data analysis proves that the pattern recognition application established by deep neural network algorithm performs very well in the field of vision and pattern recognition.

Keywords: Deep neural network algorithm · Computer vision · Pattern recognition · Technical application

1 Introduction

With the rapid development of the Internet, computer vision and pattern recognition also need rapid progress. Deep neural network algorithm innovates the algorithm structure, improves the efficiency of vision and pattern recognition, and improves the technical level of pattern recognition. This algorithm essentially improves its visual image capture ability and image discrimination ability, adopts advanced data mode, improves the performance of the vision and pattern, and promotes the progress of vision and pattern recognition. Using deep neural network algorithm, computer vision and pattern recognition from the technical essence of the improvement.

As for the research of deep neural network algorithm, many scholars at home and abroad have done research on it. In foreign studies, Mohamed E M proposed an algorithm to dynamically change the structure of neural networks. According to some characteristics of the cascade correlation algorithm, the structure is changed. So far, many researchers have proposed several growth algorithms to optimize the structure of feed-forward neural networks. The algorithm has been tested on various medical data sets. The results show that this algorithm is a better method to evaluate the accuracy and flexibility of algorithms [1]. Almas MA proposed an algorithm for denoising noisy images by using iterative median, low and high voltage boost technology and deep neural network. In the process of image transmission, noise is added in the transmission and reception process due to thermal noise of antenna or faulty equipment, intentional and interference of other signals and other factors. Gaussian noise in the noise is more prominent, can be removed. At present, the deep neural network combined with different algorithms has obtained satisfactory results [2]. Zvarevashe K proposed and developed a custom two-dimensional convolutional neural network, which can extract and classify speech features. This neural network was evaluated with deep multilayer perceptrons neural network and deep radial basis function neural network combined with Berlin Emotion Language Database and Ryerson audiovisual emotion database. The research shows that this algorithm can effectively extract the robustness and significance features of the data set [3].

Computer vision processing is the image, mainly to improve the image display effect and image identification, it has a very good application in many fields. Many application scenarios have been greatly improved by using computer vision technology. Deep neural network algorithm is conducive to the improvement of computer vision and pattern recognition.

2   Design and Exploration of Application Construction of Computer Vision and Pattern Recognition Technology on Account of Deep Neural Network

2.1   Deep Neural Network Algorithm

Artificial Neural Networks (ANNs), also referred to as Neural Networks (NNs) or Connection Model, is a kind of behavior characteristics of animal Neural Networks. Algorithm mathematical model for distributed parallel information processing [4, 5]. Depending on the complexity of the system, the network can process information by adjusting the relationship between a large number of internal nodes.

The neural network is improved at the neuron layer, which is mainly analyzed from the following points, as shown in Fig. 1:

Fig. 1. Neural networks extend the perceptron model

1. Add the hidden layer, so that the hidden layer has multiple layers and improves the level of the algorithm [6, 7].
2. There are many output items in the output layer. This algorithm can be used in the field of classification regression or machine learning, such as dimension processing or clustering processing.
3. The activation function can be improved. Now the activation function is sign(Z), which is simple to construct but limited in application. Other algorithms, such as Sigmoid function, can be adopted.

2.2 Application of Computer Vision and Pattern Recognition Technology on Account of Deep Neural Network

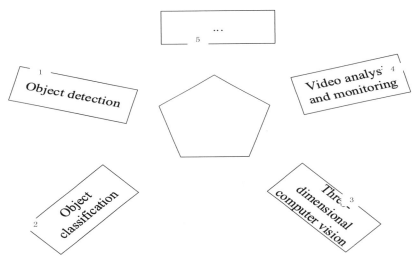

Fig. 2. Computer vision and pattern recognition research performance

Deep neural network algorithm is adopted to study computer vision and pattern recognition in the following aspects, as shown in Fig. 2:

(1) Object detection

Object detection algorithm adopts the method of interface window to detect objects, places objects of similar size inside the window, adjusts the relative position of the object and the window, and makes the object cut completely in the window, and then adopts the algorithm to extract features of the object [1, 8]. In this field of detection, there are often many problems, such as non-rigid deformation, which adopt the object detection method to achieve the result of object detection.

(2) Object classification

Object classification refers to judging objects in images and classifying them according to certain principles. Object classification is a very common problem in pattern recognition, which usually involves image search, scene identification, behavior judgment, etc. [9, 10]. The scene that this problem needs to be solved may encounter very complex classification problems. How to classify complex problems carefully and simplify them into small problems one by one is the important part of object classification. While predicting the behavior of objects is another important ability, if the behavior can be accurately predicted, then object classification will be solved quickly.

(3) THREE-DIMENSIONAL computer vision

Image 3D system is a very important tool for image processing, which includes camera coefficient, parameter point location reset, image point cloud model, etc. [11, 12]. Scene 3d vision usually extracts multiple features of the image. When the visual system processes the image, the first step is to acquire the object, the second is to extract the object features using the visual system, and the third is to correct the error of the acquired object features, so as to naturalize the features into a set. 3d computer vision usually uses nonlinear mathematical methods to optimize various parameters and coordinate objects and feature points.

(4) Video analysis and monitoring

Images often contain a lot of object points, among which the analysis and monitoring of object points is a very important work [13, 14]. Objects in static images are often in a relatively static state, so image analysis needs to be clear about what objects in the image are and what features the objects present. Video analysis often combines computer tools, machine learning, pattern recognition and other technologies to process video objects. With the help of these tools, the various behaviors, movements and trends of objects in the video are very clear.

3 Exploring the Application Effect of Computer Vision and Pattern Recognition Technology on Account of Deep Neural Network

The convolutional layer is the most important part of convolutional neural network, and feature extraction in images is completed by the convolutional layer [15, 16]. There are multiple convolution kernels in each convolution layer. Different features can be extracted by convolution operation between different convolution kernels and two-dimensional images. In addition, the activation function is introduced into the convolutional neural network to increase nonlinear factors, so as to facilitate the approximation of arbitrary functions by the convolutional neural network and enhance the feature expression energy of the network model. The convolution calculation and nonlinear transformation algorithm formula of convolution neural network is as follows:

$$Z^l = W^l \otimes Z^{l-1} \tag{1}$$

$$A^l = f(Z^l) \tag{2}$$

where, Z^{l-1} is the input of layer L, Z^l is the output after convolution of layer L, A^l represents the output after activation, and f is the activation function.

The activation function is:

$$Sigmoid(x) = \frac{1}{1 + e^x} \tag{3}$$

In convolutional neural network, the output layer is generally classified by Softmax function, so this layer is also called Softmax layer [17]. In the network training, Softmax layer normalizes the output value of the last full-connection layer and then evaluates the gap between the network prediction and the real target through the loss function, so as to adjust the network parameters in the iteration by back propagation, and finally optimize the network model to better handle the image classification task.

3.1 The Popularization and Application of Computer Vision Technology

(1) Applied in the field of visual navigation

Computer vision has made a lot of progress in many years of research, it has been applied to visual navigation, this technology is mainly used in space image recognition, space image processing and other fields; In later years, the technology was applied to missiles, transportation and many other industries. The application of computer vision has improved the accuracy of image processing, and greatly promoted the improvement of work efficiency, especially to solve the potential risk of danger.

(2) Applied in the field of human-computer interaction

Human-computer interaction (HCI) is a hot technology project, which mainly deals with the interaction between robots and workers. Its principle is that the robot through the vision of human body behavior, face shape changes to identify, so as to judge the intention of people, so that they can communicate with the staff, to complete the transaction together.

(3) Applied in the field of virtual reality

Computer vision is a very important means of high technology, which has great application value in virtual reality. Computer vision obtains the virtual scene and the real scene through its own object identification, and then makes an overall judgment of the scene, and finally assists people to complete some specific tasks.

(4) Applied in the field of satellite remote sensing

Satellite remote sensing is a geographical exploration technology. This technology mainly solves the search and identification of unknown objects that need to be detected, and excavates the potential resources among them, and finally serves people by obtaining the resources. Satellite weather forecast and disaster detection all need detection technology processing. Satellite remote sensing accelerates research and development results by collecting samples of these objects and combining them with analysis, which can effectively improve work efficiency.

4 Investigation and Research on Application of Computer Vision and Pattern Recognition Technology on Account of Deep Neural Network.

In order to verify and evaluate the effectiveness of the proposed deep neural network algorithm, it is performed on multiple datasets with random label noise. The random label noise set in the test, as the name implies, is that each sample in the data set changes independently and randomly to any category in the total category with probability P. In order to fully evaluate the algorithm, this paper selects two commonly used benchmark datasets, CAZ-10 and CAZ-100, which are widely used to evaluate the problem of tag noise. Among them, there is no verification set data in the two public data sets, so after obtaining the data set, 1000 image samples with correct labels are randomly selected from the training set as the verification set, and also as the metadata set required in the deep neural network algorithm.

In this paper, Linux is used as the interface system, flash storage mode is adopted, core dual-core processor is selected, and Matlab software is used for experimental processing. The test running data of the deep neural network algorithm is shown in Table 1.

Table 1. Evaluation index of experimental operation

DataSet	Result(%)	Iterations
CAZ-10	93.12	3
CAZ-100	92.34	5

Table 1 the results of deep neural network processing two data sets, CAZ-10 and CAZ-100, are respectively 93.12% and 92.34% higher than 90%, showing very good results. At the same time, the number of iterations is 3 or 4, which are all digits, and the effect is very good.

Figure 3 shows the number of iterations and processing efficiency of the deep neural network algorithm in processing the two data sets caz-10 and CAz-100. It can be seen that the number of iterations is in single digits and the efficiency is above 90%. It can be seen that the algorithm is very good.

The data test shows that the application of computer vision and pattern recognition technology on account of deep neural network has good performance in computer vision and pattern recognition.

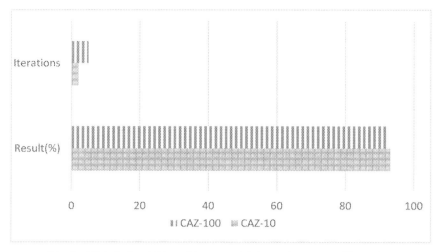

Fig. 3. Digital visual 3d teaching material dynamic resource illustration

5   Conclusions

In the continuous development of economy, computer vision is more and more valuable in the market, and its use is also very broad. In this paper, deep neural network algorithm is used to optimize the image capture mechanism of computer vision, improve the principle of image acquisition and analysis, so as to improve the technical level of computer vision and pattern recognition. The application of computer vision and pattern recognition technology on account of deep neural network effectively improves the performance of computer vision and pattern recognition.

References

1. Mohamed, E.M., Mohamed, M.H., Farghally, M.F.: A new cascade-correlation growing deep learning neural network algorithm. Algorithms 14(5), 158 (2021)
2. Almas, M.A., Sharma, V.K.: A novel algorithm for denoising image with deep neural network and spatial filters. Turk. J. Comput. Math. Educ. (TURCOMAT) 12(9), 1991–1996 (2021)
3. Zvarevashe, K., Olugbara, O.O.: Recognition of speech emotion using custom 2D-convolution neural network deep learning algorithm. Intell. Data Anal. 24(5), 1065–1086 (2020)
4. Aoa, B., Ys, A., Hz, A., et al.: Observer-based interval type-2 fuzzy PID controller for PEMFC air feeding system using novel hybrid neural network algorithm-differential evolution optimizer. Alex. Eng. J. 61(9), 7353–7375 (2022)
5. Mohammed, M.J., Mohammed, E.A., Jarjees, M.S.: Recognition of multifont English electronic prescribing on account of convolution neural network algorithm. Bio-Algorithms Med-Syst. 16(3), 182–190 (2020)
6. Skuratov, V., Kuzmin, K., Nelin, I., et al.: Creation of a neural network algorithm for automated collection and analysis of statistics of exchange quotes graphics. EUREKA Phys. Eng. 3(3), 22–29 (2020)

7. Asrianda, A., Aidilof, H., Pangestu, Y.: Machine learning for detection of palm oil leaf disease visually using convolutional neural network algorithm. J. Inf. Telecommun. Eng. **4**(2), 286–293 (2021)

8. Rajendran, B., Venkataraman, S.: Detection of malicious network traffic using enhanced neural network algorithm in Big Data. Int. J. Adv. Intell. Paradig. **19**(3), 370 (2021)

9. Alarcon, C., Shene, C.: Fermentation 4.0, a case study on computer vision, soft sensor, connectivity, and control applied to the fermentation of a Thraustochytrid. Comput. Ind. **128**, 103431–103431 (2021)

10. Méndez-Ortega, M.G., Herrera-Granda, E.P., Malte, A., et al.: Supervision and control of students during online assessments applying computer vision techniques: a systematic literature review. Univers. J. Educ. Res. **9**(5), 1000–1013 (2021)

11. Banfi, F., Mandelli, A.: Computer vision meets image processing and UAS PhotoGrammetric data integration: from HBIM to the eXtended reality project of arco della pace in milan and its decorative complexity. J. Imaging **7**(7), 118 (2021)

12. Noreen, K., Umar, M.: Computer vision syndrome (CVS) and its associated risk factors among undergraduate medical students in midst of COVID-19. Pakistan J. Ophthalmol. **37**(1), 102–108 (2021)

13. Kim, S.J., Kim, H.: Effect of online learning environment on subjective symptoms of computer vision syndrome(CVS) in the Era of COVID-19. Korean J. Vis. Sci. **23**(2), 159–169 (2021)

14. Harris, M.D., Luka, M., Markham, A.N.: Pattern recognition: using rocks, wind, water, anxiety, and doom scrolling in a slow apocalypse (to learn more about methods for changing the world). Qual. Inq. **27**(7), 914–927 (2021)

15. Tomita, S., Kurita, R.: Pattern-recognition-based identification of proteases and their complexes by a one-component array composed of a Dansyl-modified charged polymer. Sens. Mater. **33**(1), 233 (2021)

16. Shatilina, T.A., Tsitsiashvili, G.S., Radchenkova, T.V.: Application of interval approach to pattern recognition for identification of preceeding baric structures that determine extreme thermal modes in the South-Kuril area in summer. Izvestiya TINRO **201**(2), 470–483 (2021)

17. Setiawan, F.B., Kurnianingsih, F.A., Riyadi, S., et al.: Pattern Recognition untuk Deteksi Posisi pada AGV Berbasis Raspberry Pi. J. Nasional Teknik Elektro dan Teknol. Inf. (JNTETI) **10**(1), 49–56 (2021)

Design of 3D Image Visual Communication System Based on Computer Image Technology

Shuangxiao Gou[1] and Ling Mei[2(✉)]

[1] College of Fine Arts and Design, Chongqing University of Arts and Sciences,
Chongqing 402160, China
[2] Large Data Institute, Chongqing Water Resources and Electric Engineering College,
Chongqing 402160, China
1778564313@qq.com

Abstract. Computer imaging technology is a kind of use of digital photography, using a computer as a medium to realize interactive communication and interaction between humans and machines through the collection and processing of images and the editing and storage of graphic information. The purpose of this paper to study the design of the 3D image visual communication system based on computer image technology is to improve the mastery of 3D image technology and design the visual communication system. This article mainly uses experimental and comparative methods to analyze the feature extraction situation of the 3D image visual communication system, and finds that the error of the improved RANSAC algorithm in image feature extraction is about 54%, while the unimproved algorithm and other algorithms The error is greater. This shows that the improved algorithm proposed in this paper is incomparable in the 3D image visual communication system.

Keywords: Computer image technology · 3-dimensional image · Visual communication · System design

1 Introduction

In today's information society, people need to use a variety of advanced science and technology when accessing external things. Image processing and recognition is a computer-based human-computer interaction system. Analyze the data from the original state and extract the required information, then perform a series of operations, and finally output the obtained results to the user.

There are many theoretical results in the research on the design of the three-dimensional image visual transmission system of computer image technology. For example, A ndo Y, Fuse Y said that the effective combination of image processing technology and visual communication system can achieve good design effects [1]. Panda D K, Meher S takes improving the accuracy of traffic sign image recognition as the main goal, and proposes an intelligent traffic sign image recognition method [2]. Lochhead IM, Hedley N said that with the passage of time, people's requirements for entertainment and aesthetics have become higher and higher. Visual communication is technically supported

N. Khare et al. (Eds.): MIND 2022, CCIS 1763, pp. 170–177, 2022.
https://doi.org/10.1007/978-3-031-24367-7_17

by modern science and technology to reflect the internal and external manifestations of things represented [3]. Therefore, this article intends to study the design of the 3D image visual communication system from the perspective of computer technology. This is a new round of research with a certain theoretical support.

This article first studies the classification of 3D modeling methods. Secondly, the feature-based image matching algorithm is analyzed and described. Then I studied the combination of photographic pictures and visual communication design. Afterwards, the overall design of the medical image 3D visualization system is carried out. Finally, the system designed in this paper is tested whether it meets the requirements through experiments, and the relevant data results are obtained.

2 Design of 3D Image Visual Communication System Based on Computer Image Technology

2.1 Classification of 3D Modeling Methods

Computer vision, computer graphics, image processing and virtual reality are the main research directions of 3D image modeling. The image-based modeling and rendering process uses a set of digitized images to create a virtual reality model. Due to the use of photos of real scenes, the drawn virtual scenes have a strong sense of immersion [4, 5].

Typical reconstruction methods based on 3D images generally include: image acquisition, camera calibration, image matching, 3D reconstruction and other steps.

Image acquisition is a prerequisite for image processing and computer vision. The calibration of camera parameters is used to determine the corresponding relationship between the camera position, attributes and its image points on the image plane. Feature extraction is the premise of stereo matching. When calculating stereo vision, the correspondence between the corresponding parts of two or more images is very important. After knowing the camera image model and the appropriate relationship, 3D reconstruction is relatively easy [6, 7].

2.2 Feature-Based Image Matching Algorithm

(1) Image feature extraction based on SURF algorithm

The SURF algorithm uses an approximate method based on the Hesse matrix in the identification of feature points, and the identification of feature points is based on the scale space theory. Calculate the integral graph first, which can speed up the calculation of all rectangle operations [8, 9]. For image A and point (m, n), the integral image A_c is the sum of the brightness values of all points in the range from the origin to this point.

$$A_c(\mathrm{m}, n) = \sum_{\mathrm{a}=0}^{\mathrm{a}\leq\mathrm{m}} \sum_{\mathrm{k}=0}^{a\leq n} \mathrm{A}(\mathrm{m}, n) \tag{1}$$

Therefore, for the calculation of the sum of the brightness of any rectangular area, the corresponding four vertices on A_c can be directly used. This calculation time does not change with the size of the image, so it can get a very fast speed when calculating large-area convolution calculations [10, 11].

(2) Feature point matching based on RANSAC algorithm

Feature-based image matching is used to solve the transformation matrix between feature matching images and find the feature points that match the two feature matching images. At present, the widely used RANSAC algorithm filters out these initial matching points and eliminates the poorly matched points [12].

The RANSAC algorithm requires that under a certain confidence probability P, at least one set of data in the N sets of samples are all interior points, and N is obtained by the following formula:

$$M = \frac{\log(1 - Q)}{\log(1 - (1 - \omega)^a)} \tag{2}$$

Among them, ω is the proportion of external points, and a is the minimum amount of data required to calculate model parameters.

(3) Improved RANSAC algorithm

The calculation range of RANSAC is determined by two factors: one is that the proportion of incorrect data samples determines the need for more random sampling periods to ensure confidence in the optimal results, and the other is whether each parameter of the hypothesis model and the sample data verification process conform to. In this process, the failure model parameters required by a large amount of failure model data also go through this verification process. Although these model parameters are only a small part of the data, they greatly increase unnecessary calculations. The steps to improve the R-RANSAC algorithm using location information constraints are as follows:

1) Randomly select 4 pairs of characteristic points to solve the homography matrix to see if there are 3 collinearities, and if there are collinearities, select the points again.
2) Use the boundary conditions of the location information to test the 4 pairs of feature points. If the constraints are met, the current hypothetical model is calculated; if the conditions are not met, then return to step (1).
3) Randomly select 10 sets of feature points to pre-test the hypothesis, namely
4) For each hypothetical feature point pair, it is used to calculate the symmetric transformation error and calculate the number of points within the error.
5) Find the standard deviation of the symmetric transformation error of the interior points obtained in the last step of the loop.
6) If M > M_inlier or M = M_inlier and cur_std < min_std, the model is assumed to be the best model currently, and the inlier is saved.

2.3 The Combination of Photographic Pictures and Visual Communication Design

Photographic images have become an element of communication in the entertainment, information, and advertising industries. Designers, including business owners, believe that it can easily attract people's attention. The term "reporter" not only informs the print media of this change. What's more noteworthy is that when designers and owners communicate their products, these design directors abandon traditional narrative methods and rely solely on photography to reach a wider audience. Photography plays a particularly important role in the execution of these elements. This conceptual transition is so smooth that photography has been seamlessly integrated into the visual communication design.

The illustrations, graphics, magazines and advertisements in photography have created a visual culture for modern people. In order to maintain its status or value in all respects, these foundations must be transferred to interests. Whether this behavior is to increase subscriptions or to convey information, attractive images and designs reveal their uniqueness. Ultimately, narrative skills, whether it is illustrations or photos, play an important role.

The use of photographic images in visual communication design is as follows: The goal of modern visual communication design is to use mechanized printing for mass production. People's demand for publications, magazines, posters, etc. is very high. The improvement of printing presses is inevitable, and the number of printings is gradually increasing.

2.4   Overall Design of Medical Imaging 3D Visualization System

The 3D medical image visualization system is a complex system. In the actual application environment, the basic function that the medical image three-dimensional visualization system must perform is: acquiring and storing image data from medical imaging equipment such as computed tomography or MRI. Allow doctors to manage patient information and images perfectly; store visual reconstruction of 3-D model image data to perform 3D model rotation, scaling, cutting and surgical windowing operations. Finally, a complete diagnostic report is generated.

According to the actual requirements of the hospital, a complete 3D medical visualization system should include image acquisition, database management, online storage, offline archiving, display and processing.

(1)   Medical imaging 3D visualization system generally has the following functions:

   1)   The images generated by the existing medical imaging equipment in the hospital are directly or indirectly converted into a digital form that the system can store and process.
   2)   The storage and management of the image data generated by the inspection is a very important function of the medical 3D visualization system.
   3)   Viewing and processing images are the most commonly used functions for doctors. Medical 3D image viewing system software must be able to perform the most commonly used functions of doctors, including retrieving patient information or image data sets from a database, and visually reconstructing stored image data.

(2) According to the above requirements, the system can be divided into the following modules:

The network subsystem is responsible for information interfaces such as image acquisition and device network communication. The memory management subsystem is responsible for patient information and image database, model management, diagnosis report management, statistical information management, reports, etc. The image display subsystem is mainly responsible for image display and reconstruction, image analysis and processing, etc.

3   System Implementation

3.1   System Development Environment

This system develops the system interface based on the MFC basic class library in the VS2018 integrated environment, and selects the OpenCV development kit, OpenGL graphics package and Matlab as auxiliary development tools to shorten the development cycle.

3.2   System Functional Structure Design

According to the previous design and algorithm research of the 3D model retrieval system based on 2D images, the system can be divided into the following four main interfaces. The functional structure of the system is shown in Fig. 1:

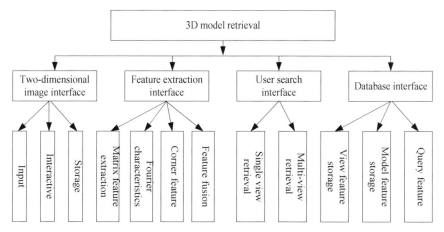

Fig. 1. System function structure

    Two-dimensional graphical interface. In this part, the user selects the input two-dimensional image data, and then selects the target area of interest in the image through simple interaction. Once the region is selected, the foreground target image is extracted through the image segmentation algorithm in this document.

Feature extraction interface. After receiving the foreground target image, the image can be preprocessed (filtering and denoising, binarization, normalization, etc.) to obtain conditions for extracting suitable features. The feature extraction interface mainly includes the three feature extraction algorithms and feature merging algorithms mentioned above.

User recovery interface. Since a single image may not be able to reflect the attributes of things well, this article uses two user recovery methods for recovery, namely single-view recovery and multi-view recovery. By comparing the similarity of the feature vectors, the comparison results are finally sorted and output according to the similarity.

Database interface. This part mainly stores the feature vector of the 3D model library and the associated data of the input 2D view.

3.3 System Test

In order to test the effect of the improved RANSAC algorithm based on location information constraints, the actual effect of the improved RANSAC algorithm is verified by the robust estimation of the homography matrix. The overall method includes obtaining a clean set of corresponding points obtained after the initial corresponding points and the coordinates of the points and the filtering algorithm of the provided real homography matrix.

4   Analysis of System Test Results

4.1   Feature Matching Comparison Before and After Using the RANSAC Algorithm

(1) refers to the number of matched pairs, and (2) refers to the average error. IMFPP is the initial matching feature point pair, and IRANSAC is the improved RANSAC algorithm. Two sets of images of Graf and Boat are used to verify the improved RANSAC algorithm (in Table 1).

Table 1. Characteristic matching contrast before and after using the RANSAC algorithm

	Graf	Boat
IMFPP(1)	451	714
IMFPP(2)	1.7856	1.5213
RANSAC(1)	135	289
RANSAC(2)	0.5901	0.5831
IRANSAC(1)	142	261
IRANSAC(2)	0.5746	0.5419

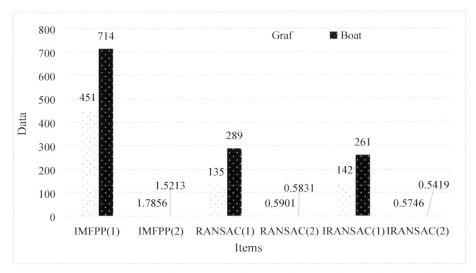

Fig. 2. Characteristic matching contrast before and after using the RANSAC algorithm

As shown in Fig. 2, we can see that with the improvement of the algorithm, the matching logarithm becomes smaller and the average error is also decreasing. Moreover, the feature matching error of graf is greater than that of boat. This shows that the accuracy of feature extraction for still images is higher, and the improved algorithm has a stronger matching ability.

5   Conclusion

The three-dimensional image transmission system is a brand-new tool with strong practicability, relatively low operation difficulty, and very practical significance and application value. As a new computer graphics image processing and analysis system, 3D imaging technology has a very wide range of applications in the field of modern science and technology. It uses a two-dimensional space as a unit and uses information technology such as digitization and informatization to observe objects in all directions and extract useful information. The RANSAC algorithm is improved using pre-check and location information constraints to obtain accurate matching points between images, and the improved algorithm is verified through experiments.

References

1. Ando, Y., Fuse, Y., Yamamoto, T.: An intraoperative three-dimensional imaging system for better image sharing and protection of reconstructive surgeons' neck. Plast. Reconstr. Surg. **142**(5), 811e–812e (2018)
2. Panda, D.K., Meher, S.: A new Wronskian change detection model based codebook background subtraction for visual surveillance applications. J. Vis. Commun. Image Represent. **56**, 52–72 (2018)

3. Lochhead, I.M., Hedley, N.: Modeling evacuation in institutional space: linking three-dimensional data capture, simulation, analysis, and visualization workflows for risk assessment and communication. Inf. Vis. **18**(1), 173–192 (2019)

4. Tsuchiya, K.: Image processor, image processing method, image processing program, and image processing system. And Then Becomes A Constant Value after Time, vol. 1, no. 1, pp. 65–70 (2018)

5. Kaashki, N.N., Safabakhsh, R.: RGB-D face recognition under various conditions via 3D constrained local model. J. Vis. Commun. Image Represent. **52**, 6–85 (2018)

6. Pages, R., Amplianitis, K., Monaghan, D., et al.: Affordable content creation for free-viewpoint video and VR/AR applications. J. Vis. Commun. Image Represent. **53**, 192–201 (2018)

7. Rabbouch, H., Saadaoui, F.: A wavelet-assisted subband denoising for tomographic image reconstruction. J. Vis. Commun. Image Represent. **55**, 115–130 (2018)

8. Oszust, M.: No-reference image quality assessment with local features and high-order derivatives. J. Vis. Commun. Image Represent. **56**, 15–26 (2018)

9. Rana, S.P., Dey, M., Siarry, P.: Boosting content based image retrieval performance through integration of parametric & nonparametric approaches. J. Vis. Commun. Image Represent. **58**, 205–219 (2018)

10. Reibman, A.R., Bai, C.: Image quality assessment in first-person videos. J. Vis. Commun. Image Represent. **54**, 123–132 (2018)

11. Rao, P.S., Yedukondalu, K.: Hardware implementation of digital image skeletonization algorithm using FPGA for computer vision applications. J. Vis. Commun. Image Represent. **59**, 140–149 (2019)

12. Kim, D.H., Han, T.Y., Lee, S.H., et al.: Infrared image super-resolution using auxiliary convolutional neural network and visible image under low-light conditions. J. Vis. Commun. Image Represent. **51**, 191–200 (2018)

Optimization Algorithm of Integrating Folk Art into VR Vision Under Deep Learning

Ren Li[✉]

Academy of Art and Design, Shaoyang University, Shaoyang, Hunan, China
lr465823778@163.com

Abstract. With the vigorous development of social economy and science and technology, the protection and inheritance of folk art are facing great challenges. Folk art has a long history. In the context of in-depth learning, the protection and development of folk art has also reached a new level. Using advanced and new technology to serve folk art is one of the effective ways to revitalize and develop folk art. This paper analyzes the virtual reality technology, and puts forward to inherit and protect the folk art by using the visual direction optimization method in the virtual reality technology and its characteristics of perception, existence and interactive operation.

Keywords: Deep learning · Folk art · VR vision

1 Introduction

Chinese folk art has a long history of civilization and is the matrix of all cultures and arts. It was born due to the formation of human civilization and condensed the folk customs of human generations. The cultural emotion contained in it is based on the actual survival needs of the people. It is not only created by the people according to the actual survival needs, but also widely used by the people. However, at this stage, due to the continuous progress of human society and the further development of industrialization, the folk art form characterized by traditional agricultural civilization has become increasingly lack of social soil for survival.

2 Overview of Deep Learning

Neural network in learning is a key technology of artificial intelligence developed by imitating the correlation between neural networks of the brain. The neural network in the brain is a very complex network organization, and a large number of signals are often transmitted between neurons [1].

Learning regards each neuron node in the network system as a single weight parameter, and a large number of neuron nodes constitute a rich number of weight parameter network systems. Training these systems and optimizing the parameters of each neuron is the key step of in-depth study and research of the system. A very basic neural network

N. Khare et al. (Eds.): MIND 2022, CCIS 1763, pp. 178–185, 2022.
https://doi.org/10.1007/978-3-031-24367-7_18

structure can be roughly divided into three layers: input layer, hidden layer and data layer. The input layer describes all the information that needs to be provided. The data layer may be graphics, data, or other processed information. The hidden layer is usually connected with the input layer, and all neurons in the input layer can transmit the input signal to the hidden layer.

Therefore, the hidden layer usually includes a multi-layer neural network, and there are the most complex types of neurons in this layer. In the final training, an output layer is usually connected, and the data of the output layer here is provided by the front hidden layer in order to transfer the data from the final training. The basic structure of the neural network is shown in Fig. 1. The number of layers of the hidden layer can be multiple network structures. There are links between each neuron in the network and between layers. These links are called full links [2].

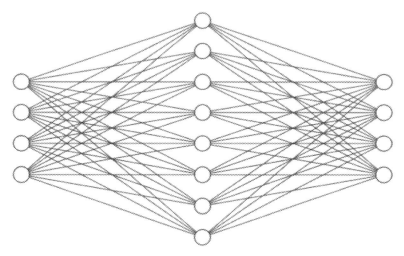

Fig. 1. Structure of neural network

Each layer of the learning network is connected by a group of neurons, and each neuron includes some weight parameters. In the whole training, the parameters are continuously transmitted to the deep layer, and finally reach the output layer [3]. For the lower layer network connected by this layer, the parameters of the first neuron will be displayed as:

$$a0(i + 1) = g(w0a0(i) + w1a1(i) + ... + wnan(i) + bias0(i + 1)) \qquad (1)$$

3   VR Optimization Algorithm Based on Visual Effect Improvement

In order to improve the operation effect of virtual reality human-computer interaction interface, human visual attention mechanism is integrated into virtual reality human-computer interaction interface, and an optimization mode of virtual environment human-computer interaction interface based on human visual attention mechanism is provided.

Based on the mechanism of human visual attention, by selecting three main influencing factors: the color, distance and visual attention level of human-computer interaction components, a function model aiming at meeting the highest visual attention of users is constructed. The eye movement test is carried out for the optimized interface, and the results prove the feasibility of this mode. Therefore, the optimized human-computer interaction interface meets the visual attention mechanism [4, 5].

3.1 Optimization of 3D Geometric Model

At present, there are mainly two ways to express 3D geometric models: face representation and volume representation. Both have their own advantages and disadvantages. Although volume representation can fully express the surface properties and internal attributes of objects, it has a large space, so the computational cost is also high. The surface representation only represents the surface properties of the model, but occupies much less space than the volume representation, so it has become a more common representation of 3D geometric model at this stage [6]. In the face representation, the triangular mesh representation in computer graphics is the most common representation, which can directly represent most complex mesh models. Therefore, this paper mainly selects triangular mesh as the research content to carry out model representation design and optimization [7]. Taking the triangular mesh model as an example, the representation diagram of the mesh model is shown in Fig. 2. Where: V1, V2 and V6 represent each topological vertex and contain spatial position signals; F1, F2 and F6 represent the number of the triangle, which is composed of three vertices of the triangle.

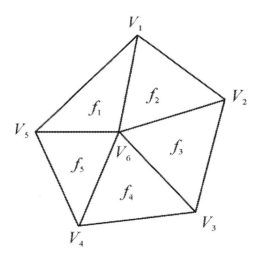

Fig. 2. Schematic diagram of grid model

Let any two vertices (P1, P2) in the triangular model satisfy any of the following conditions: (P1, P2) is the same edge; P 1, P2 < T, T represents a certain threshold, then (P1, P2) is a correct edge. The error measurement calculation from a vertex Q on the 3D model to the adjacent plane of a correct edge (PI, PJ) is shown in the following Fig. 2:

$$\Delta(q) = 1 \in (i, j)(ltq) \tag{2}$$

3.2   Optimization of Scene Hierarchical Model Selection

Generally, the appropriate level of detail modeling LOD is selected for the scene area center according to the distance d from the viewpoint to the scene area center. However, if we only transfer one level of detail to another level of detail according to the value of the center distance D, it is easy to cause significant changes in the grid mode of the geometric scene, and even a very strong jitter phenomenon, which will greatly weaken the experience of the whole system and users, and in many cases, it will even lead to the physical body of users such as "dizziness" and "vomiting", which does not adapt to the current situation [8, 9]. This paper does not use the simplified level of detail modeling, but introduces similar calculation results, which gives play to the depiction power of the core image in the graphics card GPU, and then improves the operation speed. Height difference μ I projection value on the display ε I represents, as shown in Fig. 3.

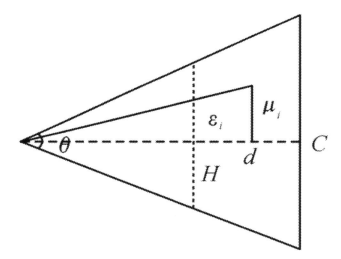

Fig. 3. Shadow of height difference on the screen

4   The Demand of Integrating Folk Art into VR Vision

No matter how widely the application scope of virtual reality is, it will always be an image of the real world. Only by giving full play to and with the help of the rich and colorful human art forms, thoughts and emotions in the real world, the virtual world will become more and more artistic and emotional. Works expressing folk art in the virtual world can not only enrich the artistry and emotion of the virtual world, but also VR technology has the characteristics of perception, presence and interaction. Using these characteristics and technologies, we can better inherit folk art [10].

4.1   Enhance the Perception of Folk Art

The so-called multiple perception refers to that in addition to the visual perception generated by general computer technology, there are also hearing perception, force perception, touch perception, movement perception, and even taste perception, smell perception and so on. The perfect virtual reality technology must have the sensory functions of all people. At this stage, due to the continuous progress of China's urbanization, the traditional building materials unique to the original agricultural conditions in many places may begin to be few or never found again, and the lack of building materials also makes some traditional folk art works gradually extinct. Virtual reality technology can overcome this defect. At present, virtual reality technology divides its cognitive functions into vision, hearing, force perception, touch, movement and so on [11]. These multi sensibilities can not only let human beings directly see the art works made of special materials, but also touch the tactile feeling it conveys and listen to the sound it makes, so that they can see the art works comprehensively and stereoscopically from different perspectives. In the virtual real world, such works of art are often not restricted by materials [12].

4.2   Enhance the Immersive Experience of Visitors

Immersion is also known as immersion, that is, the degree of fidelity that users feel as protagonists in illusory situations. The perfect virtual environment can make people completely unable to distinguish between true and false, and make people devote themselves to the three-dimensional virtual situation made by the computer. Everything in the situation looks true, reads true, moves true, and even all the feelings that smell and taste are true, just like all the feelings of people in the real world. Many forms of folk art rely on various blood relatives and oral and experiential inheritance methods, which are the result of people passing on from generation to generation. These unique traditional methods make some unique skills die out due to the death of old artists, which is not only the death of memory, but also the death of culture [13]. However, similar tragedies can also be prevented by means of virtual reality. The telepresence produced by virtual reality can not only enhance the expressiveness of folk art, but also enable us to participate in an artistic work, understand and master its workflow. Through the special effects of video and audio, the virtual world becomes more real. The use of virtual reality technology can not only break through the disadvantages of traditional blood transmission, but also broaden the scope of application of oral transmission. At the same time, it is not constrained by time and space, so that more people can join it. This not only contributes to the preservation of folk art, but also promotes the development of folk art [14].

4.3   Enhance the Interaction Between Works and People

Interactivity refers to the usability of the objects in the simulated environment and the natural degree of the viewer's response to the surrounding environment. Therefore, the audience can directly capture the virtual objects in the simulated environment with their fingers.

At this time, because the fingers have the feeling of grasping the objects and can also perceive the weight of the objects, the objects captured in the line of sight can immediately move with the movement of the fingers. It is such an interactivity that enables the audience to personally practice in the illusory real world and complete an art work by hand. For example, the viewer can pick up a pair of scissors to hinge and cut a beautiful window flower in the virtual world, or take out an embroidery needle to embroider a beautiful pattern in the virtual world. At the same time, many folk art works are difficult to preserve for a long time due to the constraints of materials. However, there is no such limitation in the virtual world. Viewers can create all kinds of art works without the constraints of time and place, and such art works can be preserved for a long time [15].

For traditional tasks, the objectives of image quality assessment can be divided into two categories, one is degenerative loss, and the other is the main purpose of the image evaluation task is to identify the image caused by the operation of saving, transmitting, decompressing, etc. The prime level loss generally includes fixed loss types such as fuzzy and white noise.

The characteristics of such losses are local or global the pixel level distortion is not reflected in the picture structure and content structure. Only when the noise is large to a certain extent only then will the content structure of the image be destroyed. The second type is generalized loss, which has no fixed class all factors that hinder people from obtaining information from images can be listed as the loss of generalization of images, such as too bright and too Dark, blurring caused by camera and other equipment shake, etc. illustrates these two different types of image loss. Although the target images of these two types of assessments are different inapplicable scenarios, they have one thing in common, that is, the content is often natural scenes from the real world.

For the generated images based on deep learning, it is generated by the computer according to some features and constraints are usually obtained by upsampling and other operations. Such images often appear in content and structureIt is very different from the natural scene in reality. Therefore, the methods used for traditional image quality assessment are directly migrated in the generated image quality assessment, there are likely to be problems such as insufficient generalization and different results from human subjective perception, How to design a special image quality evaluation algorithm based on the characteristics of the generated image is a major challenge.

These pictures can be easily obtained from the real world, so we only need to select one If the common features of these pictures can be well counted by the two methods, then all other pictures without such features Can be considered as "distortion", and the degree of this distortion varies with the statistical characteristics of the picture and the common characteristics of the natural scene As the gap between them increases. This idea can be applied to the task of image quality assessment. As shown in Fig. 4.

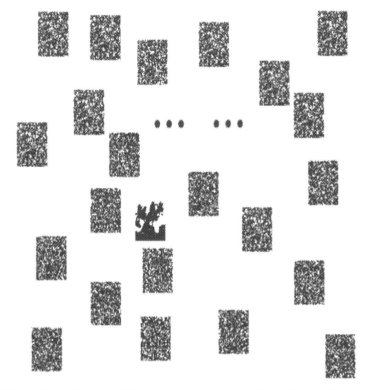

Fig. 4. Scale diagram of pictures and noise maps in line with natural scenes

5 Conclusion

Integrate traditional folk art and educational VR, so that the audience can understand the traditional folk culture and its value connotation in fun. Therefore, from the perspective of organically combining China's folk traditional culture and VR, this paper puts forward the idea of starting with the sense of experience, and then taking the folk as the background, so that the audience can understand the folk with the pace of science and technology. Nowadays, the development of VR technology has become more and more perfect. With the help of new technology characteristics such as "high speed", "low delay" and "large capacity", it will bring new opportunities for the development of VR technology combined with folk art.

References

1. Schmidhuber, J.: Deep learning in neural networks: an overview. Neural Netw. **61**, 85–117 (2015)
2. Albukhanajer, W.A., Jin, Y., Briffa, J.A.: Classifier ensembles for image identification using multi-objective Pareto features. Neurocomputing **238**, 316–327 (2017)

3. Bahdanau, D., Cho, K., Bengio, Y.: Neural machine translation by jointly learning to align and translate. Comput. Sci. (2014)
4. Garland, M., Heckbert, P.S.: Surface simplication using quadric error metrics. Comput. Graph. **31**(3), 209–216 (1997)
5. Hoppe, H.: Progressive meshes. Comput. Graph. **30**(1), 99–108 (1996)
6. Corke, P.: Image feature extraction. In: Corke, P. (ed.) Robotics, Vision and Control. Springer Tracts in Advanced Robotics, vol. 73, pp. 335–379. Springer, Heidelberg (2011). https://doi.org/10.1007/978-3-642-20144-8_13
7. Bharati, M.H., Liu, J.J., Macgregor, J.F.: Image texture analysis: methods and comparisons. Chemom. Intell. Lab. Syst. **72**(1), 57–71 (2004)
8. Sarkar, N., ChaudhuriB, B.: An efficient differential box-counting approach to compute fractal dimension of image. IEEE Trans. Syst. Man Cybern. **24**(1), 115–120 (1994)
9. Mallat, S.G.: A theory for multiresolution signal decomposition the wavelet representation. IEEE Trans. Pattern Anal. Mach. Intell. **11**(7), 674–693 (1989)
10. Ojala, T., Pietikäinen, M., Mäenpää, T.: Multiresolution gray-scale and rotation invariant texture classification with local binary patterns. IEEE Trans. Pattern Anal. Mach. Intell. **24**(7), 971–987 (2002)
11. Gatys, L.A., Ecker, A.S., Bethge, M.A.: Neural algorithm of artistic style. arXiv preprint arXiv:1508.06576 (2015)
12. Gatys, L.A., Ecker, A.S., Bethge, M.: Texture synthesis using convolutional neural networks. In: International Conference on Neural Information Processing Systems (2015)
13. Gatys, L.A., Ecker, A.S., Bethge, M.: Image style transfer using convolutional neural networks. Comput. Vis. Pattern Recognit. (2016)
14. Johnson, J., Alahi, A., Fei-Fei, L.: Perceptual losses for real-time style transfer and super-resolution (2016)
15. Al-Saffar, A.A.M., Tao, H., Talab, M.A.: Review of deep convolution neural network in image classification. In: 2017 International Conference on Radar, Antenna, Microwave, Electronics, and Telecommunications (ICRAMET). IEEE (2018)

Design of Calisthenics Choreography and Recording System Based on Action Recognition Algorithm

Yigang Mao[✉]

Physical Education College of Bohai University, Jinzhou 121000, Liaoning, China
jzzhuyingwei@163.com

Abstract. Traditional algorithms of human action recognition and also have many other technical problems, for example, there are traditional human motion image acquisition processing equipment susceptible by some outside factors such as light intensity, the impact of human motion features of the function is not entirely clear, human motion feature recognition susceptible factors affected by physical deformation and so on many problems. Gymnastics complete is a to skill dominant class difficult art XiangQun constitute a comprehensive program, the combination of the contents and forms of the complete set of movements in the choreography is also directly determines the effect of aerobics game the complete set of movements in the form of combination ultimately achieve successes, athletes personal and professional coaches team in strive to produce each set of unique design of novel and practical aerobics movements, drawn to the view The eyeballs of the judges and the high attention of the expert judges. As we all know, the beauty of content and layout method of complete sets of aerobics movement fluent and novel and unique competitors such as the ability of independent action choreography, a complete set of quality is the core of competitive game is directly determined how many key, in this paper, in order to grasp the latest international development trend of new aerobics competition, arrangement of the latest development practices systematically sorting rules and international competition, After careful study and study summary, the main changes in the content of the complete set of aerobics movements of the current national aerobics athletes are systematically summarized, summarized and strengthened to learn, to improve the basic sports theoretical knowledge of the content and rules of the complete set of movements of competitive aerobics and gymnastics. In view of the above problems, this paper tries to study the human motion recognition algorithm from the three aspects of action data information collection, feature recognition extraction and action classification feature recognition, in order to reduce the influence of the above problems. Therefore, in this paper, Kinect is selected to extract human skeleton data to overcome the problem of illumination, CNN is selected to automatically extract advanced human movement features, SoftMax is selected to complete multi-classification tasks, and on this basis, the calisthenics programming system is developed.

Keywords: Movement recognition · Aerobics movement choreography · Intelligent algorithm · Recording system design

1 Introduction

The research of human motion recognition is of great significance. A famous scholar pointed out that 55% of information transmission among human beings is completed by means of action or expression, 38% by means of tone or speed, and only 7% by means of language [1, 2]. At present, artificial intelligence is becoming more and more popular. In order to enter an increasingly intelligent society and complete the perfect interaction between humans and machines, in-depth research on human motion recognition is indispensable [3, 4]. China's aerobics rules should have a certain range of new changes in each Olympic cycle in the future. First of all, in terms of difficulty, the score of the difficult movements is more and more high, and many more difficult movements have been added, and some movements have been eliminated [5, 6]. In art, the comprehensive scoring standards of art will become more clear and detailed and scientific, each professional art discipline points deduction points will also be in the professional scoring rules system to get more detailed and specific refinement of the division; In terms of the completion of action and the difficulty, the details of all aspects of the action and points requirements are more stringent, action consistency and standards of minus one points of action points will also become will require more strict, the two authors also offers up some of their own about aerobics collective project action and scheduling rules on some improvements and Suggestions Can also be used to supply the rest of us can learn from, do these rules change main purpose is to hope to be able to make this traditional sports gymnastics project also will become more specification more perfect, make our country gymnastics in categories of team will present a set of the gymnastics movements have become rich will be more wonderful, aerobics to complete the traditional gymnastics Sports events will also become more and more demanding, and the forms of the development of sets will become more diversified [7, 8].

Due to its promising development prospects, pedestrian motion recognition has attracted extensive attention from scholars and researchers at home and abroad. In order to combine pedestrian movement recognition with other fields and promote the continuous development of intelligent life, the government, enterprises and universities have invested a lot of human and financial resources in the research of this subject and put forward various relevant algorithms and schemes [9, 10]. Early pedestrian motion recognition methods basically use traditional manual features, and then obtain feature vectors after a series of correlation processing, and finally send them into various classifiers for learning and training [11, 12]. These traditional manual features can not fully express the spatio-temporal information, and it is difficult to analyze and identify more complex action sequences. With the continuous development of research on advanced technologies and methods such as human machine learning system and computer artificial intelligence analysis, deep learning has been widely and deeply applied to the detection and classification tasks of image and video data and achieved great success [6, 7]. After seeing these algorithms, many scholars also applied deep learning to the research of pedestrian motion recognition. The following introduces the domestic and foreign research status of pedestrian motion recognition based on RGB video and bone sequence respectively.

Competition organization rule system has been playing an important role in strengthening restricting factors and effectively promoting the standardization and scientific level of organizational competition behavior. Each new version of the gymnastics competition rules guiding the direction of the small change, will indirectly influence on complete and action choreography relates to match some bias, coaches at all levels should be their first aerobics competition rules to research thoroughly, to consider in this talk about action choreographer, on top of any athletic sports events must have its own rules, aerobics in the project system in our country, rules orientation and choreography to game is absolutely inseparable is broken, so today we're going to focus on orientation arranged down to talk about the rules of competition, and more to take advantage of today's information age, the gesture recognition algorithm reference into aerobics action choreographer, calisthenics movements become more intelligent.

2 Discussion on the Design of Calisthenics Choreography and Recording System Based on Action Recognition Algorithm

2.1 Overview of Motion Recognition

The intelligent identification and analysis of human motion information testing refers to a kind of means with machine technology device (computer, robot, etc.) to establish real-time accurate sensors from computer and get to any group of human motion data for centralized storage to real-time intelligent identification and analysis and inspection right reflects the current human system is in some sort of desired Yao's technical movement state of a work process, it involves can be a lot of application and some related knowledge background information and technology, such as computer vision technology, machine brain action learning and analysis of detection technology, pattern recognition, artificial intelligence technology and so on, many researchers have devoted to explore of human action recognition, for many years, they collect human movement data from different equipment, extract advanced features of human movement from different angles, and verify the feasibility of human movement recognition in different scenes by using different action recognition methods. Therefore, human motion recognition can be divided into three processes: data collection, feature extraction and action recognition. Data acquisition is the basis of human motion recognition and the selection of appropriate data acquisition means is an important guarantee for accurate human motion recognition. At present, common data collection methods mainly include the following.

(1) Surveillance video

Surveillance video is the most intuitive reflection of human movements, but it is also most vulnerable to the influence of light intensity, occlusion and other external factors. At present, surveillance video is the main data collection method to study human movements.

(2) Kinect

The depth image and bone data collected by Kinect can overcome the influence of external factors such as light intensity, but the deficiency is that the bone data of multiple people (more than 6 people) cannot be obtained, and the collection range is limited, leading to the limitation of applicable scenarios.

(3) Wearable devices

The sensor data such as acceleration collected by wearable devices can only reflect human movements indirectly, so it is difficult to accurately identify complex human movements.

2.2 Problems Encountered in the Recording of Calisthenics Movements

Rules are the basic rules for coaches and athletes to train and create whole sets. Through the study of the group events of the 14th and 15th world aerobics Championships, this paper explores the characteristics of the content arrangement of complete sets of movements under the rules of competitive aerobics, which is the key point of the research of aerobics movement arrangement and record system. The rules of the competition are more and more detailed and strict. In the process of continuous development and improvement, all the contents, whether difficulty or operation, are in order to get a more beautiful performance, higher difficulty and more innovative performance. It is difficult to find out the contents of the complete set of calisthenics movements of the top 20 or 8 athletes in the 14th and 15th world calisthenics championships and the characteristics of their movements.

3 Experiment

3.1 The System Design

Based on previous research results, CNN is built and optimized on the basis of Caffe framework, Kinect2.0 is used as real-time data acquisition equipment, and C++ language is used as the link to realize a real-time human motion detection system combining human motion acquisition and human motion recognition.

3.2 Caffe is Introduced

The full English name of Caffe is Convolutional Architecture for Fast Feature Embedding. Caffe is a clear, simple, efficient and practical deep machine learning system framework. The core language is C++, which ensures seamless switching between CPU processor and graphics engine GPU processor. Caffe's four components are a container (Blob), a Layer (Layer), a Network (Net) and a solver (Slover). The deep network is a composite model, naturally represented as a collection of interconnection layers that process blocks of data. Caffe defines a network layer by layer in her model pattern. Slover is used to define the optimization of the model. It includes selecting the training scheme and testing scheme of the model, adjusting the number of iterations of the model training and testing, periodically testing and evaluating the model, and periodically recording the training and testing results. The most important of these is the development of training and testing protocols. Model of optimization is the key to minimize losses, D for a data set, the optimization goal is to make the whole data set all ‖ D average loss minimization, average loss is defined as:

$$L(w) = \frac{1}{|D|} \sum_i^{|D|} f_w(X^{(i)}) + \lambda r(w) \quad (1)$$

where () is the loss function of the instance of data (), and rW is a regularization term with a weight of. D may be very large, so in practice, each training iteration uses the random approximation of this goal to plot the average loss of small batches of N

$$L(W) = \frac{1}{N} \sum_i^{N} f_w(X^{(i)}) + \lambda r(w) \quad (2)$$

The model calculates the loss fw in forward propagation and the loss gradient FW' in back propagation. Update of model parameters depends on error gradient FW' and regularization gradient rW'. Model optimization algorithms such as stochastic gradient descent, Adaptive Learning rate adjustment (AdaDelta), Adaptive Gradient adjustment (AdaGrad), Adam and RMSprop have been included in Caffe. On the basis of error gradient and regularization gradient, different optimization algorithms can update model parameters in a more detailed way.

3.3   Network Structure of Action Recording System

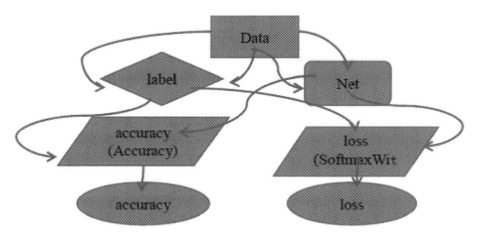

Fig. 1.   System network structure

The Caffe network code is stored in the train_test.prototxt text, where the paths to the training and test databases are specified in the Data layer. Caffe evaluates the network periodically as she trains it, so the network consists of two parts: a training network and a test network. Training network in the right part, where Net box is the figure). Take 50 groups of data each time to train the network, and at the same time take 50 groups of labels (label boxes) to calculate the loss to optimize the network. In the left half of the test network, 160 groups of data are entered into the Net box, and the classification results are output for comparison with labels to get the classification accuracy (Fig. 1).

4   Discussion

4.1   Analysis of System Experimental Results

Table 1. Comparison of human action recognition results between the proposed method and other methodson NTU RGB-D dataset

Methods	Cross-subject (%)	Cross-view (%)	Year	Conference
Part-aware LSTM	62.6	70.2	2016	CVPR
ST-GCN	81.4	88.1	2018	AAAI
SR-TSL	84.7	92.6	2018	ECCV
DPRL+GCNN	83.4	89.7	2018	ECCV
ARRN-LSTM	81.9	89.8	2019	ICME
FO-GASTM CNN	82.6	90.7	2019	ICME
Motif-STGCN	84.3	90.4	2019	AAAI
Si-GCN	84.4	89.2	2019	IJCNN
STGR-GCN	86.6	92.1	2019	AAAI
CGCN	90.2	96.5	2020	CVPR
MST-GCN	91.4	96.3	2021	AAAI
methods	85.7	93.4	2021	

It can be seen from the table that in the NTU RGB-D data set, the action recognition accuracy of this method is higher than that of most other methods. Except CGCN method and MST-GCN method, this method is at the highest 23% higher and at the lowest 1.7% higher than other methods under cross-subject. Under cross-view, the highest value was 22.9%, and the lowest value was 0.9%. The algorithm proposed in this paper combines the bone point detection module and the motion recognition module into an end-to-end network, and uses two levels of loss in the training process: Skeleton point detection of return loss and gesture recognition classification loss, optimize the whole end-to-end network, which not only optimize the gesture recognition module, and optimize the skeleton detection module, the purpose of this design is to reduce the two networks are directly related to the series mistakes caused by bone detection gesture recognition error, the experimental results in the table also prove the effectiveness and necessity of the end-to-end network proposed in this paper (Table 1 and Fig. 2).

Fig. 2. Comparison of human action recognition results between the proposed method and other methodson NTU RGB-D dataset

5   Conclusions

In the intelligent era, human motion recognition ushered in a research upsurge. Nowadays, motion intention recognition has been regarded as the most indispensable part of deep learning methods and artificial intelligence applications, and has been widely used in video surveillance and intelligent security. In recent years, with the development of motion recognition data sets, researchers have studied motion recognition algorithms based on various inputs. Future research can be carried out from more and more extensive aspects, which has high research value and application prospect. Aiming at the shortcomings of the traditional algorithm and combining with the new products of the development of The Times, this paper studies the movement recognition algorithm and designs a recording system of aerobics movement choreography. The training system will be able to quickly and efficiently shorten the learning practice time of complete sets of movements, reduced the number of repeated practice hold the complete set of movements, the complete set movement training sets of content structure and the arrangement of the training structure, compact will further toward a more flexible direction of scientific development, if the action is in order to make the style is more vivid, the specialized practice content The structural arrangement of the form must be a little innovative, rich operation content, through the various and complex arm movements and foot steps, to achieve a visual stimulation effect. In practice the number of units as much as possible to ensure that the athletes hold quality based on the premise, enriching the content of its operating action, combining with the personal characteristics of athletes, the plait compose one by one with a range of personalized connotation of complete sets of training action, through diverse vivid and complex esoteric interpretation of the sports theme content, reach a certain visual psychological stimulation training effect. The ability of the athletes to get a perfect display.

References

1. Sun, Y., Chen, J., Chen, M.: Human movement recognition in dancesport video images based on chaotic system equations. Adv. Math. Phys. **2021** (2021)
2. Shi, Y.: Research on human movement recognition and posture analysis based on CR model. Sci. J. Intell. Syst. Res. **3**(5) (2021)
3. Han, Q.: Research on the algorithm of motion track recognition in football video. J. Phys. Conf. Ser. **1992**(3) (2021)
4. Ting, H.Y., Sim, K.-S., Abas, F.S.: Kinect-based badminton movement recognition and analysis system. Int. J. Comput. Sci. Sport **14**(2) (2015)
5. Wang, Y., Zhu, X., Qu, C.: Fitness movements recognition and evaluation based on LSTM. J. Phys. Conf. Ser. **1302**(3), 032057–032057 (2019)
6. Schmidt, A.: Movement pattern recognition in basketball free-throw shooting. Hum. Mov. Sci. **31**(2), 360–382 (2012)
7. Moeslund, T.B., Hilton, A., Krüger, V.: A survey of advances in vision-based human motion capture and analysis. Comput. Vis. Image Underst. **104**(2), 90–126 (2006)
8. Lv, L.: Research on aerobics movement choreography based on embedded network technology. Appl. Mech. Mater. **3207**(556–562), 5685–5689 (2014)
9. Gang, J.: Dynamic monitoring of football training based on optimization of computer intelligent algorithm. Comput. Intell. Neurosci. **2022**, 2199166–2199166 (2022)
10. Yu, J.: Auxiliary research on difficult aerobics exercise training based on fpga and movement recognition technology. Microprocess. Microsyst. **81** (2021)
11. Zhu, S.: Real-time detection of aerobics posture based on strain sensor. EURASIP J. Adv. Signal Process. **2021**(1) (2021)
12. Zhou, W., Lv, H.: Aerobics exercise posture tracking and recognition system based on wireless smart sensors. J. Sens. **2021** (2021)

Construction of 3D Model of Ice and Snow Landscape Based on Interactive Algorithm

Weidan Chang[✉] and Zhiheng Zhang

Jilin Agricultural Science and Technology University, Jilin, China
63999279@qq.com

Abstract. As computer technology was rapidly developing, research and development and application of technology by measuring, a significant breakthrough with mature, complete, and useless noodles was obtained. Humanization and economics of technology; Interactive algorithm refers to the motion state estimation of an object. Most of us will use a filter plus a target motion model to estimate the motion state of the object. The 3D model construction of ice and snow landscape based on interactive algorithm discussed this paper can be simply understood as determining the 3D model shape of ice and snow landscape by predicting the movement mode of objects.

Keywords: 3D model · Inter active algorithm · Ice and snow landscape

1 3D Model Construction Background

The three-dimensional three-dimensional model, that is.3Dtechnologyis constantly developing, which provides the main direction for the construction of modern science and technology. In essence the world we live in is three-dimensional, and all objects exist based on length. Width and height. Computer technology is rapidly developing today, 3D technology is increasingly mature, 3D or 3D digital technology, it is the basic common technology of modern equipment based on computer/network/digital platform. 3D software development technology, 3D hardware development technology, 3D software application technology, 3D hardware integration with other software and hardware digital platform/equipment to different industries and different needs.

In recent years, with the rapid development of computer technology, the R & D and application of 3D technology have experienced the early exploration stage of decades, and a sound system has been formed; [1] With the rapid popularization of computer network application, 3D application has become a basic computer tool that ordinary college students can easily control, just like computer typing; The consumption and use of 3D.

Interactive algorithm refers to the estimation of the motion state of an object. Most of us will use a filter and a target motion model to estimate the motion state of an object. However a single motion model has different representation of object motion.

N. Khare et al. (Eds.): MIND 2022, CCIS 1763, pp. 194–202, 2022.
https://doi.org/10.1007/978-3-031-24367-7_20

They do not have a very universal model that can describe the motion state of the vehicle at any time The interactive model algorithm is a method that can fuse multiple models and adaptive transform them to represent the motion state of the target [2].

Since the common design platform can't draw the stereoscopic image according to the location of the landscape [3]. The research on several technologies of 3D landscape interactive design is based on the needs of dimensional information visualization of the earth, 3D virtual construction and engineering design. The research of 3D landscape interactive design technology is closely related to the current research hot spot 3Dvisualization technology, virtual reality and visual simulation technology, and 3D technology. Therefore, the construction of 3D model of ice and snow landscape based on interactive algorithm can be simply understood as determining the shape of 3D model of ice and snow landscape by predicting the movement mode of objects. This method of judging the parameters of ice and snow landscape through the intersection of multiple models is interactive algorithm.

3D refers to a three-dimensional system composed of a three-dimensional two-dimensional system with another direction vector. A directional vector is a mathematical concept, and the direction of the spatial straight line is represented by a nonzero vector parallel to this straight line, which is called a unidirectional vector of this straight line. The three dimensions have three dimensionality, but before and after the common language of our slang. Based on the design of the previous stage, a piece of animation is produced through the related production software in the computer, and the flow of the production is modeling, material, lighting, animation, camera control, rendering, etc. This is characteristic of the production of the three-dimensional animation, and 3D animation software first created one virtual world in the computer, the designer created models and scenes according to the dimensions of the shape of the object to express in this virtual three-dimensional world, the model motion trajectory, the virtual camera motion, and so on To set other animation parameters, assign a specific material to the model as needed and light up the light.

2 Build Process

2.1 Interactive Algorithm

The application of the dialogue algorithm in the model construction is mainly the Markov transfer matrix method. The Markov transfer matrix method is a method to analyze the market trend of market share by using transfer probability matrix. Russian mathematician Markov discovered that several elements of the system were relocated in the early 20th century. Nth confectionery is only affected by the N-1 confectionery and is related to the current state and is not related to any other state. Markov analysis introduces the concept of state transition. A state means the state in which an objective thing may appear or exist. A state transition refers to the probability that a target object transitions from one state to another.

The transition probability is an important concept in Markov chain. When the Markov chain is divided into m States, the history data is transformed into an array consisting of these m states. Transition from any state inevitably causes one of the states 1, 2,..., M. The transition of these States is called transition probability. In actual analysis, it is necessary to know the possible state of the market trend analysis object after a fixed period, and it is necessary to establish the mathematical model which can reflect the change rule. Markov market trend analysis model establishes a random time series model using stochastic process and is used for market trend analysis. This model is applicable only to time series with Markov characteristics, and it is pointed out that the state transition probability at each time is stable. This method must not be used if the time series transition probability varies at different times. Since the actual purpose is difficult to maintain the transition probability of the same state for a long time, this method is generally applicable to short-term tendency analysis and prediction.

The main application order is generally summarized as follows: first, the survey of the divination situation, the mathematical model based on the divination situation and other coordinates, and the construction of the future state of the future through this method are decided, and the future shape of the three-dimensional model is intuitively planned and summarized. The basic model of Markov analysis is x (K + 1) = x (k) * P. In this equation, X (k) is used to predict the predicted trend through rational trend analysis and the state vector of the predicted subject at t = K + 1, and to specify the future model of the future snow and snow landscape. Of course, this method is not applied when the state transition probabilities of the time sequence changes with time, while the state transition probabilities for each hour remain stable and the time transition probabilities are stable.

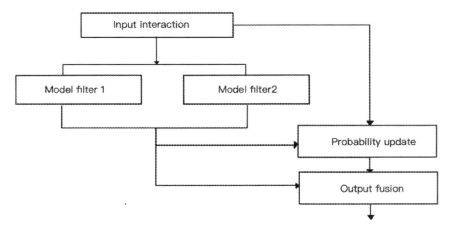

Fig. 1. Detailed explanation of algorithm

This method is generally applied to short-term trend analysis and prediction, because it is difficult for real objective objects to maintain the same probability of transfer over the long term. The market has many excellent modeling software, such as 3 dma, ArcGIS, Maya, AutoCAD, and so on, usually provides basic geometry elements such as cube and sphere, and also builds complex geometry scenes through a series of geometry operations (Pan, rotation, stretching). The usual 3D model is considered to represent the best effect on the least side. The appropriate material texture is sequentially added to the model, the UV is expanded, the various maps such as color and normality are supported, the light effect is made, the model is made finer, and the animation is set, and it is finally rendered and written. Modelers are looking for a number of tools to perform the 3D models for faceted down, UV expansion, bake processing, and format conversion. The purpose is to make the model smaller and avoid the effect and to display it quickly.

Here, after you build your model to fulfill the maximum role of the 3D model, you can do the old broom cloud to help you complete the rest of the process quickly and efficiently and to achieve the best effect (in Fig. 1).

2.2   Construction of 3D Model of Ice and Snow Landscape

3D model is made of light and text. It's made of a lot of clouds from the points of an object that is made of a three-dimensional Latin model. The network is finally painted using three-dimensional displays. These cycles are usually connected to three angles, four or several simple angles. It can simplify the image process. However, the light may also include things that are made of ordinary polygons with a hole. The texture not only includes the texture of the object surface in the general sense, even if the object surface presents uneven grooves. But also includes the color patterns on the smooth surface of the object. When the texture is mapped to the object surface in a specific way, it can make the object look more real. The technique of texture mapping mesh assigning image data; After processing the image obtained by photographing the object, the texture on each mesh is mapped. and finally a three-dimensional model is formed. Of course, in order to make a complete 3D model more convenient in use, actions and physical states need to be added to make the 3D model of ice and snow landscape more comprehensive. The picture is the basic 3D model of ice and snow landscape constructed by using interactive algorithms. In the basic model construction and game the model can already cope with most algorithms [4].

What is the composition of the 3D model?

Figure 2 shows an example of character modeling:

Fig. 2. Character modeling

Mean. The grid is composed of different points of the object, an d the model grid is made by measuring through the point program. Three-dimensional (XYZ) coordinates are taken into account in the punch point, brightness (glass) and colour information (RGB), and are finally expressed as a mixture. These sizes can normally be made up of triangles, triangles or other convex simple polygons to simplify the production process. However, the keyboard may include ordinary political uses with holes.

Texture. The texture is also referred to as a color pattern (texture) that is included in the smooth surface of the object, along with the texture of the object surface (in the normal sense), and mapping the texture to the surface of the object in a specific manner, as shown in Fig. 5 to The object can be more realistic. After the texture mapping mesh is applied to the image data and the image processing by the photographing of the object, the three-dimensional mapping is finally formed by texture mapping on each mesh.

How do you build a 3D model?

There are almost three methods of modeling the present object. The first way is software modeling using 3D animation. The second method is to model by measuring instrument equipment. The third method is to model using an image or video.

Currently, you can see many excellent modeling software in the market, including 3ds max, softmage, Maya (this book is actually working on this software), UG and AutoCAD. These common features are to use complex geometry elements, such as cube and spheres, to build complex geometry scenes by a series of geometry operations such as translation, rotation, expansion, and Boolean operations, as shown in Fig. 3. The modeling of the 3D model using the modeling software mainly includes geometric modeling, behavior modeling, physical modeling, object behavior modeling, model segmentation, and so on. Here, the creation and explanation of geometry modeling is an emphasis on virtual scene modeling.

Fig. 3. Ice and snow landscape

3   3D Model and Interactive Algorithm

3.1   Practical Application of Interactive Algorithm

Three dimensional visual interactive landscape model. This kind of visual model is the product of rational design thinking and computer aided design. Therefore, based on the interactive visual model, combined with landscape environment analysis, and according to the proposed environmental constraints, rules, parameter settings and landscape designer's design thinking, by feedback the design process, change the parameters and rules. And generate a variety of optional schemes By recording the design data. Avoiding the rupture of the design thinking process, and then selecting the results by the landscape designer, a set of landscape design process with clear thinking logic can be constructed. Whether it is snow visualization, terrain visualization, water flow visualization or glacier visualization, the application of interactive algorithm can be better solved, because the interactive algorithm is used to calculate the change trend of objects, while the change trend of ice and snow landscape is obvious, and the direction is difficult to predict. We might as well regard the ice and snow landscape as a whole as a container with a capacity of V Then the total value of V remains unchanged which means that the overall content of water remains unchanged in the process of condensing into ice and then into water. Using this method, the ice and snow landscape can be refined more intuitively and effectively. The role of ice and snow landscape is in Table 1.

Table 1. The role of ice and snow landscape

Landscape of ice and snow	Effect
Game	Ice and snow landscape that can interact in the game
Movies	It can be used as a background in film and television

3.2   3D Model Construction Purpose

Interactive network streaming media provides a good platform for people's communication [5]. The consumption and use of 3D models, such as games, movies, architecture, automobiles, mobile phones, and clothing, have already become a part of a wide public work and life. Application of 3dmodeltechnology: through the rapid development and extensive applications of many years, the current 3D technology has already been remarkably mature and popular: 3D takes place at 20 in 3D. "3D" and "virtual" simulation "reality" rapidly appear in each field instead of "flat noodle". The application and dissemination of 3D model technology is used for the interaction between the person and the environment, including the development and production of visual expression culture art products such as movies, animations, games, and design and production of real products such as automobiles, aircrafts, appliances, furniture, and virtual reality simulation and simulation.

Simulation technology is a simulation model technology which reflects the behavior and process of the system by using some numerical calculation and problem solving through simulation experiment by applying simulation hardware and simulation software. Simulation technology has an initial application in the early 20th century.

For example, a water model is constructed in a laboratory, and a water - like study is carried out. The development of climate, airspace and nuclear energy technologies promotes advanced technologies. The rapid development of computer technology in the 1960s, since the 1960s, used more analogue computers than analogue computers, accelerating the development of analogue technology and supplying analogue hardware.

Hybrid computer systems have been stagnant once in the seventies and have been developed since the 1980s. For example, it is possible to simulate a large-scale and complex flight system in real time using joint work of the micro machine vax11-785 and the peripheral processor Ad-10.

Based on the development of interactive configured language and more powerful configured software systems, configured technology and integration of free information into configured software In other words, the production of similar software with the application of system experts is an important trend. Increasing the scale and complexity of similar models and test systems will continue and their efficiency and reliability will be very important. It is becoming more important to evaluate the system by setting applicable standards at the same time.

Three dimensional graphic technology has attracted much attention as the development of 3D video technology. 3D animation is more intuitive than the plan view, so you can give viewers a sense of presence. In particular, it is suitable for unimplemented projects and implemented projects, and allows you to understand the best results after implementation.

3D animation consists of 3D models, 3D animation, 3D walkthrough, 3D animation, from 3D models, static, single model presentations, 3D models, from simple geometric models, such as generic product exhibitions, art show exhibitions, complex personality models Displays dynamic and complex scenes such as character animations. All of these animations can be achieved through powerful technical power.

3D technology has developed rapidly in recent years. We found the following data to estimate the future trend. The development of 3D technology in the past three years is shown in Table 2.

Table 2. Application trend of 3D technology in recent three years

Changes of 3D industry in recent three years	Animation	Game	Movie
Application rise	20%	23%	21%
Earning asset rise	44%	47%	50%

4 Conclusion

3D animation technology makes real objects a useful tool. As a result of its meetings, authenticity and unlimited operation, it is widely used in various fields such as medicine, education, military business and entertainment. In the production of film and television ads, this new technology can give people a new feeling and is welcomed by a majority of companies. 3T animation may be used to produce special effects (stimulation, tobacco, white, light effects, etc.), advertisements, films and television dramas, special effects (car collision, deformation, illusion, character, etc.), display of advertising products, film title flights, etc. The main reason for developing research technology is the huge social and economic benefits.

In the 1950s and 1960s, simulation was mainly used in engineering technology fields such as aviation, aerospace, electric power, chemical industry and other industrial process control.

Using virtual reality technology the interactive algorithm is studied with 3D model deformation technology and 3D model mesh simplification technology. Using the grey relational analysis method, we calculate the weight of the evaluation index of the environmental efficiency index, and construct the evaluation index body [6].

The deformation technology of 3D geometric entities is studied. The local scaling torsion and bending of 3D entities are realized by hierarchical division and deformation operation of geometric entities. In the reconstruction of traditional village couplet landscape, taking the repair of village cultural landscape gene as the starting point [7].

The 3D solid deformation technology based on hierarchical operation can accurately control the deformation of solid, and can implement combined deformation operation on geometric entities to realize complex 3D solid deformation [8].

The three-dimensional reconstruction technology based on the image has already been applied to many scenes of civil engineering works [9].

The edge folding mesh simplification algorithm of 3D model is studied. The edge folding cost is defined as the product of the length of the edge and the importance of its starting point [10].

Acknowledgments. This work was supported by the. 2022 Scientific Research Project of Education Department (General Topics). Exploring on Artistic Innovation of Landscape Architecture of Ice and Snow Tourism in Jilin Province [JJKH20220408SK].

References

1. Wang, K., et al.: Construction and application of landscape models based on visualization. J. Northw. Forestry Univ. **32**(4), 8 (2017)
2. Peng, W., et al.: Study on construction of the model of collaborative visual learning environment based on interactive whiteboard. In: International Conference on Information Science & Engineering. IEEE (2009)
3. Changhao, L.I., Song, H., Xue, Y., et al.: Construction of interior design platform based on 3D virtual vision and interactive design. J. Modern Electr. Tech. **42**(7), 53–56 (2019)
4. Shih, N.J., et al.: The integrated 3D as-built representation of underground MRT construction sites. J. Build. Constr. Plan. Res. **01**(4), 153–162 (2013)

5. Zhi, M., Ping, W.: Construction of the English teaching model based on the interactive network streaming media. In: Xu, Z., Choo, K.R., Dehghantanha, A., Parizi, R., Hammoudeh, M. (eds.) CSIA 2019. AISC, vol. 928, pp. 30–36. Springer, Cham (2020). https://doi.org/10.1007/978-3-030-15235-2_5

6. Wang, S.: Quantitative evaluation of landscape architecture environmental benefits based on multi-criteria decision-making. Int. J. Environ. Technol. Manag. **25,** 95-107 (2022)

7. Wang, X., Jin, X., Feng, Y.: Landscape reconstruction of traditional village couplets based on image recognition algorithm. J. Opt., 1–9 (2022)

8. Dong, Q., et al.: Construction of ecological and recreation patterns in rural landscape space: a case study of the Dujiangyan irrigation District in Chengdu, China. Land, 11p (2022)

9. Li, H.: Rapid reconstruction of 3D structural model based on interactive graph cuts. Buildings **12** (2012)

10. Luo, G., et al.: Application of computer simulation and high-precision visual matching technology in green city garden landscape design. Environ. Technol. Innov. **4,** 101801 (2021)

Classroom Learning Situation Analysis System Based on Computer Vision

Yixin Chen[✉] and Xi Hu

School of Artificial Intelligence, Jianghan University, Wuhan, Hubei, China
blairchen@126.com

Abstract. With the continuous progress of society and the change of learning methods and teaching environment, research on the analysis of College Students' learning situation in the classroom is emerging in endlessly. The real-time learning situation analysis (LSA) system of college students mainly analyzes college students' learning status and behavior in the classroom, which can provide college teachers with the basis and means to effectively manage the classroom. Based on computer vision (CV) technology, this paper takes the students' listening behavior in college theory class as the research object, and uses CAMSHIFT tracking algorithm to analyze the behavior of college students in class. On this basis, the system of classroom learning situation analysis (CLSA) based on CV is designed and implemented. Through the simulation experiment, the traditional algorithm is compared with the CV CAMSHIFT tracking algorithm; The test results show that the recognition rate of this algorithm is about 10% higher in the case of facial interference, which proves the accuracy, availability and effectiveness of the classroom real-time LSA system designed and studied in this paper, and provides a new way of LSA for college teachers and students.

Keywords: Computer vision · Classroom · CAMSHIFT tracking algorithm · Learning situation analysis

1 Introduction

With the development and progress of society, the traditional teaching evaluation mechanism in Colleges and universities is basically unable to analyze and summarize the learning situation of a single student in a timely and long-term way. Especially for students whose academic performance is not particularly excellent, the traditional teaching evaluation mechanism can only catch up with them if they want to timely feedback the students' performance every day and even every class to make them reflect. But these feedback work is extremely important to the growth of students. Based on the above shortcomings of traditional teaching management and LSA, there is an urgent need to design a CLSA system based on student video analysis to assist college students and college teachers in evaluating the effect of theoretical classroom teaching. Therefore, this paper studies and analyzes the CLSA method based on CV.

Many scholars at home and abroad have studied and analyzed the CLSA method based on CV. Chaynikovagr analyzes how blended learning technology enables students to better adapt to the conditions of distance learning. Through the analysis of the peda-gogical literature on blended learning, we can determine some important principles that the learning process in the flipped classroom model should be based on. The analysis of these principles shows that they fully comply with the principles of distance learning [1]. Khans introduced CNN and discussed case studies related to the application of CNN in CV, including image classification, object detection, semantic segmentation, scene understanding and image generation [2].

This paper mainly introduces the overall design idea, the overall framework of the system, and the overall workflow of the system based on CV; The overall design idea mainly introduces the overall application scenarios and requirements of the system, and specifically describes the design of the main functional modules of the student side, the teacher side and the server side; Carry out real-time analysis on students' classroom learning and constantly feedback the results to students and teachers. On the one hand, it can remind students to pay attention to their own learning status at any time, adjust their learning status, make good use of limited classroom time and improve learning efficiency; On the other hand, it can provide teachers with a fair and convenient basis for evaluating students' classroom performance. The most important thing is to provide teachers with first-hand information, analyze students' learning, adjust teaching content and means, and improve teaching quality [3].

2   Design of CLSA System Based on CV

2.1   Main Problems of the CLSA System in the Smart Classroom

Single function without practical application: the existing smart classrooms in Colleges and universities are nominally able to analyze students' classroom behavior, but in fact they are only applied to a single student's classroom attendance. There are few applica-tions in analyzing students' classroom learning behavior, and the application of real-time analysis of students' classroom behavior is almost zero.

Wide coverage and inadequate data analysis: the current student behavior analysis system developed for the application of the smart classroom is mainly to install a camera at a fixed position in the classroom and use the data collected by the camera for analysis and processing. The main drawback is that the camera has a large coverage, and the fine beat is not in place. In particular, the shooting of students' facial expressions sometimes cannot well identify their characteristics, and the data analysis is inaccurate.

There are many subjects to be photographed, and the pertinence is not strong: in the process of video shooting, the camera in the smart teacher faces all the students in the classroom, and most of the time it collects video for the whole classroom. In the process of video analysis, most of it analyzes the whole class, so it is difficult to analyze the whole class for a student, let alone the whole semester for a student.

2.2   Overall Design Idea of Students' Real-Time LSA in Class

The campus wireless network is used for data transmission. First, the student's mobile terminal is used to collect the student's personal class video or image, then the video or image is compressed and uploaded, and then the wireless network is used to send the video or image to the server. After the server performs processing and calculation, the server can use the wireless network to return the analyzed class status to the teacher, Teachers selectively and timely use the wireless network to push prompt messages to students according to the specific situation fed back by the server. At the same time, the teacher can view the data on the server at any time [4, 5].

Overall Structure Design of LSA Based on CV. The real-time CLSA system based on CV technology is mainly composed of three parts: Student client, teacher management and video server. Specifically, it includes three types of user roles: students, teachers and managers. Different user roles correspond to different system functions. The overall structure diagram of the system is shown in Fig. 1:

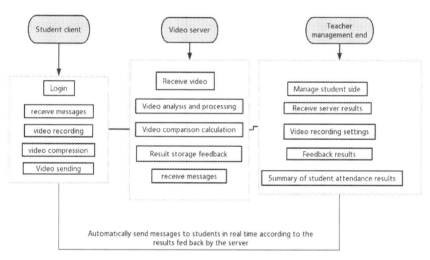

Fig. 1. System overall structure diagram

The basic workflow of the system is as follows: the student side registers and logs in before class, views the messages sent from the teacher side, and carries out corresponding operations according to the content of the message feedback; The server side is used to receive the video / picture data collected from the student side, compare and analyze the collected data, and synchronize the analysis results with the teacher side [6–8].

2.3 Overall System Function Design

The student classroom real-time LSA system based on face recognition includes three parts: Student client, teacher management and video server,

The student side requires students to register information in advance, log in to the app before class, start the camera to record videos or take photos according to the instructions sent by the teacher side during class, compress and upload the videos and pictures to the server side, and timely receive the result messages pushed by the teacher side.

After confirming the student's login, the teacher mainly sets the time point for recording video or taking pictures and the duration of video shooting during class, receives the result feedback from the server, and pushes messages to the student in real time according to the feedback results.

Message management: the message management function includes message pushing and receiving. The teacher automatically selects appropriate messages to push to students according to the specific analysis results returned by the server; Push the set time point and duration of recorded video before class. The received message in the message management function is to receive the analysis results from the server [9]. Video viewing: the video viewing function enables the teacher to access the video and video analysis results in the server at any time. Report analysis: the report analysis function enables teachers to view the statistical results of students' attendance in a class, which can be divided into analysis for a student and class situation.

The server mainly manages the user information of students and teachers, and also stores and analyzes the video. File management: the file management function is mainly used to save, query, analyze and calculate the video/picture files uploaded by students and the results. Statistical analysis report: the statistical analysis report function is mainly used to analyze and summarize the analysis results of students' class behavior, mainly including the analysis of a student in different time periods and the analysis of a class in different time periods.

2.4   Overall Algorithm Design of LSA System

According to the existing face recognition algorithms, we mainly judge from several features. The main features include macro and micro aspects. The macro aspect is to compare the positions of forehead, jaw, neck, shoulder and arm to ensure the correct sitting posture of students; Microscopically, it mainly compares eyes, nose and mouth to analyze students' listening behavior [10, 11]. The analysis of students' behavior in class first uses the object detection algorithm based on CV technology to detect faces. The advantage of this object detection method is to accelerate the speed of feature extraction, so as to achieve real-time face detection. The main flow chart of this target detection algorithm is shown in Fig. 2.

The specific class behavior is analyzed and judged by CAMSHIFT algorithm. The algorithm is based on the template method, that is to compare the actual detected objects with the standard template objects, and judge by their similarity.

The comparative analysis and judgment process of class behavior described in Fig. 2 is to make a comprehensive judgment based on the similarity of the two results. If the similarity of the two results is high, it indicates that the actually detected pictures are consistent with the standard template, that is, the sitting posture is correct; If one similarity is high and the other similarity is not high, it can be judged that the sitting posture is not standard; If the similarity of the two results is not high, the sitting posture is not correct.

The feature point detection algorithm in CAMSHIFT algorithm can be used to judge the boundary region of each part marked by the body according to the marked feature points. Using this algorithm, feature points are annotated for students' personal images from the microscopic aspect, mainly from the students' facial expression features, mouth and eyes, especially from the eyes' line of sight, that is, the position of black eyes [12].

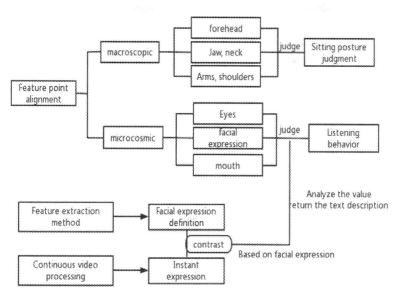

Fig. 2. Video / picture behavior algorithm design

3   CAMSHIFT Tracking Algorithm Based on CV

CAMSHIFT algorithm in the continuous tracking process, the algorithm will adaptively adjust the size and position of the search window in the frame according to the results of the previous frame. Given n (n = 1,2,3,,, n) sample points of d-dimensional space SD, select any point a in the space, then the basic form of meanshift vector is defined as:

$$M_v = \frac{1}{H} \sum_{a_i \in R_h} (a_i - a) \tag{1}$$

where RH is a high-dimensional region with radius J, which satisfies the set of points B of Eq. (2).

$$R_j(a) = \left\{ b : (b - a_i)(b - a_i)_T (b - a_i) < j^2 \right\} \tag{2}$$

H means that h of the n sample points AI fall into the RH region. Meanshift algorithm is transformed into:

$$\hat{g}_{w,h}(a) = \frac{C_{h,d}}{nw^d} \sum_{i=1}^{n} w\left(\left\| \frac{a - a_i}{w} \right\|^2 \right) \tag{3}$$

where H (a) is a kernel function; Is the unit density; W is the radius.

CAMSHIFT algorithm tracks all video frames to get the motion trajectory of the moving target. CAMSHIFT algorithm needs to make color projection map (direction projection) for the video frame first. After determining the centroid of the tracking target, the size setting of the search window also has a great impact on the experiment. In order to improve the accuracy, this paper sets the initial search window to the complete area containing gesture targets.

4   Design of CLSA System Based on CV

After the overall design of the LSA, the detailed description of each part of the function and the realization of each part of the system function, the terminal function of the classroom real-time LSA system based on CV technology is basically developed. This paper will test the real-time CLSA system based on CV technology, test the realization of each functional module of the system, record the test content and test results, and analyze the test results. After the research of dynamic gesture recognition method based on CV is completed, a whole experiment needs to be done to verify the superiority of the method proposed in this paper, and the analysis of the experimental method and the final results of the system.

In this paper, the whole experiment of dynamic gesture recognition method based on CV is carried out. This experiment also takes into account the situation that simple threshold segmentation is used in the dynamic gesture segmentation and only CAMSHIFT algorithm is used in the dynamic gesture tracking. The academic analysis of the traditional algorithm is analyzed and compared with the CV CAMSHIFT tracking algorithm. The comparison results are shown in Table 1 and Fig. 3.

Experimental process: start the dynamic gesture recognition program; Draw the corresponding track in the camera frame with the palm of your hand according to the predefined gesture. When drawing the corresponding track, you need to meet the requirements of the experimental attention section below; Record the results of each experiment for the later analysis of the experimental results.

The experimental results show that there is little difference in the recognition rate between the two cases without facial interference. The difference between the two is between 1%–4%. The experimental results are in line with expectations, which verifies that the CV algorithm in this paper has better adaptability to the changes of the external lighting environment; In the case of facial interference, the recognition rate of this algorithm is about 10% higher, because when encountering facial interference, the CAMSHIFT algorithm based on CV can better track the motion trajectory of dynamic gestures. When encountering interference, this algorithm can predict the position of the next gesture, so as to avoid the interference of skin color to a certain extent. Therefore, this paper proposes a CLSA method based on CV, which has achieved good experimental results and is of great significance for efficient LSA in the future.

5   Conclusions

The real-time CLSA system studied and designed in this paper is based on the mature CV CAMSHIFT tracking algorithm, and the server is designed and analyzed in detail;

Table 1. Result data sheet of facial interference

Recognition rate without facial interference

	play	suspend	Volume increase	Vol	Next song	Previous song
Traditional algorithm	85%	72%	74%	96%	94%	91%
CAMSHIFT algorithm	87%	76%	78%	98%	97%	94%

Recognition rate with facial interference

	play	suspend	Volume increase	Vol	Next song	Previous song
Traditional algorithm	59%	52%	61%	70%	72%	70%
CAMSHIFT algorithm	70%	61%	76%	86%	84%	84%

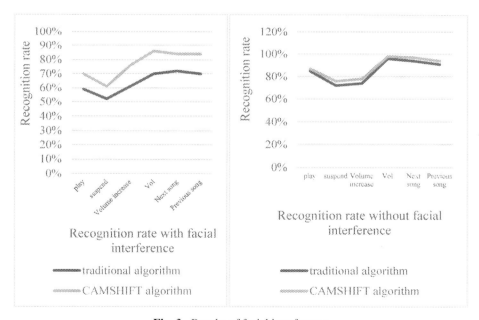

Recognition rate with facial interference

traditional algorithm

CAMSHIFT algorithm

Recognition rate without facial interference

traditional algorithm

CAMSHIFT algorithm

Fig. 3. Results of facial interference

According to the characteristics of College Students' classroom real-time LSA system, the function and performance of the system are tested to create a practical college classroom real-time LSA system. However, there are also some deficiencies in the design and research of the system: the test samples and test time of the system are limited, so the number of test samples and test time should be further increased, so as to continuously improve the accuracy of the system algorithm and the availability of the system, and finally make the system be put into practical application to effectively help classroom teaching; This paper mainly uses the existing CV face recognition and behavior analysis algorithms to judge students' behavior in class. Although it has been improved and perfected from the macro and micro aspects, it still needs a lot of tests and continuous improvement in practical application, which makes it more perfect and accurate to judge students' behavior in class, makes the system more perfect, and gives full play to the advantages of the system research technology, Make the system more valuable.

Acknowledgements. This work was supported by the Jianghan University project-based teaching reform course "Java development platform".

References

1. Chaynikova, G.R.: Analysis of adaptation of students studying under the flipped classroom model to the conditions of distance learning. Open Educ. **24**(5), 63–71 (2020)
2. Khan, S., et al.: A guide to convolutional neural networks for CV. Synth. Lect. CV **8**(1), 1–207 (2018)
3. Wldchen, J., Mder, P.: Plant species identification using CV techniques: a systematic literature review. Arch. Comput. Methods Eng. **25**(2), 507–543 (2018)
4. Ricker, M.: Statistical analysis of growth curves with mathematica. Actas Urologicas Espaolas **18**(9), 855–860 (2018)
5. Metatla, O., et al.: Toward classroom experiences inclusive of students with disabilities. Interactions **26**(1), 40–45 (2018)
6. Murugesan, L.J.: Investigation on enabling intelligence through deep learning and cv-based internet of things (IoT) systems in a Classroom Environment. Bioscience Biotechnology Research Communications **13**(6), 80–91 (2020)
7. Jeong, L.O., Kim, Y.M., Kang, M.K.: The analysis of flipped learning centered on prospective study. Int. J. Mob. Blend. Learn. **10**(3), 38–45 (2018)
8. Gomoll, A., Šabanović, S., Tolar, E., Hmelo-Silver, C.E., Francisco, M., Lawlor, O.: Between the social and the technical: negotiation of human-centered robotics design in a middle school classroom. Int. J. Soc. Robot. **10**(3), 309–324 (2017). https://doi.org/10.1007/s12369-017-0454-3
9. Yu, Q.: Development of computer aided classroom teaching system based on machine learning prediction and artificial intelligence KNN algorithm. J. Intell. Fuzzy Syst. **39**(6), 1–12 (2020)
10. Brunetti, A., et al.: CV and deep learning techniques for pedestrian detection and tracking: a survey. Neurocomputing **300**(July 26), 17–33 (2018)
11. Goulart, C., et al.: Literacy, discourse and the production of social senses: dimensions and guidelines for research and for teaching writing. Bakhtiniana Revista de Estudos do Discurso **15**(4), 76–97 (2020)
12. Hallal, K., Hajjhussein, H., Tlais, S.: A quick shift from classroom to google classroom: SWOT analysis. J. Chem. Educ. **97**(9), 2806–2809 (2020)

Application of VR Virtual Technology in 3D Panoramic Roaming Design System of Rural Ancient Buildings

Lei Han[✉]

School of Art and Design, ShaoYang University, Shaoyang 422000, Hunan, China
hanlei123_007@163.com

Abstract. The development of VR technology in our country has gone through nearly 60 years. From the initial 3D display to the current virtual reality interaction to today's omni-media stereoscopic display, 3D display technology has become the mainstream trend of VR applications. In terms of virtual reality, the VR three-dimensional panoramic roaming system is based on the principles of interactivity and authenticity. Through virtual reality, the computer system is used to realize real-time communication between humans and machines, that is, to convert three-dimensional scenes into two-dimensional images. The virtual reality interaction is realized through the computer system, which enables the real-time interaction between the user and the device. The 3D display design is based on a dynamic solid space three-dimensional model established in two-dimensional image processing software, which is the application of virtual reality technology in architectural 3D display design, and the system roams the scenes through the interaction between virtual objects and the real world. This paper mainly discusses the application of VR virtual technology in the design of three-dimensional panoramic roaming of rural ancient buildings and in the application of VR virtual technology and full-media stereoscopic display design.

Keywords: VR technology · Rural ancient architecture · 3D panoramic roaming design system

1 Introduction

VR technology is a new 3D interactive virtual scene roaming system design method that has emerged in recent years. This approach allows users to easily access the required information at home through mobile devices. In the VR interactive design system, the three-dimensional interaction between the user and the building and environment can be accomplished through virtual operation technology [1]. Traditional ancient architecture roaming work needs to rely on two-dimensional plan and three-dimensional three-dimensional scene map in order to achieve the transmission and interpretation of the entire spatial information and get the required data point location and other related content. But these ancient buildings have undergone a long period of development and change, and the development process of its three-dimensional interactive technology

© The Author(s), under exclusive license to Springer Nature Switzerland AG 2022
N. Khare et al. (Eds.): MIND 2022, CCIS 1763, pp. 211–219, 2022.
https://doi.org/10.1007/978-3-031-24367-7_22

has caused many problems, such as the conflict problem between the technology of architectural roaming and the traditional two-dimensional spatial scene map [2]. The VR virtual roaming system can solve these problems, through the way of virtual operation technology to achieve three-dimensional panoramic information interaction of the building space, so as to achieve real-time interaction between the user and the device, which can provide new ideas for the traditional two-dimensional plane scene map and three-dimensional display [3].

The existing general display of ancient architectural relics is mainly applied to dynamic web pages, Flash technology, streaming media technology, etc. These technologies can achieve a simple display of three-dimensional panoramic view of large cultural relics [4]. However, there are many shortcomings in the creation of realistic environment, three-dimensional interactive display and simulated experimental operation, such as lack of flexibility and real-time, lack of security, etc., which cannot meet the requirements of modern society [5]. VR technology is applied to the architectural three-dimensional panoramic display design system, simulates the natural environment through virtual reality, and realizes the all-round display of the architectural environment, which can not only effectively solve the problems existing in the traditional method, but also improve the construction efficiency and reduce the project cost [6]. At the same time, it can also promote the combination of traditional construction technology and modern virtual reality, thus providing new ideas for the construction of modern cities in our country [7].

2   VR Virtual Technology and Ancient Building Simulation Algorithm

2.1   VR Virtual Technology

VR virtual technology is a three-dimensional panoramic image simulation and display for the purpose, it will be the camera ingested scenery, sound and other information through the computer processing to generate images, presented in a virtual way, and through the computer system processing and analysis, so that objects and three-dimensional images to interact. It can bring people to a realistic environment for interactive interaction, allowing people to interact in a realistic environment, thus achieving the purpose of virtual reality and human interaction design. This way not only can make more contact experience between people and buildings, but also can improve the user visually to the overall design of the building, and it can be more intuitive from the construction process to feel the existence of scene elements, which enhance the entire VR virtual technology application effect and the use of value, so that users can get more experience from the visual [8].

VR virtual technology is a computer simulation as the main hand, it simulates the 3D information of the real environment through sensors, cameras and other equipment. Firstly, the projector is used in the building roaming system combined with the mobile platform. For example: the use of robots for real-time photography and sent back to the control center computer, and then according to the need to modify and optimize the model processing to make it consistent with the geometric relationship and physical characteristics of the actual situation, and then finally the parameters into the database to save to the VR virtual technology development board can be through the PC interactive terminal device, the virtual scene into a three-dimensional model, so as to achieve human-computer interaction. The advantages of this technology are: it can visually display the building roaming, and it is easy and convenient to operate, and also has a strong visual and three-dimensional sense [9]. The principle of VR technology is shown in Fig. 1.

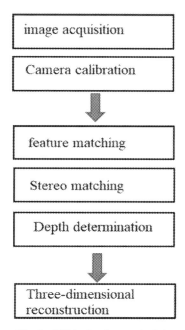

Fig. 1. VR technology principle

2.2   Ancient Building Simulation Algorithm

The traditional building simulation technology is mainly completed through digital models, in VR virtual reality, it can transform the three-dimensional scene into a limited amount of information. Through the computer network, the transformation of the operation process and the spatial relationship of the three-dimensional object construction, projection and extraction is realized. Through the real-time interactivity and high efficiency of the computer, the application of virtual reality technology in space modeling in the process of 3D object construction and extraction is realized. Three-dimensional sense and interactivity, thus providing users with a more convenient and efficient experience. In the ancient architecture roaming system, the establishment of architectural building 3D panoramic information model based on sensing technology is widely used, and this system realizes the interactivity between virtual architecture and traditional visual environment based on VR technology. Through the comprehensive use of computer sensing technology, 3D printer and other advanced equipment, it is applied to the design of rural architectural roaming. The simulation manufacturing of models in ancient architecture includes the simulation of natural scenery and the simulation of fractal terrain.

The simulation of natural scenery refers to the use of computer technology to simulate the architectural model on the basis of the three-dimensional scene, which is displayed through projectors and 3D printing equipment. This series of models is colorful, it can be simulated in two-dimensional or three-dimensional, and it can also display architectural models in virtual scenes. The modeling methods for natural landscapes can generally be divided into three categories: modeling with regular landscape shapes, modeling based on natural landscape features, and modeling with irregular landscape shapes. The modeling method with regular landscape shape is through the simulation of geometric shapes, which combines natural and human landscapes to present the physical image of the building in three dimensions. The modeling method based on the characteristics of natural landscape refers to processing the shape, size, color and other information of the scene, and then combining it with the physical image of the building, and then using 3D printing technology to display it in three dimensions. The modeling method with irregular landscape shape refers to the physical simulation of the irregular natural landscape and display it in a three-dimensional scene, so as to achieve architectural realism and visual impact [10].

A fractal terrain model is one in which buildings in nature have many variations in shape and size, characterized by objects in different orientations that exhibit different sizes, shapes and colors. Natural terrain is likely to be a typical fractal surface. In the terrain description model established by Berry and Hannayca, the well-known variational function is given as shown in Eq. (1), and the power spectral density of the off terrain profile is calculated as shown in Eq. (2).

$$E[X(x) - X(x+d)]^2 = k(|d|)^{2H} \tag{1}$$

$$G(w) = 2\pi k w^{-3} \tag{2}$$

Fractal terrain modeling can be roughly divided into Poisson step method, inverse Fourier transform method, midpoint displacement method, successive random addition method and band-limited noise accumulation method. Among them, the midpoint displacement method is commonly used. The midpoint displacement method is characterized by the position, size and angle of the point, establishes a space rectangular coordinate system, determines the spatial relationship between objects through the mid-coordinate transformation, and establishes a space rectangular coordinate system. Where the position and angle of the midpoint can be determined directly by coordinate transformation, it can also be achieved by superposition and translation method, while etc. is carried out on two-dimensional or three-dimensional objects. The basic principle of midpoint displacement method is based on the power law relationship of variance, as shown in Eq. (3).

$$E[(X(t + \Delta t) - X(t))^2] = \Delta t^{2H} \sigma^2 \tag{3}$$

Midpoint displacement method is the standard fractal geometry method, and its basic principle is to use the displacement information of points for analysis. In the 3D panoramic roaming system, multiple object image sequences as well as relationship models and coordinate converters between entities at different locations are established by virtual reality technology, which is used to realize the interactive design of architectural 3D scenes, thus realizing the 3D display of architectural roaming graphics. The 2D fractal terrain model can be obtained by the simplest 1D random fractal curve extension, and this method can visualize the location, size and 3D terrain of the building site on the 2D plane with high accuracy, which can be applied to the rural building roaming system [11]. Assuming that the two endpoints of the given initial line segment are Pi and Pi + 1, one iteration is completed by randomly perturbing the midpoint of the line segment, whose iteration is shown in Eq. (4).

$$fmid \cdot \frac{fi + fi + 1}{2} + roughnes \times Rand() \tag{4}$$

The roughness is used to control the amount of disturbance at the current level, which can be expressed by the formula as shown in Eq. (5).

$$roughness = pow(2.0, -h), h \in [0, 0.1, 0] \tag{5}$$

3 VR-Based Three-Dimensional Panoramic Roaming System of Rural Ancient Buildings

VR technology is based on the computer-aided realization of three-dimensional panoramic roaming design. Through the virtual building model can be realized in two-dimensional plane for roaming, it does not need complex mechanical movement, and does not need complex construction process, which greatly saves the three-dimensional space three-dimensional modeling production cycle. Through the analysis and research on the application of VR virtual technology in rural architectural roaming design system, we found that 3D printing technology as a new digital information processing method and means has been applied in various fields, and it has achieved a wider application prospect and development space. 3D stereo modeling technology also has a high starting research value in computer graphics, which is a new research method and means, and its application in the field of architecture is of great value. Virtual technology has many advantages compared with the traditional two-dimensional flat three-dimensional visual representation: such as strong interactivity, visualization and other characteristics, it can realize three-dimensional geometric modeling as well as high-resolution image processing functions.

3.1 Virtual Three-Dimensional Scene Structure

Different object models inside the virtual scene of the antique market 3D architecture system need to be generated using different modeling methods, using 3DSmax and VRML combined to achieve real-time interaction of architectural information, and through three-dimensional modeling technology to complete the virtual scene roaming. The overall structure of the system modeling is shown in Fig. 2.

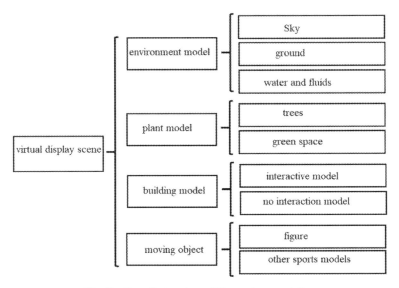

Fig. 2. Overall structure of the system modeling

3.2 Overall Design

The 3D panoramic display of rural ancient architecture based on VR technology uses Three.js to create and render 3D scenes of ancient architectural relics. The flowchart of Three.js is shown in Fig. 3. 3D scene creation and 3D panoramic display are effects that cannot be achieved by traditional methods. VR stereoscopic roaming technology can solve the problems of traditional visual intuition that is difficult to achieve and poor interactivity. By panning and rotating the virtual reality simulation of the internal environment of the building and the model of the external scenery of the building to improve

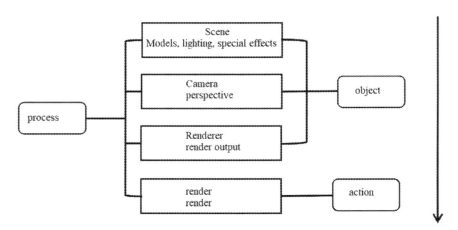

Fig. 3. Flowchart of three.js

the user experience, so as to achieve the organic integration of virtual architecture and the environment.

4 The Application of VR Technology in the Design of Three-Dimensional Panoramic Roaming of Rural Ancient Buildings

The application of VR technology in the three-dimensional panoramic roaming system of rural buildings is mainly through the virtual camera to obtain information about buildings and equipment, and analyze and process this information, so as to complete the physical map of the building and establish a three-dimensional model on the computer, thus providing users with the function of virtual roaming.

First of all, virtual reality technology can simulate real objects in various environments. Such as: greenhouse scenes, ground stage background and large event venues. The application of virtual reality technology in the countryside scene roaming system can simulate the real objects in a variety of environments. For example: greenhouse, ground stage background and large event venues and other scenes can be completed by VR interactive three-dimensional panoramic visual model to complete the virtual space roaming function, so that it has the characteristics of high resolution and real-time. Traditional building construction drawings are generally made of two-dimensional plane or semi-3D surface, while the digital technology is to realize the generation and processing of graphic information on the computer screen.

Second, the use of different types of cameras to obtain more image data and graphics parameters, so as to come to realize a variety of functional needs, to achieve the application of VR virtual technology in the rural three-dimensional panoramic roaming system, which can achieve the goal of saving costs and improving the user experience. At the same time, this can also solve the workload and difficult to achieve the time demand. By analyzing and extracting different types of data to obtain more comprehensive information content. Combined with the spatial perception effect to establish a model and use 3DMax software to build a solid building model, and finally realize the purpose of 3D panoramic roaming in the virtual scene, which can bring a new experience to change the traditional countryside environment, indoor pattern, etc., and at the same time, it also improves the user participation and comfort.

The application of VR technology in the countryside 3D panoramic roaming system is mainly for the traditional village 3D virtual modeling, which takes 2D images as the information carrier and realizes the interaction through computer software. This method can effectively improve the three-dimensional sense of architectural objects and visual impact, at the same time this can also save the footprint of the three-dimensional space, thus bringing a new meaning to the rural architecture virtual roaming. At present, many regions in China have their own digital display machines for ancient buildings and have established VR virtual technology systems specifically for demonstrating architectural scene models or simulating tourist scenic spots. Virtual reality panoramic 3D printing device (AR) has appeared in Beijing Palace Museum, the emergence of virtual reality technology makes the three-dimensional panoramic display of architecture more intuitive and visible, providing great convenience for tourists. Therefore, the application of VR virtual technology in the three-dimensional panoramic roaming system of rural architecture has become an inevitable trend in the coming digital era.

5   Conclusion

VR virtual technology is an emerging research direction. In the architectural 3D panoramic roaming system, the conversion between traditional 2D images and 3D works is realized based on computer vision, interactive video processing software and image synthesis software. The display of virtual scenes is completed through three-dimensional interactive software, so as to save labor costs and improve work efficiency and quality. This method can improve the efficiency and reduce the input of personnel, it also has great advantages in cost saving and resource allocation. The three-dimensional panorama refers to the use of computer technology to achieve the display of three-dimensional scenes of the building, in this process, the user can see the entire object, objects, etc. on the screen, but also through the virtual scene to achieve the entire object roaming, which has great advantages in the traditional three-dimensional display technology and computer vision combined. At the same time, VR technology also has great advantages in the traditional three-dimensional scene display, which can realize the integration of reality and reality through the combination of virtual reality interactive software and computer vision. The future application of VR technology in the three-dimensional panoramic roaming system of rural architecture will combine the traditional flat two-dimensional display with 3D virtual reality, thus improving the efficiency and quality.

Acknowledgements. Project No. 20YBX020, Research on the local social memories and meaning Change of ancestral hall buildings in Dongkou, Hunan Province, Philosophy and Social Science Planning Fund Project of Hunan Province, China.

Project No. 21YBB17, Research on the red architectural cultural heritage of Shaoyang from the perspective of the heritage corridor--taking the ancestral hall of Dongkou County as an example, Project of the Social Science Achievement Review Committee of Shaoyang City, Hunan Province, China.

References

1. Kim, D., Jae, Y.: The impact of virtual reality (VR) technology on sport spectators' flow experience and satisfaction. Comput. Hum. Behav. **93**, 346–356
2. Costanzo, V., Evola, G., Marletta, L., et al.: The effectiveness of phase change materials in relation to summer thermal comfort in air-conditioned office buildings. Build. Simul. **11**, 1145–1161 (2018)
3. Hong, T., Langevin, J., Sun, K.: Building simulation: ten challenges. Build. Simul. **11**, 871–898 (2018)
4. Gersak, G., et al.: Effect of VR technology matureness on VR sickness. Multim. Tools Appl. **79**, 14491–14507 (2000)
5. Carugati, F, et al.: Building legal order in ancient Athens. J. Legal Anal. **7**, 291–300 (2015)
6. Farronato, G., et al.: Three-Dimensional Virtual Treatment Planning.Journal of Craniofacial Surgery, **29**, 11–14 (2018)

7. Guzmán, G., et al.: Evaluation of three-dimensional printed virtual setups. Am. J. Orthod. Dentofacial Orthoped. **155,** 288–295 (2019)
8. Englund, C.: Exploring approaches to teaching in three-dimensional virtual worlds. Int. J. Inf. Learn. Technol. **134,** 40–151 (2017)
9. Liyu, T., et al.: Three-dimensional Forest growth simulation in virtual geographic environments. Earth Sci. Inform. **12,** 55–58 (2018)
10. Psaltis, S., et al.: Three-dimensional virtual reconstruction of timber billets from rotary peeling. Comput. Electr. Agric. **152,** 268–269 (2018)
11. Xia, J., Wang, P., Chen, Q.: Neural correlates underlying size constancy in virtual three-dimensional space. Sci. Rep. **7,** 443–450 (2017)

Ear Recognition System Using Averaging Ensemble Technique

Ravishankar Mehta[✉] and Koushlendra Kumar Singh

Machine Vision and Intelligence Lab, Department of CSE, National Institute of Technology Jamshedpur, Jamshedpur 831014, Jharkhand, India
rmehta.online@gmail.com, koushlendra.cse@nitjsr.ac.in

Abstract. Ear recognition system based on deep learning approaches attracted the researcher in recent years due to its enormous application areas especially in security and surveillance. In this paper, ensemble based ear recognition system is proposed for person identification task. Here, a pool of three classifiers based on deep CNN is generated and prediction is done by averaging the prediction from each classifier. Each classifier is trained with training data independently and extracts very discriminant features. The combined approach of this ensemble models perform well even in scarcity of enough data. To overcome the scarcity of training data, we have applied augmentation technique which generates variety of image for training purpose. For entire experiment, we have used IITD-II dataset of ear image which contains total 793 images. The proposed model shows an improvement in performance accuracy over the individual model. It achieves an accuracy of 96.83 for weighted average ensemble and 95.68 for average ensemble technique that shows an improvement in accuracy of 2% over the individual model. It also achieves precision as 96.25, recall as 95.86 and f_score as 95.84 for average ensemble technique. Similarly, it achieves precision as 96.86, recall as 96.53 and f_score as 96.93 for weighted average ensemble technique.

Keywords: Ensemble · Feature extraction · Recognition · Accuracy · Precision

1 Introduction

Deep learning-based ear recognition system has become an interesting area in the field of biometric. Traditional approaches for such recognition system requires specific biometric modalities which perform the detection of ROI (ear region), segmenting it from profile image and analyzing it to differentiate them for unique identity. Among the other biometric modalities, ear is considered as a distinctive and promising biometric modalities that provide reliable and stable information including the shape structure that does not show drastic change over the time [1]. Also capturing the ear images is contactless and non-intrusive task which does not require much cooperation of user. Many works have been proposed starting from geometric, holistic to descriptor-based by the researcher in recent years [2–4]. Deep learning-based methods process the input images to extract the relevant features and compute the descriptors in the output. To perform this task, it uses combination of convolution and MaxPooling layers for feature extraction and classification [5–7]. Further, development of ear recognition system requires domain knowledge of how different models treat the input images when image are captured in unconstrained environments. Various types of challenges like pose variations, illumination changes; occlusion and ethnicity are considered for such environments [8]. In last decades, deep CNN based approaches for ear recognition outperform over the traditional approach [9–11]. Sharkas in his work applied two tracks for classifying the ear images [12]. First is classical machine learning for feature extraction from the discrete curvelet transform and passing the extracted features to a classifier. Second is deep learning based approach for classification purpose. In the field of ear recognition, when deep learning based single model fails to outperform the classification task due to diversity of features, ensemble methods works fine in this circumstances. In additions, it overcomes the problem of pose variations, illumination changes, and scaling. The obtained result from the proposed model is found to be more robust and reliable as compared to the single model.

Priyadharshini et al. Proposed a CNN based ear recognition model which requires very less memory [13]. Alkababji et al. in his paper used faster R-CNN for ear detection. They applied principal component analysis (PCA) and genetic algorithm for feature reduction and selection task and finally applied fully connected artificial neural network for matching purpose [14]. Semwal et al. proposed ensemble learning based hybrid deep learning models and achieves 99.34% classification accuracy [15]. Their CNN-LSTM based ensemble model seems very effective for the lower extremity activities recognition task and archives accuracy around 99.25%, 8.48% and 97.44% respectively on three different datasets [16]. In the proposed work, authors tried to solve the technical challenges like high variance, low accuracy for limited dataset, addition of features noise and bias while making a prediction faced by a single model. Because it is not always possible for a single model to make perfect prediction on a given dataset. By combining the multiple models, we have a chance to boost the overall accuracy that reduces the model error by maintaining the model's generalizations. Most of the ensemble based technique uses deep learning models which are pretrained (Transfer learning) which is computationally complex and requires highly configured machine and GPU.

The contributions of this work are summarized as follows: (i) We present three simple CNN model for feature extraction tasks (ii) We ensemble these three proposed CNN model for multi-class classification that require minimal pre-processing and no hand crafted features (iii) The performance of the proposed work demonstrated that proposed ensemble model significantly outperforms the conventional approaches and boosts the performance of the conventional CNN-based method.

The rest of the paper is organized as follow: Sect. 2 introduces materials and methods; Sect. 3 gives the description about the dataset; Sect. 4 describes the experimental result and analysis. Section 5 finally concludes the work.

2   Materials and Methods Used

In this section, we describes the ensemble technique that we have used in our work to improve the performance of ear based recognition system. Generally ensemble learning uses two or more models to produce the final prediction which is more robust and accurate than the individual model. The architecture of proposed ensemble technique and each model is illustrated in the below section.

2.1 Proposed Ensemble Technique

The proposed ensemble technique uses three deep CNN models for ensemble purpose as shown in Fig. 1. The ear images go for pre-processing stage where normalization is performed to remove the non-uniformity present in the images. In pre-processing stages, we resized the input image to 100 × 100. After resizing all the input data to fixed size, we split these image dataset to training and test set with ratio 80% and 20% respectively. Then apply augmentation technique where we apply different parameter like rotation, flipping, zooming and fill mode. After these pre-processing stages, these three models are trained with this training set. Each of the model act as a classifier which gives its own prediction for test set data. Final prediction is obtained by averaging the predictions obtained from each of the three classifiers.

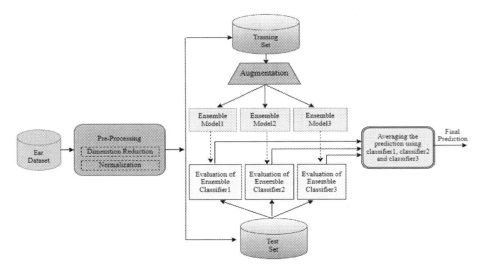

Fig. 1. Architecture of proposed ensemble technique

2.2 First Model Used for Ensemble Technique

The first model of presented ensemble technique contains three convolutional layers. There exists one MaxPooling layer after each convolution layer. ReLu activation function is applied after each convolution operation. Its primary job is to map all the negative value to zero. The output of last convolution layer is flattened to one dimensional vector which are passed to dense layer and fully connected layer of size equal to the number of the subjects present in the dataset. The architecture of this model is presented in Fig. 2.

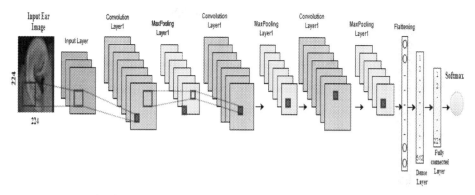

Fig. 2. First model architecture used in the ensemble learning

2.3 Second Model Used for Ensemble Technique

The second model of ensemble technique contains seven convolutional layers. A Max-Pooling layer is presented after first two convolution layers. Then again three convolution layers each followed by one MaxPooling layer are present. Finally two convolution layers are present. A ReLu activation function is applied in between each convolution layer. The output of the last convolution layer is flattened to one dimensional layer through flattening operation. This one dimensional vector is finally fed to fully connected layer that consist of number of neurons equal to number of distinct subjects present in the dataset. The architecture of this model is presented in Fig. 3.

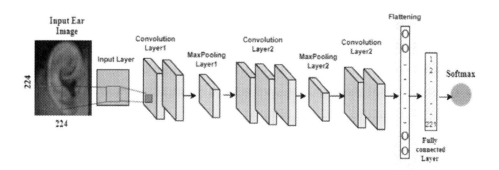

Fig. 3. Second model architecture used in the ensemble learning

2.4 Third Model Used for Ensemble Technique

The third model of ensemble technique consists of only two convolutional layers. These two convolutional layers are convolved with 32 and 64 filters respectively. Each filter has size of 3×3. Each convolutional layer is followed by MaxPooling layer that reduces the size of feature map to half. Finally, output of convolution layer is flattened and then fed to fully connected layer containing number of neurons equal to number of distinct subjects in the dataset. The architecture of this model is shown in Fig. 4. After fully connected layer of each model, a softmax activation function is applied that gives probability based out which are averaged from individual model to give the final prediction.

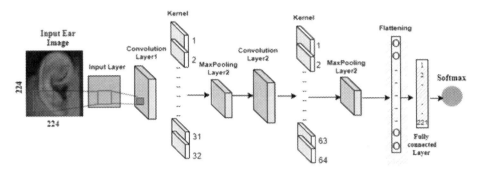

Fig. 4. Third model architecture used in the ensemble learning

3   Dataset Description

IITD-II ear dataset has been used for evaluating the performance of proposed work. This dataset contains total 793 images with 221distinct subjects. Each subject has at least three images. All the images are labeled and taken under indoor environment. The age groups of all the subjects in this dataset are between 14–58 years. All the images in this dataset are normalized and cropped with resolution of 50×180 pixels. Some sample images of this dataset is shown in Fig. 5.

4   Experimental Result and Analysis

The proposed technique improves the performance of ear recognition system through ensemble of three models descriptions of which are already illustrated in the above sections. For the entire experiments we have used IITD-II dataset which contains total 793 cropped images of 221 distinct subjects. Since the number of training sample in this dataset is very less for deep learning based approach. So we apply augmentation technique to generate more samples of training data. Different parameters of augmentation used for generating this sample images are illustrated in Table 1.

The classification accuracy of each model is highly dependent on the features extracted by each classifier for the input images. Each model of ensemble technique contains a number of convolution layers. After each convolution layer we have used ReLu activation function which maps the negative value to zero. At last layer of every model, softmax activation function is used that gives numeric value as output which is of probability type. We run first and second model till 50 epochs and third model till 100 epochs. We set the batch size as 256 for first and second model. For third model it is set to

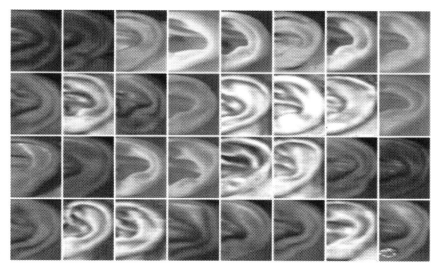

Fig. 5. Sample images of IITD-II ear dataset used in the experiment

Table 1. Different parameters of augmentation techniques

	Parameters	Values
IITD-II Dataset	Rotation range	$15°-45°$
	Flipping	Horizontal
	Zoom range	0.2–0.8
	Fill mode	Nearest

128. We have used categorical cross entropy as a loss function. Adam optimizer is used for first and second model and RMSprop is used for third model. Different parameters used for each model contributing in the ensemble model are illustrated in Table 2.

Table 2. Different parameters used by each model of proposed ensemble model

Hyper parameters	Values
Optimizers	RMSprop/Adam
Dropout	0.1/0.2/0.3
Batch size	128/256
Rescaling	1/255
No. of epochs	50/100

For the proposed work, we have conducted our experiments on a system having 64 GB RAM and 3.70 GHz processer. Each model is build using tensor flow framework. For each of the model, we have plotted the model accuracy vs epoch and model loss vs epoch. The plot of model accuracy and model loss for each of these models are illustrated in Fig. 6, 7 and 8.

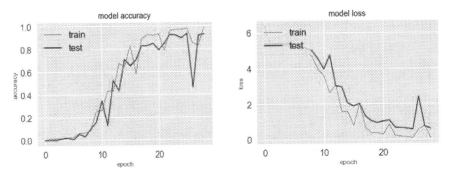

Fig. 6. Plot of model accuracy and loss Vs. epochs for model1 used in ensemble technique.

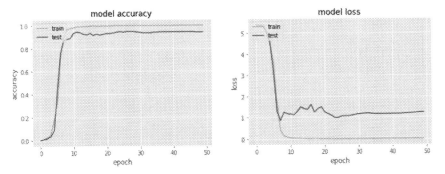

Fig. 7. Plot of model accuracy and loss Vs epochs for model2 used in ensemble technique.

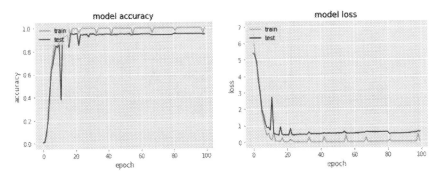

Fig. 8. Plot of model accuracy and loss Vs epochs for model3 used in ensemble technique.

Further, to determine the effectiveness of the proposed system, we have also calculated the Precision, Recall, and F_score which are defined as follow:

$$Precision = \frac{TP}{TP + FP} \times 100 \tag{1}$$

$$Recall = \frac{TP}{TP + FN} \times 100 \tag{2}$$

$$F\_score = 2 \times \frac{Precision \times Recall}{Precision + Recall} \times 100 \tag{3}$$

$$Accuracy = \frac{TP + TN}{TP + FP + FN + TN} \times 100 \tag{4}$$

To calculate the performance metric of the proposed model, we have applied averaging ensemble and weighed average ensemble technique. Result of obtained precision, recall, f_score and accuracy for each of this technique are illustrated in Table 3.

Table 3. Performance metric for average and weighted ensemble technique in proposed model

Dataset	Ensemble technique	Accuracy	Precision	Recall	F1-score
IITD-II Dataset	Average ensemble	95.68	96.25	95.86	95.84
	Weighted average ensemble	96.83	96.86	96.53	96.93

In weighted ensemble method, we have tested our model with different weights as illustrated in Table 4. We randomly checked the weights from 0.0 to 0.5 for each model. It has been observed that the ideal weights for different models are assigned with value $w1 = 0.3$, $w2 = 0.1$ and $w3 = 0.0$ and it gives the max accuracy which is 96.83%.

Table 4. Different weights used by each model in the ensemble technique

Model	CNN1	CNN2	CNN3	Ensemble accuracy
Accuracy	94.27	95.31	95.37	95.86
W1	0.2	0.1	0.1	94.27
W2	0.1	0.1	0.3	95.87
W3	0.2	0.1	0.2	95.41
W*	**0.3**	**0.1**	**0.0**	**96.83**

We have also plotted the ROC curve that shows the performance of the proposed ensemble model at different classification threshold value as shown in Fig. 9.

The performance of proposed work is compared with other existing methods as illustrated in the Table 5. It has been observed that the proposed ensemble model further improves the accuracy when dataset are augmented and achieves recognition accuracy of 96.83% which is better and acceptable for this limited dataset.

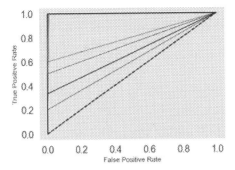

Fig. 9. ROC curve for the proposed model

Table 5. Performance comparison of the propose model with other existing methods

Article	Dataset	Accuracy
Log-Gabor Feature with Weighted Sum matching [17]	IITD-II	95.93
SUMrule based fusion [18]		92.40
Ear recognition with ensemble classifiers ResNet features [12]		93.50
Ear recognition with ensemble classifiers ResNet50 [12]		93.57
Ear recognition with ensemble classifiers AlexNet [12]		94.29
Proposed ensemble model		**96.83**

5   Conclusion and Future Work

In this work, authors proposed three simple CNN model and ensemble them for ear recognition tasks. Accuracy of each model is observed and predictions are averaged to give final accuracy. It has been observed that ensemble based ear recognition system performs better than the individual model. If any model in ensemble learning works poorly, the overall performance of the model does not degrade. Since ensemble learning combines the mapping functions learned by different classifiers to generate an aggregated mapping function. Hence, ensemble of models gives better performance as compared to the individual models in most of the cases. Also it gives more robust and stable result. The performance of proposed technique is validated on IITD-II dataset which contains variety of images like very dark and very bright images that may cause deterioration in performance. It has been observed the proposed model works well with such variety of images. It achieves the performance accuracy up to 96.83% which shows an improvement in accuracy of 2% over the individual model. However, selection of individual model for building the ensemble is really challenging task in terms of time and complexity. Sometimes, it may happen that improvement in accuracy is relatively less than the individual model. For future task, we are planning to obtain access to different public datasets and more complex model that can give more accurate results even in challenging environments like rotation and pose variations.

References

1. Pflug, A., Busch, C.: Ear biometrics: a survey of detection, feature extraction and recognition methods. IET Biom. **1**(2), 114–129 (2012)
2. Alaraj, M., Hou, J., Fukami, T.: A neural network based human identification framework using ear images. In: International Technical Conference of IEEE Region, vol. 10, pp 1595–1600 (2010)
3. Rastogi, A., Bhoumik, U., Choudhary, C., Akbari, A.S., Kumar Singh, K.: Ear localization and validation using ear candidate set. In: Bajpai, M.K., Kumar Singh, K., Giakos, G. (eds.) Machine Vision and Augmented Intelligence—Theory and Applications. LNEE, vol. 796, pp. 109–120. Springer, Singapore (2021). https://doi.org/10.1007/978-981-16-5078-9_10
4. Mehta, R., Garain, J., Singh, K.K.: Cohort selection using mini-batch k-means clustering for ear recognition. In: Advances in Intelligent Computing and Communication, pp. 273–279 (2022)
5. Dodge, S., Mounsef, J., Karam, L.: Unconstrained ear recognition using deep neural networks. IET Biom. **7**, 207–214 (2018)
6. Eyiokur, F.I., Yaman, D., Ekenel, H.K.: Domain adaptation for ear recognition using deep convolutional neural networks. IET Biom. **7**, 199–206 (2018)
7. Kumar Singh, K., et al.: Deep learning capabilities for the categorization of microcalcification. Int. J. Environ. Res. Public Health **19**(4), 2159 (2022)
8. Prakash, S., Gupta, P.: An efficient ear recognition technique invariant to illumination and pose. Telecommun. Syst. **52**(3), 1435–1448 (2013)
9. Krizhevsky, A., Sutskever, I., Hinton, G.E.: ImageNet classification with deep convolutional neural networks. In: Advances in Neural Information Processing Systems (NIPS), pp. 1097–1105 (2012)
10. Saikia, T., Kumar, R., Kumar, D., Singh, K.K.: An automatic lung nodule classification system based on hybrid transfer learning approach. SN Comput. Sci. **3**(4), 1–10 (2022)
11. Szegedy, C., et al.: Going deeper with convolutions. In: IEEE Conference, CVPR, pp.1–9 (2015)
12. Sharkas, M.: Ear recognition with ensemble classifiers; a deep learning approach. Multi-media Tools Appl., 1–27 (2022)
13. Priyadharshini, R.A., Arivazhagan, S., Arun, M.: A deep learning approach for person identification using ear biometrics. Appl. Intell. **51**(4), 2161–2172 (2021)
14. Alkababji, A.M., Mohammed, O.H.: Real time ear recognition using deep learning. TELKOMNIKA **19**(2), 523–530 (2021)
15. Semwal, V.B., Gupta, A., Lalwani, P.: An optimized hybrid deep learning model using ensemble learning approach for human walking activities recognition. J. Supercomput. **77**(11), 12256–12279 (2021)
16. Jain, R., Semwal, V.B., Kaushik, P.: Deep ensemble learning approach for lower extremity activities recognition using wearable sensors. Expert Syst. **39**(6), e12743 (2022)
17. Kumar,A., Wu, C.: Automated human identification using ear imaging. Pattern Recognit. **45**(3), 956–968 (2012)
18. Meraoumia, A., Chitroub, S., Bouridane, A.: An automated ear identification system using Gabor filter responses. In: 13th IEEE Conference on NEWCAS, pp. 1–4, June 2015

IoT and Machine Learning-Based Covid-19 Healthcare Monitoring System Using Face Recognition

Chahat Vaswani[1]([✉]) [ID], Shalini Chimaniya[1] [ID], Rajnish K. Ranjan[2] [ID],
and Yachana Bhawsar[1] [ID]

[1] Government Women's Polytechnic College, Shivaji Nagar, Bhopal 462016, India
vaswanichahat03@gmail.com
[2] LNCT University, Bhopal 462042, India

Abstract. After facing the horrible COVID-19 pandemic, steadily life is getting back to normal again. This pandemic came with opportunities as well, especially for researchers to come out with novel ideas and handle the situation. Many researchers have contributed with their dedicated research work with the help of recent technology to overcome similar circumstances. This paper presents a novel idea for proper monitoring and detecting normal/abnormal health using AI-based models. Proper monitoring and detection of symptoms are essential to ensure the health of members. This model is devised using several IoTs components and various ML (Machine Learning) techniques have been used to get comparative enhanced results. The hardware used Raspberry Pi 4 model B, which is the main hardware connected to several sensors like MLX906014 non-contact thermal sensor and MAX30100 pulse oximeter and heart rate sensor to measure body temperature without contact and to calculate the level of oxygen in the blood and measuring pulse rate respectively. Additionally, a Camera module for facilitating face recognition features for devices has been used. An Alert will be sent to Admin if someone has an abnormal temperature and oxygen level. The Firebase database is used to store information and it gets updated in real-time. People's health history can be further analyzed through graphs for visualization and monitored by the administrator.

Keywords: Machine learning · Internet of things · Sensors · Support Vector Machine · Face recognition

1 Introduction

1.1 Overview

The most essential thing for everyone is their health. According to the well-known proverb "Health is Wealth", the recent squirt of the COVID-19 pandemic have been affected all aspects of our day-to-day life. It made it very difficult for any organization to run safely. Fear of the spread of coronavirus in the office made people not prefer to

N. Khare et al. (Eds.): MIND 2022, CCIS 1763, pp. 230–244, 2022.
https://doi.org/10.1007/978-3-031-24367-7_24

work on-premises as proper monitoring measures are not available and if one is infected others may also get impacted leading to an urge for finding a new solution for proper monitoring of COVID-19 symptoms among the organizational members. This era is an era of ML and IoT that can find solutions for many problems that are difficult to manage manually. Internet of things results to tackle the COVID-19 rife by including smart solutions based on IoT [3, 6]. This work is based on COVID-19 health monitoring using face recognition, and contactless body temperature [9], and monitors and visualizes data every week/month. We used a Raspberry Pi with a MAX30100 pulse oxygen sensor and MLX90614 non-contact IR Temperature Sensor.

The main intention of our work is to develop a self-regulating automated monitoring system to monitor the health of employees in an organization and also to predict the possible outbreak. Thus, people at risk can be notified with alerts. Our main goal is to adapt IoT technology in the monitoring of COVID-19 pandemic symptoms [16]. This model is all about capturing faces and registering (in case of a new face), finding their temperature, pulse rate, and oxygen level, and predicting if a person is healthy or not. This model can be operated by any technical or non-technical member or admin. Furthermore, our COVID-19 monitoring system can be used in other sectors such as the public sector, hospitals, and clinics too. Now we will see different components either hardware or software, used for the completion of this project below.

1.2 IoTs Hardware

1.2.1 Raspberry Pi 4 Model B [13, 14]

Raspberry pi is not simply a microcontroller for IoTs projects, but a small single-board computer. With the advancement of technology and ide, raspberry pi is used for programming languages and even making its software. it's running on Linux which makes it more secure. In our project raspberry pi is used as the main controller to derive functions

Fig. 1. Raspberry Pi 4 Model B with its component.

like face recognition and detection, database management, and different connected sensors are connected to it. Below Fig. 1 is illustrating various components of 'Raspberry Pi 4 model B'.

1.2.2 OV5647 5MP 1080P IR-CUT Camera Module

Camera Module supports all Pi embedded IR-CUT filters and also upgrades, and removes color distortion in daylight. Possesses an infrared LED and facilitates a night vision OV5647 sensor with 5 megapixels (Fig. 2. (a)), when using Night Vision Mode, you can attach IR LEDs. Color distortion during the day caused by IR light during the day eliminated by the IR-CUT filter. The infrared lights are attached to the camera using the screw hole, also used to pass electricity to the lights. Due to the lack of an IR filter in the CCD, typical cameras would produce reddish images during the day, but our RPi IR cut camera can capture images with up to 1080 p resolution during the day or night.

1.2.3 MAX30100 Pulse Oximeter Heart Rate Sensor [11]

There are two LEDs in the device, one of them emits infrared light and the other one emits red light. Only infrared lights are needed to measure the pulses. Infrared and red lights are used to measure blood oxygen levels. A FIFO buffer of up to 64 bytes is used to store absorption data for IR and red light. Two modes of operation are offered by it, the first is heart rate and the other one is heart rate & oxygen saturation mode. The IR LED is ON in the heart rate mode, while both IR LED and the LED mode is on in dual mode. A built-in 60Hz low-pass filter is also there. Although power line noise can be filtered by it, noise and environmental fluctuations are ignored. When the heart pumps blood, the amount of oxygen in the blood increases due to the larger amount of blood in the human body. The amount of oxygenated blood decreases when the heart relaxes.

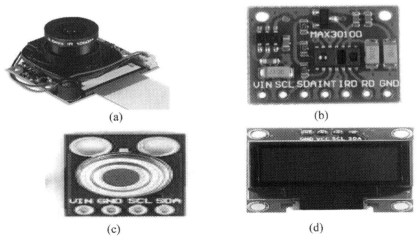

(a)   (b)

(c)   (d)

Fig. 2. Different sensors used as - (a) OV5647 5MP 1080P IR-CUT camera module, (b) MAX30100 sensor, (c) MLX90614 thermal sensor, and (d) OLED display.

Knowing the time interval from increase to decrease in blood oxygen, one can measure the pulse. MAX30100 sensors are shown below in Fig. 2 (b).

Working Processes of MAX30100 [15]: Absorption levels of both light sources are read and stored by it in a buffer. Then the I2C communication protocol reads the buffer. The ratio of red light absorbed to infrared light is used to calculate Hemoglobin Blood Oxygen concentration. With the help of a change in the amount of blood in the finger, heart rate is detected, which is then quantified by the amount of light passing through the finger.

1.2.4   MLX90614 Thermal Sensor

The thermometer can measure temperatures with excellent precision and resolution using a noise amplifier, 17-bit ADC, and robust DSP unit. But an infrared thermometer to measure temperatures without touch is the MLX90614. Two Melexis technology developed and produced chips make up the MLX90614, which was created especially to process IR sensor data. This hardware device is shown in Fig. 2 (c) above.

1.2.5   OLED Display

An OLED diode is made up of six different layers, two of which retain organic properties. When current is passed through these diodes, these organic layers produce light that passes through a color refiner, producing a picture on the screen. This can be seen in Fig. 2 (d) above.

1.3   Software and Library

This is one of the core parts to implement our work. Various software and compatible libraries have been used such as Visual Studio Code through which we have developed GUI for the acquisition of data and face recognition, OpenHABian, VNC Viewer, PuTTY, Geany Python IDE, Telegram, and firebase. Apart from these softwares, we have several libraries used such as Opencv, NumPy, Pandas, PIL/Pillow, Tkinter, Matplotlib, seaborn, Adafruit Python SSD1306, etc.

This paper has been organized as, next Sect. 2 is about related research, our methodology has been proposed in Sect. 3, followed by results and discussion in Sect. 4, and last but not the least section is turned up with the conclusion of our work.

2   Literature Review

Many researchers have done successful work and continuously trying to overcome the covid-19 pandemic situation with the help of IoT to make smart health monitoring systems. We have recorded some important features from a related paper, which is displayed in below Table 1. After going through different research papers in this particular area, we are coming up with this idea that raises the question: why do we need this device when we have safer options such as lockdowns? We further studied the need for

Unlocking most of the countries and the impacts of the Lockdown on the economy and Life of an individual. The work [1] proposed by Dr. Nikita Arora, and Vaishnavi Gupta in 2020 cast awareness on the monetary status of India in the tough time of covid-19 and explains the economic activities in the country. It shows how COVID-19 is impacting the Indian budget, the later consequences that the Indian finances will have to hurt and how some sectors bear major economic crises. This paper helped us to understand the urge for finding solutions that can deal with economic crises with minimizing the risk of contamination. Bhardwaj et al. [4] designed an IoT-Based COVID-19 Smart Health Monitoring System to save people from common visits to medical doctors and conferences among sufferers and scientific professionals. It is primarily based totally on IoT and allows medical doctors to acquire real-time information effortlessly. When any adjustments arise in an affected person's fitness primarily based totally on general values, then the health practitioner or medical doctor keeps alerted by IoT devices. This paper was useful for monitoring the health of an individual patient. Our objective was different from this but it gave us a great understanding of different methodologies and components that can be used. Another inspiring approach was smart doors, which are IoT-Enabled and used for body temperature monitoring and detection of face masks [5]. These doors are created using machine learning models for body temperature monitoring and detection of face masks, the suggested framework was performed using the TensorFlow software library by a face mask detection algorithm. Additionally, a non-contact temperature sensor is used to monitor personal body temperature. This conjectural system can detect COVID-19 infected by sanctioning Internet of Things technology (IoTs Technology).

Table 1. Comparative study and features identified in the context of IoT-based Covid-19 health monitoring system.

S. no.	Author	Year of publication	Title	Features
1	Joshi et al. [2]	2020	Indian economy amid COVID-19 Lockdown: A review perspective	This paper tries to verify the effect of lockdown on the Indian financial system and discover destiny's perspective
2	Bhardwaj et al. [4]	2022	IoT-based smart health monitoring system for COVID-19	A clever fitness tracking device that can track blood pressure, coronary heart rate, level of oxygen, and a person's temperature and alert the health practitioner or medical doctor accordingly

(*continued*)

Table 1. (*continued*)

S. no.	Author	Year of publication	Title	Features
3	B Varshini et al. [5]	2021	IoT-enabled smart doors for monitoring body temperature and face mask detection	This article presents a smart door that is IoT-enabled. Temperature is monitored using a machine learning model through a smart door and it also detects face masks. This proposed system can detect COVID-19 users by capacitating Internet of Things technology
4	Abdulrazaq et al. [8]	2020	Novel Covid-19 detection and diagnosis system using IoT based smart helmet	Automated detection of coronavirus is detected by this proposed system from thermal images. This system uses a smart helmet with a Mounted Thermal Imaging System for less human interaction and detection
5	Muhammad Zia Ur Rahman et al. [10]	2022	Real-time artificial intelligence-based health monitoring, diagnosing, and environmental control system for COVID-19 patients	An automatic injection system is designed to handle emergency conditions, this system is artificial intelligence-based and provides feedback in absence of a doctor, injects the dose to the patient, provides GSM messages, and live location, and also sends emails during emergency conditions

Abdulrazaq et al. [8] suggest the layout of a system to detect the coronavirus from thermal images automatically and without much human interaction. This system uses a smart helmet with a Mounted Thermal Imaging System. To monitor the screening process and to get real-time data, the smart helmet is integrated with thermal camera technology and it is combined with IoTs technology. The proposed model is also furnished with facial recognition technology; it can take pedestrians' temperatures automatically by displaying the pedestrian's personal information. To prevent spreading coronavirus, the proposed design has high demand from the healthcare system. It is now becoming feasible to detect routine parameters of isolated remote area-based COVID-19 patients. An Artificial intelligent based system is proposed [10] in which in the absence of a doctor a feedback action can be taken, during emergency an automated injection system injects the dose into the body of the patient, GSM messages and live locations are also provided, and emails also sent during emergency conditions. The Blynk application is used to show some parameters to the doctor remotely in case of any abrupt change in parameters. The IoT system is capable to send the location to relatives and the emergency team, in case of non-availability of the doctors.

3 Proposed Methodology

The proposed work is divided into two parts- First part is a model setup using various IoTs hardware devices and the second part is to recognize faces. An algorithmic flowchart can be seen in Fig. 3 and Fig. 4 below. Initially, the system activates face recognition program that runs constantly until it recognizes a face, once a face recognizes it activates both the sensors connected to it and displays Temperatures, SpO2 level/BPM with name of recognized person on the OLED display connected to raspberry pi, also they get stored in firebase Real-time database. Temperature and SpO2 levels are checked using conditional statements, if the values are suspicious then the program calls a function where an alert is sent through telegram to the admin regarding the potential symptoms of COVID-19 positive person. The working flowchart (Fig. 3) of the model is illustrated below. There is another flowchart (Fig. 4) that explains the working of one of the important modules in our novel work that is responsible for temperature surveillance of people using the device. Initial two steps- interfacing the sensors with the Raspberry Pi single board computer system and enabling I2C communication between them. While a user is using the device and his/her face got detected the program runs this module that activates the sensor and measures temperature of human body surface further it checks if the person is safe and do not have fever that is one of the common and easily ignored symptom of COVID-19 virus, It compares measured values with the standard value and if the values are within normal range it displays measured temperature with name of the person on OLED display and also updates daily health data on firebase real-time database But if the values are suspicious abnormal then an alert is sent to the admin regarding the suspicious temperature measured.

3.1 Algorithm Used for Face Detection

Histogram of Oriented Gradients [17] method invented in 2005, has been used for face detection. Steps are as follows-

STEP-I: Converting images into black and white.
STEP-II: Replacing the pixels with gradients, while only considering the direction that changes the brightness, the same exact representation is obtained by both truly dark images and truly bright images.

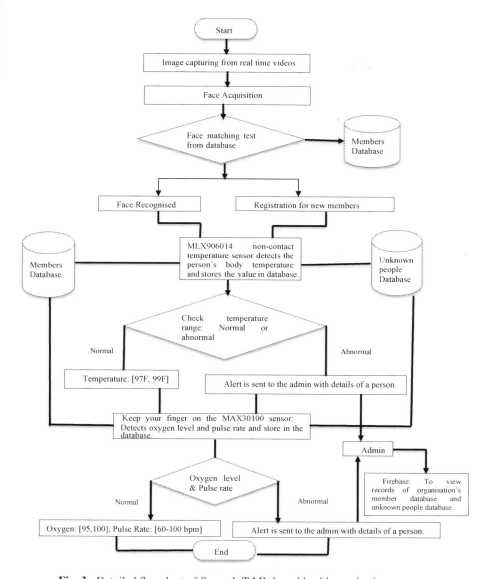

Fig. 3. Detailed flowchart of Smart IoT-ML based health monitoring system.

STEP-III: Turn the basic or original image into representations which will be simple by capturing the basic structure of a face. It will be achieved by breaking the image into small squares of 16x16 pixels each.

STEP-IV: Count gradients points in all major direction in each square and replace the square in the image that was strongest with the arrow directions, using this technique faces can be found.

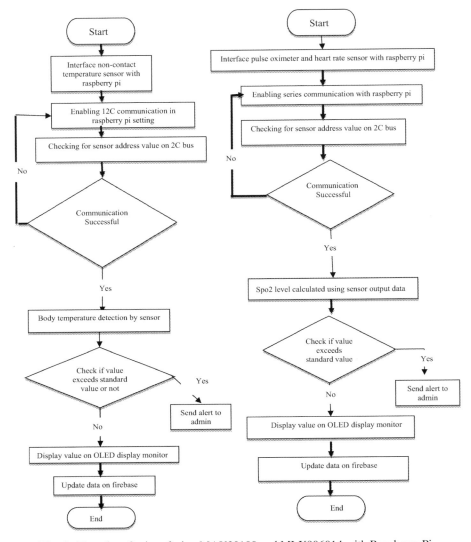

Fig. 4. Flowchart for interfacing MAX30100 and MLX906014 with Raspberry Pi.

STEP-V: Face landmark estimation [18] is used to overcome the difference occurred in different poses identified differently to the computer system (Fig. 5).

3.2 Algorithm Used for Face Recognition [7]

STEP-I: Processing each frame of a video [19–21] as it is being captured.
STEP-II: Scale the image down to a quarter of its original size.
STEP-III: Change the BGR of the image to RGB format.

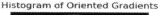
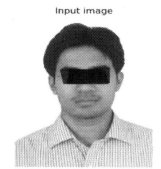

Fig. 5. Input image and its corresponding histogram of oriented gradients image.

STEP-IV: Provide a data array of 128 bytes for each face that is found.
STEP-V: Evaluate array against the arrays already present in the local database.
STEP-VI: Determine the index of minimal distance by calculating the Euclidean distance from each face in the local database.
STEP-VII: Obtain the best match index's name (Fig. 6).

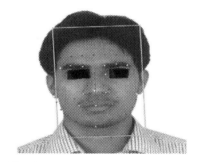

Fig. 6. Face detection with annotation.

4 Result and Discussion

During the COVID-19 pandemic the three factor Temperature, Oxygen and Heart Rate is the most important. We are unaware which person is COVID positive or negative without having an initial medical check-up. The proposed model is ready to produce normal/abnormal COVID results of a person as per mentioned three parameters. After deploying this type of system at an organization, we can easily monitor the health of members of an organization and provide basic medical check-up facilities. As per Fig. 7; we analyze the records over a month of these factors that help us to visualize data that can be easily understood by everyone. The Monthly bar plot and line plot of the person's health parameter can be shown in below Fig. 8. The bar of temperature, oxygen level and heart rate values is plotted according to the dates. The bar and line graph is made by taking the mean of values of one-day repeating this for oxygen and heart rate of 30 days.

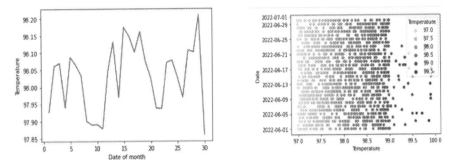

Fig. 7. Line plot and scatter plot of one-month temperature data.

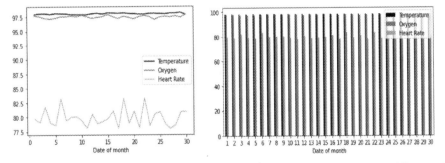

Fig. 8. Temperature, oxygen and heart rate data visualization through bar graph and line graph.

4.1   Performance Metric

To analyze the proposed ML and IoT-based smart health monitoring system, certain samples were taken. The explanations is given in detail below-

4.1.1   Confusion Matrix

Confusion matrix is a technique for measuring the performance in a machine learning classification. it is represented in a kind of a table which helps us to know the performance (Fig. 9 below) of the classification model on the test data. The classification method in the model shown here has been trained to distinguish between "normal, abnormal" value. The produced confusion matrix might seem as follows when using a sample of 300 data sets, 256 of which are normal, 44 of which are abnormal values.

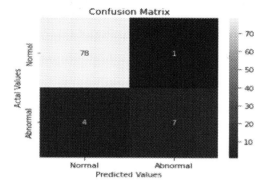

Fig. 9. Illustration of proposed work through confusion matrix.

Accuracy: From the various evaluation measures of the performance, one of the most crucial is accuracy, it is used to determine how well a machine learning algorithm is working. To calculate it, divide the total number of correctly classified occurrences by the sum of all instances. It is represented mathematically as follows:

$$Accuracy = (TP + TN)/(TP + TN + FP + FN)$$
$$= (78 + 7)/(78 + 7 + 4 + 1)$$
$$= 85/90 = \mathbf{94.44\%}$$

Precision: Precision is used to measure the effectiveness of supervised learning algorithms. It is the ratio of the total positive values to the correctly anticipated positive values. It is demonstrated mathematically as follows:

$$Precision = TP/(TP + FP)$$
$$= 78/(78 + 4)$$
$$= 78/82 = \mathbf{95.12\%}$$

Recall: It is yet another performance indicator that can be used to measure of the effectiveness of a supervised machine learning algorithm. The ratio of accurately predicted positive class values to all actual class values. It is demonstrated mathematically as follows:

$$Recall = TP/(TP + FN)$$
$$= 78/(78 + 1)$$
$$= 78/79 = \mathbf{98.73\%}$$

F1-Score: A supervised machine learning algorithm's performance is determined by the F1 Score performance metric. It is calculated using two metrics, namely precision and recall. It can be calculated using precision and recall in mathematics with harmonic mean as follows (Table 2):

$$F1\text{-}Score = 2 * Precision * Recall/(Precision + Recall)$$
$$= \mathbf{96.39\%}$$

Table 2. Confusion matrix using different algorithms result

ML algorithm	TP	TN	FN	FP	Support
Logistic regression	76	8	3	3	90
Decision tree	77	9	2	2	90
SVM	78	7	4	1	90
Random forest	74	11	2	3	90

To ensure that the suggested model works well in every circumstance, the biases in the dataset are removed via shuffling. The Decision tree in our suggested system has demonstrated the best outcome in terms of false negative. The first position uses the Decision Tree technique and Random Forest, which has two false negatives, whereas, the second and third place uses logistic regression and SVM respectively.

4.1.2 Accuracy

The different performance measures are generated as result using a novel dataset, in which the Decision Tree has the highest accuracy 95.5%, Support Vector Machine achieved the highest accuracy as 94%, and Logistic Regression has achieved the lowest among all ML techniques as 93% (Table 3 and Fig. 10).

Table 3. Comparative study of accuracy using different algorithm

ML algorithm	Accuracy
Logistic regression	93.3333
Decision tree	95.5555
SVM	94.4444
Random forest	94.4444

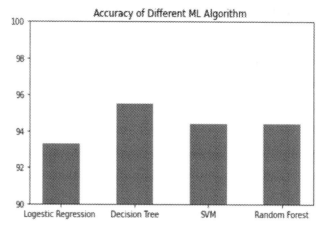

Fig. 10. Accuracy bar graph plot for different machine learning techniques.

5   Conclusion

AI facilitated a smart dedicated gateway to challenge the Covid-19 Pandemic. The goal of this work is to advance an AI-based smart health monitoring system that can provide real-time health monitoring in an organization or any public places. This device is useful to preserve quality managements with real-time information, with the implementation of this device the security of the organization can be improved, as health services are important in any place. Automating health services helps reduce the burden on human beings and also provides an accurate result. With this strong interconnectivity, devices are linked to the internet. All the data is stored and monitored at the firebase database in real-time. The temperature level, oxygen level, and heart rate is the most common health measure in covid-19. Real-time interface is enabled at the edge to provide critical alarm notifications when there is abnormal heart, temperature and oxygen levels measures of any person. Using decision tree machine learning algorithm, our model accuracy is 95.5%. Along with a firebase database stored in the cloud, IoT provides an opportunity to add more recent advanced features and sensors to this system that will make this device more updatable and flexible in future. With the appropriate implementation of this device, schools, government, and academics can create a better positive environment to fight with similar disease.

References

1. Arora, N., Gupta, V.: Study on impact of COVID-19 on Indian economy. Int. J. Sci. Res. (IJSR) **9**(7) (2020). ISSN: 2319-7064
2. Joshi, A., Bhaskar, P., Gupta, P.K.: Indian economy amid COVID-19 lockdown: a perspective. J. Pure Appl. Microbiol. **14**(Suppl. 1), 957–961 (2020)
3. Singh, R.P., Javaid, M., Haleem, A., Suman, R.: Internet of things (IoT) applications to fight against COVID-19 pandemic. Diabetes Metab. Syndr. Clin. Res. Rev. **14**(4), 521–524 (2020)

4. Bhardwaj, V., Joshi, R., Gaur, A.M.: IoT-based smart health monitoring system for COVID-19. SN Comput. Sci. **3**(2), 1–11 (2022). https://doi.org/10.1007/s42979-022-01015-1

5. Varshini, B., Yogesh, H.R., Pasha, S.D., Suhail, M., Madhumitha, V., Sasi, A.: IoT-enabled smart doors for monitoring body temperature and face mask detection. Glob. Transit. Proc. **2**(2), 246–254 (2021)

6. Khan, M., Mehnaz, S., Shaha, A., Nayem, M., Bourouis, S.: IoT-based smart health monitoring system for COVID-19 patients (2022)

7. Kumar, K.S., Semwal, V.B., Tripathi, R.C.: Real time face recognition using AdaBoost improved fast PCA algorithm. arXiv preprint arXiv:1108.1353 (2011)

8. Mohammed, M.N., Syamsudin, H., Al-Zubaidi, S., Karim, S., Ramli, R., Yusuf, E.: Novel COVID-19 detection and diagnosis system using IoT based smart helmet. Int. J. Psychosoc. Rehabil. **24**, 2296–2303 (2020)

9. Semwal, V.B., Gupta, A., Lalwani, P.: An optimized hybrid deep learning model using ensemble learning approach for human walking activities recognition. J. Supercomput. **77**(11), 12256–12279 (2021)

10. Rahman, M.Z.U., et al.: Real-time artificial intelligence based health monitoring, diagnosing and environmental control system for COVID-19 patients. Math. Biosci. Eng. **19**(8), 7586–7605 (2022)

11. Bakhri, S., Rosiana, E., Saputra, R.: Design of low cost pulse oximetry based on Raspberry Pi. J. Phys. Conf. Ser. **1501**(1), 012003 (2020)

12. Li, F., Valero, M., Shahriar, H., Khan, R., Ahamed, S.: Wi-COVID - A COVID-19 symptom detection and patient monitoring framework using WiFi. Smart Health **19**, 10014 (2021)

13. Connecting the MLX90614 infrared thermometer to the Raspberry PI. https://olegkutkov.me/2017/08/10/mlx90614-raspberry/. Accessed July 2022

14. PyMLX90614 · PyPI. https://pypi.org/project/PyMLX90614. Accessed July 2022

15. Pelayo, R.: How to use the MAX30100 as Arduino Heart Rate Sensor. Microcontroller Tutorials, 23 July 2021. https://www.teachmemicro.com/max30100-arduino-heart-rate-sensor/. Accessed 1 Aug 2022

16. Otoom, M., et al.: An IoT-based framework for early identification and monitoring of COVID-19 cases. Biomed. Signal Process. Control **62**, 102149 (2020)

17. Dalal, N., Triggs, B.: Histograms of oriented gradients for human detection. In: IEEE Computer Society Conference on Computer Vision and Pattern Recognition (CVPR 2005), vol. 1. IEEE (2005)

18. Kazemi, V., Sullivan, J.: One millisecond face alignment with an ensemble of regression trees. In: Proceedings of the IEEE Conference on Computer Vision and Pattern Recognition (2014)

19. Rajnish, K.R., Agrawal, A.: Video summary based on F-sift, Tamura textural and middle level semantic feature. Procedia Comput. Sci. **89**, 870–876 (2016)

20. Gupta, A., Semwal, V.B.: Multiple task human gait analysis and identification: ensemble learning approach. In: Mohanty, S.N. (ed.) Emotion and Information Processing, pp. 185–197. Springer, Cham (2020). https://doi.org/10.1007/978-3-030-48849-9_12

21. Kumar, K.S., et al.: Multiple cameras using real time object tracking for surveillance and security system. In: 2010 3rd International Conference on Emerging Trends in Engineering and Technology. IEEE (2010)

Implementation of SARSA-HMM Technique for Face Recognition

Anil Kumar Yadav[1]($\boxtimes$), Shiv Shankar Prasad Shukla[1], Vikas Kumar Jain[1], and Rajesh Kumar Pateriya[2]

[1] School of Computing Science and Engineering, VIT University, Bhopal, India
anilkumar.yadav@vitbhopal.ac.in
[2] Computer Science Department, Maulana Azad National Institute of Technology, Bhopal, India

Abstract. SARSA (State-Action-Reward-State-Action) is a Markov Decision Process Strategy learning method (MDP). There can be discrete, permanent, stationary, time variable or noisy observations in real-time processes. The main difficulty is to characterize observations by estimating their parameters using a well-defined mathematical model as a parametric random process. The hidden Markov model is one such statistical model to interpret the (unobserved) process by examining the pattern of a sequence. HMM-based methods frequently used in the study and prediction of the most likely sequence of states, such as usage and activity patterns, as well as transitions between different process stages. In this paper, we proposed SARSA facial recognition technique used to select overlapping subsets from each image, which estimates the hidden attributes for each image. In the result section, represent that our proposed algorithm having better recognition rate than PCA. It can be used for solving complex feature selection and other solution for the development of further image.

Keywords: Hidden Markov Models (HMM) · Self-learning · SARSA learning

1 Introduction

During the training for mathematical model production, HMM defined unattended feature. Two methods exist, first defining unnoticed or hidden characteristics based on a specific state. Another based on the function of state probability for any state. Reinforcement learning based on interaction between test and error to solve complex decision-making issues [1]. Unlike controlled learning where a variety of practical challenges (e.g., backgammon games, grid world problems etc. It also addressed and developing effective reinforcement learning approaches is critical to the advancement of artificial intelligence [2]. The decision-making process interacts based on state assessment with the unknown environment. It also used to make policy decisions for optimal purposes. An agent to identify an optimal strategy can still use time differences [3, 4]. Agent's response based on the movement towards action in the form of a reward and penalty over the given environment predicts a certain future reward. Model Marko described behavioral psychology that helps to learn skills in training. Time-based learning in different circumstances defines very quickly, given the conditions of archived optimality.

N. Khare et al. (Eds.): MIND 2022, CCIS 1763, pp. 245–254, 2022.
https://doi.org/10.1007/978-3-031-24367-7_25

Temporary approaches to difference methodology used for off-the-shelf strategies, such as Q-learning. The behavioral approach used during the learning process for controlling the representative approximate state by defining a specific parameter [5]. The advantage of the suggested method is that it uses a research strategy to ensure that information diversified sufficiently. Model hidden Marko used for policy-making it offers numerous benefits, such as the absence of line-strategy approaches. Many to estimate future benefits have used it and the non-iterative process [6, 7]. The identification of faces and video images becomes popular with a variety of applications related to navigation and complex problem identifying [8]. Facial system recognition that can work in different situations such as different lighting systems and facial system recognition. FRS allowed a coordinative facial picture mechanism or semi-mechanism procedure. A distinctively organized range connected, such as entertainment, safety information, enforcement and intelligence (surveillance), forensic, sensitive environment, business, and government and wearable recognition frameworks. Entertainment: Pc game, virtual reality, young people the definition of stimulation space Tools for learning, coaching, workshops and human robot associations. Interaction with the human computer. Information Security: Privacy and safety of information play an important role in the uninterrupted exchange of information from one place to another. It includes application security, security of information, encryption of documents, computer network security, network access, restoration records, secure exchange terminals, etc. [14–16]. Law social control and Surveillance: Legal authorization largely refers to any framework in which a number of people in society are involved. It extends propelled observation of features, CCTV camera, portal control, theft, suspect and testing. Forensic: It uses the key problem of identifying shorter proof. It examines the preventive law on the basis of specific gadgets. Basic concept based on the evidence chain to discover the exact matter exactly what happened and who are the main culprits for specific cases on the basis of fingerprinting, other blood test lines DNA tests etc. Some criminal cases include body ID, criminal investigation, recognizable evidence of terrorists, identification of parenthood, and missing children [14, 17–19]. Smart Environment: At present, scientists effectively structure bright situations such as the sound, functionality and haptic interfaces to various platform situations such as home, car workshops etc. This system's basic aim is to create perceptual capabilities to detect basic population characteristics. A brilliant framework essentially gives fast external appearance to recognize in different states. Commercial: Day considerations, missing youth, gaming industry, private security, internet, e-commerce, social insurance, charge cards, mobile phones, ATM, administration of therapeutic records, security and login systems [20]. Government Applications: Different government application definitions are UID cards, PAN cards, Voter ID cards, driving license, Passport, sign-on individual gadgets, office mechanization, representative participation, movement and detention, etc. Wearable Recognition System: The wearable devices can be adapted to a particular customer and are incorporated in the customer's exercise more effectively and personally. PCs, cameras, mouthpieces and various sensors place themselves in a man's clothing. In case you add an eye lens to a camera, then face recognition programs can help you to collect the name of the person you whisper so you can take a gander in your ear. Confront recognition is therefore a vital part of wearable frames such as memory partners, specialists in recognition and the establishment of careful frameworks. In this manner, it is required for bunches of future acknowledgment frameworks to be coordinated with the client's garments and extras [20–22]. Robotics and Controls: In multi robot frames and controls, the FRS may be the most prominent application. Perceptibly, the recognition force of robots will be expanded to help build the utility, strength and knowledge of others. 3D-FRS: encourages patterns in the programming of facial recognition that pretend to be more accurate. In this way, a constant 3D image of the facial surface of a man was found, and a short time later a few kinds of elements were connected to the nose, eye and so on. These are all remarkable areas and after some time they do not change [23]. Biometric Attendance Machines: It can contribute to saving time and expenses. These systems promote reliability in the company [24–29]. Access control vehicle: This zone meets the expectations of the vehicle's access control on safe premises. The framework co-ordinates tags against a recorded database without human mediation. The lighting could use to check the personality of the driver in the face. Field Analyst like Age & Gender Classification: With their age and their sexual orientation, Field Analyst gradually recognizes the face pictures. It provides customer properties with CCTV cameras. The awards for the arrangements are speed, precision and the ability to coordinate constant research. Automated Border Clearance: Is the Frameworks of FRS and Fingerprint Acceptance the best biometric innovation in the world? This offers customers fast, leeway frameworks that only change. As part of Japanese and other Asian world aero plane terminals, the migration of biometrics as demonstrable and leeway frameworks is as frequently as possible used. Factory for cyber security: This framework continuously dissects and collects data from digital attacks, offers innovation and know-how to prevent unapproved access. Smart City Solution: The first arrangement that was sought from the earliest base of offices to the general population will be the development and development of the smart city. After a time, development slows down and new problems emerge, which force urban communities to reclassify themselves and to undergo a consistent restauration and restoration cycle. FRS supports are added to some settings, such as Vehicle Access Control, Field Analyst, Enforcement and Monitoring, shrewd situations etc. In social associations, recognitions are crucial to our knowledge of the individual's personality, mindset, sexual orientation and age [29]. It is currently perceived throughout that individual have developed an intellectual and unbiased tool for face recognition. Again, the memory recognition of people is usually not correct. We must then prepare a machine to perceive the faces. The importance of face recognition is demonstrated by various applications. Importance and its elements persuade us to do so. Computer vision propellers and improved sensor procedures have now led to a restored enthusiasm for the creation of a facial recognition framework. Face recognition, since the facial component of people are not extremely special from each other, is exceptionally unpredictable. Therefore, before transmitting any new framework, it must know the essentials of FRS.

2   Proposed Model and Algorithm

Hidden Markov Models and SARSA major algorithms for voice recognition, action identification and time learning. Now we propose new approaches to recognize the face as a grey scale based on HMM with SARSA. Feature in the face such as hair, forehead, eyes, nose and mouth represent the image shown in Fig. 1 sequentially, upwards and downwards. Aij also proved to be a non-zero probability of transition.

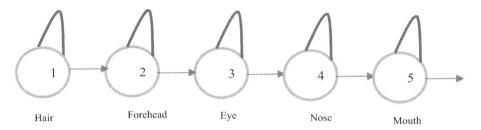

Fig. 1. Proposed model of HMM

2.1   Extraction of Features

The first face is grey and divided into contact blocks of width and height. Number of blocks recovered from the sample observed by the techniques proposed. Proposed method used to accurately identify and detect the specific image in the given image number. A little observer vector can produce insufficient discrimination, whereas the large absence of a certain sample of the image can lead to insufficient discrimination. The frontal faces in the training set photographed in various lighting conditions. The observation obtained and used to train the given face in Fig. 2 using HMM combined with SARSA learning after segmentation of the given picture in the training set extraction of observation.

Model of Training:

Data for Training Input

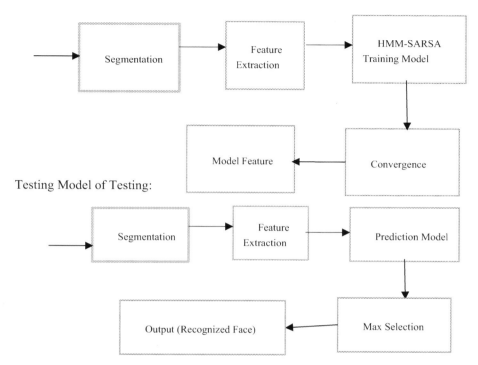

Fig. 2. Training and testing scheme for HMM-SARSA

The probability computation done using the SARSA method for ease of use. As possible, face locations. In this paper, we present the HMM-SARSA Learning algorithm as follows:

Define the discount rate $0 > 1$ as an input parameter.

1. For each state and action, randomly initialize state action pairings Q(s, a).
2. For all iterations, loop for each episode.
3. Set up the current state (si)
4. Each episode's iterative process
5. Decide on a greedy policy (π)
6. Move forward (a)
7. Updated state action pairs (look up table) and greedy policy-

$$Q\pi(s, \ a) = \gamma(x1 - i) \sum \pi a' \ Qt(st + 1, \ at + 1) \tag{1}$$

8. Until the goal state is reached
9. Come to an end

HMM-SARSA Learning Algorithms Implementation

For each set of learning parameters, a random state action pair is selected using a greedy strategy and loop. Learn the rate and rate of discount ($\alpha > 0$, & $0 < \gamma > 1$), policy ($\varepsilon > 0$);

Every state, create state Q (s, a) and perform action a;

Begin (each state si: s)

Initialize; start state (s,a);

{

current state and action are defined in the supplied Q table as (si), (ai), respectively.

{

Updated   search   results   for   "greedy   policies"   -

$Q\pi\,(s,\ a)\ =\ R\gamma\,(x1-i)\sum \pi a'\ Qt\,(st+1,\ at+1)$

{

Using action for updates

}

}

}

If final state = goal state; then stop.

3 Comparison and Result

The following table and graphic use the HMM-SARSA Learning Performance Algorithm to assess the accuracy of learning efficiency.

The accuracy of the HMM-SARSA learning and PCA algorithm with various episodes presented in Table 1 and 2 so that these data compared, and the accuracy shown as a percentage in Fig. 3.

Table 1. SARSA learning algorithm- HMM table of comparisons between episodes

Recognition rate	For Epoch E = 1000	For Epoch E = 3000	For Epoch E = 5000	For Epoch E = 7000	For Epoch E = 9000	For Epoch E = 11000
R_1	93.50	68.72	73.41	94.73	95.21	96.23
R_2	68.23	73.32	69.31	78.70	82.39	83.55
R_3	66.51	70.31	81.54	72.51	83.35	92.62
R_4	72.11	82.71	84.43	78.26	89.55	85.14
R_5	91.14	93.70	63.12	93.28	93.89	93.55
Average	80.60%	82.83%	74.59%	86.35%	88.69%	92.69%

Tables 1 and 2 illustrate the accuracy of the learning algorithms SARSA and HMM with different episodes so that data compared and accuracy as a percentage shown on Fig. 3. Figure 4 shows yet another comparison.

Table 2. PCA technique over different episodes

Recognition rate	For Epoch E = 1000	For Epoch E = 3000	For Epoch E = 5000	For Epoch E = 7000	For Epoch E = 9000	For Epoch E = 11000
R_1	72.40	94.90	84	93.78	83	94.71
R_2	71	73	73	84	95.82	92.82
R_3	76	69.80	92.72	93.62	91.76	84.61
R_4	90	79.81	95.62	85.80	96.82	93.72
R_6	96.99	96.81	80.62	86.86	97.73	95.54
Average	79.87%	82.52%	81.72%	92.59%	89.71%	96.32%

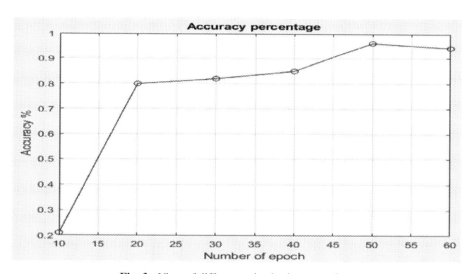

Fig. 3. View of different episodes in comparison

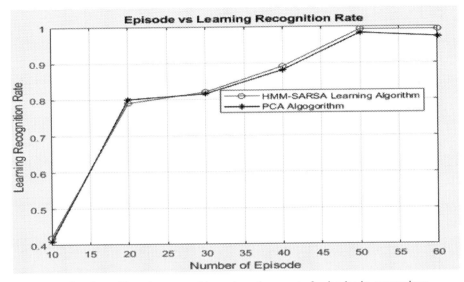

Fig. 4. View of learning recognition rate and amount of episodes in comparison

4 Conclusion and Future Work

A new face recognition strategy based on HMMs and SARSA Learning proposed in this research. The HMMs given a model selection approach. To discover the optimal model for the data without having to think about it. The efficiency of HMMs in solving the challenge of face identification based on accurate features. In comparison to the PCA method, the HMM-SARSA algorithm discovered that it reduced the number of iterations and episodes while also improving the learning recognition rate. In order to evaluation of different learning techniques the result section, represent that our proposed algorithm having better recognition rate than PCA. It can be used for solving complex feature selection and other solution for the development of further image prediction.

References

1. Kaelbling, L.P., Littman, M.L., Moore, A.P.: Reinforcement learning: a survey. J. Artif. Intell. Res. **4**, 237–285 (1996)
2. Bellman, R.E. A Markov decision process. J. Math. Mech. **6**, 679–684 (1957)
3. Fitzner, G.: Homepage. In: Start als Hausarzt, pp. 277–280. Springer, Heidelberg (2021). https://doi.org/10.1007/978-3-662-62874-4_42
4. Sutton, R.S.: Learning to predict by the methods of temporaldifferences. Mach. Learn. **3**, 9–44 (1988)
5. Watkins, C., Dayan, P.: Q-learning. Mach. Learn. **8**(3–4), 9–44 (1992)
6. Boyan, J.A., Moore, A.W.: Generalization in reinforcement learning: Safely approximating the value function. In: Advances in Neural Information Processing Systems, pp. 369–376 (1995)
7. Rummery, G., Niranjan, M.: Online Q-Learning Using Connectionist Systems. Cambridge University, Tech. Rep. CUED/F-INFENG/TR166 (1994)

8. Hamid, Berenji, R., Vengerov, D.: Learning, cooperation, and coordination in multi-agent systems. In: Proceedings of 9th IEEE International Conference on Fuzzy Systems (2000)
9. Vidhate, D.A., Kulkarni, P.: Enhancement in decision making with improved performance by multiagent learning algorithms. IOSR J. Comput. Eng. 1(18), 18–25 (2016)
10. Tokarchuk, L., Bigham, J., Cuthbert, L.: Fuzzy Sarsa: an approach to fuzzifying Sarsa Learning (2015)
11. Padmapriya, T., Saminadan, V.: Inter-cell Load Balancing technique for multi-class traffic in MIMO-LTE-a networks. Int. J. Electr. Electr. Data Commun. 3(8), 22–26 (2015). ISSN:2320-2084
12. Manikanthan, S.V., Baskaran, K.: Low cost VLSI design implementation of sorting network for ACSFD in wireless sensor network. CiiT Int. J. Program. Device Circ. Syst. 3 (2011). PDCS112011008. Print: ISSN: 0974-973X & Online: ISSN: 0974-9624
13. Rajesh, M., Gnanasekar, J.M.: Congestion control in heterogeneous wireless ad hoc network using FRCC. Aust. J. Basic Appl. Sci. 9(7), 698–702 (2015)
14. Jagadesh Kumar, M.: Face recognition by machines: is it an effective surveillance tactic? IETE Tech. Rev. 30(2), 93–94 (2013)
15. Jain, A.K., Dass, S.C., Karthik, N.: Can soft biometric traits assist user recognition? In: Proceedings of SPIE, vol. 5404, pp. 561–572 (2004)
16. Kanya Bennett, A., Comment: can facial recognition technology be used to fight the new war against terrorism? Examining the constitutionality of facial recognition surveillance systems. North Carolina Kornal of Law Technol. 3(1), 115–174 (2001)
17. Rutherford, E.: Facial-recognition tech has people pegged. North Carolina J. Law Technol. (2001)
18. Watson. A.B.: Image compression using the discrete Cosine transform. Math. J. 4(1), 81–88 (1994)
19. Khayam, S.A.: The Discrete Cosine Transform (DCT): Theory and Application. Technical Report, Michigan State University (2003)
20. Rowley, H.A., Baluja, S., Kanade, T.: Neural network-based face detection. Comput. Vis. Pattern Recogn. 20(1), 23–38 (1996)
21. Lu, Y., Zeng, N., Liu, Y., Zhang, N.: A hybrid wavelet neural network and switching particle swarm optimization algorithm for face direction recognition. Int. J. Neurocomputing, 155, 219–224 (2015)
22. Kasar, M.M., Bhattacharyya, D.: Kim, T-h.: Face recognition using neural network: a review. Int. J. Secur. Appl. 10(3), 81–100 (2016)
23. Shen, L., Bai, L., Ji, Z.: A SVM face recognition method based on optimized Gabor features. In: Qiu, G., Leung, C., Xue, X., Laurini, R. (eds.) VISUAL 2007. LNCS, vol. 4781, pp. 165–174. Springer, Heidelberg (2007). https://doi.org/10.1007/978-3-540-76414-4_17
24. Heisele, B., Ho, P., Poggio, T.: Face recognition with support vector machines: global versus component-based approach. In: Proceedings of 8th International Conference on Computer Vision, vol. 2, pp. 688–694 (2001)
25. Hafed, Z.M.: Face recognition using DCT. Int. J. Comput. Vis. 43, 167–188 (2001)
26. Guodong, G., Li, S.Z., Chan, K.: Face recognition by support vector machines. In: Proceedings Fourth IEEE International Conference on Automatic Face and Gesture Recognition (Cat. No. PR00580), pp. 196–201 (2000)
27. Jonathon Philips, P.: Support vector machine applied to face recognition. In: Advances in Neural Information Processing System, PP. 803–809. Technical Report NISTIR, MIT Press (1999)

28. Yang, M.-H., Moghaddam, B.: Gender classification using support vector machines. In: Proceedings 2000 International Conference on Image Processing (Cat. No. 00CH37101), vol. 2, pp. 471–474 (2000)
29. Kim, K., Jung, K., Kim, H.J.: Face recognition using kernel principal component analysis. Signal Process. Lett. IEEE **9**(2), 40–42 (2002)

A Novel BiLo-T Based Gradient Method for Identifying Diverse Shape Variants of Ovarian Cyst in Female Pelvic MRI Imaging

Lidiya Thampi[1]([envelope]) [iD] and Amel Antony[2]

[1] Indian Institute of Information Technology, Kottayam, Kerala, India
lidiya@iiitkottayam.ac.in
[2] Lisie Institute of Radiology Research and Imaging Sciences, Kottayam, India

Abstract. A unique fully automatic segmentation method for different shape variants of ovarian cyst is presented. Ovarian cyst is a common abdominal cyst occurs at all stages of life including infants and fetuses. The present work focuses on the identification of arbitrary shaped ovarian cystic masses and further carried out the segmentation task for feature extraction and classification. Identification is carried out using a Luminance oriented Low-Threshold (BiLo-T) based gradient method which further utilizes texture and shape features in achieving the objective. In addition, the findings of shape similarity indices between manual and automatic segmentations are shown. The average similarity index is 91.92%, the JSI is 85.6%, and the DSC is 88.48% in the comparison. The experimental results demonstrate that our proposed scheme is very robust in segmenting diverse shape variants of ovarian cysts, indicating its good performance in real medical applications. The algorithms developed for segmenting the ROI from female PMRI have been tested and evaluated using real image datasets and also compared with other existing segmentation methods.

Keywords: Segmentation · Female pelvis · MRI imaging · Ovarian cyst

1 Introduction

Female pelvic abnormalities have been linked to benign and malignant neoplasms of the uterus, ovaries, fallopian tubes, and cervix. These malignancies are expected to rise worldwide particularly in low- and middle-income countries (LMIC's) like India and China. Cervical cancer was estimated to be the second most common female malignancy in India with 96,922 new cases annually, after breast cancer and it ranks as the second leading cause of female cancer deaths (about 60,078 deaths) (Bruni et al. 2019). Figure 1 depicts a graph comparing age-specific cervical cancer incidence and mortality rates in India. The graph shows that the majority of occurrences occur between the ages of 50 and 60. Nonetheless, behind breast cancer, it is the second most frequent female-specific malignancy (World Cancer Report 2014). The incidence rate has tended to fall from 20,863 cases in 2012 to 13,619 cases in 2018 among women aged 50 to 54.

© The Author(s), under exclusive license to Springer Nature Switzerland AG 2022
N. Khare et al. (Eds.): MIND 2022, CCIS 1763, pp. 255–267, 2022.
https://doi.org/10.1007/978-3-031-24367-7_26

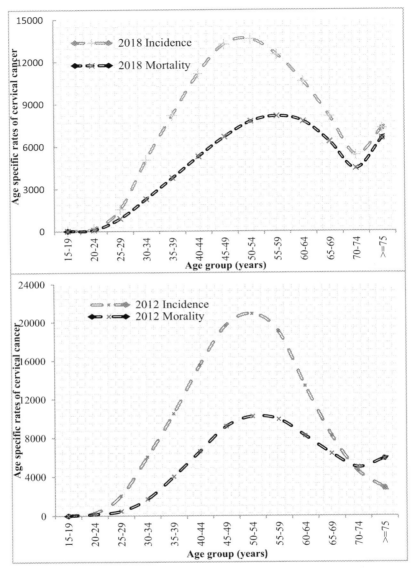

Fig. 1. Comparison of age-specific cervical cancer incidence and mortality rates in India. Estimates for 2012 and 2018. Redrawn from (Bruni et al. 2016, 2019).

India, the world's second most populous country, currently has a population of 1.37 billion people and is expected to reach 1.53 billion by 2030. With the increase in population growth, the chance of acquiring cancer is also increasing, and women aged 15 and older are at risk of developing cancer (Thampi et al. 2018).

The diagnosis of gynecology related symptoms is normally performed through periodic pelvic examinations by an expert radiologist. The doctors suggest additional diagnostic treatment or testing as part of this pelvic examination. Experts and gynecologists recommend a routine pelvic examination for all women unless any medical problem, preferably after 21 years. A routine pelvic exam can definitely help to find the possible signs of ovarian cysts, sexually transmitted infections, uterine fibroids or early-stage cancer. However, this clinical or physical examination overestimates or underestimates the actual extent of disease and getting troubled with wrong decision (LaPolla et al. 1986). For this reason, several imaging modalities like transvaginal ultrasonography (TVUS), computed tomography (CT), and magnetic resonance imaging (MRI) have been used as a diagnostic tool for the pre-treatment work-up of cervical cancer all over the world (Faria et al. 2015).

A priori the diagnosis on female pelvic malignancies was based on the outcomes derived from the Pap smear, colposcopy and other biopsy tests (Bourgioti et al. 2016). Over a period of time lots of positive breakthrough has occurred in the field of imaging. MRI has complemented other existing diagnostic techniques like CT, sonography in monitoring anomalies in female pelvis (Brocker et al. 2011, Chou et al. 1997). It's better tumor delineation and improved tissue contrast helps in further therapy planning. The challenges for abdominal pelvic imaging at 3 T system in contrast to 1.5 T have been discussed (Brown et al. 2006). An increase in signal-to noise ratio (SNR) is the peak advantage of high field MR imaging and at the same time it creates problem of shading artefacts and signal inhomogeneity's when compared with 1.5 T system. A 1.5 T system MRI device was used to capture the images for this entire research project. Ultrasound should be utilized as the primary imaging assessment for patients with suspected gynecological pathology, while computed tomography (CT) is rarely employed in female pelvic imaging due to its low contrast in identifying soft tissues. (Xyda et al. 2015).

The rest of the paper is laid out as follows. The relevant work proposed by various researchers is presented in Sect. 2. The dataset definition and CAD system implementation are covered in Sect. 3. Section 4 contain the performance evaluation, results, and discussion, while Sect. 5 concluded with limitations and future work.

2 Related Works

MRI was one of the proven imaging modalities that can be employed for early diagnosis and staging of female pelvic cancers, despite the availability of other imaging modalities such as transvaginal ultrasonography (TVUS) and computed tomography (CT) (Xyda et al. 2015, Umutlu et al. 2019). Automatic detection of anomalies in PMRI plays a crucial role in the computational processing of images because manual reading and analysis of MRI images by radiologists is time-consuming due to the vast volume of data. The radiologist's experience and competence are essential for a successful diagnosis. MRI has its own set of artefacts, just as other imaging modalities. These artifacts need to be identified and certain necessary steps should be taken to eliminate the root of its origin or at least minimize them. Since the noise reduction is vital and necessary, the reduction methods are carried out either in acquisition mode or in the post-acquisition mode. The literature mainly targeting on the filtering-based approach rather than transform and statistical based approaches of denoising methods. Different reviews of MRI denoising methods can be found in (Mohan et al. 2014). The initial use of median filtering in image processing was first suggested by (Frieden et al. 1976). Many more fast algorithms are also evolved from these basic enhancement methods (Huang et al. 1979). This simplest median filtering approach (Mustaqeem et al. 2012) was used to address the denoising problem in MRI images. The effect of median filtering with a mask size of 5×5 pixels has a greater impact on their accuracy values (Ozer et al. 2010). A combination of both median and mean filters can be seen in (Yousuf et al. 2011; Gupta et al. 2018) to remove the noise from MRI medical images. An attempt was made to reduce the spatially varying Rician noise in MRI image (Manjón et al. 2012). Here the denoising strength of the filter depends upon the local noise information of images.

Although there are many demonstrated methods for detecting and locating the cancerous tissues from different MRI images, the exploration in the field of female pelvic MRI (PMRI) is very less. We developed an abnormality recognition method for extracting tumor from female pelvic ultrasound (PUS) images in (Thampi et al. 2018), where texture and shape features are mined from the segmented region. The range of values for each feature is note down. An attempt for uterine region segmentation and volume measurement in uterine fibroids can be seen in (Fallahi et. al. 2010). This combined method initially uses FCM (fuzzy C mean) algorithm to segment out the uterine region and then applied morphological procedures to filter out the fibroid part. Segmentation algorithms can be chosen according to the region of interest, tumor intensity, shape and position (Thampi et al. 2018). A review of diverse segmentation methods is presented before (Balafar et al. 2010; Liu et al. 2014), which mainly targeted on brain segmentation.

A multiscale gradient algorithm is presented (Wang et al. 1997) which efficiently improves segmentation accuracy and significantly reduce the computational cost of watershed-based methods. A simple and efficient brain tumor detecting algorithm is presented (Mustaqeem et al. 2012), a threshold-based watershed segmentation method was applied to the median filtered image. For conducting the experiments, the authors stored MRI scan images in JPEG format, which is not recommended since the JPEG format is in compressed form. The approach reported in (Asaturyan et al. 2019) describes the automatic pancreas segmentation of CT and MRI scans. The method utilizes morphological and geometrical characteristics of abdominal tissue to classify the contour. After identifying the major pancreas region, a contrast enrichment method is applied to differentiate pancreas from the neighboring tissue. The authors point that the method is applicable to other abdominal MRI or CT sequences.

3   Materials and Methods

3.1   Dataset Description

In this research work, we used real female pelvic MRI (PMRI) dataset, which is based on two-dimensional MRI images. The dataset containing 320 T2 weighted MRI images (slices) of 175 patients. All the patients were examined with OPTIMA 360-INSPIRE GE Healthcare 1.5T MRI scanner. The scanned MRI images in the dataset are displayed in matrix format. The size of each image is 512 x 512 pixels, with a pixel size of 47 mm

× 47 mm. The radiology department team preferred images in sagittal direction for examining female pelvic region. We also considered images in that plane for algorithm development or method evaluation. All the images for this research work are provided by radiology department in LIRRIS-Lisie Institute of Radiology Research and Imaging Sciences.

3.2 Implementation of CAD System

The functional block diagram of the proposed computer aided detection system is shown in Fig. 2. Segmentation of region of interest from female pelvic MRI or PMRI plays an important role in the diagnosis of diseases like cyst, fibroid, cervical cancer etc. The authors developed a BiLo-T based gradient method to segment ovarian cyst type of abnormality from female PMRI images.

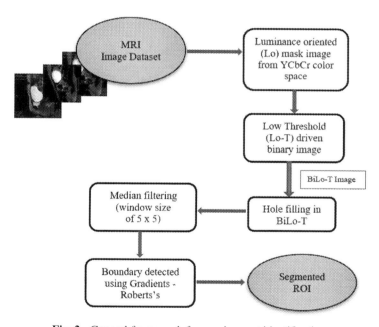

Fig. 2. General framework for ovarian cyst identification

The acquired MRI scanned image, stored in a database is in RGB color space form. There are other color models besides RGB which also represent colors numerically namely, HSV, YCbCr, YIQ, CMYK etc. Among that, our image dataset is showing more accurate results on YCbCr color space and therefore as a preprocessing step, input RGB image is first transformed into YCbCr color space. The standard way to perform YCbCr conversion is as follows:

$$Y = (77/256)R + (150/256)G + (29/256)B \tag{1}$$

$$Cb = -(44/256)R - (87/256)G + (131/256)B + 128 \qquad (2)$$

$$Cr = (131/256)R - (110/256)G - (21/256)B + 128 \qquad (3)$$

Y represents the luminance, Cb and Cr represents the blue and red components of chrominance and R, G, B are the values of the current pixel in the original color input image. Luminance contains the most important gray-scale information of the original image and it is represented in an 8-bit range of 16 to 235 and that of chrominance has scaled to a range of 16 to 240. A mask image is formed by iterative thresholding the luminance and chrominance values of YCbCr color space. This mask image is also used to evaluate goodness of segmentation and to improve image quality in the following steps. The threshold values used for creating a mask image from Y, Cb, Cr values is given by,

$$x(i, j) >= 147 \,\&\&\, x(i, j) <= 237) \,\&\&\, (q(i, j) == 128) \,\&\&\, (z(i, j) == 128 \quad (4)$$

$x(i,j)$ is the luminance and $q(i,j)$, $z(i,j)$ represents the values of chrominance red and blue components. Cyst type of lesions appeared as bright regions in T2 weighted MRI images, which need to be separated from the structured background. In order to focus on these bright objects, thresholding technique has been used. For that, a method of binarization can be done based on pixel intensity values and is given by:

$$bin(x, y) = \begin{cases} 1 & if\ I(x, y) >= Th \\ 0 & if\ I(x, y) < Th \end{cases} \qquad (5)$$

bin(x,y) is the resultant binary image based on the threshold value *Th*. Here the luminance threshold value can be estimated based on the region of interest of mask image and input image *I(x,y)*.

Elimination of holes in the resultant binary image is performed using morphological image filling operation. A pixel connectivity of '4' is selected to finish the process. Then a median filtering approach is introduced to remove the unwanted pixels. Each output pixel contains the median value in a specified neighbourhood around the corresponding pixel in the input image. The selection of window size has a greater impact on median filter outputs. The window size can be 3×3, 5×5, 7×7, 13×13 etc. So before applying the gradient operation, we perform median filtering with a mask size of 5×5 pixels on the binary image. To get the true edges from median filtered image, a gradient method of edge detection is initialised.

There are lot of gradient operators like Roberts's gradient, Sobel gradient, Prewitt gradient etc. In our work we are pointing to Roberts's method of gradient operator to get the best results of ROI detection. Figure 3 shows the stage by stage results of ovarian cyst extraction of female PMRI images.

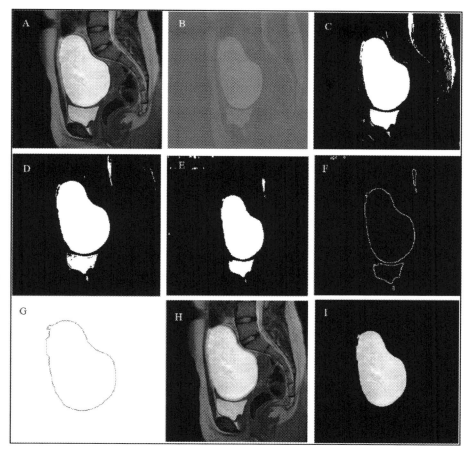

Fig. 3. Segmentation image outputs. **A.** Input MRI image **B.** YCbCr image **C.** Mask image using YCbCr values **D.** Binary image using threshold **E.** Median filtered image **F.** Gradient image **G.** Contour of the final ROI **H.** Final ROI marked on original image **I.** Tumor separated.

3.3 Algorithm

……… …… …… ……… …… …… …… ……… …… …… …… …… …… …… …… ……… …… …… …… …… …… ……

1: *Input RGB image is converted to YCbCr image.*
2: *Separating YCbCr into three planes*
3: *Let R, C be the size of input image, x be luminance plane, q be chrominance blue and z be the chrominance red plane*
4: *set i=1*
5: *Repeat steps 6 through 8 until i<=R and j<=C*
6: *If (x(i,j)>=147 && x(i,j)<=237) && (q(i,j)==128) && (z(i,j)==128)*
7: *Set final mask roi (i,j) =1,*
8: *else, set final mask roi (i,j) = 0*
9: *Input RGB image is separated into red, green, blue planes // threshold driven binary image*
10: *Each plane is multiplied with the obtained mask roi (i,j)*
11: *red* uint8 (roi (i,j)), do the same for other two planes*
12: *Set the luminance threshold value as 0.68*
13: *Step 13 is converted to binary using im2bw function*
14: *Fill the holes in the obtained binary image, specifying connectivity of 4*
15: *median {I (x, y), [m n]}. set the window size [m n] ==> [5 5] // Median filtering*
16: *Gradient operation is performed using 'roberts' operator*
17: *Steps 16 to 19 are separately done for three planes*
18: *Concatenate three planes*
19: *Using area and entropy the important ROI is filter out*

……… …… …… ……… …… …… …… …… …… …… …… …… ……… …… …… …… …… …… …… …… ……

4   Experimental Results and Discussion

The proposed system assists in detecting the abnormalities present in female pelvic MRI imaging systems. All image processing result analysis was carried out in MATLAB R2022b. The publicly available datasets are unsuitable for testing algorithms. As a result, we completed our research work using real medical images. The dataset for this work was collected during the period of 2017–2018.

Input MRI image with stage by stage results of algorithm is pictorially represented in Fig. 3. We considered 370 MRI input images with cyst type of lesion to carry out this work. Different input images having different texture and shape. Segmentation results of five female PMRI samples are given in Fig. 4. From the results it can be clearly seen that the proposed system can able to segment the tumor with different sizes and shapes.

The Features like area and entropy are giving better results in segmentation of ROI. So, a threshold value is set for both area and entropy to find out the final part. An average of both entropy (A_e) and area (A_a) are taken for setting a threshold value. A tolerance of 15% and 20% is chosen according to the characteristics of image. Our experiments show that a threshold value of 0.68 is fairly good choice. The results of shape similarity indices between manual and automated segmentations can be seen in Table 1. For brevity the similarity measures were carried out on six female PMRI samples which is reviewed and validated with the aid of radiologists.

We have considered Similarity index, Jaccard similarity index and Dice similarity coefficient or (Zijdenbos similarity index) to evaluate the similarity check process (Thampi et al. 2018). The comparison result gives an average similarity index of 91.92% and JSI of 85.6% and a DSC of 88.48%. The proposed method achieved a good similarity result and JSI value when compared to 74.5% and 76.5% obtain in (Gu et al. 2016, Thampi et al. 2018).

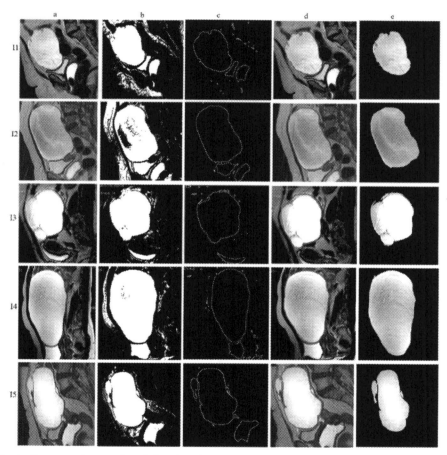

Fig. 4. Segmentation results of five female PMRI samples. Column 'a' shows the five input images I1, I2, I3, I4, I5. Column 'b' Mask image using YCbCr values. Column 'c' Gradient image. Column 'd' final contour. Column 'e' separated ROI part.

Table 1. Comparison of manual segmentation and automated segmentation using similarity measures

Test tmage	I1	I2	I3	I4	I5	I6	Average
SI (%)	91.2	93.8	92.3	88.2	89.69	96.3	91.92
JSI (%)	80.1	85.6	86.1	87.5	86.82	87.5	85.6
DSC (%)	91.67	91.36	88.3	87.69	85.65	86.21	88.48

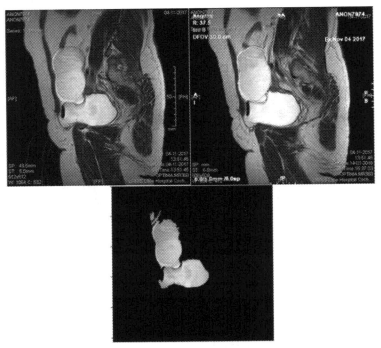

Fig. 5. Wrongly segmented cyst results. Top row shows input image and its corresponding Ground Truth Image. Bottom row shows segmented output.

The suggested BiLo-T based segmentation method is compared with existing segmentation methods include K-Means Clustering, Marker controlled watershed segmentation and Fuzzy C Means algorithms (see Fig. 6). Image I1 with different values of k (2, 4 and 8) have been used for doing k means clustering algorithm. From the results it is clear that the proposed method can able to produce better ovarian cyst in comparison with others.

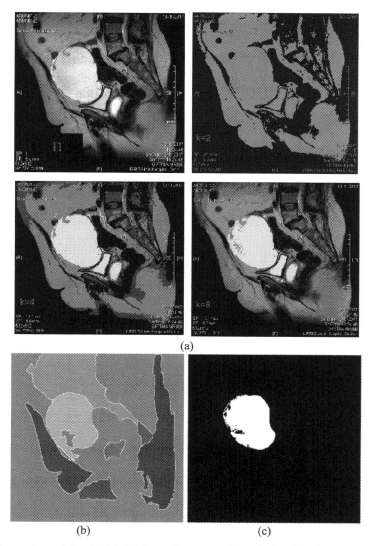

(a)

(b)   (c)

Fig. 6. Comparison of I1 with (a) K-Means Clustering- (K = 2, 4 and 8) (b) Marker controlled watershed segmentation (c) Fuzzy C Means

5   Conclusions, Limitations and Future Work

Our research work is based on the finding of important diagnostic region from real medical images. A luminance oriented low threshold (BiLo-T) based gradient method is chosen for identifying the different shape variants of ovarian cyst in MRI images. The developed algorithm has been tested and evaluated using real image datasets and also compared against gold standards.

The drawbacks of this study can be summarized as follows: First, the presented algorithm couldn't able to segment all the images in the dataset. Out of the 320 MRI images considered, around 290 images produce correctly segmented results. Since the shape and size of the ovarian cyst varies from patient to patient the authors couldn't able to solve these issues at the present study (see Fig. 5). From the figure it is quite clear that, apart from the ovarian cyst another pelvic area is also coming and this should be rectified in the future work. Second, the authors need to consider more number of features other than the main features like area and entropy for detecting the ROI part.

The presented work in this paper can also be extended to classification part by incorporating a greater number of features from the correctly segmented ovarian images. Also, a stage-by-stage prediction ie, from ovarian neoplasm (initial stage) to granulosa cell tumor (malignant stage) is also possible via a supervised classifier.

Statements and Declarations. This research did not receive any specific grant from funding agencies in the public, commercial, or not-for-profit sectors.

Data Availability Statement. The data that support the findings of this study are available on request from the corresponding author.

References

Asaturyan, H., Gligorievski, A., Villarini, B.: Morphological and multi-level geometrical descriptor analysis in CT and MRI volumes for automatic pancreas segmentation. Comput. Med. Imaging Graph. **75**, 1–13 (2019)

Balafar, M.A., Ramli, A.R., Saripan, M.I., Mashohor, S.: Review of brain MRI image segmentation methods. Artif. Intell. Rev. **33**, 261–274 (2010). https://doi.org/10.1007/s10462-010-9155-0

Bourgioti, C., Chatoupis, K., Moulopoulos, L.A.: Current imaging strategies for the evaluation of uterine cervical cancer. World J. Radiol. **8**, 342 (2016)

Brocker, K.A., Alt, C.D., Eichbaum, M., Sohn, C., Kauczor, H.U., Hallscheidt, P.: Imaging of female pelvic malignancies regarding MRI, CT, and PET/CT. Strahlenther. Onkol. **187**(10), 611 (2011)

Brown, M.A., Martin, D.R., Semelka, R.C.: Future directions in MR Imaging of the Female Pelvis. Magn. Reson. Imaging Clin. N. Am. **14**, 431–437 (2006)

Bruni L., et al.: ICO/IARC Information Centre on HPV and Cancer (HPV Information Centre). Human Papillomavirus and Related Diseases in India (2019)

Bruni L., et al.: ICO/IARC information centre on HPV and cancer (HPV Information Centre). human papillomavirus and related diseases in India (2016)

Chou, C.Y., Hsu, K.F., Wang, S.T., Huang, S.C., Tzeng, C.C., Huang, K.E.: Accuracy of three-dimensional ultrasonography in volume estimation of cervical carcinoma. Gynecol. Oncol. **66**(1), 89–93 (1997)

Fallahi, A., et al.: Uterine segmentation and volume measurement in uterine fibroid patients MRI using fuzzy C-Mean algorithm and morphological operations. Iran. J. Radiol. **8**, 150–156 (2011)

Faria, S.C., Sagebiel, T., Balachandran, A., Devine, C., Lal, C., Bhosale, P.R.: Imaging in endometrial carcinoma. Indian J. Radiol. Imaging **25**, 137–147 (2015)

Frieden, B.R.: New restoring algorithm for the preferential enhancement of edge gradients. J. Opt. Soc. Am. **66**, 280–283 (1976)

Gupta, M., Taneja, H., Chand, L., Goyal, V.: Enhancement and analysis in MRI image denoising for different filtering techniques. J. Stat. Manag. Syst. **21**, 561–568 (2018)

Gu, P., Lee, W.M., Roubidoux, M.A., Yuan, J., Wang, X., Carson, P.L.: Automated 3D ultrasound image segmentation to aid breast cancer image interpretation. Ultrasonics **65**, 51–58 (2016)

Huang, T.S., Yang, G.J., Tang, G.Y.: A fast two-dimensional median filtering algorithm. IEEE Trans. Acoust. **27**, 13–18 (1979)

LaPolla, J.P., Schlaerth, J.B., Gaddis, O., Morrow, C.P.: The influence of surgical staging on the evaluation and treatment of patients with cervical carcinoma. Gynecol. Oncol. **24**(2), 194–206 (1986)

Liu, J., Li, M., Wang, J., Wu, F., Liu, T., Pan, Y.: A survey of MRI-based brain tumor segmentation methods. Tsinghua Sci. Technol. **19**, 578–595 (2014)

Manjón, J.V., Coupé, P., Buades, A., Louis Collins, D., Robles, M.: New methods for MRI denoising based on sparseness and self-similarity. Med. Image Anal. **16**, 18–27 (2012)

Mohan, J., Krishnaveni, V., Guo, Y.: A survey on the magnetic resonance image denoising methods. Biomed. Signal Process. Control **9**, 56–69 (2014)

Mustaqeem, A., Javed, A., Fatima, T.: An efficient brain tumor detection algorithm using watershed and thresholding based segmentation. Int. J. Image Graph. Signal Process. **4**, 34–39 (2012)

Ozer, S., et al.: Supervised and unsupervised methods for prostate cancer segmentation with multispectral MRI. Med. Phys. **37**, 1873–1883 (2010)

Thampi, L., Paul, V.: Abnormality recognition and feature extraction in female pelvic ultrasound imaging. Inform. Med. Unlocked **13**, 133–138 (2018)

Umutlu, L., Antoch, G., Herrmann, K., Grueneisen, J.: PET/MR imaging of the female pelvis. Semin. Nucl. Med. **49**, 512–520 (2019)

Wang, D.: A multiscale gradient algorithm for image segmentation using watersheds. Pattern Recogn. **30**(12), 2043–2052 (1997)

World Cancer Report 2014: World Health Organization, p. 2014 Chapter 5.12 (2014)

Xyda, A., Moyle, P., Addley, H., Freeman, S.: Imaging of the female pelvis. Obstet. Gynaecol. Reprod. Med. **25**, 283–294 (2015)

Yousuf, M.A., Nobi, M.N.: A new method to remove noise in magnetic resonance and ultrasound images. J. Sci. Res. **3**, 81 (2010)

Network and Cyber Security

Elaborated Distributed System-Activity Synchronization Among Different Distributed Systems

Surjit Paul$^{(\boxtimes)}$ (iD) and Binod Kumar

Department of Computer Science and Engineering, National Institute of Technology
Jamshedpur, Jamshedpur 831014, Jharkhand, India
paul.surjit55@gmail.com

Abstract. A distributed system is the collection of different nodes distributed independently to solve a common agreed problem. The bully algorithm is used to establish communication within the distributed system. However, no algorithm helps to establish communication among the different distributed systems; establishing communication among different distributed systems is challenging. In this paper, we proposed an elaborated bully algorithm (process). The proposed algorithm works under any load. It also takes care of the super coordinator's or boss's failure using proper rules and handles the synchronization among distributed systems. With the help of the proposed algorithm, we can establish communication among inter-distributed systems. The analysis shows that although resource utilization increased by the proposed algorithm, the algorithm still achieves the same time complexity $O(n^2)$ as the existing Bully algorithm.

Keywords: Elaborated distributed system · Bully algorithm · Synchronization

1 Introduction

Some problems are complex in nature that cannot be solved using a single system. The distributed system is a collection of all the independent entities that coordinate to solve different problems. It becomes easy for the system (called a node in a distributed system) to work in coordination for the perfect solution to complex problems that need collaborative efforts. Some examples of a distributed system are the solar system, college management system, and ecosystem. Due to Internet technology, distributed system word became very popular because of its problem-solving capability with maximum performance at significantly less cost, so it fascinated researchers and academicians attention. However, nowadays there is an exponential growth in the size of the distributed systems that leads to different challenges regarding its proper management, controlling its functioning, and resource handling.

Distributed system architecture contains an interconnected network of processors, each having local memories. Each processor communicates in the network using the message passing technique. In order to establish communication between one node to another node in the distributed system very popular bully algorithm is used. This algorithm is not only used to establish communication but also used to synchronize the whole system. The functioning of the distributed system is based on the selection of leaders. Then this leader helps in finding the coordinator of the distributed system. This coordinator keeps an eye on the functioning of the distributed system. This algorithm was fine for establishing communication within the one distributed system.No algorithm helps establish communication among distributed systems. To our knowledge, no algorithm exists that helps one distributed system establish communication among other distributed systems. Hence, in this paper, we proposed an enhanced form called an elaborated-distributed system (e distributed system) to help in establishing communication among inter distributed system.

The rest of the paper is organized as follows. In the subsequent section, background work has been presented. In Sect. 3, the working of the Bully algorithm has been shown. Section 4 deals with the proposed work. The fifth section represents the result and analysis. Finally, Sect. 6 concludes the paper.

2 Background Work

The distributed system is defined as a group of different nodes interacting with each other, participating in communication, and working collaboratively to achieve a common goal [1]. The interaction is performed among the nodes under the guidance of a guardian named as coordinator. The selection of a leader for communication among the node is the central theme of the distributed system [2]. Mamun et al. presented an algorithm upon the elimination of the duplicate election of the coordinator to overcome the maintenance problem of crashed or overlapped processes. This help in maximizing the utility of our golden bully algorithm [3]. In the event of failure of the coordinator system in the distributed system, the following high-priority process in the distributed system is elected as the coordinator [4]. Gholipour et al. directed while electing the leader, and work was progressively performed [5]. EffatParvar et al. proposed a new method for improving the algorithm for the election of the coordinator by implementing a heap tree mechanism [6]. Basu proposed an efficient algorithm for passing the message to establish communication using the coordinator [7]. Katwala & Shah selected an active process that acts as a leader that performs the management work of the remaining processes in the distributed system [8]. To establish communication in the distributed system, we need synchronization between different nodes. The coordinator process is responsible for synchronization between different nodes of the system. As we interact among different nodes depending upon the leader so, all the nodes should accept and have a mutual understanding with the leader [9]. Rahdari et al. proposed that the global coordinator coordinate access to multi-site shared resources [10]. The importance of distributed networks reveals to everyone, so there is a need for an algorithm that helps in establishing communication among them. Social networking sites (SNS) have been rapidly increasing in recent years, providing a platform to connect people worldwide and share their interests [11]. Hence, to establish communication, there is a need to perform some changes in the algorithm to control the network traffic. In place of selecting the node with high priority, select the node with a low priority that reduces the number of messages within the distributed system [12]. However, this has some disadvantages, such as increasing the process's complexity and facing issues like redundant messages and long interval time, so the author proposed an announcer-based bully algorithm [13]. To reduce the complexity, different authors proposed different forms of bully algorithms such as modified bully, ring and Well-Organized Bully Leader Election process algorithm [14].

Nowadays bully algorithm is used as an application among web servers. This help in finding out the best server that handles most of the work and has high priority. This ease the task of website hosting [15]. Many authors proposed combining different algorithms, such as bully and ring, to eliminate the different drawbacks [16]. These days focus shifted to the new environment, and become easy to detect the failure in the distributed system by implementing the hardware-based algorithm [17]. When we shift the environment, we need to calculate the time, so it needs a timer-based leader election bully algorithm [18]. When selecting a node for the leader, there is no need to reveal its information, but with the introduction of an anonymous leader election algorithm, there is no need to do it. Without disclosing, the identity became accessible to a selection of the leader and performed synchronous activity [19]. As two essential factors, reliability and availability, help maintain the robust and fault-tolerant system, this author proposed leader election using ordered delivery (LEOD) [20]. Further, improvement to bully algorithm with fault detection feature was proposed [21]. This method continuously detects crashed nodes to maintain a fresh list of live nodes. However, it increases the number of messages while doing this and which eventually increased the message passing cost. In [22], authors proposed an improved bully algoritm that uses a system identification number (ID) to order the list of candidates for election, and the leader is chosen from the available list, but the process does not provide any information about the maintenance cost of that list. Further, EffatParvar et al. [25] proposed a novel election method with an improvement in the Bully and Ring election algorithm to find a method for the election process. The method used a max-heap tree for election process of the coordinator. The total memory used by the proposed algorithm was 4n and the election is completed in $O(\log n)$ messages, while the Bully and Ring algorithm take $O(n^2)$ messages to elect a coordinator.

In [23], the proposed algorithm takes a long time to elect a new leader node and does not consider some more exceptional cases that could arise in the system. Though the bully algorithm was proposed in 1982, it is still a very useful and preferred algorithm for some important applications. Madisetti and Panda [26] proposed a dynamic leader selection algorithm by selecting a set of future leaders which are then notified before the failure of the present leadership and handed over the leadership. In [24], the author proposed a called Fast Bully Algorithm (FBA) to implement a Web Service Community. To make the web service faster, convenient and available, some web services that are functionally similar were grouped together as a community. In this application, one of the web services plays the role of the Master Web Service (Coordinator) and FBA was used to elect a new Master Web Service in case of coordinator failure.

3   Bully Algorithm

Elaborated distributed system or process internally uses the Bully algorithm principle, therefore before starting the proposed work let's see the working of the bully algorithm [1].

1. Every node in the system has a unique priority number
2. Every node in the system knows the priority of the other nodes
3. Whenever an election is held, the node having the highest priority number among the currently live nodes are elected as the coordinator
4. On recovery, a failed process can take appropriate actions to re-join the set of active processes

In the e-distributed system (algorithm), there is a need to select the leader among the different distributed systems.

Suppose there are N distributed systems, each runs bully algorithm internally to choose leaders. As mentioned above if there are N distributed systems then N leaders would be selected. To establish communication between N different selected leaders, we have to run the elaborated distributed system (also called e-distributed system, which is an enhanced form of Bully algorithm) algorithm among them to select a super coordinator/leader. The below Fig. 1 represented the whole concept.

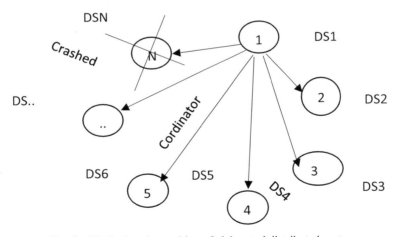

Fig. 1. Displaying the working of elaborated distributed system

Here, as given in the Fig. 2, L1, L2, L3…. LN are the coordinators of DS1, DS2, DS3…. DSN. For establishing the communication, we need to Select the Super coordinator using the elaborated distributed system algorithm. Here, L5 is elected as the super coordinator or Super leader.

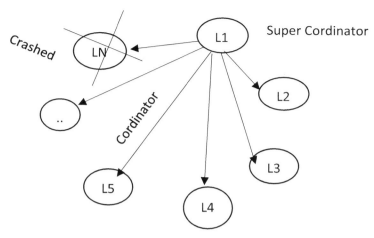

Fig. 2. Displaying the working of elaborated distributed system to select the super coordinator

After finding out the different distributed system leaders and electing one as super coordinator or leader. To coordinate the communication for proper operation among different distributed systems, a leader must know about their super leader. As shown in the above Fig. 2, how the super leader or coordinator is elected. All the synchronization is controlled by the super leader among the distributed system. What will happen if the super leader fails or crashes, there is a requirement to quick fix this problem by electing a new super leader for short time or temporarily till the new super leader election takes place. Hence, an election is conducted to find out the next super leader or coordinator among different distributed systems. The following assumptions are considered:

1. There is a need to assign the unique priority number to each member of elected leaders
2. In the election each member priority nu evaluated. Result favour for the highest priority number 3
3. The leader who assigned the highest priority number is declared as Super leader or coordinator
4. In case any leader is crashed with the priority then they can rejoin the system with proper action

Operation
Lets's assume there are 6 nodes in the distributed system, node 1 is inactive and node 6 has the highest priority, so it is declared as coordinator of the process. However, due to some reason, node 6 gets crashed and it is realized by the node 2 then the leader election message is transferred to all the nodes 3, 4, 5, and 6 in the distributed system as shown in Fig. 3.

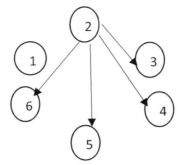

Fig. 3. Message sending by node 2

Node 2 receives the ok message from all the active nodes except node 6. Those nodes who receive the election message compare the priority of the sender of the message with its priority of the message. Node 3 find that its priority is greater the node 2 as shown in Fig. 4.

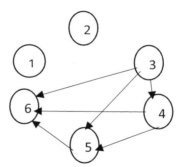

Fig. 4. Message sending by node 3

Above step is repeated by the node 4, 5. Finally, node 5 gets the highest priority and it sends election message to all the nodes and declared itself as a coordinator as shown in Fig. 5.

4 Proposed Work

In this paper, an enhanced distributed system algorithm is applied to find a Super coordinator among three different distributed systems. Below are the generalized steps:

Step 1. Consider a distributed system (DS-1) that contains many processes. Applying bully algorithm [1] on this system to find a coordinator
Step 2. Similarly, consider two more systems as DS-2 and DS-3 and find their respective coordinators using the bully algorithm

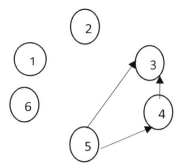

Fig. 5. Message sending by node 5

Step 3. Now assume the respective coordinators of DS-1, DS-2, and DS-3 as processes that form a new virtual distributed network system (DS-4).

Step 4. Now applying the elaborated distributed system algorithm on this newly formed virtual distributed network, DS-4 to find the super coordinator or boss. The Fig. 6 as shown below presented the whole concept

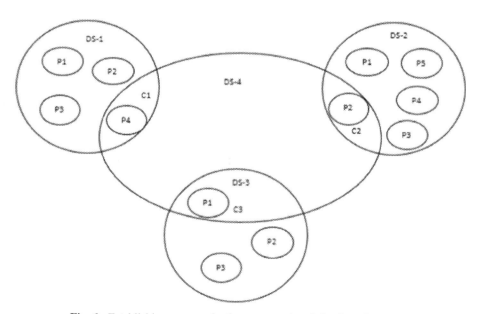

Fig. 6. Establishing communication among virtual distributed systems

Algorithmic Steps of the Implementation

Step 1. Defined a distributed system with a certain number of processes.
Step 2. Assigned priority to each process along with status as 1 (for every active process in the network).
Step 3. The bully algorithm is applied to find the leader or coordinator for the system [1].
Step 4. Step 1, 2, and 3 are repeated twice to create two more distributed systems and find their respective coordinators
Step 5. Another virtual distributed system is defined which consists of three processes. The coordinators of the first, second, and third distributed system are the active processes or the member of the virtual distributed system DS-4
Step 6. The enhanced distributed system or process is applied to find the super coordinator for the newly defined system
Step 7. The final super coordinator will coordinate the activities amongst the three systems.

5   Result and Analysis

We considered the total number of resources required for executing the algorithm in three different distributed systems. We executed the bully algorithm on three distributed systems and on a virtually distributed system [6]. The proposed algorithm was implemented and tested. The system configuration details are shown in Table 1.

Table 1. System configuration details

Processor name	Intel i5 3.2 GHz 64 bit
Operating system	Windows 10
RAM	4 GB
Hardisk	1 TB

1. Total memory consumed $= 3n^2$
2. Minimum message required $= 4(2n - 2)$
3. Maximum message required $= 4n2$
4. Approx. no of message when leader has crashed $= N(i) = (4n - i + 1)(4n - i) + 4(n - 1)$

We find that even though the number of resources consumption increases, but complexity remains the same [8].

1. Best case $= O(4n) = O(n)$
2. Worst case $= O(4n^2) = O(n^2)$
3. Recovery $=$ Best Case-$O(n^2)$, Worst case-$(n - 1)$

6   Conclusion

The bully algorithm is vital in establishing communication in the distributed system. However, no algorithm has been proposed to help establish communication among inter-distributed systems. The proposed algorithm shows super coordinator or boss among the leader helps establish communication among N distributed systems. The proposed algorithm works under any load; it also takes care of the failure of the super coordinator or boss using proper rules and handles the synchronization among distributed systems. It uses $O(n^2)$ complexity simultaneously even when it handles three different distributed systems. Further, the proposed algorithm could be improved to minimize the time complexity for establishing inter and intra-communication among and within the distributed systems.

References

1. Garcia-Molina, H.: Elections in distributed computing system. IEEE Trans. Comput. **31**(01), 48–59 (1982)
2. Peleg, D.: Research-note on time-optimal leader election in general networks. J. Parallel Distrib. Comput. **8**(1), 96–99 (1990)
3. Mamun, Q.E.K., Masum, S.M., Mustafa, M.A.R.: Modified bully algorithm for electing coordinator in distributed systems. WSEAS Trans. Comput. **3**(4), 948–953 (2004)
4. Sepehri, M., Goodarzi, M., Sepehri, M.: Leader election algorithm using heap structure. In: 12th WSEAS International Conference on Computers (2008)
5. Gholipour, M., Kordafshari, M.S., Jahanshahi, M., Rahmani, A.M.: A new approach for election algorithm in distributed systems. Commun. Theory Reliab. Qual. Serv. (2009). CTRQ'09. Second International Conference on, IEEE, pp. 70–74 (2009)
6. EffatParvar, M., Yazdani, N., EffatParvar, M., Dadlani, A., Khonsari, A.: Improved algorithms for leader election in distributed systems. In: 2nd International Conference on Computer Engineering and Technology (ICCET), vol. 2 (2010)
7. Basu, S.: an efficient approach of election algori thm in distributed systems. Indian J. Comput. Sci. Eng. (IJCSE) **2**(1), 16–21 (2011)
8. Katwala, H., Shah, S.: Study on election algorithm in distributed system. J. Comput. Eng. (IOSRJCE) **7**, 34–39 (2012). ISSN: 2278-0661, ISBN: 2278-8727
9. Soundarabai, P.B., Sahai, R., Venugopal, K.R., Patnaik, L.M.: Improved bully election algorithm for distributed systems. Int. J. Next Gener. Netw. (IJNGN) **5**(1) (2013)
10. Nandhini, B.S., Sheeba, J.I.: Online social network bullying detection using intelligence techniques. In: International Conference on Advanced Computing Technologies and Applications (ICACTA), vol. 45, pp. 485–492 (2015). Procedia Computer Science
11. Rahdari, D., Rahmani, A.M., Aboutaleby, N., Karambasti, A.S.: A distributed fault tolerance global coordinator election algorithm in unreliable high traffic distributed systems. Inf. Technol. Comput. Sci. **7**(3), 1–11 (2015)
12. Kabashi, Q., Zeqiri, A., Zabeli, M.: The reduction of number messages in election bully algorithm. Syst. Int. J. Comput. Commun. **1** (2016). ISSN: 2074-1294
13. Khan, M., Agarwal, N., Jaiswal, S., Khan, J.A.: An announcer based bully election leader algorithm in distributed environment. In: Bhattacharyya, P., Sastry, H., Marriboyina, V., Sharma, R. (eds.) NGCT 2017. CCIS, vol. 827, pp. 664–674. Springer, Singapore (2018). https://doi.org/10.1007/978-981-10-8657-1_51

14. Numan, M., Subhan, F., Khan, W.Z., Assiri, B., Armi, N.: Well-organized bully leader election algorithm for distributed system. In: International Conference on Radar, Antenna, Microwave, Electronics, and Telecommunications, (ICRAMET), pp. 5–10. IEEE (2018)
15. Shukla, K., Sahoo, B.: Dynamic selection of the best server out of multiple servers available using bully algorithm in any geographical area. In: Pradhan, G., Morris, S., Nayak, N. (eds.) Advances in Electrical Control and Signal Systems. LNEE, vol. 665, pp. 871–877. Springer, Singapore (2020). https://doi.org/10.1007/978-981-15-5262-5_66
16. Subramanian, E.R.S., Sri Gurubaran, B., Sayee Shruthi, A.S., Aishwarya, V., Balaji, N., Umamakeswari, A.:. A novel hypergraph-based leader election algorithm for distributed systems. In: Saini, H., Sayal, R., Buyya, R., Aliseri, G. (eds.) Innovations in Computer Science and Engineering. LNNS, vol. 103, pp. 437–445. Springer, Singapore (2020). https://doi.org/10.1007/978-981-15-2043-3_48
17. Johansson, B., Rågberger, M., Papadopoulos, A.V., Nolte, T.: Heartbeat bully: failure detection and redundancy role selection for network-centric controller. In: Conference of the IEEE Industrial Electronics Society, pp. 2126–2133 (2020)
18. Biswas, A., Dutta, A.: A timer-based leader election algorithm. In: Conferences on Ubiquitous Intelligence & Computing, Advanced and Trusted Computing, Scalable Computing and Communications, Cloud and Big Data Computing, Internet of People, and Smart World Congress, pp. 432–439 (2016)
19. Mitra, D., Cortesi, A., Chaki, N.: ALEA: an anonymous leader election algorithm for synchronous distributed systems. In: Choraś, M., Choraś, R.S., Kurzyński, M., Trajdos, P., Pejaś, J., Hyla, T. (eds.) CORES IP&C ACS 2021 2021 2021. LNNS, vol. 255. Springer, Cham (2022). https://doi.org/10.1007/978-3-030-81523-3_5
20. Verma, S., Yadav, D., Chandra, G.: Leader election algorithm in fault tolerant distributed system. In: Gupta, D., Khanna, A., Kansal, V., Fortino, G., Hassanien, A.E. (eds.) Proceedings of Second Doctoral Symposium on Computational Intelligence. AISC, vol. 1374, pp. 471–480. Springer, Singapore (2022). https://doi.org/10.1007/978-981-16-3346-1_38
21. Park, S.H., Yoo, S.C., Lee, J.Y.: The design of an election protocol in wireless cellular networks. In: 2014 11th International Conference on Information Technology: New Generations, pp. 59–65. IEEE (2014)
22. Arghavani, A., Ahmadi, E., Haghighat, A.T.: Improved bully election algorithm in distributed systems. In: ICIMU 2011: Proceedings of the 5th international Conference on Information Technology & Multimedia, pp. 1–6. IEEE (2011)
23. EffatParvar, M., Effatparvar, M., Bemana, A., Dehghan, M.: Determining a central controlling processor with fault tolerant method in distributed system. In: Fourth International Conference on Information Technology (ITNG'07), pp. 658–663. IEEE (2007)
24. Subramanian, S.: Highly-available web service community. In: 2009 Sixth International Conference on Information Technology: New Generations, pp. 296–301. IEEE (2009)
25. EffatParvar, M., Yazdani, N., EffatParvar, M., Dadlani, A., Khonsari, A.: Improved algorithms for leader election in distributed systems. In: 2nd International Conference on Computer Engineering and Technology, pp. V2–6. IEEE (2010)
26. Madisetti, V.K., Panda, S.: A dynamic leader election algorithm for decentralized networks. J. Transp. Technol. 11(3), 404–411 (2021)

Multimodal Fake News Detection on Fakeddit Dataset Using Transformer-Based Architectures

Sakshi Kalra[1]([✉]), Chitneedi Hemanth Sai Kumar[1], Yashvardhan Sharma[1], and Gajendra Singh Chauhan[2]

[1] Department of CSIS, BITS Pilani, Pilani Campus, Pilani 333031, Rajasthan, India
`p20180437@pilani.bits-pilani.ac.in`
[2] Department of HSS, BITS Pilani, Pilani Campus, Pilani 333031, Rajasthan, India

Abstract. Real-time information is transforming due to technological advancements and widespread internet access. In our increasingly digital culture, fake news and misinformation are more common in journalism, news reporting, social media, and other online information consumption platforms. The spread of misinformation can have harmful impacts or even control public events by using multimedia content to deceive readers and gain dissemination. The question here is how to spot fake news about recently occurring events and it is one of the special difficulties in Fake News Detection (FND) on social networking sites. Recent study has considerably increased our ability to identify fake news, because of less emphasis on utilizing the relationship between the textual and visual information in news samples. It is possible to spot fake news by giving importance to similarity among textual and visual features. In this paper, we study the task of identifying fake news using the Fakeddit dataset, which is a collection of full-length articles and related images. We propose a multimodal approach that makes use of transfer learning to gather semantic and contextual data, develop stronger hidden representations between the words in news samples and the images, and tries to improve the accuracy of FND task. We carefully evaluate the performance of our model on the Fakeddit dataset. The results demonstrate that the proposed model learns more accurate textual features and outperforms the most current textual results on that dataset.

Keywords: Natural Language Processing (NLP) · Fake News Detection (FND) · Transfer learning · Deep learning · Social media analytics

1 Introduction

"Fake news" has existed for a while. Although the cause of it was established in society for a very long time, the harm it caused to people made it a pressing problem that needed to be resolved by the scientific community [1]. The definition of this term has changed slightly from the earlier studies, but it has now become jargon. Earlier, any type of unique content, including satires, hoaxes, news propaganda, and clickbaits, was referred to as fake news. The term "fake news" refers to news stories that are deliberately and clearly inaccurate and have the potential to mislead readers. The rise of online news in the early 2000s brought about a new set of worries, among them the possibility that an excessive diversity of viewpoints would make it simpler for people with similar opinions to form "echo chambers" or "filter bubbles" where they would be shielded from opposing viewpoints [2].

Most recently, social media has been under investigation. Comparing social media platforms like Facebook to earlier media technologies reveals how drastically different their structures are. Users can share content without any significant fact-checking, editorial review, or third-party screening. Recent years have seen a significant increase in the amount of fake news due to the quick and explosive expansion of social media. Misinformation is ubiquitous, intrusive, and distracting in today's world. Both people and society are profoundly affected by it [3]. The FND task faces a number of challenges: 1. It is difficult to identify fake news because it can take many different forms, including text, image, video, and more. 2. The abundance of false information: Anyone can readily post misinformation online without any verification procedures. There are many websites that were created specifically to publish false news and stories. There is an urgent need for automated FND since the volume of online-generated material exceeds the capacity of human verification.

More false information has been spread during the extraordinary COVID-19 worldwide pandemic due to the corona virus's mysterious origin and extreme infectiousness [4]. A popular strategy for debunking COVID-19 myths is fact-checking by domain experts. In addition to reputable fact-checking organizations like PolitiFact[1] and Press Information Bureau[2] (PIB), the Infodemic has inspired numerous social media platforms, news organizations, and even governments to release specialized tools to debunk wrong information [5]. Figure 1 illustrates a case study of a fact check conducted by the PolitiFact.com in which a tweet was uploaded on the Instagram[3] and claimed that Covid-19 vaccine increases the syncytial virus in children. However, PolitiFact.com confirmed it and made it into a false claim by claiming that Covid-19 vaccine is not causing RSV in children. The majority of current studies mostly concentrate on exploiting textual features to identify fake news. But the social media news stories now include information in many media formats, including texts, images, and videos. Between various modalities, there are increased and balanced interactions. More significantly, news that includes visual information is more likely to catch consumers' attention and spread faster. However, little research has been done on using visual data to validate the veracity of news [6].

This study makes a contribution to the field of FND by focusing on multimodal viewpoints and utilizing deep learning in relation to transformer-based architectures for improved multimodal feature fusion. The contributions of our study, in brief, is as follows: 1. This paper suggests a method for identifying social media postings that just considers the post's content, which includes the text and any related images. In order to learn sequences and hidden internal representations of words more effectively, this paper leverages deep learning-related transformer-based architectures. We thoroughly assess our model's performance using the Fakeddit dataset. The outcomes show that the

---

[1] Http://www.politifact.com.

[2] Https://www.pib.gov.in/indexd.aspx.

[3] Https://www.instagram.com/.

suggested model outperforms the most recent textual results on that dataset and learns better textual features.

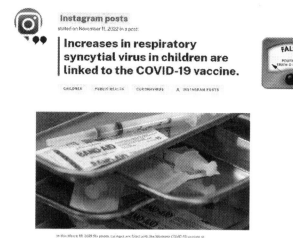

Fig. 1. An instance related to the fact-check done by PolitiFact.com[4].

The rest of this work is structured as follows: In Sect. 2, we go over earlier research on multimodal architectures and FND. We go into considerable detail on the dataset in Sect. 3. We present our suggested model and its various components in Sect. 4. Results and analysis are presented in Sect. 5, and Sect. 6 provides a concise summary.

2 Related Work

The task of spotting fake news is comparable to a number of other intriguing problems, including spam identification [7], rumor detection [8], and satire detection [9]. Each paper accepts its own definition because every person may have their very own intuitive definition of such linked concepts. The major constraint in FND tasks is how to classify news based on features. Posts, social context, and even associated images can all be used to extract the features. As a result, we examine the literature on Unimodal and multimodal FND.

2.1 Unimodal FND

The majority of earlier work on FND relied mainly on text and user metadata features. Such research has covered several linguistic levels within a conventional statistical Natural Language Programming paradigm. In order to describe and classify news information, numerous hand-crafted features have been extracted from it [10]. These features

---

[4] https://www.politifact.com/factchecks/2022/nov/21/instagram-posts/no-covid-19-vaccinati
onnot-causing-rsv-children/.

have been employed, for example, by SVM and random forest, to distinguish fake news from authentic news in terms of linguistic and writing styles. It is challenging to generalize hand-crafted linguistic features across topics and domains for FND tasks [11]. The results of [12] discussed how an author's writing style affects the perspectives and opinions of readers of such articles. This is crucial in influencing how the general public feels.

To automatically learn the hidden representation of temporal textual features, an RNNbased model was developed, outperforming techniques relying on manually created features [13]. Another study [14] used soft attention and RNN to learn only some of the temporal feature representations of post series in order to capture the long-range dependency among variable length sequential information.

Using knowledge graphs, authors of [15] are able to improve fact analysis in news content. Text content can be made to make sense by using entity relation information that is retrieved from these graphs. To identify fake news, [16] employ an LSTM network over propagation channels to infer embedding's of social media user profiles. A multivariate time series is used by [17] to represent the propagation path of a news story, and they use a combination of RNNs and CNNs to classify the propagation path in order to identify fake news. As a further effort, the authors of [18] use text summarization approaches in combination with transformer-based architectures to enhance the FND task. Ensembling of different Transformer-Based Models for the Urdu Language FND Task is carried out in [19].

Recent research has demonstrated that visual elements, such as images, are crucial for spotting fake news [20]. However, there has been less focus on examining the authenticity of multimedia content on social media. One common method of tampering with news is to create false images. Image splicing approach [21], which assesses whether or not the image is self-consistent based on input such as the EXIF metadata information, was utilized to detect such events.

2.2 Multimodal FND

Even while all of the Unimodal strategies listed above were able to produce encouraging results, the informal and brief nature of social media data makes information extraction difficult. The researchers began experimenting with features taken from other modalities (such as text and image) and merged them together for richer data representation to get over this limitation.

Att-RNN [22] is an attention-based RNN-based automated multimodal FND model that combines joint representations of textual, user profile, and visual information. Another attempt by the [23] is the Multimodal Variational Autoencoder (MVAE), a multi-task learning, multimodal fusion FND system. By using VAE to rebuild the textual and visual feature representations from the common latent representation, the modal seeks to identify relationships between modalities.

An event-level multi-modal architecture called Multi-modal Knowledge-aware Event Memory Network (MKEMN) [24] uses visual data and outside knowledge to help with the challenge of detecting fake news. For the purpose of learning event invariant characteristics, the authors used an event memory network.

The Event Adversarial Neural Networks (EANN) is a multi-task learning FND model that seeks to discover shared feature representations between all postings by employing an extra adversarial component [25]. By combining a CNN-based textual features extractor and a VGG-19 network, respectively, textual and visual feature representations are obtained.

3   Dataset Used

For the FND task, we have examined a broad range of datasets, starting with LIAR [26] for textual content and COVID19 fake news dataset [27] for multimodal FND. We utilized the Fakeddit [28] dataset in this study because we noticed that it offers a wide range of categories, making the training of new models considerably more reliable. Fakeddit dataset obtained from Reddit[5], a social news and debate platform where users can submit content to multiple subreddits. Over 1 million submissions from 22 distinct subreddits comprise Fakeddit. The pushshift.io[6] API was used to gather submissions, the oldest of which dates back to March 19, 2008, and the most current from October 24, 2019. In addition to the score, the author's username, the source subreddit, the sourced domain, the number of comments, and the up-vote to down-vote ratio were also collected. They also obtained the submission title and image. They regarded both submission and comment data from the photoshopbattles subreddit[7] as submission data. Users submit entries with real images to the subreddit photoshopbattles. The images from the submission are then altered by other users, who submit the edited images as comments on the submission page. These comments also include written information relating to or describing the image. These comments from the photoshopbattles subreddit are gathered, and they considered them as submission data to include in their submission dataset, greatly increasing the quantity of multimodal samples. The datasets described below are included in Table 1. Under multiple categories.

Table 1. Comparative analysis of Fakeddit with different datasets under multiple categories

Dataset	Size	#of classes	Modality	Source	Data category
LIAR	12836	6	Unimodal	PolitiFact	Political
COVID-19	10700	2	Unimodal	Multisource	Pandemic
Fakeddit	1063106	2, 3, 6	Multimodal	Reddit	Variety

4   Proposed Architecture

In this study, we provide an architecture for text classification that makes use of a distilled version of RoBERTa, DistiBERT, XLNet and fine-tuning. To extract image features,

---

[5] Https://www.reddit.com/.

[6] Reddit Statistics - pushshift.io.

[7] Https://www.reddit.com/r/photoshopbattles/.

ResNet50 [29] is used. We employ DistilBERT together with VGG16 for text and image feature extraction followed by a stack of dense layers for the multimodal FND task.

4.1 Exploratory Data Analysis (EDA) of Fakeddit Dataset

First, we conducted an EDA on the Fakeddit dataset and discovered that a two-way labelling scheme results in 74,882 duplicate records, whereas a three-way and six-way labelling schemes result in 74,844 and 72,176 duplicate records, respectively. At a greater depth 878,218 records for training, 92,444 records for testing and 92,444 records used for test data. The number of words per sentence is then calculated to examine the distribution of word lengths across the training dataset, and 80 was found to be the best fit. By truncating the words in phrases that are longer than 80 characters, the text part was tokenized using the RoBERTa tokenizer.

4.2 Unimodal Classification

To begin building the model, tokens are used as input. Next, the pre-trained Distil RoBERTa[8] is supplied as input, and the ensuing features related to the text are extracted and passed through a few dense layers. The Hyperparameter tuning carried out using the keras tuner determines the number of layers and the number of neurons per layer. The final dense layer's output is sent to the layer with the same number of neurons as class labels, where the logits are calculated. The probabilities are then obtained by running these logits through the softmax. The components of the hyperparameters are stated in Table 2, and Fig. 2. Depicts the architectural flow graphically.

Table 2. Hyperparameters tuning

Hyperparameter	Value
Optimizer	Adam
Loss function	Sparse categorical cross entropy
Epsilon value	0.000006(6e−6)

4.3 Multimodal Classification

We employ DistilBERT [30] along with VGG16 [31] for text and image feature extraction followed by a stack of dense layers for the multimodal FND task. We experimented with several fusion variations for the fusion of the extracted features, including adding the features, multiplying, concatenating, and taking the maximum of both features. Concatenate is determined to function better after some testing with the current architecture. This might change if we apply Hyperparameter tuning to other experiments and add denser layers. Figure 3 depicts multimodal architecture designed for the Fakeddit dataset.

---

[8] https://huggingface.co/sentence-transformers/all-distilroberta-v1

5 Experimental Analysis

In this study, we tested with three different textual data architectures, including XLNet [32], DistillBERT, and DistilRoBERTa, and compared the outcomes to the BERT architecture used in the [28] as shown in Table 3. And results show that proposed architectures are providing the better results than the baseline paper itself. Table 4. Illustrates the performance of the model in the context of image data, where ResNet50 architecture has been improved using part data and the same data has also been used for multimodal architecture. Figure 4 displays the multimodal accuracy using DistilBERT to extract textual features and VGG16 to extract visual features.

5.1 Error Analysis

A thorough analysis of the textual data using EDA revealed several duplicate entries, which were all removed. There was also a significant imbalance in the data as shown in Fig. 5, which was balanced using under-sampling, oversampling, and SMOTE techniques.

Table 3. Comparison of the outcomes for the three alternative class labelling schemes using textual data

Model/ way	2-way_ Validation	2-way_ Test	3-way_ Validation	3-way_ Test	6-way_ Validation	6-way_ Test
Fakeddit (BERT)	0.8654	0.8644	0.8282	0.8580	0.7696	0.7677
DistilBERT	0.9252	0.8798	0.8643	0.8633	0.7967	0.7982
DistilRoBERTa	0.8876	0.8860	0.8733	0.8747	0.8022	0.8032
XLNet					0.7323	0.7336

Table 4. Results on image data samples using ResNet50

Model	Validation accuracy	Testing accuracy
ResNet50	0.6329	0.6219

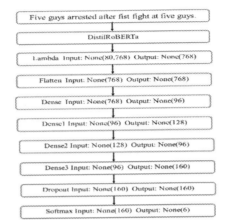

Fig. 2. Complete architecture used for classification based on text with 6 class labels

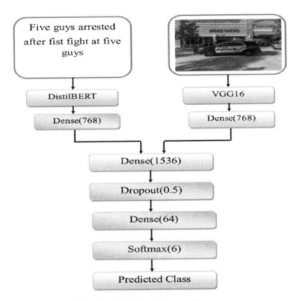

Fig. 3. Multimodal architecture

Due to the enormous amount of parameters involved, the model began to overfit and dropouts were introduced in between the dense layers. The model failed to improve training accuracy after three epochs of significant performance, which indicated under fitting and required the addition of a few denser layers using the Keras turner module (a Hyperparameter technique). The results displayed in Fig. 4. Are the performances on the part data, thus if the reason for the poor performance is a lack of data, these models have not yet been trained on the entire training set. On satire data, which the paper states are system generated, or synthetic data, the model has performed poorly.

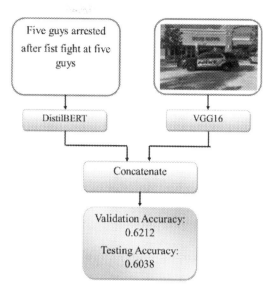

Fig. 4. Results on multimodal architecture

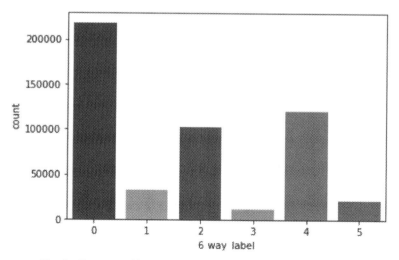

Fig. 5. Data spread in case of 6-way class label an imbalance data

6 Conclusion

In this paper, multiple architectures have been experimented with many baseline models. Maintaining the individual modal features while combining the features that are relevant to each modality is the main problem in multimodal architectures. Here, we suggested a novel architecture that makes advantage of the most recent feature extractor technologies, tested with a variety of fusion techniques, and displayed a comparison of the outcomes.

The results demonstrate that the suggested model outperforms the most current textual results on that dataset and learns better textual features. Future research in this field can use adversarial networks to improve the models resistance to new types of input with various classifications and to improve the models performance on regionally distinct languages as well.

References

1. Singhal, S., Shah, R.R., Chakraborty, T., Kumaraguru, P., Satoh, S.: SpotFake: a multi-modal framework for fake news detection. In: Proceedings of the 2019 IEEE Fifth International Conference on Multimedia Big Data, BigMM 2019, pp. 39–47 (2019). https://doi.org/10.1109/BIGMM.2019.00-44
2. Allcott, H., Gentzkow, M.: Social media and fake news in the 2016 election. J. Econ. Perspect. **31**(2), 211–236 (2017). https://doi.org/10.1257/JEP.31.2.211
3. Zhang, X., Ghorbani, A.A.: An overview of online fake news: characterization, detection, and discussion. Inf. Process. Manag. **57**(2), 102025 (2020). https://doi.org/10.1016/J.IPM.2019.03.004
4. Du, J., Dou, Y., Xia, C., Cui, L., Ma, J., Yu, P.S.: Cross-lingual COVID-19 fake news detection. In: IEEE International Conference on Data Mining Workshops ICDMW, vol. 2021-December, pp. 859–862 (2021). https://doi.org/10.1109/ICDMW53433.2021.00110
5. Siwakoti, S., Yadav, K., Bariletto, N., Zanotti, L., Erdogdu, U., Shapiro, J.N.: How COVID drove the evolution of fact-checking. Harvard Kennedy Sch. Misinform. Rev. (2021). https://doi.org/10.37016/MR-2020-69
6. Song, C., Ning, N., Zhang, Y., Wu, B.: A multimodal fake news detection model based on crossmodal attention residual and multichannel convolutional neural networks. Inf. Process. Manag. **58**(1), 102437 (2021). https://doi.org/10.1016/J.IPM.2020.102437
7. Zhu, Y., Wang, X., Zhong, E., Liu, N.N., Li, H., Yang, Q.: Discovering spammers in social networks. In: Proceedings of the AAAI Conference on Artificial Intelligence, vol. 26, no. 1, pp. 171–177 (2012). https://doi.org/10.1609/AAAI.V26I1.8116
8. Takahashi, T., Igata, N.: Rumor detection on twitter. In: 6th International Conference on Soft Computing and Intelligent Systems. International Symposium on Advanced Intelligence Systems SCIS/ISIS 2012, pp. 452–457 (2012). https://doi.org/10.1109/SCIS-ISIS.2012.6505254
9. Rubin, V.L., Conroy, N.J., Chen, Y., Cornwell, S.: Fake News or Truth? Using Satirical Cues to Detect Potentially Misleading News, pp. 7–17. https://youtu.be/2X93u3anTco. Accessed 29 July 2022
10. Zhou, X., Wu, J., Zafarani, R.: SAFE: Similarity-Aware Multi-modal Fake News Detection. Lecture Notes in Computer Science (including its subseries Lecture Notes in Artificial Intelligence and Lecture Notes in Bioinformatics), vol. 12085 LNAI, pp. 354–367 (2020). https://doi.org/10.1007/978-3-03047436-2_27/FIGURES/6
11. Sharma, K., et al.: Combating fake news. ACM Trans. Intell. Syst. Technol. **10**(3) (2019). https://doi.org/10.1145/3305260
12. Potthast, M., Kiesel, J., Reinartz, K., Bevendorff, J., Stein, B.: A Stylometric inquiry into hyperpartisan and fake news. In: ACL 2018 - 56th Annual Meeting of the Association for Computational Linguistics, Proceedings of the Conference (Long Papers, vol. 1, pp. 231–240 (2017). https://doi.org/10.48550/arxiv.1702.05638
13. MA, J., et al.: Detecting rumors from microblogs with recurrent neural networks. In: Proceedings of the 25th International Joint Conference on Artificial Intelligence. (IJCAI 2016) (2016). https://ink.library.smu.edu.sg/sis_research/4630. Accessed 29 July 2022

14. Chen, T., Li, X., Yin, H., Zhang, J.: Call attention to rumors: Deep attention based recurrent neural networks for early rumor detection. Lecture Notes in Computer Science (including subseries Lecture Notes in Artificial Intelligence and Lecture Notes in Bioinformatics), vol. 11154 LNAI, pp. 40–52 (2018). https://doi.org/10.1007/978-3-030-04503-6_4/COVER
15. Pan, J.Z., Pavlova, S., Li, C., Li, N., Li, Y., Liu, J.: Content Based Fake News Detection Using Knowledge Graphs, pp. 669–683 (2018). https://doi.org/10.1007/978-3-03000671-6_39
16. Wu, L., Liu, H.: Tracing Fake-News Footprints: Characterizing Social Media Messages by How They Propagate, vol. 9 (2018). https://doi.org/10.1145/3159652.3159677
17. Liu, Y., Wu, Y.F.B.: Early detection of fake news on social media through propagation path classification with recurrent and convolutional networks propagation path classification with recurrent and convolutional networks. In: Proceedings of the AAAI Conference on Artificial Intelligence, vol. 32, no. 1, pp. 354–361 (2018). https://doi.org/10.1609/AAAI.V32I1.11268
18. Kalra, S., Pathak, A., Agarwal, A., Sharma, Y., Singh Chauhan, G.: Comparative analysis of various text summarization techniques via leveraging transformer model for the fake news detection. In: Applications of Machine Intelligence in Engineering, pp. 511–520 (2022). https://doi.org/10.1201/9781003269793-53
19. Kalra, S., Verma, P., Sharma, Y., Chauhan, G.S.: Ensembling of Various Transformer Based Models for the Fake News Detection Task in the Urdu Language. https://github.com/Kalra-Sakshi/URduFND.git. Accessed 29 July 2022
20. Wu, K., Yang, S., Zhu, K.Q.: False rumors detection on Sina Weibo by propagation structures. In: Proceedings of the International Conference on Data Engineering, vol. 2015-May, pp. 651–662 (2015). https://doi.org/10.1109/ICDE.2015.7113322
21. ECCV 2018 Open Access Repository. https://openaccess.thecvf.com/content_ECCV_2018/html/Beery_Recognition_in_Terra_ECCV_2018_paper.html. Accessed 29 July 2022
22. Jin, Z., Cao, J., Guo, H., Zhang, Y., Luo, J.: Multimodal fusion with recurrent neural networks for rumor detection on microblogs. In: MM 2017 – Proceedings of the 2017 ACM Multimedia Conference, vol. 17, pp. 795–816 (2017). https://doi.org/10.1145/3123266.3123454
23. Khattar, D., Gupta, M., Goud, J.S., Varma, V.: MvaE: multimodal variational autoencoder for fake news detection. In: Web Conference 2019 – Proceedings of the World Wide Web Conference WWW 2019, vol. 7, pp. 2915–2921 (2019). https://doi.org/10.1145/3308558.3313552
24. Zhang, H., Fang, Q., Qian, S., Xu, C.: Multi-modal knowledge-aware event memory network for social media rumor detection. In: MM 2019 - Proceedings of the 27th ACM International Conference Multimedia, pp. 1942–1951 (2019). https://doi.org/10.1145/3343031.3350850
25. Wang, Y., et al.: EANN: Event adversarial neural networks for multi-modal fake news detection. In: Proceedings of the ACM SIGKDD Conference on Knowledge Discovery and Data Mining, pp. 849–857 (2018). https://doi.org/10.1145/3219819.3219903
26. Wang, W.F.: 'Liar, liar pants on fire': a new benchmark dataset for fake news detection. In: ACL 2017 - 55th Annual Meeting of the Association for Computational Linguistics. Proceedings of the Conference (Long Papers), vol. 2, pp. 422–426 (2017). https://doi.org/10.18653/v1/P17-2067
27. Patwa, P., et al.: Fighting an Infodemic: COVID-19 Fake News Dataset. Commun. Comput. Inf. Sci. **1402** CCIS, 21–29 (2021). https://doi.org/10.1007/978-3-030-736965_3/COVER
28. Nakamura, K., Levy, S., Wang, W.Y.: r/Fakeddit: a new multimodal benchmark dataset for fine-grained fake news detection. Lr. 2020 - 12th International Conference Language Resources and Evaluation Conference, pp. 6149–6157 (2020)
29. He, K., Zhang, X., Ren, S., Sun, J.: Deep residual learning for image recognition. In: Proceedings of the IEEE Computer Society Conference on Computer Vision and Pattern Recognition, vol. 2016-December, pp. 770–778 (2015). https://doi.org/10.48550/arxiv.1512.03385
30. Sanh, V., Debut, L., Chaumond, J., Wolf, T.: DistilBERT, a distilled version of BERT: smaller, faster, cheaper and lighter (2019). https://doi.org/10.48550/arxiv.1910.01108

31. Simonyan, K., Zisserman, A.: Very Deep Convolutional Networks for Large-Scale Image Recognition (2015). http://www.robots.ox.ac.uk/. Accessed 30 July 2022
32. Yang, Z., Dai, Z., Yang, Y., Carbonell, J., Salakhutdinov, R., Le, Q.V.: XLNet: Generalized Autoregressive Pretraining for Language Understanding. https://github.com/zihangdai/xlnet. Accessed 30 July 2022

SAFE: Secure and Fast Key Establishment for Resource Constrained Devices in Device to Device Communications

Mahanya Kochhar[1(✉)], Narendra S. Chaudhari[1], and Shubham Gupta[2]

[1] Indian Institute of Technology, Indore 453552, India
mahannya.kochhar@gmail.com
[2] SRM University, Amaravati 522240, Andhra Pradesh, India

Abstract. Device to Device Communications allows devices within certain proximity limits to communicate directly with or without cellular network infrastructure. This leads to faster data exchange and low latency delays. With ever-rising security threats that can jeopardize D2D communications, authentication of devices and initial key establishment for further message encryption is the need of the hour for secure D2D communication. In this paper, we first analyze authentication schemes for traditional Diffie-Hellman and their shortcomings in terms of performance and security for resource-constrained devices. We then propose a solution initially meant for wireless sensor networks for key issuing and establishment, which is ideal for devices with resource limitations. The principle of the protocol is based on Identity-based Key Issuing and a Key Generation Centre Model. It is observed that a secure session key is established between two devices with the above protocol. The proposed protocol eliminates the need for certificates that lead to storage, communication, and computation overheads. It is suitable in terms of computation and communication overhead with the existing literature. The proposed protocol with the proposed Key Generation Centre model can easily be integrated into devices enabled with Wi-Fi Direct further enhancing the security of D2D communications.

Keywords: Device to Device Communications · Wi-Fi Direct · Resource constrained devices · Key establishment

1 Introduction

Device to Device (D2D) Communications has been a major area of research in recent years. Two or more devices within certain proximity can communicate with each other with or without the involvement of existing cellular network infrastructure. With more devices being connected globally and ever-rising mobile subscribers, the need for fast and secure data exchange between devices is an urgent and pressing requirement.

D2D communications allow User-Equipments (UEs) within a certain proximity to communicate using a direct link without routing radio signal paths through the network infrastructure. This promises high data rates and ultra-low latency due to shorter

N. Khare et al. (Eds.): MIND 2022, CCIS 1763, pp. 293–307, 2022.
https://doi.org/10.1007/978-3-031-24367-7_29

signal paths. Till recent times, D2D communications did not appear financially feasible to network operators. However with more demanding resource-consuming applications and proximity-based services, D2D has been seen as a key complementary technology with the 5G infrastructure for peer-to-peer communication, proximity detection services, Machine to Machine Communication, coverage extensions, data and computation offloading, emergency communications and IoT enhancement (e.g., V2V communication).

5G technology promises higher bandwidth capabilities, low data rates and efficiency in the exchange of real-time data and hence is the preferred technology for IoT-based applications. The D2D Communications in 5G are possible via cellular services or Wi-Fi Direct. As cellular services are limited by partial or no coverage, Wi-Fi Direct can efficiently and reliably facilitate data exchange for the implementation of IoT-enabled smart city applications. Figure 1 illustrates the two typical D2D communication scenarios.

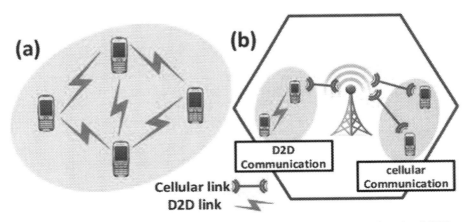

Fig. 1. D2D communications (a) without infrastructure (b) cellular network assisted D2D

With the development of emerging technologies, new security threats arise that can disrupt and jeopardize the whole communication setup. Typical D2D communication security threats include jamming, user emulation attacks, message modification and node impersonation. Man-in-the-middle (MITM) attack is an active eavesdropping attack when an attacker device disrupts the private communication between communicating devices and relays messages between those devices that still believe they are communicating with each other securely.

For secure and reliable exchange of information between nodes with protection from the security threats mentioned, key establishment via cryptographic primitives is required that authenticates the devices before any exchange of information. The security requirements of Confidentiality, Integrity and Authentication (CIA triad) are a must for any secure key establishment protocol along with robustness, privacy, non-repudiation and availability and dependability of the network.

The authors of this work propose SAFE: a secure and fast key establishment for Resource Constrained Devices in D2D communication scenarios with an identity-based key issuing model.

1.1 Technical Contribution

This article proposes a lightweight cryptographic protocol based on research work conducted for key establishment in typical D2D devices. The authors of this work use the idea of an Identity-based Diffie-Hellman Key Establishment with the latest and fastest Elliptic Curve Cryptography primitives discussed subsequently for mutual authentication and key establishment in D2D scenarios. The important contributions of this paper include:

- Analysis of the Station to Station Protocol (STS) as a possible solution to the MITM attack in traditional unauthenticated Diffie-Hellman key exchange.
- We present an underlying security issue in STS and propose a modification to the same to improve its security.
- We find issues with our proposed approach in terms of performance and suitability for resource-constrained devices with costly cryptographic primitives involved.
- To achieve a robust, lightweight authenticated key agreement we propose an identity-based solution initially meant for wireless sensor networks for our D2D communication scenarios.
- We propose a new identity-based key issuing model to the above solution to improve security and robustness for our D2D communication scenarios. We further evaluate SAFE's computation and communication overheads and compare them with existing literature works. We further analyze the latest Elliptic Curve Cryptography (ECC) primitives for fast scalar multiplication for use in our key generation and key establishment phases.

The rest of the paper is organized as follows: Sect. 2 provides a literature overview and discusses conventional and current research work for secure D2D communications. Section 3 describes a new protocol proposed by this work's authors and its performance limitations. Section 4 defines the notations and security goals for secure D2D communication. Section 5 identifies a solution initially for sensor networks and proposes the same for the key issuing and establishment phase. Section 6 discusses the results of SAFE. Section 7 analyzes the latest Elliptic Curve Cryptography primitives for performance improvements. Finally, Sect. 8 draws the conclusions.

2 Background

D2D bypasses the cellular network infrastructure or base stations enhancing spectral efficiency and reducing latency. Such enhancements to the existing infrastructure speed up the data exchange between devices. For the adoption and deployment of D2D services, security and privacy are fundamental aspects to be addressed [1].

Wi-Fi Direct has emerged as a suitable technology for D2D communications to save data exchange and communication costs. D2D communication establishment via Wi-Fi Direct is a four-stage process: discovery, GO negotiation, WPS and address configuration. D2D communications with Wi-Fi Direct are susceptible to various security threats and challenges [2]. Wi-Fi Direct relies on Wi-Fi Protected Setup (WPS) to connect two devices securely. The limitations of this setup in terms of security enable an attacker to perform a brute force attack against the WPS Pin solution [3]. Short Authentication Scheme (SAS) based Protocols [4] by S Pasini et al. require a safe and secure Out of Band (OOB) channel for string authentication and in reality, no channel can be considered to be secure in wireless communications. Hence such protocols are subject to eavesdropping and MITM which leads to a compromise in the security of the system.

Diffie-Hellman Key Exchange is based on the computational hardness of the Discrete Logarithm problem [5]. Traditionally, Diffie-Hellman Key Exchange is unauthenticated and subject to the famous MITM attack [6]. Whitfield Diffie and others introduced a protocol referred to as the Station to Station (STS) Protocol for authenticated Diffie-Hellman key exchange [7]. The STS protocol consists of traditional Diffie-Hellman key establishment along with an exchange of authentication signatures with the help of certificates issued via a trusted authority. In practice, the STS Protocol uses certificates to facilitate the distribution of users' public keys and user-specific Diffie-Hellman parameters.

Since these traditional authentication mechanisms are either costly in terms of processing speed, and resource utilization or are vulnerable to attacks, it is evident that a strong, lightweight mutual authentication scheme is required in the Wi-Fi Direct Protocol to enhance the security of D2D communications.

The authors of [8] propose a solution for secure D2D communication with Elliptic Curve Cryptography (ECC) and the lightweight AEAD cipher for efficiency. Maode Ma et al. [9] proposed an LTE-AKA scheme based on [8] for 5G D2D networks. However, both the above solutions are designed for 5G D2D networks, require the necessary 5G infrastructure, and are not suitable for Wi-Fi Direct D2D scenarios. Based on the computational hardness of the ECC Discrete Logarithm Problem, the authors of [10] propose an authenticated certificateless key agreement protocol that uses International Mobile Subscriber Identity (IMSI) as identity information.

To improve the security of D2D communications via Wi-Fi Direct, the authors of [11] proposed an authentication approach called Secure Key Exchange with QR code (SeKeQ) to enable devices to establish a shared key over public channels. Besides having large computation and communication overheads, SeKeQ requires the D2D device to scan a QR code for string authentication purposes. We typically want to avoid any OOB authentication in an authentication protocol for security reasons.

We now discuss and analyze the MAKE scheme [12] that aims to enhance the security capabilities of the Wi-Fi Direct Protocol.

2.1 Intelligent Device Filtering and Mutual Authentication and Key Establishment (MAKE)

The authors of [12] propose an intelligent device filtering mechanism and mutual authentication and key establishment scheme for preventing DOS attacks in the discovery phase and MITM attacks in the key agreement phase of the Wi-Fi Direct Protocol.

It is assumed by the authors of [12] that nodes are stationary and have unique MAC Addresses and Received Signal Strength Indicator (RSSI) values. These addresses are used to verify the legitimacy of the probe requests received at a node for further communication. With such a probe request, the authors of [12] aim to prevent bogus requests received at legitimate devices that drain battery resources and processing capabilities.

The mutual authentication and key establishment scheme (MAKE) aims to enhance the security capabilities of the SAS-based key agreement [4] with timestamps added and message authentication codes for mutual authentication and secret key establishment. The authors aim to eliminate the use of OOB channels and plaintext communication of short authentication strings.

3   Cryptanalysis of Protocols

3.1   Cryptanalysis of Intelligent Device Filtering and MAKE Scheme

While the protocol proposed by [12] enhances the security of the Wi-Fi Direct Protocol and protects devices from DOS and MITM attacks, it has some severe limitations in terms of strict assumptions.

The assumption by the authors that nodes are stationary is not feasible for D2D communications as mobile devices are at the heart of D2D communications and their RSSI values cannot be held constant ever as RSSI itself is determined by weather conditions, temperature and obstacles in the path of communication [13]. Hence the assumption that the RSSI of devices is held constant is impractical in real-life applications. Thus, the intelligent device filtering for malicious nodes to prevent DOS will fail in real-time scenarios.

The MAKE scheme employs the use of timestamps and lifetime values for authentication purposes. Timestamps put forward a huge challenge of maintaining local clocks that are periodically synchronized securely with reliable sources of time that lead to delays and tradeoffs in performance and security and are hence not recommended by the authors of [7] for any use in authentication protocols.

Cryptanalysis of STS Protocol
We have critically analyzed the STS protocol and found a vulnerability in the same. The attacker can compromise any communication between two devices. Such an attack is illustrated in Fig. 2.

1. If a powerful adversary can issue certificates in someone else's name through trusted authority or compromise the trusted authority, a successful MITM attack can be established where an adversary can impersonate one of the devices, making it appear as if a normal exchange of information is underway.
2. Let's assume a D2D communication scenario where one device (say $Device_1$) wants to communicate with another D2D device ($Device_2$) but somehow attacker device ($Device_3$) intervenes. $Device_3$ pretends to be $Device_2$ to $Device_1$ and receives the STS protocol's message (1). $Device_3$ cannot determine x (secret key of $Device_1$), from α^x. However, $Device_3$ sends α, p and $\alpha^{x'}$ to $Device_2$ where x' is $Device_3$'s

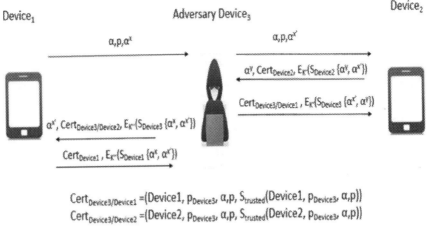

Fig. 2. MITM in STS with certificate forgery by an adversary

secret key. Device$_2$ thinks he has received this message from Device$_1$ and sends the message (2) of the STS Protocol as α^y, Cert$_{Device2}$, $E_{K'}$ ($S_{Device2}$ $\{\alpha^y, \alpha^{x'}\}$) where K' is the shared key between Device$_2$ and Device$_3$.

Device$_3$ now sends $E_{K'}$ ($S_{Device3}$ $\{\alpha^{x'}, \alpha^y\}$) to Device$_2$ along with a forged certificate (Cert$_{Device3/Device1}$) issued by him carrying Device$_1$'s name. Device$_2$ thinks he is communicating with Device$_1$, however, it is Device$_3$ who has established a connection with him. Now, Device$_3$ sends to Device$_1$ $\alpha^{x'}$, Cert$_{Device3/Device2}$, $E_{K''}$ ($S_{Device3}$ $\{\alpha^{x'}, \alpha^x\}$) where Cert$_{Device3/Device2}$ is the forged certificate carrying Device$_2$'s name and K'' is the shared secret key between Device$_1$ and Device$_3$. Device$_1$ considers this message to be Device$_2$'s and responds with $E_{K''}$ ($S_{Device1}$ $\{\alpha^x, \alpha^{x'}\}$) along with his original certificate.

Thus Device$_3$ has established independent connections with Device$_1$ and Device$_2$. As Device$_1$ and Device$_2$ are unaware of fraudulent Device$_3$, they continue the communication with Device$_3$.

Proposed Hybrid Protocol to Solve the Issue with STS
The hybrid protocol proposed by the authors of this work assumes a Public Key Infrastructure (PKI) set-up where the sender of a message can easily access the recipient's public key and use it to encrypt messages and send messages.

Encrypting the sender's exponential term and Diffie-Hellman parameters with the sender's private key first and the recipient's public key accessed via broadcast or PKI (see Fig. 3 and Table 1) mitigates the attack mentioned in the previous section. Such a modification ensures that the sender's exponential term is viewed by the intended recipient as only the intended recipient can decrypt the message with his own private key first followed by the sender's public key.

Thus any adversary can never find out the sender's exponential as he does not have the recipient's private key which is confidential information. Hence, he cannot establish independent connections with the intended targets, so the MITM attack is prevented.

Device1   Device2

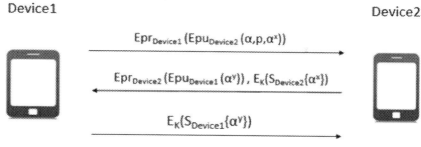

Fig. 3. Proposed hybrid scheme with encryption

Table 1. Notations and denotations

Notations	Denotations
$pr_{Device1}$	Public key of device 1
	Private key of device 1
$pu_{Device1}$	
$pr_{Device2}$	Private key of device 2
$pu_{Device2}$	Public key of device 2

The proposed protocol is secure from MITM attack but it has certain limitations described as follows:

1. Assumption that the sender initially knows the recipient's public key is not always practical without a large infrastructure set up.
2. Resource-constrained devices like mobiles, sensors and IoT devices have low processing power and battery limitations.
3. Standard Encryption algorithms like Blowfish, and AES have high processing capability requirements and are not suitable for D2D devices that are resource constrained.
4. Cryptographic certificates for authentication require additional computational effort for their authentication purposes.

Due to the resource limitations of typical D2D devices, identity-based schemes that embed the authentication in the key establishment procedure are considered ideal for D2D devices as computational overhead is minimized at the device participating in D2D.

4 Notations and Typical Security Goals

4.1 Notations of Proposed Solution

The notations and denotations of the parameters used in the proposed solution are found in Table 2 below.

Table 2. Notations and denotations for proposed solution

Notations	Denotations
H	Cryptographic hash function
E	Elliptic curve
G	Generator point on curve
q	Prime order selected
KGC	Key generation centre
d	Master private key of KGC
R	Master public key of KGC
H_{device}	Nonce generated by KGC
U_{device}	Public value of device
x_{device}	Secret key of device
KGC_i	KGC selected by device for session communication
P_{device}	Nonce generated by device
E_{device}	Random point on elliptic curve
ID_{device}	Identification parameter of device

4.2 Security Goals

The security goals of a secure authentication protocol include:

1. Secret Key Establishment: D2D devices generate and share a large amount of data that is shared with other devices through untrusted wireless channels. Therefore a secure key via a key agreement and establishment protocol between the two parties is needed for data encryption.
2. Mutual Authentication: Authentication is required to confirm the identity of a device. With the open nature of wireless channels, D2D devices need to be authenticated to ensure that the correct parties are communicating with each other. Authenticated Key exchanges are required that also authenticate the identities of parties involved in the key exchange.

   Diffie Hellman Key Exchange is unauthenticated and hence it needs a separate authentication scheme to authenticate devices.
3. Ephemeral Key Exchange: Static/Fixed keys remain the same over a long period. One key for many instances of a key establishment scheme is not good practice.

   An Ephemeral key is generated for each execution of a key establishment process. It ensures key freshness and a unique key for each session.
4. Security and Defense from Prominent Attacks:

Security protocols must be resilient against common attacks such as node impersonation, the MITM attack and authentication attacks.

The proposed solution in the subsequent section establishes a unique ephemeral key comprising of a fixed identity-based component and a random component. The Key Establishment phase achieves perfect forward secrecy and is secure and resilient against the MITM attack and other attacks as shown in [18].

5   Proposed Solution

At the end of Sect. 3, identity-based schemes were discussed that embed authentication into the key establishment and saved computational effort. ID-based encryption was first proposed by Adi Shamir in 1984 [14].

The pairing-based Boneh-Franklin scheme solved the IBE problem with pairings [15]. However, it made use of expensive bilinear maps. Two pairing-free identity-based schemes that require minimum computational effort were further introduced. One approach was introduced by Arazi, Qi et al. in 2007 [16]. Another approach was introduced by D Fiore and Rosario Gennaro in 2011 [17].

Based on Arazi, Qi solution; the protocol proposed by [18] has been considered suitable by the authors of this paper for the identity-based Diffie-Hellman Key Agreement. We now introduce Hang et al. solution for wireless sensor networks as a possible key establishment solution for D2D devices. We further propose a change to the Key Generation Centre model proposed by [18] later in this section.

The protocol introduced by [18] based on Arazi, Qi scheme consists of 2 steps: Identity-based Key issuing and Key Establishment.

5.1   Identity-Based Key Issuing

The identity-based key agreement schemes avoid the use of public certificates by making the public key computable easily from some unique identification information of the owner. The identification information can include a unique identification number or device properties. Identity-based cryptography thus avoids cumbersome certificate management infrastructure and saves computational effort.

Key Issuing Model
In this step, each device is presented with an identity, a secret key and a public value. This is an identity-based approach. For Elliptic Curve Key Establishment, a suitable safe elliptic curve E over a finite field along with an initial generator point G of prime order q is chosen by the Key Generation Center.

A cryptographic hash function H: $\{0, 1\}^* \rightarrow \{1, ..., q - 1\}$ like HMAC is further needed. The authors of [18] propose a single Key Generation Centre (KGC) for endowing all D2D participants with a secret key and public value. The KGC generates a random number $d \in \{1, ..., q - 1\}$ as the master private key of itself and computes its own master public key R as $R = d \times G$. All D2D participants are aware of the elliptic curve, the point G selected, R and the prime order q.

Let us consider two devices A and B want to participate in D2D communication. Before the D2D device is deployed, it is presented with a secret key and public value by the KGC setup. Firstly, the KGC generates a random number $h_A \in \{1, ..., q - 1\}$ and calculates $U_A = h_A \times G$. U_A is the public value of device A presented to it by KGC.

Then, the private key $x_A \in \{1, \ldots, q - 1\}$ of device A is generated by the KGC as follows $x_A = [H(ID_A, U_A) \cdot h_A + d] \bmod q$.

This public value U_A and secret key x_A are then issued to device A. This key issuing is done for every device interested in D2D communications. On receiving U_A and secret key x_A, a device can verify its issued values by checking whether

$$x_A \times G = H(ID_A, U_A) \times U_A + R \tag{1}$$

The value $x_A \times G$ is the public key of Device A. It is never used explicitly, however, it is computed from the identification parameters of a node and Key Generation Centre public information.

A single KGC was originally proposed. However, a single KGC's failure can disrupt the entire communication setup. The authors of this work propose multiple KGCs, say n KGCs, where each KGC can have an independent curve E, the point G, and master public key R. The prime order q is assumed same for all KGCs. Each D2D participant is aware of the KGC parameters when it receives n distinct (X_A, U_A) pairs and can verify each pair independently.

Such independent KGCs ensure a fault-tolerant key generation system where the compromise of a single KGC facility doesn't lead to a breakdown of the infrastructure.

Figure 4 illustrates the proposed key issuing model with n KGCs.

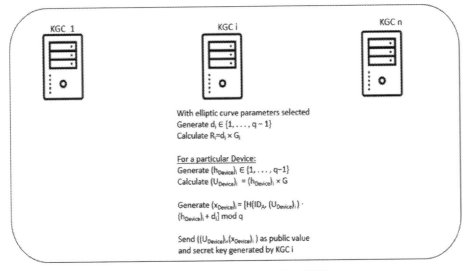

Fig. 4. Key issuing model with n KGCs

Key Establishment Procedure

For two D2D participants to communicate with each other, they should have their identity-based keys issued at first as described by the key issuing model. For key establishment between devices A and B, the protocol is as follows:

Each node generates independent numbers as follows: $p_A \in \{1, ..., q - 1\}$ is generated by device A and a nonce $p_B \in \{1, ..., q - 1\}$ is generated by device B. A indicates to B its desire for D2D communication and shares its $(ID_A, U_A, KGC_i, E_A = p_A \times G)$ where KGC_i is the KGC chosen by Device A for this particular D2D communication instance. Sending this parameter is important so that the receiving node can then select the correct secret key, public key-value pair, master public key of KGC, elliptic curve considered and initial point G from all possible pairs available to him.

Now Device B processes the message (1) and responds with $(ID_B, U_B, KGC_i, E_B = p_B \times G)$. Now both the Devices have agreed to use the (secret key, public value) pairs issued by KGC_i and public information of KGC_i for key establishment.

Device A checks whether $E_B \neq 0$, $E_B \in E$ and now calculates the current session key K_{AB} as

$$K_{AB} = \left[x_A \cdot H(ID_B, U_B) \bmod q \right] \times U_B + x_A \times R + p_A \times E_B$$
$$= x_A x_B \times G + p_A p_B \times G. \tag{2}$$

Similarly, after checking whether $E_A \neq O$ and $E_A \in E$, the session key K_{BA} is also computed by Device B as

$$K_{BA} = \left[x_B \cdot H(ID_A, U_A) \bmod q \right] \times U_A + x_B \times R + p_B \times E_A$$
$$= x_B x_A \times G + p_B p_A \times G \tag{3}$$

The two parties have now generated a common secure session key and can initiate their communication.

Since $x_A \times R$ is fixed for each session, it can be pre-stored in the device multiplication. Also, E_A can be precomputed before key establishment to save a scalar multiplication. Therefore at the key establishment, 2 scalar multiplications are required at each device.

Figure 5 illustrates the key establishment procedure between two devices.

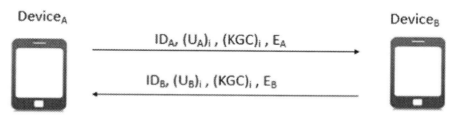

Fig. 5. Key establishment between two devices

6   Results

The authors of this work intend to implement the proposed key generation model and key agreement protocol for D2D devices shortly. For now, the quantitative and qualitative analysis of the proposed scheme is performed in terms of its communication and computation overheads. We further compare our solution with some existing solutions in the literature and prove why our solution is ideal for D2D communications with Wi-Fi Direct.

The key issuing procedure is performed at the Key Generation Centres (KGCs). It is a reasonable assumption that Key Generation Centres have enough processing capabilities and resources to generate and issue keys that embed user identity.

Key Establishment between two devices involves only two message exchanges that have minimum communication overhead. ECC Scalar multiplications are typically the most costly operations in ECC and our proposed scheme employs 2 Scalar multiplications at each stage. This is a reasonable amount of computation overhead at each device as storage overhead, verification, communication and computation overhead of certificates are eliminated with such a protocol.

Table 3 illustrates the communication overhead of some common cryptography primitives.

Table 3. Communication overhead specifications of some cryptography primitives

Parameters	No of bits required
ID_{device}	128 bits
U_{device}	256 bits
E_{device}	256 bits
N_{device}	128 bits
g^a	1024 bits
Ts	64 bits
L_T	64 bits
HMAC	160 bits

The communication overhead for key establishment at each device in our protocol amounts to overheads of $ID_{device} + U_{device} + E_{device} + KGC_i$. This amounts to a net overhead of $(128 + 256 + 256 + \log(n)$ bits$) = 640 + \log(n)$ bits at each device where n is the no of KGCs in the KGC and is implementation-dependent (depends on number of KGCs selected in the KGC model).

Assuming elapsed time for scalar multiplications to be T_{SM}, elapsed time for modular exponentiation to be T_{ME} and elapsed time for hash message function to be T_{Hash}. It is also considered that elapsed time for XOR, T_{XOR} is negligible. From the research work in [19] where the elapsed time of certain cryptographic primitives is verified by the OpenSSL [20] library written in C++, it is evident that $T_{ME} > T_{SM} > T_{Hash}$. The computation overhead for key establishment at each device in our proposed scheme is thus $2 * T_{SM} + T_{Hash}$.

We now compare our proposed scheme with the Key Establishment phase in SeKeQ [11] and MAKE [12] for communication and computation overheads in Table 4.

Table 4. Comparative analysis with MAKE at each D2D device

Protocol	Communication overhead	Computation overhead
MAKE	1696 bits	$2 * T_{ME} + 2 * T_{Hash}$
SeKeQ	1184 bits	$2 * T_{ME} + T_{Hash}$
SAFE	$640 + n$ bits	$2 * T_{SM} + T_{Hash}$

It is clear that the protocol SAFE proposed by the authors of this work is efficient in terms of computational and communication overheads and is thus an ideal choice for D2D communication technology with Wi-Fi Direct in resource-constrained devices.

7 Latest Elliptic Curve Cryptography Primitives

Elliptic Curve Cryptography (ECC) is the modern encryption technology as it is smaller, faster and lightweight than traditional cryptography primitives. As the name suggests, ECC uses the properties of algebraic elliptic curves over finite fields and the computational hardness of the Elliptic Curve Discrete Logarithm Problem (ECDLP) [21].

Elliptic Curve Diffie Hellman (ECDH), uses ECC point multiplications instead of modular exponentiations. ECDH promises very fast key generation and key agreement with smaller keys. The performance analysis by [22] reveals that to achieve a 128-bit symmetric-equivalent security level, Diffie Hellman needs a key length of 3072 bits whereas ECDH requires just 256 bits. This smaller key length improves overall performance and is thus suitable for our resource-constrained D2D devices.

Now we turn our focus to the latest underlying Elliptic curves used by ECC Algorithms. Different Elliptic Curves provide different results in terms of performance, security and resource consumption. Choosing safe elliptic curves is an important criterion to provide ECC security and avoid side-channel attacks. Notable cryptographers like Bernstein believe that most of the curves described in the NIST crypto standards are unsafe and have suspicious origins and hence have defined their own ECC security standards. Safe curves for use in ECC as studied by Bernstein and Lange are documented in [23]. Bernstein in 2005 released an ECDH key agreement protocol, X25519 with Curve25519 as the underlying elliptic curve [24]. It offers significant performance improvements compared to the NIST elliptic curves and its reference implementation is available publicly, thereby it has gained tremendous popularity recently with messaging application giants like WhatsApp.

The authors of this paper recommend Curve25519 as the underlying elliptic curve used by the KGCs for key issuing procedures.

8 Conclusions

D2D communications with Wi-Fi Direct are fast emerging as a popular mode of communication for the exchange of information between devices. Due to unsecure wireless channels and developing infrastructure for D2D communication, it is typically subject to attacks such as MITM with the traditional protocols that are in use. With the above risks kept in mind, the authors analyzed the famous STS solution to prevent the MITM attack and proposed a new protocol. As devices are resource constrained and have low processing capabilities and the above-mentioned solutions are costly in terms of communication and computation overheads, we proposed a new scheme of key establishment using the concepts of identity-based key issuing and key establishment. The proposed identity-based key issuing scheme eliminates the need for certificates for the authentication of devices with (secret key, public value) pairs now being issued by KGCs that embed device identity. With the above key issuing model and key establishment scheme, we propose using certain latest elliptic curve cryptography primitives for scalar multiplications that make the solution safe and suitable for use in D2D devices with resource limitations. The limitation of this proposed scheme possibly is the one-time setup of the key issuing model and the required infrastructure. The future extension of this work might include detailed performance analysis and implementation of the key issuing and key establishment of the proposed model with the cryptographic primitives above discussed. The authors also plan to explore D2D communication in terms of many-to-one, one-to-many and many-to-many scenarios.

References

1. Haus, M., Waqas, M., Ding, A.Y., Li, Y., Tarkoma, S., Ott, J.: Security and privacy in device-to-device (D2D) communication: a review. IEEE Commun. Surv. Tutor. **19**(2), 1054–1079 (2017). https://doi.org/10.1109/COMST.2017.2649687
2. Wang, M., Yan, Z.: Security in D2D communications: a review. In: Proceedings of the 2015 IEEE Trustcom/BigDataSE/ISPA - Volume 01 (TRUSTCOM 2015), pp. 1199–1204. IEEE Computer Society, New York (2015). https://doi.org/10.1109/Trustcom.2015.505
3. Viehbock, S.: Brute forcing Wi-Fi protected setup, Wi-Fi Prot. Setup 9 (2011)
4. Pasini, S., Vaudenay, S.: SAS-based authenticated key agreement. In: Yung, M., Dodis, Y., Kiayias, A., Malkin, T. (eds.) PKC 2006. LNCS, vol. 3958, pp. 395–409. Springer, Heidelberg (2006). https://doi.org/10.1007/11745853_26
5. Baker, K.A.: Diffie-Hellman Key Exchange. https://www.math.ucla.edu/~baker/40/handouts/rev_DH/node1.html
6. Gretes, M.: MITM Attack. https://open.oregonstate.education/defenddissent/chapter/the-man-in-the-middle/
7. Diffie, W., Van Oorschot, P.C., Wiener, M.J.: Authentication and authenticated key exchanges. Des Codes Crypt **2**, 107–125 (1992)
8. Seok, B., Sicato, J.C.S., Erzhena, T., Xuan, C., Pan, Y., Park, J.H.: Secure D2D communication for 5G IoT network based on lightweight cryptography. Appl. Sci. **10**, 217 (2020)
9. Chow, M.C., Ma, M.: A lightweight traceable D2D authentication and key agreement scheme in 5G cellular networks. Comput. Electr. Eng. **95**, 107375 (2021)
10. Li, S., Li, M., Bao, B., Yu, B., Tang, J.: An efficient authenticated key agreement protocol for D2D communication. In: 2021 7th International Conference on Computer and Communications (ICCC), pp. 199–203 (2021)
11. Belghazi, Z., Benamar, N., Addaim, A., Kerrache, C.A.: Secure WiFi-direct using key exchange for IoT device-to-device communications in a smart environment. Future Internet **11**, 251 (2019)

12. Gaba, G.S., Kumar, G., Kim, T.-H., Monga, H., Kumar, P.: Secure Device-to-Device communications for 5G enabled Internet of Things applications. Comput. Commun. **169**, 114–128 (2021)

13. Munoz, D., Bouchereau, F., Enriquez, R.: Position, Location Techniques and Applications. Elsevier, Amsterdam (2009)

14. Shamir, A.: Identity-based cryptosystems and signature schemes. In: Blakley, G.R., Chaum, D. (eds.) CRYPTO 1984. LNCS, vol. 196, pp. 47–53. Springer, Heidelberg (1985). https://doi.org/10.1007/3-540-39568-7_5

15. Boneh, D., Franklin, M.: Identity-based encryption from the weil pairing. In: Kilian, J. (ed.) CRYPTO 2001. LNCS, vol. 2139, pp. 213–229. Springer, Heidelberg (2001). https://doi.org/10.1007/3-540-44647-8_13

16. Arazi, B.: Certification of DL/EC keys. In: Proceedings of the IEEE P1363 Study Group for Future Public-Key Cryptography Standards (1999)

17. Fiore, D., Gennaro, R.: Identity-based key exchange protocols without pairings. In: Gavrilova, M.L., Tan, C.J.K., Moreno, E.D. (eds.) Transactions on Computational Science X. LNCS, vol. 6340, pp. 42–77. Springer, Heidelberg (2010). https://doi.org/10.1007/978-3-642-17499-5_3

18. Hang, I., Ullmann, M., Wieschebrink, C.: Short paper: a new identity-based DH key-agreement protocol for wireless sensor networks based on the Arazi-Qi scheme. In: Proceedings of the Fourth ACM Conference on Wireless Network security (WiSec 2011), pp. 139–144. Association for Computing Machinery, New York (2011)

19. Gupta, S., Parne, B.L., Chaudhari, N.S.: ISAG: IoT-enabled and Secrecy Aware Group-based handover scheme for e-health services in M2M communication network. Future Gener. Comput. Syst. **125**, 168–187 (2021)

20. OPENSSL-Cryptography and SSl/TLS Toolkit. Technical report. https://www.openssl.org/

21. Rabah, K.: Theory and implementation of elliptic curve cryptography. J. Appl. Sci. **5**(4), 604–633 (2005)

22. Alvarez, R., Caballero-Gil, C., Santonja, J., Zamora, A.: Algorithms for lightweight key exchange. Sensors **17**, 1517 (2017)

23. Bernstein, D.J., Lange, T.: SafeCurves: choosing safe curves for elliptic-curve cryptography. https://safecurves.cr.yp.to. Accessed 5 Aug 2022

24. Bernstein, D.J.: Curve25519: new Diffie-Hellman speed records. In: Yung, M., Dodis, Y., Kiayias, A., Malkin, T. (eds.) PKC 2006. LNCS, vol. 3958, pp. 207–228. Springer, Heidelberg (2006). https://doi.org/10.1007/11745853_14

Exploring Patterns and Correlations Between Cryptocurrencies and Forecasting Crypto Prices Using Influential Tweets

Mohit Kumar, Gurram Sahithi Priya, Praneeth Gadipudi, Ishita Agarwal, and Saleti Sumalatha(✉) ⓘD

SRM University, Amaravathi, India
sumalatha.s@srmap.edu.in

Abstract. The Crypto market, as we know, is a market full of various kinds of investors and influencers. We all know the pizza incident in 2010 where a guy purchased two pizzas at 10000 BTC, which ranges nearly around 80 million in current times. That describes how much the market has progressed in these 10–12 years. You can see drastic changes in the price of several coins in the past few years, which brings in many new investors to invest their money in this market. Crypto Market has highly volatile currencies. Bitcoin was around 5K INR in 2013, and by year 2021, it reached 48 Lakhs INR, which shows how volatile the market is. The dataset provides many fascinating and valuable insights that help us gather practical knowledge. As data scientists, we are very keen to understand such a market whose data is unstable and keeps changing frequently and making out new patterns with time. This introduction of new patterns with time makes this problem an interesting one and keeps on motivating us to find some valuable information. So, through this manuscript, we tried to analyze two specific crypto coins for a particular period, including more than 2900 records. We found several interesting patterns in the dataset and explored the historical return using several statistical models. We plotted the opening and closing prices of the particular coin by using NumPy, SciPy, and Matplotlib. We also tried to make predictions of the cost of the specific currency and then plot the predicted price line with the actual price line and understand the difference in the prediction model with the fundamental price mode. To do so, we used the Simple Exponential Smoothing (SES) model and performed sentiment analysis based on influencing tweets on Twitter. That makes our prediction more accurate and more reliable than existing techniques. Lastly, we used a linear regression model to establish the relationship between the returns of Ripple and Bitcoin.

Keywords: Crypto market · Cryptocurrency · Data mining · Data visualization · Simple exponential smoothing · Sentiment analysis · Linear regression

1 Introduction

A cryptocurrency is an encrypted string of data representing a unit of currency. It is overseen and hosted by a peer-to-peer network called the blockchain [1]. The cryptocurrency

N. Khare et al. (Eds.): MIND 2022, CCIS 1763, pp. 308–321, 2022.
https://doi.org/10.1007/978-3-031-24367-7_30

market is very similar to the stock market, where we can buy, sell and transfer digital coins instead of physical coins; these digital coins are considered digital currency [12]. Crypto is a decentralized currency which means the government of any particular country does not issue it. Cryptocurrencies are created using cryptographic algorithms that are maintained and validated through a process called mining. Cryptocurrencies have many coins, some of which are Cryptocurrencies that operate on a distributed public ledger known as the blockchain, a record of all transactions maintained and held by the owner of the currency. There are thousands of cryptocurrencies in the market; bitcoin, Ethereum, Litecoin, and Ripple are some of the famous cryptocurrencies.

Recently, we have seen the crypto market's growth peak, making this market a matter of curiosity to analyze and get to know the variations that occur there every minute. Here we have discussed data preprocessing, data reduction, finding patterns, historical results, and comparing crypto coins, namely bitcoin and ripple. We used various techniques like interpolation for cleaning data, Person correlation for data reduction, Single Exponential Smoothing for plotting predicted and actual values, and linear regression for performing a comparison of two coins. These techniques are used to analyze market data and the expected results, which we further compare with the actual data.

Bitcoin is a decentralized virtual foreign money created in January 2009 [13]. Bitcoin promises to decrease transaction costs than conventional online charge mechanisms do, and not like government-issued currencies, and its miles are operated with the aid of using a decentralized authority. Bitcoin may be very famous and has precipitated the release of masses of different cryptocurrencies, known as altcoins. Bitcoin is generally abbreviated as BTC while traded. Bitcoin makes use of the peer-to-peer generation for doing transactions.

Ripple is a financial system that functions as both a cryptocurrency and a digital payment network. Ripple's basic procedure is a payment settlement asset exchange and remittance system, comparable to the SWIFT system for international money and security transfers, which banks and financial intermediaries utilize. Ripple is a peer-to-peer decentralized open-source network that enables the frictionless movement of money in any form. It is a worldwide payments network with a customer base. XRP is employed in the company's products which allow rapid currency conversion.

We reviewed the already existing algorithms behind the proof of work which is a critical factor in mining Bitcoin/XRP, and we gathered the data and found the statistics of Bitcoin/XRP for the past five years. Then, we went to find interesting patterns in the dataset. After finding the patterns, we went to visualize closing prices and predicted vs. actual values of the coins. Later, we went on to forecast the price of crypto coins by using simple exponential smoothing and sentimental analysis model. Finally, we used an ML algorithm that is linear regression to find out the relationship between two coins, namely Bitcoin and XRP. Figure 1 describes the various tasks which we performed on the crypto currency dataset.

This document's contents are categorized as follows: In Sect. 2, we did the literature review on Bitcoin, XRP cryptocurrencies, and its mining process. It also consists of already existing algorithms and mining techniques at present. Section 3 contains a dataset description that is a detailed description of the dataset, which consists of 2 database tables. Section 4 consists of the implementation part. Section 5 is experimental result and Analysis, which consists of graphs of data collected over several simulation results and analyses. In Sect. 6, we conclude the work with the collected results and discuss the shortcomings and future work.

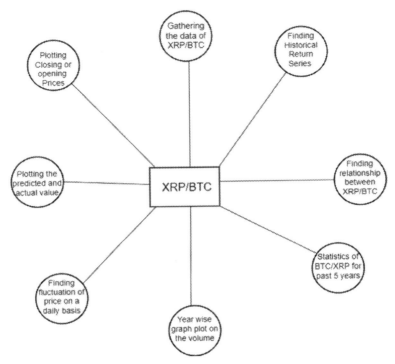

Fig. 1. Various analysis on cryptocurrencies.

2   Related Work

Blockchain technology [1] arose from the proposal of Distributed Ledger Technology (DLT) in the 1990s. Although DLT was introduced almost two decades ago, it gained traction with the deployment of Bitcoin [15]. In 2008, it was used as a crypto-currency for the first time. The data structure for the first was a hash-table was used to create a blockchain. However, as demand has grown, various other data formats have been proposed to address the constraints of the classic blockchain. Some writers advocated for the use of Directed Acyclic Graphs (DAGs) [15].

As it is scalable, lightweight, and decentralized, the Graph (DAG) keeps track of transactions. However, this option has some of the same issues as the first. At substantial sizes, the blockchain is used. RadixDLT's Tempo Ledger is designed to scale linearly in a limitless and efficient manner. In contrast to standard blockchain implementations, where the entire ledger is stored at each node, the Tempo ledger allows each node to keep a shard of the entire ledger [15].

Bitcoin is described as a cryptocurrency that was established in 2009 as the first decentralised digital money. Bitcoin enables online payments to be made without the use of banks, as well as the purchase of products and services from one party to another without the need of a financial institution [12]. Bitcoin has just lately been a topic of economic study. In computer science, the issue has piqued interest for a long time. Computer scientists have authored a modest number of theoretical articles on incentives. Mining is not incentive-compatible, and that "selfish mining" can result in better revenue for miners that conspire against one another [4]. The anonymous online marketplace in cryptocurrency, is another example of computer science research [2]. Although there has been some work on Bitcoin published in legal journals, there is relatively little in the economics literature.

Blockchain technology is a relatively new emerging technology that has the potential to transform a variety of established businesses. Since the launch of Bitcoin, which is blockchain 1.0, blockchain technology has gotten a lot of attention, and a lot of user transaction data has been collected [1]. As a result, determining the degree of value, performance, and cost of a blockchain-based application requires a thorough understanding of what and how data is stored and altered. While blockchains improve data quality by offering a transparent, irreversible, and consistent data repository, they also present new issues in terms of data management. That's why we use data and web mining techniques and algorithms to resolve emerging issues [7].

A lot of research has been conducted on the correlation between Bitcoin and other financial assets. In one such study, they discovered data supporting the long-run correlation between Bitcoin and major stock indexes using the ARDL boundary test method [3], and they also found out that there is a relation between Bitcoin prices and the leading US market and China market, which can have a major impact in their long term investment decision process. Another study used the Monte Carlo simulation to assess the structure of Bitcoin [13] dynamically. One study shows that Bitcoin does not adhere to the one-price rule [9]. There is research that is based on GARCH models to study and determine the bitcoin volatility, and their study says Bitcoin is a very speculative market [6]. Applied rolling window approach to study the time-varying long-term memory in the Bitcoin market [5]. We can see that there is a lot of scope for more research in this field. So, in this paper, we tried first to explore and bring out the hidden patterns from the crypto dataset. We used two well-known technologies: simple exponential smoothing and sentimental analysis, to outperform the forecasting for cryptocurrencies. Using these both improves the accuracy and takes into account the current news and trends of crypto going across the globe.

3   Dataset Description

The dataset contains two distinct datasets each of them describing each coin (XRP, Bitcoin). The dataset has 2894, 2992 rows of XRP, Bitcoins with 10 features (or columns). We obtained this dataset from the Kaggle website, which was obtained from "coinmarketcap," an open-source, free-to-use data site. Since April 28, 2013, the cryptocurrency price data has been gathered daily. This dataset has the historical price information of two top cryptocurrencies (XRP, and Bitcoin) by market capitalization. The features present in this dataset are the date of observation (Date), the opening price of the given day (Open), the highest price on the given day (High), the lowest price on the day (Low), the closing price of the day (Close), the volume of transactions on the given day (Volume), market capitalization in USD (Market Cap). There are a few redundant columns in this time series collection, and there is no room for missing values [11].

If we perform the statistical analysis on the bitcoin we can clearly see that the minimum value of the adjacent closing price of bitcoin in the span of 9 years is 68 dollars and the maximum value at the same time period is 63503 dollars which clearly indicates the high volatility of the bitcoin in the crypto market. Even at the seventy-fifty quartile, the value is 8576 which shows the sudden jump in the price of bitcoin within a short period of time, this creates the uneven distribution of data. Off all the 11 columns of data 7 of them are having float with 64 bit as its datatypes, 1 int (64 bit) datatype, and the rest with object datatype.

Whereas in the case of XRP or ripple the minimum value of the adjacent closing price in the span of 9 years is 0.0028 dollars and the maximum value at the same time period is 3.37 dollars. Compared to bitcoin the XRP is not too volatile in nature and it is easily predictable. Similar to that of bitcoin the off 11 columns, 7 have a float,1 int, and the rest object datatypes.

4   Preprocessing of Dataset

Data preprocessing converts data into a format that can be processed more quickly and efficiently in data mining. Before processing the data using many data mining techniques to find out the different patterns in the data, the initial step we are performing is data preprocessing.

Data preprocessing involves many steps:-

4.1   Importing the Required Libraries and Dataset

First, we imported the required libraries such as Numpy which contains mathematical functions and scipy which contains modules for interpolation, linear algebra etc. The second step is importing the dataset. The most common format for data sets is.csv. A CSV file is a plain text file that contains tabular data. To read a local CSV file as a data frame, we use the panda's library's read CSV method.

4.2   Data Cleaning

Now we perform data cleaning, in which our main aim is to remove the inconsistent data, fill in the missing values and ensure that the data is suitable for the analysis [10]. Suppose we take bitcoin, we have many values like high, low, open, close etc. If we have a missing or null value at some column, and if we are trying to remove it, there is a high possibility that it may alter our results as it is a time-series data, every data record is important for the analysis, as a result, we are using the interpolation to fill in the missing or null values. So, in the data cleaning step, we are finding all the missing values and filling them by interpolation which is taking the average value to the above and below valid value (trying to fit in between the above and the below valid value).

4.3 Data Reduction

The dataset which we are working on is of 5 years data, so it would have some redundant data and also the attributes which are not required for our analysis. As the redundant data would cause us trouble in our analysis to give accurate results, we are dropping a few attributes which are redundant or have similarities with other attributes. In order to do so, we will use Pearson Correlation Coefficient between two columns. In our dataset, when we performed the Pearson correlation coefficient between "close" and "adjacent close", the result turned out to be 1 which means they are highly correlated. So, we dropped the adjacent close attribute from both the XRP and BTC.

5 Proposed Scheme and Implementation

5.1 Finding Patterns and Historical Return Series in the Dataset

Finding patterns is quite essential in understanding the coins and making up the investing plans. The historical return series provides us with the historical analysis of both gains and losses that occurred with both the coins XRP and BTC. We first preprocessed the dataset and computed the percentage change on the adjacent closing values to compute the historical return series. To better understand the percent change, just look at the Formula 1 mentioned below.

$$\text{pct\_change} = \text{close}_{\text{Today}} - \text{close}_{\text{PreviousDay}} \tag{1}$$

After computing the percentage change in the adjacent closing values, we plotted them graphically to understand better the trend of the returns. Along with this, we also explored the closing prices trend by plotting them using a line plot. Figure 2 shows the closing price curve for BTC, while Fig. 3 shows the closing price curve for XRP. While closing observing them, we could easily see how BTC started from somewhere around 70 USD and reached 60000 USD. Similarly, one can see XRP, which started from somewhere about 0.08 USD and reached 3.5 USD. It clearly shows that the crypto market is very volatile, and its users can find a lot of fluctuation as time passing.

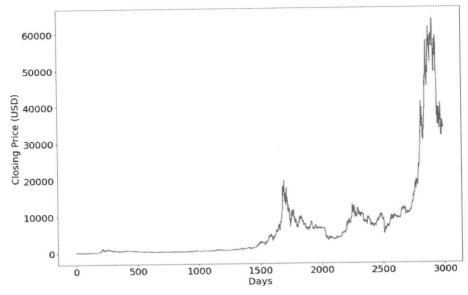

Fig. 2. Closing price curve for BTC.

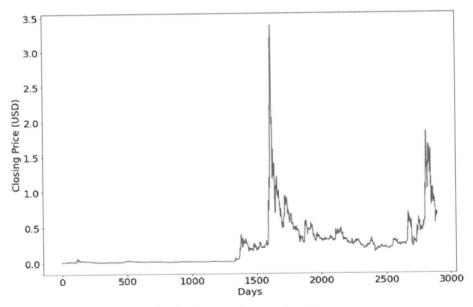

Fig. 3. Closing price curve for XRP.

5.2 Finding the Actual and Predicted Price Line Using Simple Exponential Smoothing and Influential Tweets

Simple exponential smoothing (SES) is used to predict time series when the data does explicitly not follow a trend in either an upward or downward trend, and seasonality (patterns caused by seasonal factors such as hours, days, and years. SES uses weighted averages to determine its rankings [8]. The average of the previous value and the current observation. Enormous weights are associated with recent observations, and the smallest weights are associated with older observations. The weight decrease is controlled by the smoothing parameter known as alpha or smoothing coefficient, which can be between 0 and 1. The forecast for future value is based on the average of past data. One means that the prediction of all future values is the final value.

Simple Exponential Smoothing (SES) is defined under the stats model library of python. SimpleExpSmoothing.fit (smoothing_level = None, optimized = True). The smoothing_level parameter is set, then the value is used for simple exponential smoothing. An optimized parameter of the boolean type is set to ask to go for optimizing the parameters as mentioned earlier automatically. We will be using.fit() to fit the model. Now, along with it we added sentiment analysis for each cryptocurrency to estimate the likelihood of a rise or fall in the price.

Bitcoin is a leading cryptocurrency in the crypto market. Its prices and returns are growing with the growth in the crypto market worldwide. On the other hand, Twitter has increasing recognition and predictive power for various programs related to the crypto world and the financial market [14, 16, 17]. So here we are examining how accurately public opinions on Twitter can be used to forecast Bitcoin returns. Using a sentiment analyzer on Bitcoin-related tweets and financial data, we observed that sentiment analysis on Twitter has predictive value for Bitcoin's results.

To begin with, we downloaded the historical prices of Bitcoin and the collection of Bitcoin-related Tweets, then analyzed the sentiment of the tweets. These tweets were gathered using several APIs and a little web scraping. In our dataset, we are examining the 92550 tweets which were posted virtually every minute, according to the statistics. Our objective is to use sentiment analysis to determine the subjective feelings or views regarding Bitcoin expressed in our collected tweets. We used the VADER (Valence Aware Dictionary and Sentiment Reasoner) for our processing.

Next, for evaluating our proposed model, we choose Random Forest regression. It is a type of machine learning algorithm which is effective when working with different kinds of inputs that are not related to each other at all. As inputs, we used the Sentimental Analysis score and history price of bitcoin and then implemented random forest analysis. When making predictions based on bitcoin-related tweet sentiment and historical bitcoin price, about 62.48% accuracy was observed. Price forecasting studies sometimes use sentiment analysis of tweets. Because of the enormous number of news updates per minute regarding Bitcoin, most academics use Twitter to analyze Bitcoin's sentiment [14, 17]. Similarly, we did the same analysis for XRP and tried to investigate the sentiment from XRP-related tweets.

5.3 Finding Relationship Between BTC and XRP Returns Using Linear Regression

We need to find the similarity between the two coins, BTC and XRP. To do so, we rely on a very well-known model, which is linear regression. Linear regression is one of the most fundamental regression models for predicting outcomes. It's used to build a relationship model between the independent and dependent variables. There is only one independent variable and one dependent variable in simple linear regression. One way to model the relationship between two variables is linear regression. Gradient equations are another name for equations. The equation is:

$$Y = a + bX$$

where Y is the dependent variable (that is, the variable plotted on the Y-axis), X is the independent variable (that is, the variable plotted on the X-axis), and b is the line. Gradient and y-intercept. So, keeping the above concept in mind, we applied Linear regression to analyze the relationship between BTC and XRP returns. Bitcoin is based on blockchain technology, while Ripple does not use blockchain but uses a distributed consensus ledger using a network of validation servers and a cryptocurrency token known as XRP. We kept BTC percentage returns as the independent variable while the XRP percentage returns as the dependent variable. Our ultimate goal was to analyze how the percentage return of BTC correlated to the percentage returns of XRP. As a first step, we computed the Pearson coefficient among the two variables and then calculated the slope and intercept for the best fit line. After getting the predicted y, we plotted the best fit line with the actual points. Doing so helped us to analyze the relationship between the two coins better.

6 Experimental Results and Analysis

We applied several statistical techniques and models to understand the crypto market trends better. While doing so, we examined several sub-sections like historical return series, forecasting closing prices, finding relationships between the two coins, etc. Now it's the time for us to explore all the results and draw conclusions from them. So, starting with the historical return series, we found that both XRP and BTC had comparatively similar kinds of return series except for a few outliers. Figure 4 and Fig. 5 show BTC and XRP historical return series, respectively.

We performed simple exponential smoothing on the time series crypto dataset to forecast the closing values for both BTC and XRP. Figure 6 and Fig. 7 show the plotting of both predicted and actual values of BTC and XRP, respectively. The red lines in the curves indicate the actual values, while the blue lines indicate the predicted value. We can observe that the predicted prices have coincided with actual prices for the first 1300 data rows. This means the model has performed very well at first, but the predicted values have varied. Though the model performed very well for low extremes, the model has failed to predict the prices when there is a sudden spike in the prices and at times of high volatility. One can easily conclude that the simple exponential smoothing model fits well to predict the closing values. However, there are a few moments where we see deviations in the

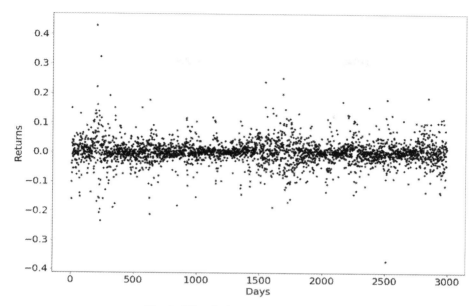

Fig. 4. Historical return series of BTC.

predicted and actual values, which can be further smoothed by considering some more parameters like current business news, war status, market volatility, etc. So, thinking the same we tried to examine influential tweets which can further improve the predictions.

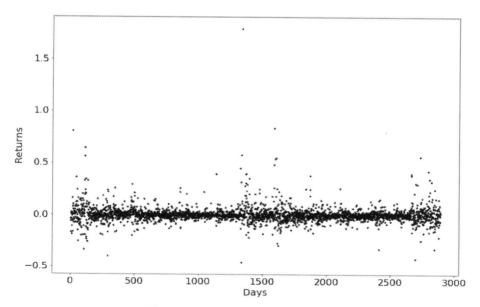

Fig. 5. Historical return series of XRP.

With simple exponential smoothing, we can easily get an exponential equation for the respective cryptocurrency, whether BTC or XRP. This equation is then used to make future predictions. We proposed a scheme that couples simple exponential smoothing with sentiment obtained from influential tweets to make the forecast more accurate. In other words, we use tweets that are related to crypto or tweets which are highly significant. To find out whether a tweet is influencing the market or not, we basically used hashtags and crypto-related keywords. We analyze the sentiment from those influential tweets and try to determine whether the tweet is affecting the market positively, negatively, or has no effect on the cryptocurrency. Figure 8 shows the obtained graph after performing sentiment analysis on influential tweets.

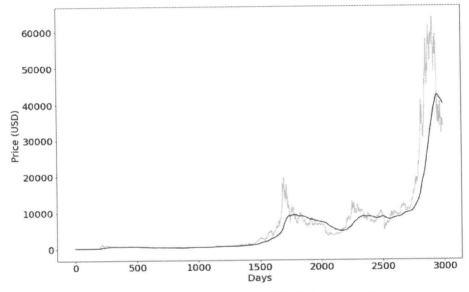

Fig. 6. Predicted vs actual values of BTC. (Color figure online)

Finally, we applied a linear regression model to analyze the relationship between the returns of BTC and XRP. We first computed the percentage change as usual and then used the seaborn regression plot module to plot the return series. Figure 9 shows the relation between the returns of BTC and XRP collectively. The X-axis consists of the BTC percentage return, while the Y-axis consists of the XRP percentage return. While closely observing the plot, we found that both BTC and XRP are highly correlated in returns and have the same percentage returns. However, if one aims to have higher profit margins, BTC shows significant fluctuations, which can be used as an advantage while trading BTC.

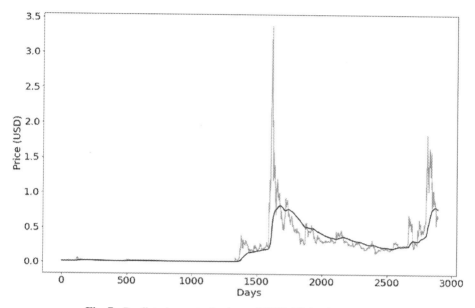

Fig. 7. Predicted vs actual values of XRP. (Color figure online)

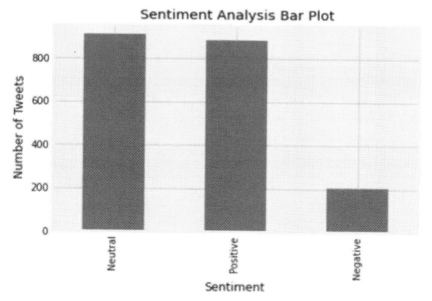

Fig. 8. Results of sentiment analysis over influential tweets.

7 Conclusion

The paper's experimental observations and results show that the crypto market is quite volatile and is susceptible to frequent fluctuations. The analysis performed on the BTC and XRP has shown a positive correlation and were following a similar trend in highly volatile times. The model built using VADER for processing and Random Forest for prediction has performed sentiment analysis on public opinions by tweets about how the subjective feelings were determining the prices of bitcoin has shown 62.48% of accuracy. Forecasting the prices helped us conclude that in the coming years, crypto market trading and the number of investors will rise. The simple exponential smoothing used to predict value has shown great results in low extremes, but it has some vulnerabilities when there is a sudden spike which we going to be tackled by adding various external factors. In the future, we would like to build a prediction model considering several factors and using current data and historical data to make better predictions of coin prices.

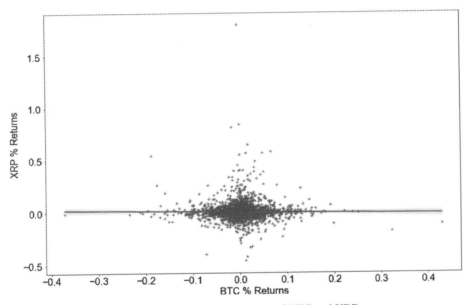

Fig. 9. Relation between returns of BTC and XRP.

References

1. Beck, R., Müller-Bloch, C.: Blockchain as radical innovation: a framework for engaging with distributed ledgers as incumbent organization (2017)
2. Christin, N.: Traveling the silk road: a measurement analysis of a large anonymous online marketplace. In: Proceedings of the 22nd International Conference on World Wide Web, pp. 213–224 (2013)

3. Dirican, C., Canoz, I.: The cointegration relationship between Bitcoin prices and major world stock indices: an analysis with ARDL model approach. J. Econ. Financ. Account. **4**(4), 377–392 (2017)

4. Eyal, I., Sirer, E.G.: Majority is not enough: bitcoin mining is vulnerable. In: Christin, N., Safavi-Naini, R. (eds.) FC 2014. LNCS, vol. 8437, pp. 436–454. Springer, Heidelberg (2014). https://doi.org/10.1007/978-3-662-45472-5_28

5. Jiang, Y., Nie, H., Ruan, W.: Time-varying long-term memory in bitcoin market. Financ. Res. Lett. **25**, 280–284 (2018)

6. Katsiampa, P.: Volatility estimation for bitcoin: a comparison of GARCH models. Econ. Lett. **158**, 3–6 (2017)

7. Lee, S.J., Siau, K.: A review of data mining techniques. Ind. Manag. Data Syst. **101**, 41–46 (2001)

8. Ostertagova, E., Ostertag, O.: Forecasting using simple exponential smoothing method. Acta Electrotechnica et Informatica **12**(3), 62 (2012)

9. Pieters, G., Vivanco, S.: Financial regulations and price inconsistencies across bitcoin markets. Inf. Econ. Policy **39**, 1–14 (2017)

10. Rahm, E., Do, H.H.: Data cleaning: problems and current approaches. IEEE Data Eng. Bull. **23**(4), 3–13 (2000)

11. Rajkumar, S.: Cryptocurrency historical prices (2021). https://www.kaggle.com/datasets/sud alairajkumar/cryptocurrencypricehistory

12. Raymaekers, W.: Cryptocurrency bitcoin: disruption, challenges and opportunities. J. Paym. Strat. Syst. **9**(1), 30–46 (2015)

13. Salman, A., Razzaq, M.G.A.: Bitcoin and the world of digital currencies. In: Financial Management from an Emerging Market Perspective, pp. 271–281 (2018)

14. Sattarov, O., Jeon, H.S., Oh, R., Lee, J.D.: Forecasting bitcoin price fluctuation by twitter sentiment analysis. In: 2020 International Conference on Information Science and Communications Technologies (ICISCT), pp. 1–4 (2020). https://doi.org/10.1109/ICISCT50599.2020.9351527

15. Yang, W., Garg, S., Raza, A., Herbert, D., Kang, B.: Blockchain: trends and future. In: Yoshida, K., Lee, M. (eds.) PKAW 2018. LNCS (LNAI), vol. 11016, pp. 201–210. Springer, Cham (2018). https://doi.org/10.1007/978-3-319-97289-3_15

16. Ye, Z., Wu, Y., Chen, H., Pan, Y., Jiang, Q.: A Stacking ensemble deep learning model for bitcoin price prediction using Twitter comments on bitcoin. Mathematics **10**(8), 1307 (2022)

17. Zaman, S., Yaqub, U., Saleem, T.: Analysis of Bitcoin's price spike in context of Elon Musk's Twitter activity. Glob. Knowl. Mem. Commun. (2022). https://doi.org/10.1108/GKMC-09-2021-0154

Design of Laboratory Identification Equipment Based on Intelligent Identification Technology

Yiyang Lin and Chunfeng Jiang[✉]

Jilin Agricultural Science and Technology University, Jilin, China
hero_jcf@126.com

Abstract. The design of an identification equipment for user of academic computer laboratory was discussed. It used fingerprint identification technique to identify the user based on present using of academic computer lab. It introduced the detailed design of fingerprint identification system, including hardware components, software functions and communication protocol developing, and how to save and handle mass data by single-chip microcomputer as well. Experimental results show that it is helpful digital campus construction.

Keywords: Identification · Fingerprint verification · Single-chip microcomputer

1 Introduction

In the present resources of colleges and universities, various types of laboratory utilization ratio is higher. Information modernization construction in colleges and universities, students can be fuzzy query name, number and other information. Due to making the campus departments can unified management of students, the universities use the campus E-card system to establish a unified database and use the student's ID as the index for precise queries. The purpose of our project is for the unified management of college laboratory to offer students an authentication fast, accurate method.

The fingerprint verification process is that the laboratories establish fingerprint characteristic database and the students scan the fingerprint identification card to the laboratories, then they press the fingerprint for the card holder authentication. If the students and the cards are matched, identification device giving prompt that the student can enter the room to use resources, otherwise, it will tell the staff that the student hold the missing card and must not enter the room, so as not to damage the rights of others.

2 The Design Scheme of the System

At present the design of the fingerprint identification system basically has the following several ways that one is the fingerprint collection device directly connected to the computer, image preprocessing, feature extraction and matching fully performed by the computer. So that we can use computer resources, such as high-speed computing power, large capacity of storage space and friendly user interface, powerful data transformation, communication, etc. Using this scheme, the design of the hardware also became simpler, only acquisition module design. The existing acquisition module there are many ways to choose from. All software on the computer, writing, debugging and testing instruments are needed to reduce to a minimum.

The fingerprint can focus on gathering on a single computer, also be collected on multiple computers to set on a server finally. The defect is fingerprint matching still need to be done on the computer, if each room with a computer is used for identification, there are so more the number of rooms that the greater the waste of resources, if put the fingerprint identification system on the LAN server, storage and data security are the main problem which must be solved. Another way is used a separate device to collect fingerprint, match student ID. That means the acquisition module, image preprocessing and feature extraction and comparison on the physical ability to work independently entity, constitutes a fingerprint identification system without the aid of a computer. This kind of design can overcome the disadvantage above, but there is a new problem that the storage capacity will be restricted by fixed hardware, it is not like a computer system which has the massive storage capacity. If the system is fully developed by ourselves, it must adopt efficient preprocessing, feature extraction and matching algorithm, so it will be used to high-speed microprocessor, and it is a longer development cycle.

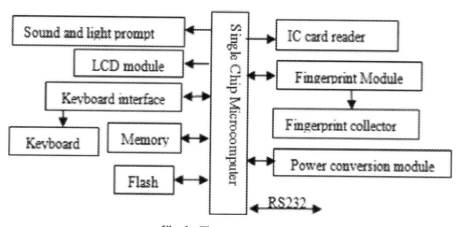

Fig. 1. The system structure

The finally adopt solution is that the system employs the existing module to collect and compare the fingerprint image, and the fingerprint data storage uses the large capacity flash memory. Because of a single module device storage capacity limited, there is the RS-232 interface and computer communication additional, the information on the module devices can be uploaded to the database on computer or server, and the data can be download from the computer to the module device. There is a built-in battery in the module device, so it can work independently. And it adopt a 16-key small keyboard for input control commands or student ID, and a display module with 16X2 LCD shows the operating results to the users of the room and it increases a speakers and light-emitting diodes (leds) tip at the same time. The specific control by MCS-51 series microcontroller [1–5], the system hardware structure diagram shows as Fig. 1.

3 Design of Hardware Structure

In the system, we used the fingerprint module M04 from changchun Hongda company [6]. The M04 fingerprint module included optics, capacitance and pressure module, fingerprint image acquisition, storage, integration of high-tech products. The module adopted the advanced fingerprint matching algorithm. And the company provided OEM cooperation. The standardized module included core foundation part of the collection and comparison, and provided the ability of second development. The mechanical extension module contained control part and could be convenient and entrance guard controller, locks, safes, security doors, gun cabinets, automobile anti-theft devices, attendance system, ATM, POS machine, fingerprint PDA, PC and other system equipment integration. The extension module could be applied to online or offline system, made traditional non-fingerprint products into the fingerprint products. In order to ensure the equipment in the absence of mains power supply to normal use, we used a sealed lead acid battery, 6v rated voltage, rated capacity of 1.2 Ah, as a backup power supply. When a mains power supplied to system, we used a small direct current power supplied to the instrument and charged to the back-up power.

In the user interface, the card reader read the student ID from the E-card, and then determined the identity of the students, so the fingerprint of the query time would be shortened. We used a 16-key small keyboard as the input part of the user interface, the 16-key press functions were shown in Table 1.

Table 1. The functions of keyboard

Key	Function
"0"–"9"	To input the number of student ID
Backspace	To deletes the last digital characters
Collection	To collect the fingerprint
Verify	To verify the fingerprint
Check	To confirm the above input
Cancel	To cancel the above input and return to the idle state
Online	To be online, and microcomputer communication

While the liquid crystal display module was as output part [7], and there was a corresponding hint in the operation of each step, such as please enter the number, successful, check, check failed and so on. In addition, a light emitting diode was added as the auxiliary output to be often bright when the instrument checked the collection, matching of the student fingerprint, in order to prompt the user not to move their fingers. It was also bright during the transmission of data with microcomputer to prompt the user that the communication was right. The system used a speaker assisted shown the various operating results.

The display part adopted common dot matrix liquid crystal display module. It integrated dot matrix LCD display and was used to control the drive for the large-scale specialized integrated circuit of dot matrix LCD and PCB board. The users only needed directly input the data and the instructions then the display what they needed could be realized. The input keyboard was a small 16-key keyboard, the purpose of setting the keyboard was to prevent the card reader to be out of order and then to lead to the system paralysis. If the readers could not read the card or the student's card problems that the reader couldn't read the student information, the system could be obtained by manual input digital keyboard student ID, then solved computer exams to enter the system such as emergencies. In order to save hardware resources, serial technique in which the single chip microcomputer interface, such as two pieces of 74LS164, serial input and parallel output shift register, was employed to convert the serial single-chip microcomputer output signal into parallel data, with the keyboard returned after the public line operations through a line back to the mouth.

The memory of the system employed the static random access memory (SRAM) chip, it had 8K bytes of storage capacity, and was used to store some temporary data, such as communications when sending and receiving data buffer, the buffer storage directory, keyboard input buffer, display buffer, read/write flash memory page buffer using the message queue, and system management, etc.

The flash memory used to store data fingerprint characteristic, and the fingerprint information, directory.

The single-chip microcomputer and serial interface needed to two devices communications, the fingerprint module and upper computer. The communication with the fingerprint module did not need to be level conversion, which only received and sent directly to the two signal lines cross connection. To communicate with microcomputer, the system used the MAX232 chip as TTL level with the RS-232C level converter, and an external standard 9-pin socket.

4   The Software Design

The software adopted modularized program design, despite the use of assembly language, in order to facilitate expansion on the function, we employed some methods of the advanced language program design.

First of all, the whole program was not a line, but with a message-loop-mechanism, it defined all the events which might be produced by external parts as the different messages, and after the message generated, put them into the message queue, then the main loop, equivalent to a scheduling module, was responsible for distribution. In addition, the system in different operation stages defined as a state of the system, and different status, and produced different response to different message, at the same time it might cause the change of state. So the application in addition to the main loop, the overall structure was independent of other modules, each module changes would not affect other modules. If the system wanted to add the new function module, it was easy to add the new definition in the state and message.

As to the count of the state, if it was too little, the program needed judgment accordingly to increase, so it had violated the modular thought. If it was too much, the program would show little and it could affect the speed of programming. The status defination by the value was shown in Table 2.

Table 2. The definition of the status value

Status value	Status meaning
s_idle	The system is idle
s_idle_wait	The sysem is waiting for idle, after user presses any key, it will return to idle state
s_idle_num_rec	When the system is idle, it will receive the user keys (keyboard command)
s_pre_read	The system is ready for reading the card
s_reading	The system is reading the card
s_read	The system finishs the reading card
s_acq_num_rec	The system receives the pressing keyboard when it collects the user's fingerprint
s_acq_prompt	The system prompts the information of the state such as number repeat when it collects the user's fingerprint
s_pre_acquire	The system is ready to collect data as the identity information is ready and it is waiting for the module reply
s_acquiring	The system is collecting the fingerprint
s_acquired	The fingerprint collection is finished
s_ver_num_rec	The system receives the user keys when it is verifying the fingerprint
s_pre_verify	The system is ready for verifying the fingerprint
s_verifying	The system is verifying the fingerprint
s_verified	The verifying of the fingerprint is finished
s_initializing	The system is initializing
s_online	The status of the system is online
s_listing	The directory information is shown on the screen by list

5   Communication Protocol Development

In the design of the fingerprint identification system, according to the previous scheme, the single chip microcomputer would transfer instructions and data to the fingerprint module, and then need complete data collection and distribution with microcomputer database. It also employed the RS-232C interface to communicate between computer and device, and all the transmission was adopted by the serial communication [8–11].

5.1   To Communicate with the Fingerprint Module

The communication between fingerprint module and single-chip microcomputer was implemented with a communication interface provided by the module. At the hand of the hardware, it provided 4 sockets. In core softwares, the fingerprint module provided a series of work instructions to control the movement. And the communication protocol adopted response mode, when the module received the order, it sent the responsed instruction first, then did the corresponding operation. The replied instruction format was a total of 6 bytes of data such as 00h, 88h, 00h, 00h, 00h, 00h. The command format for single-chip microcomputer control module was the guide code and the control code and the control instructions. After the module operation, the success or failure information returned to the single chip microcomputer. For example, to read a fingerprint characteristic information from the module, business data was as followed.

The single chip microcomputer sent the data that the guide code as 00h, aah, 00h, aah, 55h, aah, ffh, the control code as 08h, the control instruction as 00h, 00h, 00h, 00h, 00h.

The fingerprint collection module sent the response information as 00h, 88h, 00h, 00h, 00h, 00h.

Then the fingerprint collection module began to work such as colleting fingerprint image and extracted the feature from the image. When the work finished, it sent the feature data to the single chip microcomputer as 00h, 66h, 200 bytes feature data, ffh, ffh.

5.2   To Communicate with the Computer

In order to improve the anti-interference ability, the command transmitted from the computer had the specific format to different against the data sent between the single chip microcomputer and the module, the phase from devices to computer also had obvious the logo of beginning and end. It set a flag inside the identification device, when the communication with the computer, the single chip microcomputer could only receive the command which the computer sent, after receiving the command to take corresponding actions such as reading the data and transmitting to the computer, receiving data and writting to flash memory, etc.

The computer command was began as $ character, it was to say that the single chip microcomputer would enter the command receiving state after receiving the command. All the commands of single chip microcomputer were began as NEIEP followed by the command code and data.

To correspond to receive orders, all the response information from the single chip microcomputer to the computer was also began with a string as NEIEP, then the command code followed by data, the data formats depending on the command, finally ended up with two OFFs.

6   Conclusions

This project was in the research, the identification device achieved the aim of the designin when it used in the laborary daily management, it was convenient to the management of the staff, and saved the authentication time for the students, especially it had eliminated the piggybacking on other students e-card phenomenon, and made students lost card reduce economic loss. The team is researching to improve the function of the identification device, and the system will be expected to identify the instrument to the library and campus supermarket.

Acknowledgements. This work is supported by 202111439009 which was from the Science and Technology Innovation and Entrepreneurship Training Program for University Students of Jilin Province.

References

1. San, M.H., Dan, F.C., Yu, P.C., Yue, T.C., Si, Y.F.: Design and implementation of the maze patrolling with three branch roads by the smart car based on 51 single chip microcomputer. Autom. Control Intell. Syst. **2020**(8), 9–12 (2020)
2. Chun, H.Z., Xue, L.G.: Design of tracking car based on infrared reflective sensor TCRT5000. Mod. Electron. Technol. **2018**(18), 143–146 (2018)
3. Jin, T.M., Huai, X.L.: Research on indoor monitoring of STM32 single chip microcomputer. Comput. Prod. Distrib. **2018**(08), 74 (2018)
4. Chi, Y.Y., Yue, S., Rui, T.L.: Intelligent tracking car based on STC12C5A60S2. Lab. Res. Explor. **2014**(11), 46–49 (2014)
5. Ya, L.T., Bo, L.: Design of intelligent voice car control system based on single chip microcomputer. Electron. Technol. Softw. Eng. **2019**(02), 247–248 (2019)
6. Changchun Hongda High-tech Group Co., Ltd.: Fingerprint Identification Module User Manual. Changchun Hongda High-tech Group Co., Ltd. (2016)
7. Ning, L., Dong, Q.C., Ke, L.Y.: Design of serial communication display system based on STM32 minimum system. Ind. Control Comput. **2017**(08), 33–34+36 (2017)
8. Du, L.: Research and design of wireless communication module based on single chip microcomputer. In: 2019 International Conference on Artificial Intelligence Technologies and Applications (ICAITA), pp. 1–5. IOP Publishing, July 2019
9. Jing, H.Y., Wei, W., Zhi, G.W., Xin, H.: Design of hostless communication system based on STM32F103. Sci. Technol. Eng. **2017**(04), 63–66 (2017)
10. Xiang, P.M., Xin, Y.W., Ji, C.R.: Design and implementation of a fingerprint identification device for exam. Inf. Technol. Inf. **2005**(01), 20–21+51 (2005)
11. Liang, C., Jing, C.G., Zhong, H.Y.: Application of digital half-duplex communication mechanism in building intercom system. Intell. Build. **2014**(09), 27–31 (2014)

A Stacked Ensemble Method with Adaptive Attribute Selection to Detect DDoS Attack in Cloud-Assisted WBAN

Priyanka Verma[1]([✉]), John G. Breslin[1], Donna O'Shea[2], and R. K. Pateriya[3]

[1] Data Science Institute, NUI Galway, Galway, Ireland
priyanka.verma@nuigalway.ie
[2] Department of Computer Science, MTU Cork, Cork, Ireland
[3] Department of Computer Science and Engineering, MANIT, Bhopal, India

Abstract. The present era of technology improves the health care services and Wireless Body Area Network (WBAN) is one of them. It is a technology which uses wireless sensors to gather the vital signs from human body for monitoring. The WBAN is often connected with cloud to overcome processing and storage limitations. However, using cloud with WBAN opens up the door for various attacks. DDoS is one of the major threat which directly affects the availability of patient data, and harness the adoption of cloud-assisted WBAN technology. Therefore, in this work we propose a approach to detect DDoS attack in cloud-assisted WBAN and ensures the availability of patients data. The proposed approach is based on Adaptive and Supreme Attribute Selection with Stacked Ensemble Classification (ASAS-SEC). All the requests intended to use the patient data stored on cloud must have to pass through ASAS-SEC mechanism. The request classified as benign are only allowed to access the patient data and DDoS requests are passed to Intensive Care Unit (ICU), where the source of the attack is identified and blocked. Publically available NSL-KDD dataset is utilized to evaluate the proposed ASAS-SEC approach and results shows that proposed approach outperforms other state-of-the-art approaches and achieves classification accuracy of 98.86%, F1-Score of 98.3%, and false alarm of 0.017.

Keywords: Wireless Body Area Network (WBAN) · Cloud network · DDoS · Availability · Healthcare system · Classification

1 Introduction

WBAN have emerged out as a promising technology that improves the human healthcare system [1, 2] and widens their wings to a broad range of medical applications. WBAN majorly benefitted patients with older age and having chronic diseases. In WBAN, the patient's data are collected through sensors in the form of bio-signals. Further, these signals need to be stored and processed for future reference by the healthcare workers such as doctors and physicians. The applications of WBAN may include health monitoring to an emergency medical response system. Autonomous nodes such as sensors and actuators positioned in the body, clothes, or under the patient's skin are connected to WBAN through a wireless communication channel. In the medical field, for continuous monitoring of particular biological functions like electrocardiogram (ECG), Blood Pressure (BP), heartbeat rate, body temperature, etc., a patient might be equipped with WBAN. The benefit of using such a system is that the patient is not restricted to a fixed location (bed). Moreover, it allows more accurate results and sometimes even faster diagnosis since the data is collected in the patient's natural environment and over a longer period of time, thus offers more helpful information.

However, the inadequate resources of WBAN sensors [3] cannot deal with such an enormous quantity of information for storage and processing. Therefore, for the colossal data collected from WBAN sensor nodes, there is a need for secure storage and processing for such data. Consequently, to deal with such a huge amount of information produced by WBAN nodes, an innovative solution to meet this growing challenge is highly desirable. On that account, to provide a robust, hybrid, and viable platform to deal with such an enormous quantity of information collected from various nodes, the integration of cloud computing and WBANs is performed and also known as cloud-assisted WBAN [4].

Cloud computing is considered as a promising innovation to achieve the objectives mentioned above in healthcare management [5]. With the help of cloud-assisted WBAN, physicians and doctors can access the infrastructure storage and processing of health data on a pay-per-usage model [6]. Figure 1 shows the general cloud-assisted architecture for the E-healthcare WBAN system.

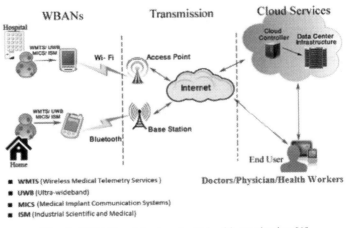

Fig. 1. WBAN architecture for E-health monitoring [1]

Nonetheless, the advent of the cloud-aided WBAN system is still in its growing stage. Recent research in this domain focuses on the framework for cloud-aided WBAN to acknowledge e-healthcare benefits. However, they do not consider the security issues. The availability of patient health data is of significant concern in such networks. A DDoS attack is the most severe threat to data availability that can directly harness the everlasting accessibility of a patient's information. Unavailability of patient's data degrades the overarching performance and credibility of the healthcare administration. The solutions currently used for traditional WBANs against DDoS attacks are not appropriate for cloud-assisted WBAN technology. There is a need for a defensive approach to detect the DDoS attacks in cloud-based WBAN that understands the varying network traffic conditions during the attack.

Therefore, an adaptive and supreme attribute selection with a stacked ensemble classification (ASAS-SEC) approach is proposed to overcome such issues. The proposed method considers various adaptive thresholding approaches to select the intermediate attribute list under the individual thresholding technique. Further, the attributes under each technique are refined using the supreme behavior approach. After selecting the most supreme attributes, a stacked ensemble classifier is used to classify the DDoS and legitimate request. In stacked ensemble classifier at level-0 Gradient Boost (GB), Random Forest (RF) classifier are used. Further, the output of these two classifiers is given as input to the level-1 classifier. At level-1, the eXtreme Gradient Boost (XGBoost) classifier is used to predict the final output. Using the adaptive approach makes the detection mechanism more robust and efficient against varying network traffic conditions during DDoS attacks. The major contributions of this work are listed as:

1. Proposed an efficient ASAS-SEC approach that can classify the incoming requests towards cloud-assisted WBAN to access patient healthcare data and detect DDoS attacks.
2. Attributes are selected based on the incoming traffic stream; hence adaptive and dynamic behavior can handle different DDoS attack intensities.
3. Also proposes a stacked ensemble classifier that integrates the advantages of different ML classifier such as RF and GB at one level and combines the output and select the dominating result at the next level as final output using XGBoost classifier.
4. ASAS-SEC achieves classification accuracy of 98.86%, F1-Score of 98.3%, and false alarm of 0.017.

The remainder section of the paper is organized as: the state of art approaches for DDoS defense in literature is presented in Sect. 2 and proposed used in this work is discussed in Sect. 3. Section 4 shows the result evaluation and observation of the proposed approach, and finally, Sect. 5 concludes the work and gives the future direction.

2 Related Work

This section presents work done in this domain against DDoS attacks. Many researchers have contributed towards the detection, prevention, and mitigation schemes against such attacks. Several attack avoidance strategies use a challenge-response approach for avoiding the DDoS attack at the entrance of the network [7]. On the other side, attack detection is performed using network traffic analysis. Further anomaly detection methods are also used for the attack detection [8]. Besides the detection and avoidance of DDoS, a great deal of work has been done regarding the mitigation methods of DDoS in the cloud domain [9].

Idhammad et al. [10] evaluated incoming network's information entropy using time-based sliding window method for handling DDoS attack. CIDDS-001 dataset was used to verify the presented approach. Verma et al. [11] offers an adaptive threshold technique that uses Mean Absolute Deviation (MAD) to select the attributes responsible for the DDoS attack. Then random forest is used for the classification, which provides the best results with the MAD threshold technique.

Sreeram et al. [30] presents a bioinspired bat algorithm that uses the bats records population-based evolution process to detect the HTTP based DDoS attacks quickly. The experiments were carried out on the CAIDA dataset to assess the model. Another bio-inspired algorithm based on the cuckoo search is proposed by Verma et al. [12] to classify the attack and benign requests. In this work, bi-variate flight instead of levy flight provides direction in the cuckoo search space to assign a label for the incoming request. Results prove the dominance proposed approach against the present bio-inspired techniques used to identify the DDoS attack.

Homogeneous ensemble classifier contains similar types of classifiers in the ensemble. A combination of homogeneous and heterogeneous classifiers called the hybrid model was used to study its performance as discussed by Aburomman et al. [13]. Identification of the source of the DDoS attack is as much important as detecting the attack. Attack detection was done using the various filter methods available to select attributes, which conglomerates the top feature in different selection techniques. The features are selected based on its occurrence in the individual filter method. If the frequency count crosses the threshold value, then the feature is selected. The requests identified as attack are sent to a special unit where the attack source is identified and blocked for future reference [14].

A deep learning based technique is presented by Shone et al. [15] called Non-symmetric Deep Auto Encoder (NDAE). The proposed method selects attributes using unsupervised learning, and stacked NDAE is used for the classification. Results shows a noteworthy progress in accuracy and deterioration in computational time. Choi et al. [16] also proposed a approach autoencoder based IDS system for unsupervised data. The proposed approach helps in detecting the anomalies in such data. It results in 91.7% accuracy for classifying the attack and benign requests when tested on NSL-KDD dataset.

The above-discussed security solutions towards DDoS attack are not directly applicable to cloud-assisted WBAN environments. The major cause for this lack of applicability are as cloud-assisted WBAN persists the shortcoming of both WBAN and cloud technology. Therefore for detecting security attacks in these networks, there is a need to develop defensive attack approach that understand and analyze the variable network traffic conditions and overcomes the limitations of both the technologies.

3   Proposed Method

This work proposes a security mechanism to ensure data availability and save the network from such attacks [17]. Figure 2 shows the detection node's placement in the cloud-assisted WBAN, and Fig. 3 shows the flowchart of the proposed approach.

The proposed approach consists of 4 sections as: (i) Preprocessing, (ii) Adaptive and Supreme Attribute Selection (ASAS), (iii) Stacked Ensemble Classifier (SEC), and (iii) Attack request processing unit (ICRPU). In the proposed approach, whenever the request to access the patient healthcare data stored in the cloud network arrives, then before passing the request, the defense mechanism is initiated.

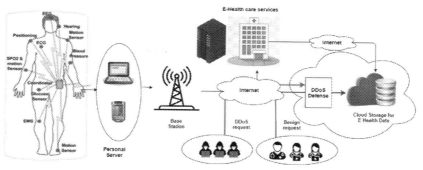

Fig. 2. Placement of defense mechanism for the detection of DDoS attack in cloud-assisted WBAN

3.1 Pre-processing

The incoming request contains multiple statistics, which helps in determining the attributes to detect the attack. These attributes need to be extracted from the incoming request for further processing. However, in this work a standard dataset NSL-KDD is used which requires the data normalization due to presence diversified attribute values. If the attributes in the dataset are spread in dynamic ranges then it does not helps proper fitting of the model and it may get bias toward a particular attributes. Thus to handle this issue, scaling of attributes is performed using Min-Max normalization before model fitting. The formula used for Min-Max normalization is:

$$X_{new} = \frac{X_i - X_{min}}{X_{max} - X_{min}} * (Y_{max} - Y_{min}) + Y_{min} \tag{1}$$

Here X is the feature that needs to be scaled, X_{min} and X_{max} are the lowest and highest values of attribute X. X_i is the current value being processed and X_{new} will be the new value. Whereas Y_{min} and Y_{max} are the minimum and maximum value in the new range. Algorithm 1 show the preprocessing steps of the data.
***

Algorithm 1: Preprocessing		
Input	:	D(x) = NSL-KDD dataset, where x ∈ {A1 , A2 ....A41}
Output	:	Preprocessed train and test datasets as $D'_{train}(x)$ and $D'_{test}(x)$
Step 1	:	Select attribute x_i from D(x)
Step 2	:	Normalize x_i with Min-Max normalization using Eq. (1)
Step 3	:	Partition normalized data $D'(x)$ into train and test sets as $D'_{train}(x)$ and $D'_{test}(x)$

3.2 Adaptive and Supreme Attribute Selection (ASAS)

Algorithm 2 shows the method for adaptive and supreme attribute selection process. Here firstly the entropy of each feature is determined. Entropy is a measure of randomness

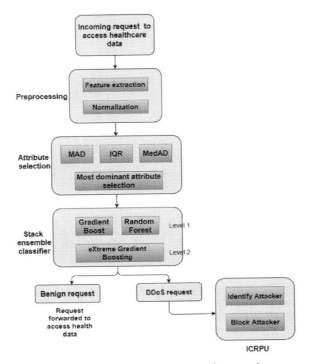

Fig. 3. Flowchart of the proposed approach

or uncertainty in the data. As the randomness increases, the value of the entropy also increases [18]. The incoming traffic activities at the time of attack can be analyzed with the help of entropy [19]. The entropy against each attribute in the incoming traffic is evaluated as:

$$Entropy(A_i) = -\sum P(A_i/x)\log(P(A_i/x)) \tag{2}$$

Algorithm 2: Adaptive and Supreme Attribute Selection (ASAS)		
Input	:	Preprocessed train dataset $D'_{train}(x)$
Output	:	Final selected attribute set f(x)
Step 1	:	Calculate entropy E(x) for each attribute in $D'_{train}(x)$ using Eq. (2)
Step 2	:	Calculate threshold value (THR) using MAD, IQR, MedAD
Step 3	:	Select attribute under each thresholding technique
		For each attribute x_i in $D'_{train}(x)$
		If $E(x_i) \geq MAD\ (THR)$
		Then x_i is added to MAD (x)
		If $E(x_i) \geq IQR\ (THR)$
		Then x_i is added to IQR (x)
		If $E(x_i) \geq MedAD\ (THR)$
		Then x_i is added to MedAD (x)
Step 4	:	Partition MAD (x), IQR (x), MedAD (x)
		If $MAD(x_i) \geq T_h$
		Then x_i is added to AMAD-1
		Else x_i is added to AMAD-2
		If $IQR(x_i) \geq T_h$
		Then x_i is added to AIQR-1
		Else x_i is added to AIQR-2
		If $MedAD(x_i) \geq T_h$
		Then x_i is added to AMedAD-1
		Else x_i is added to AMedAD-2
Step 5	:	Calculate $f'(x)$ = AMAD-1 ∪ AIQR-1 ∪ MedAD-1
Step 6	:	Calculate $f''(x)$ = AMAD-2 ∪ AIQR-2 ∪ MedAD-2
Step 7	:	Calculate final attribute set f(x)
		$f(x) = f'(x) \cup f''(x)$

Now, three threshold-based attribute selection techniques, namely Interquartile Range (IQR), Mean Absolute Deviation (MAD), and Median Absolute Deviation (MedAD), are applied to the data individually. On using MAD threshold technique on the dataset, we get a threshold value MAD (THR). Based on MAD (THR) the attributes having the entropy value greater than or equal to MAD (THR) are selected under MAD threshold-based attribute selection technique. Thereafter, attributes selected under the MAD technique are further divided into two subsets, namely AMAD-1, AMAD-2. The attributes chosen under MAD having a value greater than T_h (fixed threshold) are selected under AMAD-1 else selected in AMAD-2. Similarly, IQR and MedAD are also used to create the sets AIQR-1, AIQR-2, and AMedAD-1, AMedAD-2, respectively.

The attributes selected under AMAD-1, AIQR-1, and AMedAD-1 subsets, possess a higher score than the attributes selected under AMAD-2, AIQR-2, and AMedAD-2. Thus, the original attribute set under each threshold technique is split into two subsets. Where one subset shows more supreme attribute subsets and the other shows less supreme attribute subsets. Further, the union of more supreme attribute subsets and the intersection of less supreme attribute subsets is performed. The union of AMAD-1, AIQR-1 and AMedAD-1 gives a More Supreme Attribute Subset (MSAS) and the intersection of AMAD-2, AIQR-2 and AMedAD-2 gives a Less Supreme Attribute Subset (LSAS). Finally, the union of MSAS and LSAS gives a new subset called Final Attribute Subset (FAS).

3.3 Stacked Ensemble Classification (SEC)

A stacked ensemble model classifies unknown data by building new training data using a set of classifiers as base classifiers. The classifiers of this category are also known as multiple classifier systems. The stacked ensemble learning model creates multiple learners L1, L2,…Ln from the training process by selecting different base classifiers (or Level-0), say B1, B2,…Bn, train them using the training part of the dataset. These learners' output is merged and fed as input to the next level (Level-1) classifier.

The learners selected at the base level can be homogeneous or heterogeneous ensembles. The learners are called homogeneous learners if they are under the same type otherwise, they are called as heterogeneous learners. At level-1, the selected classifier takes the base classifier's output as input and gives the final output. At level-1, the base learner's errors are identified and then adjusted to achieve an optimal solution. A generalized model for any input data is obtained by repeating this process on level classifiers. In traditional methods, the elected classifier may not achieve good results on new and unseen data even though it has good training data performance. This problem can be eliminated by using the stacked ensemble approach.

Since the method performs averaging of all classifiers, even though one of the selected classifiers is unfit for the approach, the menace of relying on one technique can be reduced. Therefore, the ensemble approach reduces the risk of inappropriate selection of classifier. Algorithm 3 shows the steps for stacked ensemble classification.

In this work, Gradient Boost (GB) [20] and Random Forest (RF) [21] classifiers are used as learners at the base level (level-0). GB is a modern classification technique and enhanced version of AdaBoost (AB). AB starts with weak learners at the initial step for predicting the output. Further, the weak learners are improved by escalating the weight points of a higher order. GB is the minor deviation of AB, in which instead of escalating the data points, the latest learner at each step is launched. This approach can improve any differentiable loss function. At every iteration regression trees are built, and individual trees are added serially, i.e., the new tree is built, depending on the difference between the real and the projected value. Whereas the RF approach works on choosing the attributes and values that can construct some sequence of rules to create various decision trees, and finally takes the mean of the final outcomes.

Now instead of using majority voting or bayesian averaging techniques for final prediction, the learning of the level-1 model is done to combine the base model's predictions. This makes it more generalized compared to other ensemble techniques in terms of the predictions of the attack. The output of level-0 is the predictions for each record of the training dataset. To combine these outputs and predicting the final label for each request, XGBoost [22] is used.

Algorithm 3:Stacked ensemble Classification		
Input	:	$D_{train}(x)$, $D_{test}(x)$, $f(x)$
Output	:	Classify test data as DDoS and benign
Step 1	:	Learn level-0 classifier (no. of classifier used=2)
		Learn Gradient Boost (GB) classifier
		Learn Random Forest (RF) classifier
Step 2	:	Learn level-1 classifier (no. of classifier used=1)
		Learn eXtreme GB (XGB) classifier with the input from level-0 classifiers
Step 3	:	Classify test data as DDoS and benign using learned stacked ensemble classifier

XGBoost is a decision tree-oriented ensemble classification technique that utilizes the GB algorithm over a known dataset and then considers the classification decision. The major motivation behind using XGBoost is its model performance, higher execution speed, memory efficiency, and high accuracy compared to other GB algorithm models [23]. Thus XGBoost is used in this work to obtain the final prediction of the request as attack and benign.

3.4 DDoS Attack Mitigation

Once the DDoS requests are identified after the classification process, these requests need to be processed with intensive care for future reference. Therefore, this Intensive Care Request Processing Unit (ICRPU) is set up to handle such attack requests. This unit confuses the attacker and makes him believe that their requests are actually being served. This impression helps the mitigation unit identify the attack source until the attacker is busy in question and answer round by this unit. As the attack requests are in the processing state, the attacker is fooled and believes that the service provider has found no suspicious activity out. This will create an illusion to the attacker. He will continue the attack without any changes and this makes it easy for the mitigation unit to identify the attack source. Once the attack source is identified all the request belonging to that source are dropped and even blocked for future reference.

4   Experimental Evaluations

The proposed approach is tested on Windows 10 on Dell series, having 64 bit i5 processor, 8 GB RAM. Python 3.0 is the language used to implement the proposed approach. NSL-KDD [24] is a publically available dataset used to validate the proposed ASAS-SEC approach. This dataset consists of various attacks however we used DoS and normal request in the dataset, which is of our interested are used to validate the proposed approach. The metrics used to asses ASAS-SEC are classification accuracy, F1-Score, Area Under Curve(AUC), and false alarm or False Positive Rate (FPR) [11].

4.1   Performance Metrics Used

The metrics used to assess ASAS-SEC are classification accuracy, F1-Score, Area Under Curve (AUC), and false alarm, also known as False Positive Rate (FPR). These metrics are expressed in terms of True Positive (TP), True Negative (TN), False Positive (FP), False Negative (FN), respectively, where:

- TP: Specify the count of DDoS requests rightly predicted as DDoS
- TN: Specify the count of benign samples rightly predicted as benign
- FP: Count of benign requests falsely predicted as DDoS
- FN: Count of DDoS requests falsely predicted as benign

4.1.1 Accuracy

It is the percentage of correctly predicted DDoS and benign requests

$$Accuracy = \frac{TP + TN}{TP + TN + FP + FN} \tag{3}$$

4.1.2 F1-Score

This score is calculated using Precision and Recall, therefore this score takes both FP and FN into account.

$$F1 - Score = 2 * \frac{(Recall * Precision)}{(Recall + Precision)} \tag{4}$$

where recall is the ratio of correctly predicted DDoS to the all observations in actual class

$$Recall = \frac{TP}{TP + FN}$$

and precision is the ratio of rightly predicted benign request to the entire predicted benign requests.

$$Precision = \frac{TP}{TP + FP}$$

4.1.3 FPR or False Alarm

It is the ratio of falsely predicted benign requests as DDoS to the actual number of benign requests.

$$FPR = \frac{FP}{FP + TN} \tag{5}$$

4.2 Result Analysis

The proposed approach utilizes MAD, IQR, and MedAD thresholding techniques to obtain a threshold value as mentioned in Sect. 3.2, based on which attributes selection is performed under each technique. In the literature, most of the methods uses fixed threshold values for the selection of attributes. However, techniques based on fixed threshold values cannot deal with the dynamic network behavior during the attack. As the size of the packet and values of the attributes changes drastically with various kinds of DDoS attack. Therefore, fixed threshold values are not able to tackle such situations and make the predictions accurately. Thus, to handle these limitations, adaptive threshold techniques are used as a part of the attribute selection process.

After selecting attributes under each adaptive thresholding technique, the attributes are further classified in two sets based on a fixed threshold value 'T_h' as AMAD-1, AMAD-2 for MAD thresholding technique, AIQR-1, AIQR-2 for IQR thresholding technique and AMedAD-1, AMedAD-2 for MedAD thresholding technique.

The most supreme and final attributes are shortlisted based on the significance of attribute in classifying the requests from these sets. Once the final attributes are selected, the stacked ensemble classifier as discussed in the Sect. 3.3 is used to classify the incoming request to cloud-assisted WBAN as DDoS and normal.

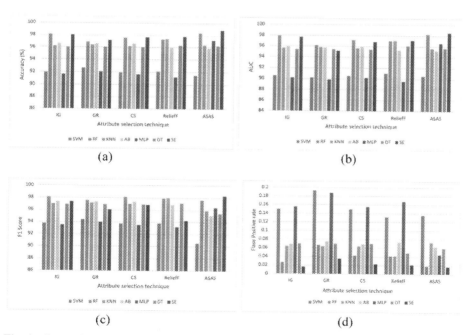

Fig. 4. Comparison between different threshold methods along side different classifier and proposed (ASAS+SE) approach for different metrics: (a) Accuracy, (b) AUC, (c) F1-Score, (d) FPR(false alarm)

After rigorous experimentations and comparisons it is observed that ASAS-SEC achieves the highest classification accuracy of 98.86%, F1 Score of 98.3%, AUC of 98.56, and lowest false alarm of 0.017. Thus ASAS-SEC is selected in the proposed approach.

Figure 4 shows the comparison of thresholding techniques with different classifiers. The classifiers used to compare the proposed approach are Decision Tree (DT), AdaBoost (AB), Support Vector Machine (SVM), K-Nearest Neighbor (KNN), Random Forest (RF), and Multi Layer Perceptron (MLP). From Fig. 4 (a), (b), (c), and (d), it is seen that the proposed ASAS-SEC attains the highest accuracy, F1-Score, Area Under Curve (AUC) in comparison to other amalgamations of thresholding technique and different classifiers. Moreover, ASAS-SEC achieves a low FPR which ensures very less false alarms.

The dominance of the proposed approach can also be seen by comparing it with the existing attribute selection techniques. The most widely used attribute selection techniques are Information Gain (IG), Gain Ratio (GR), Chi-Squared (CS), and ReliefF [25]. Figure 5 shows the comparative analysis of the proposed ASAS-SEC approach with existing feature selection and classification techniques.

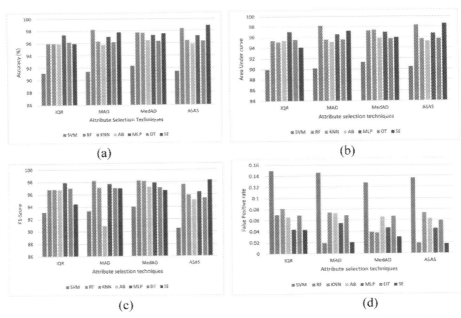

Fig. 5. Comparison between various attribute selection techniques along with different classifier and ASAS-SEC for different metrics: (a) Accuracy, (b) AUC, (c) F1-Score, (d) FPR (false alarm)

Figure 5 (a), (b), (c), and (d) shows the accuracy, AUC, F1-Score, and FPR comparison of the proposed approach with other attribute selection techniques. It is observed that the proposed ASAS-SEC proved to be superior over all the attribute selection techniques.

ASAS-SEC attains high accuracy, AUC, F1-Score, and lowest false alarm value compared to the above mentioned attribute selection techniques. As these attribute selection techniques cannot handle the dynamic behavior of traffic during the DDoS attack.

The proposed ASAS-SEC is also compared with the existing state-of-the-art approaches used to detect and classify DDoS attacks, as shown in Table 1. It is observed from Fig. 6 (a) that the proposed ASAS-SEC dominates other techniques and achieves high accuracy because it contains high TP and TN values.

Similarly, a comparative study on the F1-Score value of ASAS+SE with other existing methods is shown in Fig. 6 (b). Proposed approach attains highest F1-Score in comparison to state of the art approaches.

Table 1. Performance comparison of ASAS-SEC with state of the art techniques

Reference	Year	Accuracy	F1-Score	False alarm
[26]	2018	96.53	0.8484	0.56
[27]	2018	95.29	–	–
[28]	2018	84.25	0.8386	–
[29]	2019	75.51	0.73	2.87
[30]	2019	94.8	0.94	0.07
[31]	2018	98.23	0.7	0.32
[32]	2020	79.34	0.7888	–
[33]	2021	78.85	0.7111	–
[34]	2021	81.48	0.8523	–
[35]	2021	85.83	0.8661	–
[36]	2022	87.11	0.8533	–
Proposed	–	**98.86**	**0.983**	**0.017**

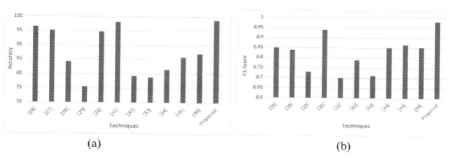

(a)   (b)

Fig. 6. Comparison of accuracy and F1-Score of ASAS+SE with state of art techniques

5 Conclusion

This manuscript presents a DDoS attack defense approach in cloud-assisted WBAN to guarantee the accessibility of patient information to the healthcare system. The proposed approach ASAS-SEC is based on adaptive and supreme attribute selection and stacked ensemble classification. The adaptive threshold technique helps to deal with dynamic network traffic conditions due to various DDoS attack intensities. However, the fixed threshold value used in the literature are not capable to deal with such conditions. Therefore, using the adaptive threshold value depending on the present network statistics identifies the effective attributes for classification. Moreover, among the selected attributes under each thresholding technique (MAD, IQR, MedAD), furthermost supreme attributes are selected. After selecting an attribute, stacked ensemble classifier is used to classify the incoming request. The advantage of using stacked ensemble classification is that it overcomes the generalization capability for the predictions of the classifiers in the ensemble. The proposed approach ASAS-SEC is evaluated on the NSL-KDD dataset and proved to be best among the other techniques in the domain and state of the art approaches. However, proposed approach is unable to detect the other attacks. Thus in future proposed approach can be modified to identify the other attacks launched against the cloud-assisted WBAN.

References

1. Latif, R., Abbas, H., Latif, S.: Distributed denial of service (DDoS) attack detection using data mining approach in cloud-assisted wireless body area networks. Int. J. Ad Hoc Ubiquitous Comput. **23**(1–2), 24–35 (2016)
2. Irum, S., Ali, A., Khan, F.A., Abbas, H.: A hybrid security mechanism for intra-WBAN and inter-WBAN communications. Int. J. Distrib. Sens. Netw. **9**(8), 842608 (2013)
3. Hayajneh, T., Almashaqbeh, G., Ullah, S., Vasilakos, A.V.: A survey of wireless technologies coexistence in WBAN: analysis and open research issues. Wirel. Netw. **20**(8), 2165–2199 (2014). https://doi.org/10.1007/s11276-014-0736-8
4. Latif, R., Abbas, H., Assar, S., Latif, S.: Analyzing feasibility for deploying very fast decision tree for DDoS attack detection in cloud-assisted WBAN. In: Huang, D.-S., Bevilacqua, V., Premaratne, P. (eds.) ICIC 2014. LNCS, vol. 8588, pp. 507–519. Springer, Cham (2014). https://doi.org/10.1007/978-3-319-09333-8_57
5. Wan, J., Zou, C., Zhou, K., Lu, R., Li, D.: IoT sensing framework with inter-cloud computing capability in vehicular networking. Electron. Commer. Res. **14**(3), 389–416 (2014). https://doi.org/10.1007/s10660-014-9147-2
6. Foster, I., Zhao, Y., Raicu, I., Lu, S.: Cloud computing and grid computing 360-degree compared. In: 2008 Grid Computing Environments Workshop, pp. 1–10 (2008)
7. Wang, H., Jia, Q., Fleck, D., Powell, W., Li, F., Stavrou, A.: A moving target DDoS defense mechanism. Comput. Commun. **46**, 10–21 (2014)
8. Sari, A.: A review of anomaly detection systems in cloud networks and survey of cloud security measures in cloud storage applications. J. Inf. Secur. **6**(02), 142 (2015)
9. Rajamohamed, R., Jose, T.J., Sumithra, S., Vijaya, J.: Multi model mitigation approach for network threats on cluster based linear chain routing protocol in wireless sensor networks at QoS development. Wirel. Pers. Commun. **102**(4), 3205–3224 (2018)

10. Idhammad, M., Afdel, K., Belouch, M.: Detection system of HTTP DDoS attacks in a cloud environment based on information theoretic entropy and random forest. Secur. Commun. Netw. (2018)

11. Verma, P., Tapaswi, S., Godfrey, W.W.: An Adaptive threshold-based attribute selection to classify requests under DDoS attack in cloud-based systems. Arab. J. Sci. Eng. 45(4), 2813–2834 (2019). https://doi.org/10.1007/s13369-019-04178-x

12. Verma, P., Tapaswi, S., Godfrey, W.W.: A request aware module using CS-IDR to reduce VM level collateral damages caused by DDoS attack in cloud environment. Clust. Comput. 24(3), 1917–1933 (2021). https://doi.org/10.1007/s10586-021-03234-2

13. Aburomman, A.A., Reaz, M.B.I.: A survey of intrusion detection systems based on ensemble and hybrid classifiers. Comput. Secur. 65, 135–152 (2017)

14. Bharot, N., Verma, P., Sharma, S., Suraparaju, V.: Distributed denial-of-service attack detection and mitigation using feature selection and intensive care request processing unit. Arab. J. Sci. Eng. 43(2), 959–967 (2018)

15. Shone, N., Ngoc, T.N., Phai, V.D., Shi, Q.: A deep learning approach to network intrusion detection. IEEE Trans. Emerg. Top. Comput. Intell. 2(1), 41–50 (2018)

16. Choi, H., Kim, M., Lee, G., Kim, W.: Unsupervised learning approach for network intrusion detection system using autoencoders. J. Supercomput. 75(9), 5597–5621 (2019). https://doi.org/10.1007/s11227-019-02805-w

17. Latif, R., Abbas, H., Assar, S.: Distributed denial of service (DDoS) attack in cloud-assisted wireless body area networks: a systematic literature review. J. Med. Syst. 38, 128 (2014). https://doi.org/10.1007/s10916-014-0128-8

18. Shannon, C.E.: A mathematical theory of communication. ACM SIGMOBILE Mob. Comput. Commun. Rev. 5(1), 3–55 (2001)

19. Sree, T.R., Bhanu, S.M.S.: Detection of http flooding attacks in cloud using dynamic entropy method. Arab. J. Sci. Eng. 43(12), 6995–7014 (2018)

20. Alamri, H.A., Thayananthan, V.: Bandwidth control mechanism and extreme gradient boosting algorithm for protecting software-defined networks against DDoS attacks. IEEE Access 8, 194269–194288 (2020)

21. Radivilova, T., Kirichenko, L., Ageiev, D., Bulakh, V.: Classification methods of machine learning to detect DDoS attacks. In: 2019 10th IEEE International Conference on Intelligent Data Acquisition and Advanced Computing Systems: Technology and Applications (IDAACS), vol. 1, pp. 207–210 (2019)

22. Chen, T., Guestrin, C.: XGBoost: a scalable tree boosting system. In: Proceedings of the 22nd ACM SIGKDD International Conference on Knowledge Discovery and Data Mining, pp. 785–794 (2016)

23. Chakraborty, D., Elzarka, H.: Advanced machine learning techniques for building performance simulation: a comparative analysis. J. Build. Perform. Simul. 12(2), 193–207 (2019)

24. NSL-KDD Dataset. http://www.unb.ca/cic/datasets/nsl.html

25. Pajouh, H.H., Dastghaibyfard, G., Hashemi, S.: Two-tier network anomaly detection model: a machine learning approach. J. Intell. Inf. Syst. 48(1), 61–74 (2015). https://doi.org/10.1007/s10844-015-0388-x

26. Hamamoto, A.H., Carvalho, L.F., Sampaio, L.D.H., Abrão, T., Proença, M.L., Jr.: Network anomaly detection system using genetic algorithm and fuzzy logic. Expert Syst. Appl. 92, 390–402 (2018)

27. Sharma, R., Chaurasia, S.: An enhanced approach to fuzzy C-means clustering for anomaly detection. In: Somani, A.K., Srivastava, S., Mundra, A., Rawat, S. (eds.) Proceedings of First International Conference on Smart System, Innovations and Computing, pp. 623–636. Springer, Singapore (2018). https://doi.org/10.1007/978-981-10-5828-8_60

28. Verma, P., Anwar, S., Khan, S., Mane, S.B.: Network intrusion detection using clustering and gradient boosting. In: 2018 9th International Conference on Computing, Communication and Networking Technologies (ICCCNT), pp. 1–7 (2018)

29. Ghosh, P., Karmakar, A., Sharma, J., Phadikar, S.: CS-PSO based intrusion detection system in cloud environment. In: Abraham, A., Dutta, P., Mandal, J.K., Bhattacharya, A., Dutta, S. (eds.) Emerging Technologies in Data Mining and Information Security. AISC, vol. 755, pp. 261–269. Springer, Singapore (2019). https://doi.org/10.1007/978-981-13-1951-8_24

30. Sreeram, I., Vuppala, V.P.K.: HTTP flood attack detection in application layer using machine learning metrics and bio inspired bat algorithm. Appl. Comput. Inform. 15(1), 59–66 (2019)

31. Idhammad, M., Afdel, K., Belouch, M.: Semi-supervised machine learning approach for DDoS detection. Appl. Intell. 48(10), 3193–3208 (2018)

32. Gohil, M., Kumar, S.: Evaluation of classification algorithms for distributed denial of service attack detection. In: AIKE, pp. 138–141. IEEE (2020)

33. Sudar, K.M., Beulah, M., Deepalakshmi, P., Nagaraj, P., Chinnasamy, P.: Detection of distributed denial of service attacks in SDN using machine learning techniques. In: IEEE International Conference on Computer Communication and Informatics (ICCCI), pp. 1–5 (2021)

34. Tonkal, Ö., Polat H., Başaran, E., Cömert, Z., Kocaoğlu, R.: Machine learning approach equipped with neighbourhood component analysis for DDoS attack detection in software-defined networking. Electronics 10(11) (2021)

35. Ahuja, N., Singal, G., Mukhopadhyay, D., Kumar, N.: Automated DDOS attack detection in software defined networking. J. Netw. Comput. Appl. 187, 103–108 (2021)

36. Pranto, M.B., Ratul, M.H., Rahman, M.M., Diya, I.J., Zahir, Z.B.: Performance of machine learning techniques in anomaly detection with basic feature selection strategy-a network intrusion detection system, J. Adv. Inf. Technol. 13(1) (2022)

A Sophisticated Framework for Document Forensics

Lokesh Yadav$^{(\boxtimes)}$ ⓘ, Shyam Mohan Azad, and Deepak Singh Tomar ⓘ

Maulana Azad National Institute of Technology, Bhopal 462003, India
lokeshcsenita@gmail.com

Abstract. Pretention of documents in today's era is a common problem for organizations as it has become so easier for fabricators to forge a document by using advanced imaging systems and softwares. Documents are very essential part of human society. These documents are images, contract deeds, identity cards, bank cheques, property papers etc. Documents also plays a very vital role in proceedings of law enforcement agencies as they are the only written roof of anything that existed or happened at some point of time or going to happen and also the proof of a person's identity. But there existed some sort of risk associated with these documents that are tempering of document, false document creation, and illegal editing.

Due to the absence of a set and specific methodology and very wide genre of documents it often found tedious for the law enforcement agencies to adopt an appropriate technique to check the authenticity of the questioned document.

In this paper, a sophisticated framework based on goal-driven approach with concept graphs is proposed. Further, attack tree is developed to present threats on document forensics. Attack scenario is also visualized by integrating computer systems and possible attacks to realize those threats. And anti-forensic model is also integrated to visualize the attack scenario in document related crime and obstruction that can be encountered while investigation process of the same respectively.

Keywords: Forensic document examination · Sophisticated framework · Attack tree · Concept graph · Anti-forensic · Alterations of documents · Computer manipulated documents

1 Introduction

A "Document" can be best taken a piece of written, printed, or electronic matter that consists of signs, signature, or any graphics that provides information or evidence or that serves as an official record, or represents ones thought. Documents and their use have become gradually dominant in the current era. It is almost impossible to avoid their use these days. These documents could be official contract images, bills and checks, etc. A digital document is easy, economical and efficient to maintain as compared to a hard copy, and both of theirs security is a challenge (illegal editing in content, illegal reprinting or unauthorized manipulation in any manner).

© The Author(s), under exclusive license to Springer Nature Switzerland AG 2022
N. Khare et al. (Eds.): MIND 2022, CCIS 1763, pp. 345–359, 2022.
https://doi.org/10.1007/978-3-031-24367-7_33

The typical available digital forensic investigation frameworks focus on the phases such as collection, preservation, examination, analysis and presentation [1, 19]. However, Casey [11] has proved with several examples in context of digital forensics that several investigations approaches traverse bottom-up and focus on collection and analysis of entire supplied media on the basis of keywords and regular expression which is a tedious task and also leads to bulky backlogs [11]. Sometimes it also have been proven inefficacious as it miss crucial evidences as prospecting low level patterns may miss crucial evidence.

The forensic investigation process should be such that it can handle all the obstacles occurred during evidence collection and their analysis both by tendentious and deliberate act that may result into incorrect, sketchy, inconsistent and unreliable evidence.

An appropriate sophisticated framework for document forensic investigation is missing related to the analysis of document forgery crime investigation requirements. This work contributes in this context by proposing a goal-driven approach in identifying the document forensic investigation requirements. The DFI process initiated with particular identification of ultimate goals of investigation and analysis of the obstacles that could hinder the achievement of these goals. To overcome the deliberate obstacles an anti-forensic dimension also been integrated in the document forensic investigation process at the level of requirements [27].

This way the proposed Methodology boost the effectiveness of the existing forensic approach by incorporating sophisticated investigation methodology for management of evidences such that it supports in achievement of investigation goals and surmount legal as well as technical obstructions in a expected manner.

Some institutions make their original documents identifiable by using some active methods such as water marking, Digital Signature Technique, Seal, and Stamps etc. But not all documents can use this approach they needs a passive approach for forensic examination of document. Most of the techniques that are previously suggested by researchers detect the source of printing of the document whereas others search for irregularities in the document [2] (Fig. 1).

1.1 Active Forensics

Active forensic approach involves detection of feature in a document such as digital signature, watermarks, seals and other explicitly infused authorship security features. Watermarking is technique to infuse additional information such as logo of issuing authority or some additional details infused into the audio, image or video. This additional information generally infused as discrete bits in the block of signal. While the actual signal goes by any illegal transformation, the infused bits gets lost or altered [6, 7]. Therefore, watermarks identify the owner of the object. Whereas visible watermarks infused in document are visible such as logo, seal etc. Figure 2 shows graphical representation of Active forensic approach. Sample Heading (Third Level). Only two levels of headings should be numbered. Lower level headings remain unnumbered; they are formatted as run-in headings.

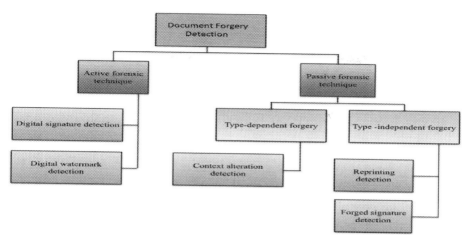

Fig. 1. Techniques of document forgery detection

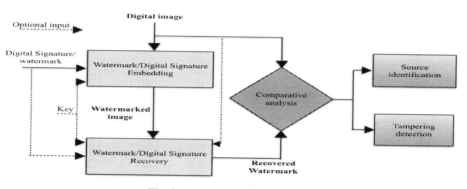

Fig. 2. Active forensics technique

1.2 Passive Forensics

Passive approaches are referred as detection of authenticity of a digitized document/image on the basis of its endogenous features that are left on the document by acquisition device such as scanners, camera etc. and the printing devices. It does not use any preventive measure in advance. These devices have various components that alter the signal in certain way and leave some endogenous fingerprints in the document. These features involve sensor noise, skew defect, edge unevenness, disturbance in pixel intensity values, area difference and relationship coefficients for individual character, ORB features, SURF features etc. No matter the acquisition methodology is unaltered still these features reside in document and are identifiable with the use of advance Artificial Technologies. Figure 3 shows graphical representation of Passive forensic approach.

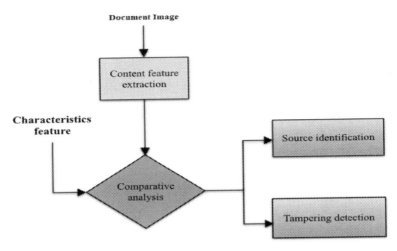

Fig. 3. Passive forensics technique

2 Background Research

Researches have focused on the Methodology of forensic investigation process and on techniques of anti-forensics. Here, this paper confers a detailed over sight throughout the approaches involved in this work.

As Kahvedić and Kechadi [13] have demonstrated digital forensic investigation ontology as an ablation of notion and affinity for the characterization, reuse and evaluation of Digital Investigation Intellect [4]. The ontological model has four dimensions that are: Crime Case, Evidence Location, Information, and Forensic Resource. Their methodology idealizes the intellect within the windows registry using keys and values.

Reith et al. [19] prepared an abstractive model for digital forensics that comprised of nine phases that are identification, preparation, analysis, presentation and returning evidence. Their model targeted non-technical observers and adhere their understanding of future digital technologies.

Carrier and Spafford [18] prepared a process model for the purpose of investigation considering digital device as a digital crime scene. Their process model incorporated five phases: Readiness phase, deployment phase, physical/digital crime scene investigation phase and presentation phase.

Harris [16] proposed methodologies to destroy hide and eliminate evidences or their resources which is considered as an anti-forensic activities. However recommended standards (mainly for investigating officers) such as educational qualifications, Domain experience in real world, and ability to reason and think in different dimensions, are underlined to handle the anti-forensic acts.

Dahuar and Mohammad [10] described challenges of investigation process as time, limitations and flaws of forensic software, privacy factor of victim and also the type of digital evidence as the key challenges of anti-forensic process.

Various researches in the forensic domain put stress on acquisition and analysis of evidence. Whereas this work different in the way that it initiated with goal identification for investigation and analyzing the anti-forensic issues that can cause hindrance at any point of time during the process of investigation. Therefore, this paper harmonize the concept of both forensic and anti-forensic methodologies to address the all the possible issues within an investigative framework with inclusion of Fraud tree to visualize the attack scenario and concept graph for better understanding of the investigation phase.

3   Risks Associated with Document Fraud

With the help of Schneier's attack trees [22] that laid the backbone for implementation of various tools for the assessment computer security attack. He investigated the scenarios of attacks contrary to an online payment system, the developed document fraud tree is a methodical way to show how or in what ways an adversary can obtain a legal document and modify its content or can create a false document to deceive others and ultimately commit a document Fraud.

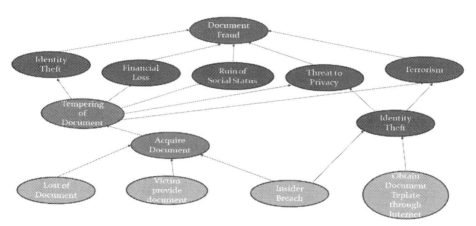

Fig. 4. Document fraud tree

Here (Fig. 4) the green ellipses shows the first level of a document fraud i.e. a document can be obtained by an adversary in any of the four ways either the victim can lose its document, victim himself provide the document to avail some service and from there the adversary may obtain it as it has been observed in case of sim-card fraud, any insider of the organization can betray and leak sensitive documents, or a template document can be downloaded from the internet.

The blue ellipses shows the second level that is acquisition of document by the adversaries after any of these four activities occurred at level one. All of these activities are in OR except those are in AND condition that has been shown by an "arc" between the edges.

The third level depicts the activity done by adversary to imitate the document and the fourth level shows the different pre-ultimate risk associated which ultimately leads to document Fraud.

Actively protected documents are easily identified as they contain secret security features such as watermarks or digital signature [5] but this paper focuses mainly on unprotected documents such as bills, ID cards, contract deeds etc. which are not actively protected and unavailability of a standard framework for forensic examination of such documents rose the need for the development of the suggested framework in this context.

4 Proposed Framework

A. Van Lamsweerde incorporated a KAOS (knowledge acquisition in automated specification) goal model [14] to help determine system requirements and obstacles for analyzing hazards to the goals. Which helps in determining the obstacles or anti-forensic goals for document forensic examination process. B. Aziz, C. Blackwell and S. Islam proposed A framework for digital forensic and investigation [9] which helps in determining the various phases associated with the forensic examination of document. The suggested framework (Fig. 5) here consists of five discreet phases that are: Identification/Acquisition of document, Preparation Phase, Examination Phase, Analysis Phase, Analysis Presentation Phase.

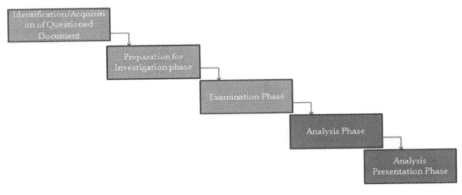

Fig. 5. Phases of document forensic investigation process

Each of these phases has its importance during the forensic examination process so that the reports that will be generated at the end of the process are acceptable in the court of law.

April Tanner and David Dampier's used Concept-maps for to model the case domain information involved in investigation to replace the classical checklist approach used in context of digital forensics. Concept-maps are actually a drawn model to organize and represent knowledge by showing the hierarchical kinship among concepts. The use of Concept-map was first carried out to comprehend the scientific knowledge obtained by children [23]. From then, concept-maps are being used as diagnosis tools and definition assistant, to frame schedules, to captivate and compile expert knowledge and to draft domain specific knowledge [23, 24]. The developed concept-graphs in this work depicts each and every activity involved in context of document forensics.

4.1 Identification/Acquisition of Questioned Document

The primary aim of identification phase is to identify the crime or crime scene but in context of document related crime the goal is to first identify weather the crime has taken place or not as in majority of jurisdictions, imitation of documents is not charged as a forgery crime unless it is done with the motive of deceiving or with the motive to commit a crime of fraud or larceny. For example, art works can be copied or imitated barely being a crime unless someone tries to sell the imitated copies as original. In such case copies will be treated as forged ones.

After the identification that a forgery crime has been committed the investigation officer will get issue a warrant and obtain prelim details of case in context of under what circumstances the crime has been committed and the parties involved in the case. The evidence concept depicts that all the evidences i.e. the questioned document and other supporting evidences if needed and available should be collected. The procedure of organization should be defined and followed throughout the investigation process and ensure that the accepted chain of custody should be followed (Fig. 6).

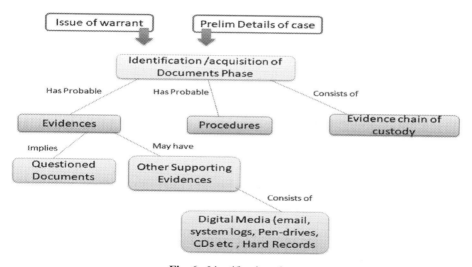

Fig. 6. Identification phase

These concept-graphs can be utilized as a quick reference cicerone by investigators in taking the decision that which evidence objects are to be searched and also as a remembrance that chain of custody should be followed and logs should be recorded.

4.2 Preparation for Investigation Phase

One of the most important task incorporated in preservation phase is chain of custody [25, 26] so as here in preparation phase. Detailed records of chain of custody enable to maintain the authenticity of collected evidences and repudiate the allegation of evidence tempering. It gives close details about custody and position of evidences during the whole lifespan of a case; these minutiae lowers the chances that the evidences will be unacceptable in court of law. It has been exhibited in Fig. 7, the establishment of chain of custody as evidences are collected by whom ("Forms" Concept), where and how the collection of evidences was done ("Forms" and "Procedures" concept), custody of evidences taken by whom ("Log Info" Concept), How and what protection and storage procedures were taken ("Forms" Concept) and evidence removed from storage by whom and the reason and purpose of removal ("Log Info" Concept).

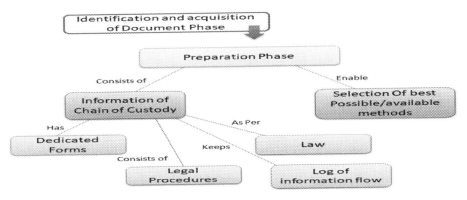

Fig. 7. Preparation phase

Another task associated with preparation phase is identification of the type of document that is whether it is actively protected or not, if actively protected use the Active forensic techniques to ensure the authenticity otherwise select the best possible passive forensic technique to fulfil the purpose. Lockdown and restrict access to the questioned documents at a secure location, which are underlined in the "Procedures," "Forms" and "Log Info" concepts, respectively.

The investigator also identifies the anti-Forensic obstacles that can hinder the investigation process. The illustration of which is shown in section-5of this paper taking a hypothetical case scenario.

4.3 Examination Phase

In examination phase specially designed tools and techniques can be incorporated to identify the evidence of forgery. For instance if the document is actively protected digital document investigator can go for identification of watermark, digital signature, metadata, system logs etc. but if it is hard document then identification of watermark, seals, paper quality, ink quality and age and verification by the issuing authority can be the supporting actors for investigator as well as investigation. But in case unprotected hard documents a very well-known methodology used is that the identification of source printer or writer (in case of hand written scripts). In such cases investigation of authentic document is a little bit complex.

Investigator should involve the legally approved methods ("Legally Approved method" concept) as per the law of the state or the law enforcement agency and maintain proper documentation of the examination process ("Proper documentation") so that the evidences collected during examination process ensure that they were collected by using legally approved methods only and no illegal practices have been involved and are acceptable by the court of law (Fig. 8).

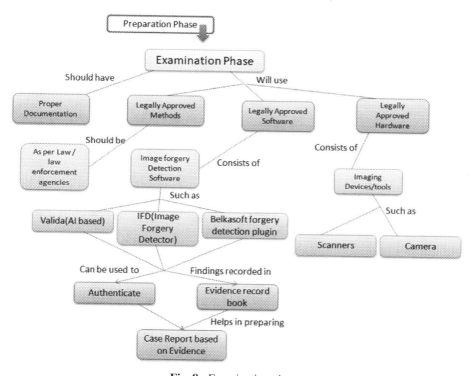

Fig. 8. Examination phase

Only legally approved softwares should be used for collection of evidences ("Legally Approved Software" concept). Some softwares suggested here may be useful for the fulfillment of purpose are VALIDA an AI based tool, IFD (Image Forgery Detector), BELKASOFT etc. and only the legally approved hardware should be used ("Legally Approved Hardware" concept).

All the evidences collected should be recorded in evidence record book and the findings obtained by the specialized tools can be used to find the authentic document. All these details should be encased in a case report based on evidence collected.

4.4 Analysis Phase

In analysis phase all the evidences found are reassembled to speculate what happened. An event timeline and kinship between evidences and criminal intention is created using the evidences collected in the examination phase. Concept graphs provide support in the analysis phase for creation timelines of events occurred by using case report based on evidences and suspect details. Beebe and Clark [16] stated that "the most complex and tedious task in digital forensic process is data analysis". Figure 9 depicts good illustration of how organization, arrangement, details of case, methods and chain of custody documentation in the course of analysis phase can be done by concept graphs.

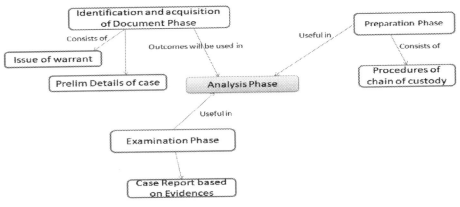

Fig. 9. Analysis phase

4.5 Presentation Phase

All the activities performed in the previous four phases are important for the presentation of collected evidences in the court of law.

Fig. 10. Presentation phase

Presentation phase is one of the most important phase of investigation as the legal consequences of suspect's activity are resolved in this phase. The investigating officer is required to demonstrate everything that happened during the identification/Acquisition of document, preparation, examination, and analysis phases of the investigation process. Generally, specially designed softwares and methods are used in the court of law to produce the findings in proceedings of court [25]. As Fig. 10 shows in presentation phase a well-documented case report based on the evidences found in examination phase and analysis phase should be presented before court which is acceptable.

5   Hypothetical Case Scenario and Application of Proposed Framework

We use a hypothesis framed on the basis of a real world case to exhibit the application of our standpoint involved two parties Party1 (P1) the petitioner and Party2 (P2) the respondent where P1 filed a complaint claiming that P2 has signed a contract with P1 so p1 is the owner of some share of p2's work. This section exhibit the methodical praxis of the five investigation phase disserted above to support the forensic investigation in case of document forgery. We will later show how the process can be followed in a different case.

P1 is a contractor who appointed P2 as his employee to do some work for him and duly signed a contract with P2 in the year XXXX. P1 paid some \$AAAA amount to P2 to work for him but claimed that he sponsored the project which is owned by P2. P1 presented a contract that is ostensibly signed by both the parties covering the two projects. According to P1, the contract describe that P1 would get 50% of the project owned by P2 against the sponsorship given by P1. They have also discussed about the P2's project in detail via emails exchanged between them.P1 presented all the assets related to his claim such as copy of contract, copy of email conversation held between them along with all the relevant electronic records. Then the investigation goes as follows:

5.1   Identification/Acquisition of Document

Firstly the issues are understood related to the investigation. The primary aim is to justify the authenticity of claims raised by P1 by checking the validity of contract and the submitted electronic media in support of the claim and also check if any of the asset is a forgery. The first goal is to acquire all the relevant evidences from P1's spot including electronic media and all hard documents to find and preserve the evidences. The subtlety of investigation huge amount of data from different spots and the necessity to safeguard and examine all the evidence collected.

5.2   Preparation Phase

The ultimate Goal of the investigation to verify that the contract of P1 is a forgery, which will deny his claim of being partner in P2's project because that contract is the only evidence competent to prove P1 is right. The ultimate goal can be divided into sub-goals related to presentation and examination of all the supporting electronic media and the contract. A preliminary general goal tree for document forgery build with the help previous cases can be helpful in determining pilot methods that concentrates on probable evidence and their locations. Three branches are demonstrated to prove the P1's contract is invalid, the other branch try to exhibit that the case should be dismissed on legal technical grounds due to dotty evidences. Division of these possibilities is shown Fig. 11. But, the forgery should be proved in multiple dimensions so that the investigation of case should be protected from unpredicted fresh evidence and any legal question. All the four Branches of goal tree are broken into sub-branches to show further investigation goals.

Identification Obstacles is also done here as various obstructions will also hinder the goal of investigation to verify that the P1's Contract was a forgery. Say if P1 doesn't have the original copy of contract but the copy of it then it will be an obstruction for the investigation as shown in Fig. 11.

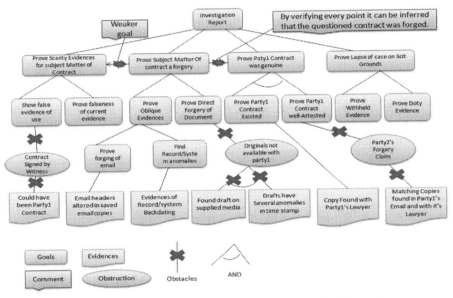

Fig. 11. Goal driven overview of case with anti-forensic obstruction

5.3 Examination Phase

To prove the authenticity of the contract the collected evidences including supporting electronic media and the contractexamined by various forensic experts such as handwriting expert and digital forensic expert [3].

Verify Email Consistency: The emails provide a good support to the P1's claim, but the header were having traces of modification. Normally header information is automatically created and updated with the creation of an email. Therefore inconsistency of email headers provided by P1 prove evidence forgery.

Verify the Evidence of Records and System Backdating: Whenever a file is created in computer system timestamps are saved as well as the sending time of email. This need endorse the verification of the contract as it is understood that the contract was created and signed before sending it as file with an email and the file size should be equally large as it is on any other electronic media. The anomalous timestamp for files was encountered and proved P1's contract a forgery. Secondly the system log of P1's computer was also inconsistence and so support P2.

Checking of Contract: The digital copy of contract is created and it was compared with the image of contract present on two different evident media presented by P1 to check th same hash value. This verification of the files can be carried out by generating the hash values for the TIFF image file of the two attached file with P1's email and the new one. But this check can also be done by specially designed software used for image analysis.

5.4 Analysis Phase

The hash values obtained were analyzed to find the similarity between the three but the outcomes were not in favor of P1. Along with that, the physical examination suggested that the page2 of contract was illegally attached from page1 of previous legitimate contract between the two. More on physical examination is not discussed here as it is out of the scope of his paper.

5.5 Presentation Phase

The evidences and findings obtained from the previous four phases are integrated to generate the forensic investigation report. The generated report must also include the taken forensic measures and their ascendancy.

6 Conclusion and Future Work

The Concept graphing can improve each phase of a document forensic investigation. The dominant advantages of CGs are a perceptive graphical representation of the investigation process and an easy technique to document and store case-related information that is evidences, case reports, and chain of custody, documents and procedures. Along with that Concept graphs lay a framework for creation of document forensic repository where case-specific concept graphs and specially designed methods will be available to be shared by the law enforcement community. There are many other advantages also, as the capacity to expose the misinterpretation in investigation process, creation of knowledge base and approaches explicit to crime investigations.

The goal model developed to show case overview can also be used to identify various goals and obstructions in Document Forensic investigation, for identification and division of whole investigation process into sub-goals and for identification of the actions required and operation, that re needed to be applied.

Document forensic investigation is a very important field of forensics but still availability of standard tools for the purpose of passive investigation technique is limited and the available tools and AI models have their own limitations in terms of accuracy. Therefore the contribution in future work of this paper, an AI based tool will be developed for the fulfillment of purpose of Passive Investigation process to provide more accurate analysis results.

References

1. Abulaish, M., Haldar, N.A.H.: Advances in digital forensics frameworks and tools: a comparative insight and ranking. Int. J. Digit. Crime Forensics (IJDCF) **10** (2018). https://doi.org/10.4018/IJDCF.2018040106
2. Saini, K., Kaur, S.: Forensic examination of computer-manipulated documents using image processing techniques. Egypt. J. Forensic Sci. **6**(3), 317–322 (2016). https://doi.org/10.1016/j.ejfs.2015.03.001. ISSN 2090-536X
3. Tajik Esmaeili, A., Ataeefard, M., Safi, M.: Recognition of sequence of print and ink strokes: investigation the effect of handwriting pressure, hue of ink, printer and paper type. Prog. Color Color. Coat. (PCCC) **12**(4), 251–261 (2019)
4. Saini, K., Kaur, S.: Examination of digitally manipulated documents using MATLAB 7.10.0 and adobe Photoshop 7.0. Probl. Forensic Sci. **111**, 31–44 (2018)
5. Singh, M., Mishra, S.: Forensic examination of digitally Fabricated signatures in printed documents. Z Zagadnien Nauk Sadowych **112**, 111–122 (2017)
6. Sánchez, Á., Vélez, J.F., Sánchez, J., Moreno, A.B.: Automatic anonymization of printed-text document images. In: Mansouri, A., El Moataz, A., Nouboud, F., Mammass, D. (eds.) ICISP 2018. LNCS, vol. 10884, pp. 145–152. Springer, Cham (2018). https://doi.org/10.1007/978-3-319-94211-7_17
7. Li, B.-M., et al.: Preliminary study on determining the sequence of intersecting lines by fluorescence technique. J. Forensic Sci. **63**, 577–582 (2018)
8. Friedberg, S.: Report of Digital Forensic Analysis in Paul D. Ceglia v. Mark Elliot Zuckerberg, Individually, and Facebook, Inc. Civil Action No: 1:10-cv-00569-RJA, 26 March 2012. http://www.wired.com/images_blogs/threatlevel/2012/03/celiginvestigation.pdf
9. Aziz, B.: Towards goal-driven digital forensics investigations. In: Proceedings of the Second International Conference on Cybercrime, Security and Digital Forensics (Cyfor-12). University of Strathclyde Publishing (2012)
10. Dahbur, K., Mohammad, B.: The anti-forensics challenge. In: Proceedings of the 2011 International Conference on Intelligent Semantic Web-Services and Applications. ACM Press (2011)
11. Casey, E., Rose, C.: Forensic discovery. In: Handbook of Digital Forensics and Investigation. Academic Press (2010)
12. Naqvi, S., Dallons, G., Ponsard, C.: Applying digital forensics in the future internet enterprise systems - European SME's perspective. In: Proceedings of the Fifth IEEE International Workshop on Systematic Approaches to Digital Forensic Engineering (SADFE), pp. 89–93. IEEE (2010)
13. Kahvedic, D., Kechadi, T.: DIALOG: a framework for modeling, analysis and reuse of digital forensic knowledge. Int. J. Digit. Forensics Incid. Response **6**, 23–33 (2009)
14. van Lamsweerde, A.: Requirements Engineering: From System Goals to UML Models to Software Specifications. Wiley, New York (2009)
15. Harris, R.: Arriving at an anti-forensics consensus: examining how to define and control the anti-forensics problem. In: Proceedings of the Sixth Annual Digital Forensic Research Workshop (DFRWS 2006). Elsevier (2006)

16. Beebe, N., Clark, J.: A hierarchical, objectives-based framework for the digital investigation process. In: Proceedings of the Fourth Digital Forensic Research Workshop (2004)
17. Ciardhuain, S.O.: An extended model of cybercrime investigations. Int. J. Digit. Evid. **3**, 1–22 (2004)
18. Carrier, B.D., Spafford, E.H.: An event-based digital forensic investigation framework. In: Proceedings of the 2004 Digital Forensics Research Workshop (2004)
19. Reith, M., Carr, C., Grunsch, G.: An examination of digital forensic models. Int. J. Digit. Evid. **1**, 1–12 (2002)
20. Technical Working Group for Electronic Crime Scene Investigation, Electronic Crime Scene Investigation: A Guide for First Responders, United States Department of Justice (2001)
21. Digital Forensics Research Workshop, A Road Map for Digital Forensics Research (2001). http://www.dfrws.org/2001/dfrws-rm-final.pdf
22. Schneier, B.: Attack trees. Dr. Dobbs J. **24**(12), 21–29 (1999)
23. Novak, J., Canas, A.: The theory underlying concept maps and how to construct and use them. Technical report IHMC Cmap Tools 2006-01, Florida Institute for Human and Machine Cognition, Pensacola, Florida (2006)
24. Kramer, M.: Using concept maps for knowledge acquisition in satellite design: translating "Statement of Requirements on Orbit" to "Design Requirements". Ph.D. dissertation, Graduate School of Computer and Information Sciences, Nova Southeastern University, Fort Lauderdale-Davie, Florida (2005)
25. Brezinski, D., Killalea, T.: RFC3227: Guideline for Evidence Collection and Archiving. Networking Working Group, Internet Engineering Task Force (2002). www.ietf.org/rfc/rfc3227.txt
26. Kruse, W., Heiser, J.: Computer Forensics: Incident Response Essentials. Addison-Wesley, Boston (2001)
27. Rowlingson, R.: A ten step process for forensic readiness. Int. J. Digit. Evid. **2**(3), 1–28 (2004)

Author Index